André Gide's Politics: Rebellion and Ambivalence

Edited by Tom Conner

palgrave

ANDRÉ GIDE'S POLITICS

First published 2000 by
PALGRAVE™
175 Fifth Avenue, New York, N.Y. 10010 and
Houndmills, Basingstoke, Hampshire, England RG21 6XS.
Companies and representatives throughout the world.

PALGRAVE™ is the new global publishing imprint of St. Martin's Press LLC
Scholarly and Reference Division and Palgrave Publishers Ltd (formerly
Macmillan Press Ltd).

Library of Congress Cataloging-in-Publication Data

André Gide's Politics : rebellion and ambivalence / Tom Conner, editor.
        p.   cm.
    Includes bibliographical references and index.
    ISBN 0-312-22708-6 (cloth)
    1. Gide, André, 1869-1951—Political and social views.   I. Conner, Tom,
1955-

PQ2613.I2 Z5282664 2000
848'.91209—dc21   00-040491

A catalogue record for this book is available from the British Library.

Design by Letra Libre, Inc.

First edition: January 2001
10 9 8 7 6 5 4 3 2 1

Printed in the United States of America.

CONTENTS

ACKNOWLEDGMENTS

This collection of essays is the result of a project that dates back at least five years in time, to a 1995 sabbatical leave in Paris and Berlin. The focus of my research then, as now, was European intellectual life in the 1930s. I was fascinated by the impact of politics on cultural life, in particular the commitment *[engagement]* of a number of progressive intellectuals and writers such as Malraux and Gide. I remember spending one dreary February afternoon in the Bibliothèque Jacques Doucet in Paris poring over some old issues of the leftist monthly *Commune*. It suddenly occurred to me that Gide's oeuvre as a whole could be construed in terms of an *engagement* and that a collection of essays like this one exploring the various ramifications of Gide's politics was long overdue.

This project finally began to take shape after I had enlisted the support of thirteen colleagues and Gide specialists. I am thankful to each of the contributors not only for their knowledge but also for their patience in seeing this project through to completion. While I would have liked this volume to appear sooner, it has been no easy task to edit a work of its magnitude. Fortunately I have been able to rely on a number of people for their expertise in the editing process. My greatest debt is to my colleague and friend Stephen Westergan, who has been an invaluable resource and collaborator. Not only has he read and reread the manuscript countless times, saving us contributors from many errors, but he has also provided wise counsel regarding style. Stephen's meticulous attention to detail and his dedication have helped make this an authoritative yet attractive volume. Indeed, it is fair to say that this book would not have been possible without his generous collaboration. I can never thank him enough.

Other friends and colleagues also read parts of the work and were, as always, helpful with their comments and criticisms. I should like particularly to mention my gratitude to René Pomeau of the Institut de France. Over the years he has always offered helpful advice and gentle correction and has been a constant source of inspiration.

I am most grateful to the Interlibrary Loan Department of the Todd Wehr Library at St. Norbert College, without whose efficiency it would have been hard to find all the books by or on André Gide that I have consulted in the proofreading process. I also wish to thank my faithful student research assistants who have done everything from typing and proofreading to tracking down translations of quotes in hard-to-find editions of Gide's works. Jim Bott, Russell Duncan, Mary Claire Hall, and Francesca Monteleone all deserve credit for their hard work. Finally, I owe a great debt to Gayle Lenz, Boyle Hall secretary at St. Norbert; her meticulous but speedy help in collating all the manuscript's passages from Gide's works is much appreciated.

Financial support from the Office of Faculty Development at St. Norbert College in the summer of 1996 helped me to get started. In-house grants of this kind provide a valuable incentive for professors in small, teaching-intensive institutions to carry out research. In this respect I also wish to thank Dr. Thomas J. Trebon, Academic Vice President and Dean of St. Norbert College, who has believed in this project from the outset and whose generous funding has helped offset costs involving proofreading and editing.

Finally, on a more personal note, I wish to thank my parents, Ethel and Charles Conner. If there are any readers to whom all my writing is addressed, it is to them. They first introduced me to French culture and not only instilled in me a love of learning but also stimulated my interest in the history of contemporary Europe, in particular the ambiguous relationship between intellectuals and their times.

Throughout the preparation of this book my wife Ikuko Torimoto has lent support and good humor. She believed in me and in the integrity of my work even when progress seemed uncertain. Our life together provides a wonderful balance to the rigors of the academic profession and its many pressures. It is to her that I dedicate this book.

Nockeby, Sweden, January 2000

PREFATORY NOTE

Most of the French terms used in these essays are followed by an English version in square brackets; those widely known or clear from the context, however, are left untranslated. An essay's use of published translations is duly credited; all renderings into English not followed by a parenthetical citation are the author's. And unless indicated otherwise, ellipsis dots within quotations have been inserted by the author, whereas italicized words belong to the source.

INTRODUCTION

Tom Conner

1

André Gide was more than a writer of fiction who showed an occasional interest in society. Beginning in the 1920s, at the peak of his career, after having established himself as an accomplished writer, astute *moraliste,* and the foremost spokesperson of his generation for personal freedom and self-realization, Gide became aware, first, that his particular brand of bourgeois individualism was becoming increasingly irrelevant in the contemporary world and, second, that social commitment and even revolution could serve as a powerful source of inspiration and self-renewal. Over a ten-year period that ended with his public break with the Soviet Union in 1936, Gide, the committed intellectual, interacted with society in what were for him unprecedented ways.

Gide's commitment can be seen in his public actions, as Europe's conscience and *"contemporain capital"* [outstanding contemporary], and in his writing, in a type of committed literature that transformed traditional genres such as the novel and theater but also included the essay, the travelogue, the journalistic reportage, the public speech, and the petition. His commitment to what he believed to be not only right but also humanly possible to achieve in his lifetime constituted a "politics" because Gide's intention manifestly was to *change* society by changing the forces that shaped it, whether public attitudes or institutions like the law courts or the *compagnies concessionnaires* that exploited the Congo. Is this not why he published books like *Souvenirs de la cour d'assises* (1914) and *Voyage au Congo* (1927)?

Gide's intention was to satisfy the moral imperative of his own conscience and, equally important, to have an impact on his world and on the life of his contemporaries as well. Gide clearly was in a position to influence public opinion through his writing, and he intended to take full advantage of his reputation to do so. As François Mauriac wrote in his eulogy of Gide, "he was a man deeply involved in a specific struggle, a specific fight, who never wrote a line which he did not think was of service to the cause he had at heart" (19).[1]

The origin of Gide's commitment was personal, and his ambition, at all times, was to remain faithful to his own integrity, that is, to the truth. In point of fact, Gide's commitment evolved from the affirmation of his own sexuality to a sensitive, informed, and sometimes activist critique of a host of issues that confronted France in the first half of this century: the emancipation of women, the shortcomings of the French justice system, French ambivalence toward colonialism, the Fascist threat to Western civilization and the fellow-traveling movement, the Communist temptation, and World War II.

However, Gide did not always follow the straight and narrow. From beginning to end, Gide's politics were characterized by ambiguity and fraught with contradiction: Gide refuted Barrès's conservative nationalism but still believed in French exceptionalism; Gide deplored the excesses of colonialism but clearly believed in the civilizing mission of France; Gide condemned Stalin but still extolled the fundamental ideals of Communism. Gide's presence in our twentieth century is as complex and fraught with uncertainty as the very events that make up what the BBC in its award-winning 1998 documentary called "the people's century."

2

Paris. July 1935. The First International Congress of Writers for the Defense of Culture was getting under way at the Palais de la Mutualité on the Left Bank, in the heart of the Latin Quarter. Every writer with left-wing sympathies had been invited, it seems, and this was arguably the greatest intellectual happening of the 1930s in France. In the words of one participant, the writer Jean Guéhenno, "We didn't stop talking for five days and nearly five nights" (Lottman 86). Gide was presiding and was an integral part of the French home team, which, in addition to himself, included Malraux, Guéhenno, Aragon, and Barbusse. Ostensibly, everyone had gathered to express concern about the decline of culture under Fascism, but this was also a call to arms in support of the Soviet Union—in a way this was *la levée en masse* [mass mobilization] all over again, a call to defend the ideals of the French Revolution against the forces of reaction everywhere.

The International Congress of Writers for the Defense of Culture was perhaps the high point of Gide's career as an engaged intellectual writer. Gide was controversial, to be sure; yet no one in France commanded the same degree of moral authority not only for his literary achievements but also and above all for his influential views on a wide range of social and political issues. His prestige abroad was at least as great. For all practical purposes Gide was indeed a *"contemporain capital"* (as André Rouveyre described him). Less than a year later, however, after publishing his blasphemous travelogue on the Soviet Union, *Retour de l'U.R.S.S.,* he was to become *persona non grata* on the Left and would never again regain the stature he had once had, not even after receiving the Nobel Prize for Literature in 1947. A modern-day Oedipus, Gide was banished from the city of intellectuals. "A corpse has just died," the Communist daily

L'Humanité wrote upon the author's death in 1951,[2] but this diatribe could hardly efface Gide's well-documented record of courage under pressure.

Perhaps the most rewarding approach to Gide's *engagement* [commitment] is to consider its many different inroads. If one inverts the terms of André Rouveyre's epithet, Gide becomes a *"capitale contemporaine"* [capital of the contemporary world], which may be even more apt to define his importance as intellectual godfather. All roads in the early-to-middle 1930s led to André Gide. What is more, like any capital city, Gide (like Oedipus) found himself at a crossroads, in this case an "intellectual crossroads" where many different and no doubt basically contradictory avenues of thought merged. Gide was involved in a wide range of activities normally associated with the intellectual: writing, editing, translating, publishing, speaking, traveling, petitioning, marching—so much so that he rather neglected his vocation as an author of fiction, as did Malraux and most other engaged writers in these troubled times. Certainly there were other and more important things to think about in the years that led up to World War II! Besides, as Gide himself remarked, "it is with fine sentiments that bad literature is made" (*Journals* 3: 322).[3]

It would be easy to idealize Gide's perception of his political integrity. Gide often said that his function was to disturb *[inquiéter]*,[4] and although this *profession de foi* attests to the conviction and character of Gide the iconoclast, it does not warrant a view of him as a paragon of moral courage. Gide was a paradox. On the one hand, he emphatically stated that his main concern was always to remain faithful to the truth and to himself, to his own integrity, whatever the consequences, no matter how high the price. For example, to publish the *Retour de l'U.R.S.S.* in 1936, at a time when the Republicans in Spain were quite literally fighting for their lives and were in desperate need of assistance from men and women of good will everywhere, made Gide appear selfish and unfaithful to the anti-Fascist cause. Nevertheless, as Gide saw things, he had no choice but to reveal the truth about the Soviet Union, no matter what the cost was to himself or to the cause of the anti-Fascist struggle. Gide was, in the words of J. Touchard, the epitome of a free man: "free against families, against convention, against judges, against the churches and conspicuous converts, against parties and prejudices, against nationalism in the style of Maurice Barrès, against dogmatism, against authority, against fanaticism" (Lottman 47). Moreover, Gide, like his mythological father Oedipus, had somehow brought this curse upon himself. Nonetheless, as he himself wrote in his 1931 version of Sophocles' tragedy, "Whoever they may be, they are men. I shall be glad to bring them happiness at the expense of my suffering" (*Two Legends* 43).[5] We can assume that these "men" are Gide's contemporaries whom Gide seeks to guide, thereby washing himself of original sin and redeeming himself in the eyes of posterity and in the eyes of God, too. Gide's autobiographical discourse is steeped in a kind of secular Protestantism that more than one critic would recognize as a point of departure on the long road that would lead Gide to Africa and then on to Moscow.

On the other hand, it is impossible not to question the authenticity and even the sincerity of Gide's good faith. Gide was not a martyr. At times he deserves our admiration for his moral courage, but there is much more that calls for attention and has not been sufficiently addressed by critics: his contradictions, his ambivalence, his occasional lapses, his restlessness, his ignorance of fundamental political realities, his vanity, his guilt, his predatory sexuality. From the very beginning of his career, Gide justifies a certain critical skepticism on our part as we try to assess the true impact of his political commitment. In fact, to shed light on this complexity is precisely what this volume seeks to accomplish: to revisit, that is, to revise and refine our understanding of Gide's overall integrity. Gide's *Journal* was recently reedited in a new Pléiade edition (1996–1997), a testimony that his example remains relevant today. The present volume is unique in that it can be read as a complement to the *Journal,* illuminating the portrait that emerges from this work from a number of different angles, some more flattering than others, but all equally revealing.

Yes, Gide's naiveté and presumption were enormous, even by the standards of his own time. But André Gide, this aesthete *rentier* who, in the words of his detractors on the staff of *L'Humanité,* "lived dangerously under three layers of flannel vests,"[6] retained a dignity and a passion for the truth that most all of his fellow-traveling contemporaries ought to have envied. What is Gide's lesson today? "Dare to be wrong"? That would be arrogant and downright dangerous. Perhaps it is enough not to be afraid to admit when you *are* wrong and not ever settle down on your moral high horse. The lesson is that the end does not always justify the means; the lesson of Communism suggests that unjust means compromise the end, obscure it, and ultimately postpone it indefinitely.

3

This collection of thirteen essays examines the outcomes of Gide's evolving commitment to controversial issues ranging from the sexual to the political, from the literary to the social. Essays are arranged roughly in chronological order (according to their place in Gide's own biography and oeuvre), and each will address a specific theme of "Gide's politics," such as French colonialism in Africa or the French justice system, just to name two areas in which Gide's commitment was especially vigorous.

In his last essay (sadly, he died before this book appeared), noted Gide critic Daniel Moutote argues that Gide's commitment is personal, social, and political. In fact, Gide's oeuvre as a whole may be construed as "engaged." Certainly the political nature of his "immoralism" escaped none of his conservative critics, who were quick to denounce Gide as a cancer on traditional French society. Following his death in 1951 the Vatican was still sufficiently incensed with Gide to place the totality of his oeuvre on its Index of Forbidden Books!

It is a fact that Gide always remained committed to himself and always appeared more concerned with his own liberation, self-affirmation, and self-creation in both fiction and nonfiction than with anything else. However, by the 1920s Gide's inspiration seemed to have dried up. Perhaps by now he had perceived the hollowness of his idiosyncratic brand of sincerity? This realization on his part coincided with a change of mood in French society that followed in the wake of the Great War. At the same time Gide's "message" had gained in public appeal—his novels were suddenly selling extremely well—and his detractors on the Right refused to let go, thus providing additional free publicity. As Gide's public persona grew in stature, the author turned to society to have a closer look at the forces that shaped life as most of his contemporaries knew it and that he had ignored for far too long, coming from a privileged background. For more than ten years Gide tried—with varying degrees of success—to speak out on behalf of victims of injustice everywhere. Ultimately the factual truth was more important to Gide than any political commitments to parties or organizations, and so he broke with that symbol of progress, the Soviet Union, yet remained faithful to the hope of peace and justice that she at first had represented to him and to a whole generation of Western intellectuals.

When does Gide's commitment begin? In the 1890s, at the very beginning of his career, Gide was not interested so much in becoming politically involved on the domestic scene as in challenging the moral and literary authority of Barrès and disputing some of the values and issues around which *Les Déracinés* is organized. However, to stake out a position in this debate was a move rife with political implications. For Gide, to leave home and country was a creative incentive, not its opposite, and French exceptionalism and imperialism were actually conducive to the civilizing mission of France in the name of *liberté, égalité,* and *fraternité.* As M. Martin Guiney argues in his essay on Gide and nationalism, the 1890s marked the beginning of an interest in French society on Gide's part because he chose sides, as it were, and adhered to the secular and democratic values of the French Republic, which, in Guiney's view, were also the values of classicism. Moreover, the roots of Gide's ambiguous position on colonialism, obvious in *Voyage au Congo,* extended all the way back to the oedipal struggle with Barrès for prominence in the cultural domain.

In Gide's case sexuality is central to an understanding of commitment. As Daniel Moutote suggests in the first essay of this volume, the origin of Gide's commitment was personal and revolved around his homosexuality. Mauriac, too, was of the same opinion and wrote: "The fact of the matter is that Gide's particular form of erotic satisfaction lay at the very centre of his drama. The struggle he waged was about that and about nothing else. For him the point at issue was the legitimization of a special type of desire" (27).[7] While we today are aware of the full impact of Gide's sexual orientation on his life and work, there was a time when Gide's sexuality was suppressed by the literary community, by critics, scholars, and editors. In an original essay that explores a new dimension of Gide's sexual politics, Michael Lucey takes as his starting point the restored journal entry for November 24, 1918, and argues that the author and the literary community at large together are responsible for molding posterity's image of an author by the way they choose to present a text. After discovering the extent and nature of her husband's relationship with the young Marc Allégret, Gide's wife destroyed their correspondence, and in this rightly famous journal entry Gide wrote that nothing now prevented him from publishing *Corydon* and *Si le grain ne meurt.* Thus began Gide's traumatic quest for sexual affirmation and recognition, a struggle that closely affected not only his posterity but also his literary career in his own lifetime.

As I stated at the beginning of this introduction, by the 1920s Gide felt that he had exhausted his interest in himself and turned to the evolution of French society for inspiration and self-renewal. Herein lies a curious duality in Gide's politics. To what extent was he (to use his own term) *"sincère"* in his political allegiances, and to what extent was he just looking for a change of scenery? Though not a Christian in any institutional sense, Gide always claimed a Christian ethos and would never renounce the ideals of truth and social justice. As a juror, Gide would become exposed firsthand to the shortcomings of the French justice system. While Gide certainly drew on these experiences to enrich the psychology of his literary characters, he also decided to speak out and expose the arbitrary and class-oriented justice exercised in the French law courts. John Lambeth studies Gide's critique of the French justice system in *Souvenirs de la cour d'assises* (1914) and also argues that this work, along with *La Séquestrée de Poitiers* (1930) and *L'Affaire Redureau* (1930), inspired Gide to propose much needed reforms.

But it was his intervention in the debate on French colonialism that gave Gide a public persona. Walter Putnam, in his essay on *Voyage au Congo* (1927) and *Le Retour du Tchad* (1928), examines Gide from a critical perspective that draws on Foucault and attempts to situate these intriguing forms of literary colonialism in the "political, historical, and anthropological debates of his time." Equally important, Putnam sheds light on the contradictions that make up Gide's own attitude toward both Africa and French colonial policy. While Gide's travel journals occupy an important position in the overall history of African studies, Gide has probably received more credit as a critic of colonialism than he deserves. Gide seems to decry the abuses of colonialism rather than the system of colonialism itself, resorting to many of the same arguments for French exceptionalism and cultural superiority that characterized his famous debate with Barrès at the turn of the century. Actually Gide embarked on his African odyssey for personal reasons rather than political ones, but he was outraged at what he saw and at his own inability to comprehend African reality fully. The political impact of the travel journals stems from the polemics in which Gide engaged upon his return to France in order to draw public attention to the worst abuses of the concessionary companies that exploited the French colonies in Equatorial Africa.

As Walter Putnam argues in his essay, Gide was quite literally at a loss to represent the African reality that confronted him during his travels and was unable or unwilling to move beyond a superficial "fauna and flora" approach to the Congo. On the one hand, Gide saw himself as a rebel against bourgeois French sensibility; on the other, once in Africa he feared going native and maintained an uncharacteristic colonial civility. In a second essay dealing with Africa, Jeffrey Geiger reads Gide's travel journals as "ethnographic spectacle," defined as a specifically European representation of the African Other, and shows how Gide's colonial politics can be further explored from an anthropological vantage point. The photographs that accompany the journals and especially Marc Allégret's documentary film *Voyage au Congo* suggest that Gide's colonial politics are grounded as much in textual representation as they are in the act of actually witnessing or seeing primitive reality. Studying Gide's reaction to Africa, therefore, helps reveal his evolving sense of self and permits new insights into how Europeans write about Africa. As it turns out, Gide is an unwilling player in this ethnographic spectacle by reproducing primitivist stereotypes about Africans. By casting himself in the privileged position of an outside observer, Gide perpetuates a subject/object dialectic that reinforces the very system of oppression that he himself is credited with attacking in the first place.

In a sense, Gide is typical of a host of left-wing French intellectuals in the period between the two World Wars. Jean-François Sirinelli draws on his extensive research on the subject to present an overview of intellectual commitment on the Left, specifically in the 1930s. Sirinelli situates Gide's fellow-traveling career in its proper historical and ideological context and argues that Gide epitomized the 1930s much the same way Jean-Paul Sartre would later come to epitomize the postwar period. The committed intellectual had been a fixture of French society ever since the Dreyfus affair, and during the 1930s intellectuals would once again take up arms. The reasons for this are obvious enough: the specter of Fascism forced many high-profile intellectuals to take sides or at least to express themselves in public. Many chose to become actively involved in the anti-Fascist struggle, but a surprising number sided with the political Right. As Sirinelli writes, left- and right-wing intellectuals were quite evenly matched in these years, in terms of both numbers and influence. Unlike an Aragon or even a Malraux, however, Gide was prepared to publicly acknowledge his poor judgment with regard to the Soviet Union. No doubt he did so out of political naiveté but also out of a moral imperative that deserves recognition and praise. As will become clear, Gide had various reasons for acting the way he did, so I will not go so far as to say that he was the moral conscience of his times. However, he did not hesitate to use a public forum to air his conscience, which sometimes had the effect of galvanizing his contemporaries.

The 1930s were indeed momentous times when both good will and hypocrisy abounded. A brilliant case in point is the 1935 First International Congress of Writers for the Defense of Culture, held at the Mutualité on the Left Bank. Hundreds of intellectuals from all over the world gathered to show solidarity with the Soviet Union and, ostensibly, to devise ways in which they could combat the rise of Fascism. The Congress lasted three days and, as expected, made little progress, if any, towards its stated goals. Moreover, the event quickly deteriorated into a happening in the best tradition of the 1960s, accompanied by the same media hype and unrealistic expectations. What is more, the Congress was corrupted from within by what can only be called the bad faith of many of its organizers and key personalities. The French Communists ran the show, aided by Soviet agents, and few, if any, French intellectuals unaffiliated with the Party either knew enough about the oppressive nature of the Soviet system or dared to speak out. Gide, to some degree, was again the brave exception and intervened on behalf of Belgian-Russian novelist Victor Serge, who had fallen victim to Stalin's purges. While the Congress shows the determination of

French intellectuals in these years to resist Fascism, it also shows how easily they were manipulated by Moscow. Roger Shattuck's essay on the Congress, therefore, sets the stage for Gide's own disappointment in the Soviet Union, following his first and last trip to the Promised Land in the summer of 1936.

Like most other progressive intellectuals of his day, Gide was fascinated by the Soviet experiment. In his essay, Paul Hollander argues that Gide's support of the Soviet Union as a critical fellow traveler must be understood in both personal and political terms. To Gide the Soviet Union at first held out the evangelical promise of peace and justice for all. Moreover, the Soviet Union alone appeared willing and able to withstand the Fascist menace that consumed much of Europe in the 1930s, and it behooved men and women of good will everywhere to rally to her defense. Soon it became clear, though, that the Soviet Union did not live up to the high expectations of intellectuals in the West. Stalinism had quelled the hopes of the October Revolution. Gide denounced Stalinism in two famous travelogues, *Retour de l'U.R.S.S.* and *Retouches à mon Retour de l'U.R.S.S.;* however, he did not denounce the ideals of the Revolution itself. This ambiguity creates a tension in the text, a critical dialectic that enables Gide to remain faithful to his ideals of human dignity while maintaining his own high standards of truth.

Not surprisingly, Gide's politics carried over into his aesthetics. While one could argue that much of Gide's writing is political in the sense that it expresses sometimes controversial moral positions, Peter F. DeDomenico limits his inquiry to Gide's flirtation with Socialist Realism. As one of the leading intellectuals of his generation, André Gide was passionately interested in the life of his times. Moreover, he wanted to be more than just a passive spectator who looked on from the sidelines. If possible, he wanted to participate firsthand. In the other essays that make up this volume, we see ample evidence of Gide's attempts to involve himself in the affairs of the City; however, we also note a certain reluctance on his part to give up his artistic vocation. Gide was never comfortable in his role as public persona and frankly regretted not being able to remain faithful to his calling as an artist. Gide soon found a way to reconcile his art with his politics. He had experimented with the fundamentals of the novel and produced *Les Faux-Monnayeurs,* which still ranks as one of the great twentieth-century French novels. Why should he not try his hand at Socialist Realism and aim for another metamorphosis of his creative genius more suited, no doubt, to the radical values of his times?

Peter F. DeDomenico explores the challenges posed by Socialist Realism and shows that Gide, after all, was still and always would be a bourgeois dilettante. Actually Gide had said as much when he tried rather naively to reconcile individualism and Communism; *L'École des femmes* and, especially, *Geneviève* bear him out. At the same time, Gide's genius is unmistakable, and the reader of this feminist triptych is treated to a panoply of lifestyle issues that trigger typically Gidean responses and maneuvers that shed new light not only on Gide's politics but also on his evolving conception of the struggle between the demands of human sexuality and the constraints of bourgeois French society in the period between the wars.

The relationship between Socialist Realism and feminism could be a dynamic one and seems promising. Naomi Segal studies the drama of revolt and submission in a French bourgeois family at the beginning of this century as portrayed in Gide's trilogy of "engaged" novels—*L'École des femmes, Robert,* and *Geneviève*—and finds new constellations of gender roles. In these three novels Gide represented a new type of woman who attempts to accommodate herself to the ruling patriarchal system and thereby reinvent her identity. However, Gide's family romance in no way amounts to a full-fledged feminist politics. Far from it. Gide had set out to study what he called, for lack of a better term, *"les problèmes de la femme"* [women's problems], but in the end he was unable or unwilling to envision and commit to a coherent and persuasive body of feminist thought. As for Geneviève, she has a child out of wedlock but still accommodates herself to the patriarchal norms that shape woman's place and role in French society.

After falling out with the Left Bank following his public denunciation of Stalinism, Gide kept a low profile. However, World War II forced him to rethink his earlier commitment, indeed to try to explain the decline and fall of France in 1940 in light of his and other intellectuals' commitment in the 1930s. World War II put Gide on the defensive. After the *débâcle* in 1940, writers on the Left like Gide were widely blamed for the defeat, for having corrupted French youth and being morally responsible for the decadence that afflicted the nation. In numerous journal entries Gide himself seemed to concur and, as if that were not already enough, opened himself to charges of collusion by continuing to write for the *NRF*, now in the hands of the collaborator Drieu La Rochelle. Gide himself was not immune to charges of anti-Semitism, having deplored the Jewish influence on French culture on more than one occasion.

As always, Gide's point of view was ambivalent, and in her magisterial reading of "Gide's war," Jocelyn Van Tuyl brings out the complexity and ambiguity of Gide's position. He would spend part of the war in North Africa, in Tunis and Algiers, and it was during this period, when quite literally Gide felt himself "under siege," that he would pen his most compelling and complex memoir of these years. Writing in his *Journal* during the 1942–1943 siege of Tunis, Gide would chronicle the progress of the war but also, more importantly, in the story of his hosts' adolescent son "Victor," would offer a personal allegory of French society's moral and intellectual decadence in the prewar years. "Victor" represented all that had been wrong with France in the 1930s: he was self-indulgent, disrespectful of authority, lazy, and spoiled silly. However, this was not to say that Gide and his generation were to blame. He had only tried to do what Socrates said to his accusers that he had wanted to do; Gide aimed to educate French youth by challenging them to think and act accordingly. In a scathing memoir of his own, "Victor" would later denounce Gide's pedagogical imperative as empty and as an excuse for his predatory sexual nature. As Naomi Segal has shown elsewhere, in Gide's case pedagogy and pederasty were intimately linked.

Thus Gide's war was not exactly glorious, and it was a far cry from the courage he had exhibited throughout the 1930s, especially when he broke ranks and denounced the Soviet Union. Gide now chose to remain above the fray, if

possible. Still, he let himself be used by the Right by decrying the moral bankruptcy of the French Republic and never went beyond a neutral and detached
attitude toward the Allies, though they would be quick to publish his portrayal
of the liberation of Tunis. Curiously, de Gaulle's V-Day proclamation is never
recorded in Gide's *Journal*.

In the concluding essay of the volume, Pamela A. Genova reveals another
dimension of Gide's commitment and shows how after the war Gide returned
to the Theseus myth to explore a homoerotic thematics further. This closes the
circle in a sense: Gide's commitment began and ended with an affirmation of
his sexuality. Myth was a constant in Gide's literary imagination, so it is significant that in his last work (*Thésée,* 1946) he should return to the world of Greek
myth to express a new form of commitment through literature. The Theseus
myth has received many different interpretations throughout history. More often
than not, Theseus has been seen as a contradictory figure, "depicting in various
texts the champion over monsters, judge of criminals, faithful friend, unfaithful
lover, and brilliant statesman." Genova shows how Gide subverts the myth to
bring out its homoerotic appeal. While Gide experimented with a variety of
different forms of commitment, some of them more active than others, his aristocratically inclined bourgeois personality usually got in the way of any lasting
social or political involvement. The story of Theseus provided Gide with an
ideal opportunity, perfectly suited to his personality, to explore a homoerotic
theme vicariously, through myth, which Genova defines as a "subtle and unexpected discourse . . . that transmits an effective and subversive power." Myth by
definition is inscribed on a higher level of human experience, which confers
added dignity and universal appeal to Gide's positions. Thus Gide, to the very
end of his life, remained committed to exploring the moral problems of contemporary life.

As I hope I have shown, Gide continues to be relevant today. Each and every
essay in this collection speaks to this effect. Moreover, the variety of approaches
taken by contributors here ensures a fresh new look at a host of issues spanning
the gamut of the humanities: intellectual history, literary studies, poetics, cultural
studies, African studies, gender studies, feminism, and queer theory. This volume
does not propose a perfectly coherent view of Gide's politics. Rather, it seeks to
bring out the ambiguity of many of Gide's positions. While Gide's approach to
politics was seldom as straightforward as we would like, he demonstrates a sensitivity to the complexities of human nature and a concern for leading a moral
life that most of us still find profoundly engaging. Despite often murky personal
reasons for doing what he did (even visiting the Soviet Union), Gide's public
interventions were sincere and well-intentioned. While we may enjoy reading
his novels for many years to come, the impact of his writing seems to be of a
distinctly moral nature. He was far from perfect himself, but he did and does
make us think about how to live our lives. As Sartre wrote in his eulogy "Gide
vivant" in 1951, "he displeases and will continue to displease for a long time to
come" (15).[8] Sartre's "displeasure" rather reminds one of Gide's avowed purpose in life to "disturb" *[inquiéter]* his readers, to shake them, quite literally, and
make them reflect on who and what they are.

There is one area that I have not mentioned in which Gide's commitment was significant, indeed fundamental with regard to his own evolution: religion. Gide would not have become Gide had he not chosen to revolt against the Church at an early age and adopt an anti-Christian outlook on life. This decision must be considered political. And here, too, Gide's attitude was ambiguous. There is far more than meets the eye. At times Gide even flirted with the idea of conversion. Certainly, his sincere interest in Christianity is obvious in works such as *La Porte étroite, La Symphonie pastorale,* and *Numquid et tu . . . ?* Equally obvious are the devious ways in which Gide used religion as a literary subject.

Gide's complicated relationship with religion should not be dismissed as somehow outdated and could well become the focus of an exciting new inquiry. The reason I decided against pursuing this relationship has to do less with the changing fortunes of Christianity in the West and more with Gide's (and not only his) victory over the kind of moral absolutism that was the rule rather than the exception in the days when he struggled to affirm his freedom. Today it is possible to be religious and a liberal at the same time. I wonder, too, whether Gide's atheism ought not to be construed as self-liberation rather than as an outright attack on Christianity. Gide's empathy with Christianity has often been credited with forming his social conscience. Lastly, Gide's battle with the Church is so well-known to the scholarly community, if not to the general public, as to offer few novel insights. Among the many critics who have commented incisively on Gide's anti-Christian commitment, Jean Delay, Wallace Fowlie, Catharine Savage Brosman, Claude Martin, and Alan Sheridan deserve special mention.

In the final analysis, reading Gide is a matter of personal choice. We read Gide for the same reason that Montaigne read the Ancients: not because these authors always have the answers but because they ask the right questions. We are all *"ondoyant et divers"* [fluctuating and multifaceted]. The quality of our moral life depends on how we take these words to heart. Gide matters to us today because we want him to and make him matter. He remains our G(u)ide.

Notes

1. "[U]n homme engagé à fond dans une certaine lutte, dans un certain combat, il n'a pas écrit une ligne qui n'ait prétendu servir la cause à laquelle il s'était donné" (180).
2. "« C'est un cadavre qui vient de mourir »" (quoted in Sartre 1537).
3. "[C]'est avec les beaux sentiments qu'on fait la mauvaise littérature" (*Journal* 495).
4. "Fine function to assume: that of *disseminator of unrest*" [Belle fonction à assumer : celle d'*inquiéteur*] (*Journals* 3: 318; *Journal* 490). "My role is that of a provocateur" [Mon rôle est celui d'un inquiéteur] (Genova 282; Marty 315).
5. "Quels qu'ils soient, ce sont des hommes. Au prix de ma souffrance, il m'est doux de leur apporter du bonheur" (*Œdipe* 304).
6. "« [V]ivait dangereusement sous trois épaisseurs de gilet de flanelle »" (quoted in Sartre 1538).

7. "Oui, sans doute, mais parlons net : la convoitise de Gide fut le centre même de son drame. Le combat de Gide a été celui-là et non un autre : il s'agissait de légitimer une certaine convoitise" (189).
8. "[I]l déplaisait encore et déplaira longtemps" (1537).

Works Cited

Genova, Pamela A. "Theseus Revisited: Commitment through Myth." Pp. 263-283 of this volume.

Gide, André. *Journal 1926–1950*. Ed. Martine Sagaert. Paris: Gallimard, Bibliothèque de la Pléiade, 1997.

———. *The Journals of André Gide*. Ed. and trans. Justin O'Brien. Vol. 3. New York: Alfred A. Knopf, 1949.

———. *Œdipe. Théâtre*. Paris: Gallimard, 1942.

———. *Two Legends: "Oedipus" and "Theseus."* Trans. John Russell. New York: Vintage, 1958.

Lottman, Herbert. *The Left Bank: Writers, Artists, and Politics from the Popular Front to the Cold War*. San Francisco: Halo Books, 1991.

Marty, Éric. *André Gide : Qui êtes-vous? avec les entretiens Jean Amrouche et André Gide*. Lyon: La Manufacture, 1987.

Mauriac, François. "The Death of André Gide." *Gide: A Collection of Critical Essays*. Ed. David Littlejohn. Englewood Cliffs, NJ: Prentice-Hall, 1970. 19–29.

———. *Mémoires intérieurs*. Paris: Flammarion, 1959. 179–191.

Sartre, Jean-Paul. "Gide vivant." *Les Temps Modernes* 65 (1951): 1537–1541.

———. "The Living Gide." *Gide: A Collection of Critical Essays*. Ed. David Littlejohn. Englewood Cliffs, NJ: Prentice-Hall, 1970. 15-18.

CHAPTER 1

The Meaning and Impact of
André Gide's *Engagement*[1]

Daniel Moutote

André Gide's commitment *[engagement]* represents nothing more than another, deeper version of his artistic activity. It became evident late in his prime and unfolded in three stages, each of which culminated in books that immortalize what he had accomplished: personal commitment from 1908 to 1918, leading to *Corydon;* social commitment from 1925 to 1929, revealed in *Voyage au Congo* and *Le Retour du Tchad;* and finally, political commitment, realized from 1930 to 1937 and concluded with *Retour de l'U.R.S.S.* and *Retouches à mon Retour de l'U.R.S.S.* All this is a brilliant demonstration of André Gide's sincerity and the indisputable value of his oeuvre.

1

One might have reservations about Ramon Fernandez's famous formula: "André Gide, or the courage to commit oneself."[2] Not that Gide ever lacked courage; quite the contrary. But for Gide, homosexuality was not a cause for which he would have campaigned in the streets or waved a banner and fought. Gide never advocated homosexuality; he only defended the amorous freedom of certain famous homosexuals, just as he fought on behalf of human freedom through his writings. In his *Journal* he states that the "drama" that he wants always to consider anew deals with what hampers human integrity: "that which is opposed to human beings' integrity, to their wholeness."[3] The aspect of homosexuality that concerns him is first and foremost a personal issue—the sensuality that provoked him as a ten-year-old child to cry out, as he experienced the *Schaudern* of difference: "I am not the same as the others."[4] All of Gide's literary works—short stories, *soties,* and novels—reflect this secret, which *Corydon* would problematize.

Corydon, which Gide considered his most important work, marks the author's break with the rest of his literary oeuvre. Far from being a step backwards, it must be considered a fundamental advance in his oeuvre. This Gidean break is analogous to Valéry's 1892 decision to give up composing verses in order to dedicate himself to the daily reflections that would lead to his *Cahiers*. Gide and Valéry are the two twentieth-century artists who have done the most to free literature from its traditional artistic superficiality and confer upon it its modern status as a work of human discovery. In 1892, on the advice of Mallarmé, Valéry decided not to publish his poetry, as the Master found it to be simplistic; instead, he undertook an investigation of the "orphic secrets of the universe" (in Mallarmé's words),[5] the secrets of the poets, by analyzing the forms and laws of the structuring faculty we call "mind" *[esprit]*. Gide devoted himself to a parallel search concerning sensibility *[sensibilité]*, which would lead him in 1918 to *Corydon*.

Corydon is both a scientific and historical study of human sensuality, and this work examines its most general form prior to sexual differentiation: homosexuality. From childhood on, Gide continually had a revelation about this particular form of human sensuality, during times like the one mentioned earlier, times when he experienced the *Schaudern* of difference. This revelation was the secret of his personality; it was something that he never, even in his literary works, stopped studying as a fundamental human mystery. His study of this secret begins in 1908 with the cryptic book *C.R.D.N.*, which in 1911 he printed in an edition of eleven copies, without any publisher's name or place of publication. At that time, the book consisted of only a first chapter and part of a second. It was completed in 1918, the same year in which Gide finished other projects begun earlier—important books that in 1915 he had noted were still to be written, in particular *Numquid et tu . . . ?*

Corydon begins with a defense of famous homosexuals condemned by the judicial system of their times, the most important being Oscar Wilde, who had attempted to shatter the moralism of Victorian society and allowed himself to be condemned to hard labor. Gide emphasizes the health and normalcy of these men, whom he considers martyrs on behalf of the moral emancipation of humanity. His discussion seeks, unsuccessfully, a scientific foundation by referring to studies of homosexuality in animals, probably at Roger Martin du Gard's instigation. The book concludes with a reminder that homosexuality among the Greeks in classical antiquity was supported by philosophers, politicians, and the general customs of the time.

In this inquiry and particularly in the *Journal*, Gide's commitment is expressed in his assiduous attention to numerous adolescents to whom he wrote letters and from whom, to his regret, he did not always receive a response. Certain young men, like Johnny B., seem in the 1930s to show remorse for what I believe is their failure to grasp the import of this great man's devotion to them. Now let us not be naive! Gide is a homosexual. But he is not a sodomite. To understand fully Gide's attitude towards young men, it is essential to be wary of simplistic jokes about the behavior of homosexuals in general. The significance of Gide's "homosexuality" can be understood only from the perspective of a careful study of human sensuality. Paul Valéry's strange confession in one of his notebooks from the beginning of the war is worth pondering:

Love and me. I could have made a contribution to Love if destiny had willed it: a cruelty towards myself and a rigorous conscience, which, coupled with my natural understanding of human physics and that mysticism without object that exists within me, could have perhaps, if some woman had been of the same opinion, having an analogous understanding of body and soul, an intelligent and experimental passion, a premonition of sensual pleasure as *means*—that's what would be new—could have, I say (and I was saying this to P[ierre] L[ouÿs] the day before yesterday), perhaps been able to make something of Love . . . as I also say that music could become a means, etc.[6]

This sense of confidence or, rather, this whim inspired by Pierre Louÿs's presence is unique in Valéry's writings. Valéry's implausible project is to use love for scientific purposes, to approach it as part of his inquiry into "Mind" *[l'Esprit]*. Gide accomplished a similar aim with reference to *sensuality*. He engaged in an inquiry that the mystery of his own profound sensitivity imposed on him. And he engaged in this inquiry by focusing on beings whose sensuality is the liveliest: adolescents. That is why he gave so much of his time to adolescents, as his *Journal* reveals. He wrote to them and was distressed when he received no answer. He stayed close to the sensuality of young boys as it developed to the point of blossoming in social situations. One can see this in the case of Marc Allégret, whom he loved to distraction during the time when he was composing *Corydon* (1917–1918), and whom he subsequently made a well-known and important filmmaker.

Valéry also speaks of the role that music could have in the study of human sensuality, and Gide played Chopin's music from this perspective. During certain periods of his life, at Cuverville, we see him working furiously on some Chopin scherzo for days on end, pushing himself beyond reasonable limits, until he plays the piece as he judges it should be played. It is not Chopin that he is studying; it is himself. He works on the Chopin piece until it becomes a deeply personal piece of evidence for his own feelings, a way of justifying who he is. These studies of Chopin's music are identical to those on homosexual sensuality. To understand this, one must recall his mother forbade him access to Chopin's music. Gide explains in *Si le grain ne meurt,* in which the study of music plays such an important part, that his mother refused to take him to a Chopin concert given by Rubinstein, under the pretext that it was "unhealthy music."[7] Indeed, Chopin's music is very sensitive, even delicately sensual. But to call it "unhealthy"! To understand her attitude, one must remember that the preceding year, or some years earlier, the young Gide had been suspended from the École Alsacienne for having repeated in class the improper practices mentioned at the beginning of *Si le grain ne meurt.* Thus, one must admit that the prudent Mrs. Paul Gide, widowed at the time, did not want to run the risk of tempting her son's rather lively sensuality. Her prohibition left an unmistakable mark on the young Gide's psyche. For him, Chopin's music became associated with that inverted sensuality that had been troubling him since the *Schaudern* of difference: "I am not the same as the others." What's more, for Gide, Chopin's music remained the long-lasting and fundamental sign of his difference from others.

From this grew his long study of Chopin's music, which was, in a sense, an experience of his own homosexual sensuality. An experience founded on a maternal prohibition became a fundamental trait of Gide's "nature."

This early homosexual sensibility, manifesting itself prior to sexual differentiation, is a permanent feature of Gidean "debauchery," which is the zero point of existence that all Gide's characters return to, or fall back into, after the final catastrophe they experience: from Michel to Jérôme, to the Pastor in the *Symphonie pastorale,* to Lafcadio and Édouard—though such is not the case for Éveline, that monument of purity, nor for Robert, that monument of infatuation, nor for Geneviève, whose story remains unfinished; and as for Thésée, debauchery is so familiar a part of his heroism that he has no need to wait for the end of his trials to taste it.

This tendency of Gide's characters to experience sensuality leads one to suspect the existence of a profound homosexuality within Gide. This imputation has no doubt harmed the reputation of Gidean morality. Rightly or wrongly, compromising statements have been attributed to him. He even appeared in the 1930s to travel afar—to Calvi, for example—in search of compromising company. But what matters here is not that Gide was morally drifting. The same point applies to the *Carnets d'Égypte,* jotted down during his trip in early 1939, which in my opinion marks a return to the homosexual experience that had been interrupted by the war. It is not appropriate to see in this an old man's surrender to the vice of homosexuality; rather, it is a return to the fundamental experience of sensuality that I am trying to substantiate in Gide's behavior. The three-year exile in Tunisia and North Africa, his stay with a family who were friends of the Reymond de Gentiles (though this stay also included the temptation posed by the famous Victor!), the precarious nature of life during the war—these put an end to Gide's experience of sensuality, which, after his return to Paris, was no longer anything more than the object of self-indulgent conversations with his friend Jean Amrouche. Add to this the fact that the Nobel Prize must have poured water on the homosexual fire which Roger Martin du Gard had no doubt stirred up too much during the period when *Corydon* was written.

In the end, are we forced to return to Ramon Fernandez's formulation and acknowledge Gide's courage to commit himself in defense of a discredited cause, homosexuality? In my view, Gide's commitment tarnished the pure radiance of his classic work. What's more, because of this commitment he conferred upon his classic characters a bit of Dostoevskian impenetrability. For example, why does the character of Alissa shine so brightly in the Christian consciousness of the twentieth century, if not because one can feel her trembling, her very foundations shaking, because of a strange unconscious love that is stronger than love? Gidean love sometimes owes its disconcerting greatness to such uneasy foundations. Let each individual judge for himself or herself. But perhaps human love owes the sense of its greatness to the share of immense weakness that it conceals.

<u>2</u>

Homosexual commitment is a constant in Gide's life once he publishes *Corydon* in the 1920s (published commercially in 1924); and homosexual commitment forms the basis of André Gide's further commitment. His departure for central Africa occurs in July 1925. Gide leaves without really knowing, he says, what he is looking for in the faraway Congo. Landscapes for the poet? Plants and butterflies for the museum? The two companions must await their arrival to find out. But they have designed their expedition grandly: they leave for a one-year trip with considerable means (thirty porters!) and cinematographic materials; their enterprise is highly dangerous, and so they carry arms. Gide claims not to know what he is looking for in the heart of darkness in central Africa. However, he has read Conrad's work, and he is not ignorant of the precedent set by Malraux in Indochina. Surely he expects a great adventure—perhaps a human one, as Pastor Allégret whispers to him.

Gide has received an assignment from the Ministère des Colonies, which confers on him an official status in the eyes of the colonial administration. In addition, he is a friend of Marcel de Coppet, the Gouverneur général of the Congo. This explains both the strength of his relationship with the colonial authorities and the complete freedom he enjoyed throughout his long journey. As was his wont, Gide could look leisurely behind the scenes of the official situation and have direct contact with the indigenous lower classes, who were exploited as gatherers of rubber by the powerful Compagnie Forestière du Congo. Gide's journey to the Congo is best characterized by this direct contact with the exploited lower-class population. He welcomes the courageous Africans who come to him at night to tell him what they have been compelled to do, how they have been victimized.

It is in this way that Gide is informed of the "Bambio Ball," which has to do with a severe punishment inflicted in Bambio upon gatherers whose harvest was too small, as they were obliged to go farther and farther to harvest the precious latex. The Forestière found no better solution for this problem than to condemn the unsatisfactory harvesters to spending the whole day circling the factory while bearing an enormous beam; those who fall are made to get up by being lashed with a whip. This practice has a name: forced labor. When he is informed about it, Gide alerts the Gouverneur général and the Ministre des Colonies. The Africans come to call him "Governor." What is astonishing is that the powerful Société Forestière makes no protest. Not yet! Gide and his companion are assailed by complaints at every stage of their journey. But not once does Gide protest or shirk his responsibility.

Otherwise, there is almost no official contact with the local colonial authorities. Gide remains in contact only with the indigenous lower classes. And note that he engages in no equivocal relationship with any black children—not the least indulgence. Here and there Marc films or photographs typical scenes, which they will present in Paris or Belgium upon their return. Gide walks in order to let his chair carriers rest, or does miles on horseback, noting down his impressions of the day during stops. He is not insensitive to the fauna; he tries, for instance, to capture in words the cry of a bird. He is in communion with his surroundings. Seeing clear water on a fine beach, he bathes; the crocodiles accord him the hospitality of not disturbing his bath. He is never ill. He has excellent relations with his cook, and even makes time to teach him to read. His days are very busy, spent either protecting black children or defending the indigenous women against the exactions of the guards who make them work for their own benefit. He also reads—La Fontaine in the middle of the Virgin Forest! Or he sends a congratulatory telegram to Valéry, who has just been elected to the Académie Française—big news that he learns at a rest stop from some issue of *Le Figaro.* Reading *Voyage au Congo* and *Le Retour du Tchad,* who would suspect that the author is an older gentleman of fifty-six, a lost artist with a companion and thirty porters, in the heart of the virgin forest?

The adventure ended with a return to Paris because of problems with the Compagnie Forestière, whose exploitation of the indigenous workers Gide had denounced. Gide got the authorities to adopt his point of view thanks to the support of the *NRF* and Léon Blum's *Populaire.* Gide's report to the Ministre des Colonies served as the basis for fixing the rates granted to indigenous labor in central Africa by the Bureau International du Travail de Genève.

The publication of the Congo writings was accomplished with Marc Allégret's assistance: first *Dindiki,* appearing in 1927 in *La Lampe d'Aladin,* and then, also in 1927, *Voyage au Congo,* published first in the *NRF* and subsequently as a book by the Librairie de la *NRF; Le Retour du Tchad* appeared in a first version in the *NRF* in 1928, and then in book form together with *Voyage au Congo* in 1929. The work of Daniel Durosay on this subject is most useful.

3

The most important and significant part of André Gide's commitment remains to be considered: his political commitment during the years 1930–1937, his leanings toward Communism and the U.S.S.R. *Corydon* was a book that searchingly elucidated its subject and had, above all, a personal significance for Gide. *Voyage au Congo* and *Le Retour du Tchad* were books that bore the stamp, above all, of an immense charity toward the African people. *Retour de l'U.R.S.S.* and *Retouches à mon Retour de l'U.R.S.S.* speak out with a lucidity that enlightened European politics until the fall of the U.S.S.R. in our own time.

The origin of André Gide's political commitment is also personal. It is in 1895, with Ménalque's cry, "Families, I hate you,"[8] that one finds the origin of Gide's attachment to a system that perhaps did away with families, as it certainly did away with God and classes, a system creating a country of complete equality and happiness. Gide never spoke of this as the beginning of his commitment—any more than he ever spoke about the October Revolution. But the innermost part of a man is revealed not in his speech but in his demeanor. Thus, I find the photograph of Gide at Lenin's Tomb in Red Square, as he spoke in front of Stalin at Gorky's funeral, very revealing. In this photograph Gide stands with his mouth half-open, speaking into infinity. (This image is so familiar as to have become a cliché; see it on the cover of my book, *André Gide : L'Engagement*.) Gide stands there declaiming, as if he were speaking in support of the Russian Revolution. He is performing, and this unconscious performance, this "spectacle" he creates, is highly indicative of the meaning he is secretly giving his actions. Naturally, he will never speak about it. Nevertheless, the enormous significance of his conduct seems to reveal itself in this moment. And the efforts that he would make throughout his period of political commitment worked in the same way. He would never be content to follow his fellow travelers—the Students of Moscow, for example, or the Russian Writers—as he demonstrates in a speech that he was not authorized to make, a speech that was judged to be "neither in line nor in tune." [9] In this speech Gide did not follow Party directives, extolling the dogma of the veracity of the dogma; rather, he was advising, shedding light on the official line, in order that it might become the truth that it claimed to be. In his eyes, his words never lost their essential dignity, which, according to him, came from enlightening and guiding human beings.

Gide was never seduced by the flattery he received during his triumphal visit to the Russian countryside. He understood very well that the banners wishing him well at every stage did not mean that the Russian populace was honoring him anew in place after place; he was keenly aware that these were promotional welcoming banners, always the same ones, transported in the car that preceded his.

What was the impact of Gide's trip to the U.S.S.R.? There is a strong possibility that he had already returned before he left. For Gide, indeed, had patiently tried to give himself a Communist soul. He sincerely believed that a person could not belong to a party without making his or her soul one with it. Thus, during the 1930s we see him trying in vain to acquire a Communist soul. He did this first in his *Journal,* where formulas abound of a hyperbolic allegiance to the articles of the Communist credo. These formulas can be read in the collections of excerpts he published: *Pages de Journal* (1929–1932) and *Nouvelles Pages de Journal* (1932–1935). It is easy to laugh at such ridiculous formulas of passionate devotion to the dogmas of proletarian thought; but doing that would indicate a failure to understand the meaning that Gide gave those pages. He does not write them because he is convinced of their truth, *but in order to convince himself of their truth.* He will end up recognizing this in his *Journal:* something essential will always be missing for him to feel a Communist soul in himself, namely, the fact that he has never had to earn a living. He admits, not without a certain bitterness, that he was born on the wrong side of the barricade. He will never feel in himself a Communist soul because he was not born a Communist. One does not become a proletarian: one *is* one. And so Gide never becomes a member of the Communist Party.

Gide, then, has mostly set his dreamy illusions aside by the time he leaves for Moscow in June 1936. His trip is a verification rather than a discovery. He was accompanied by five companions: two spoke fluent Russian, two others were card-carrying members of the Communist Party, and the fifth, who had for six months been the director of an important Russian journal that spread Communist propaganda, was fully versed in the intrigues of power. Gide thought that six pairs of eyes and ears were not excessive in order to see and understand things clearly. "So much cunning enters the soul of a devotee . . . of the truth!"[10] The notion of truth was no doubt so foreign to his Soviet comrades that they did not suspect Gidean duplicity and so let him do as he pleased. Gide was no longer keeping his journal, perhaps out of indifference; he was content to record in his memory what he observed. Besides, he had been trained by his trip to the Congo to look behind the scenes as he considered institutions and customs. He gives an example of the spirit of inquiry that guided him. The setting was in Odessa, in a magnificent "four-star" hotel reserved for dignitaries of the regime. They were served excellent green vegetables from a *kolkhoz* adjoining the hotel. At the end of the meal, Gide takes his companions on a tour of the property. They cross the small stream separating the hotel grounds from the *kolkhoz* and question the workers there. They lose no time informing themselves about the living conditions of the workers: the poor men slept four to a room, in quarters measuring only four meters by three, the rent costing a significant portion of their salaries; and for sustenance, they had to be content with a little bread and a dried herring. Similar experiences persuade Gide and his companions that the government of the U.S.S.R. is not providing its people with the happiness it has been promising. Upon returning to France, Gide and his companions confront their enormous disappointment. And without delay, while his memories are still fresh, Gide lets them flow from his pen and drafts his *Retour de l'U.R.S.S.;* the title expresses, above all, his disappointment. Malraux is consulted and finds the book unpublishable: this was the time when the Spanish Republic was in agony and, more than ever, was awaiting aid from the U.S.S.R. Gide did not allow himself to be stopped, however: in political terms, the Spanish War had gotten off to a bad start. Who would suppose that the United States of America would let the U.S.S.R. gain a foothold in Spain? In spite of everything, *Retour de l'U.R.S.S.* was published near the end of 1936, provoking an enormous scandal and leading to a polemical exchange between Gide and Jean Guéhenno, who vigorously reproached Gide for his lack of political fidelity.

Gide's political commitment was misunderstood; it really was more of an inquiry than a commitment. Moreover, the situation was complex. Gide's pro-Soviet attitude is understandable enough in light of the dangers mounting in Europe because of German rearmament. Yet, as always, Gide was motivated by more than politics; it is the ardent concern for truth that explains the nature of his commitment. And it is important to recognize that beginning in 1936, Gide had personally discovered the truth about the U.S.S.R., a truth he proclaimed fifty years ahead of his time and exposed to European consciousness—a consciousness that has not always known how to let itself be enlightened. It was one thing for French and European Communists to let themselves be deceived; after all, the U.S.S.R. held all their hopes. But how could so many educated Catholics like Althusser allow themselves to be duped as well!

In truth, the regime of the U.S.S.R. did not have the humanity to match the immense hope it inspired. The Soviet State was an artificial state, one lacking any relation to basic human strengths, established with the help of a large police force by noble utopians, pledged to Marx, who were zealously intent on making humankind happy in spite of itself. This enormous and noble construct of the October Revolution took fifty years to start crumbling. Up until May 1968, the mass of leftist intellectuals in France docilely allowed themselves to be deluded by the beautiful mirage that had arisen to the east of Europe. The fall of the U.S.S.R., like that of the Berlin Wall, is still for many of them the most disconcerting political mystery of the twentieth century.

It is Gide's glory—one forgets this too often—to have made known to people everywhere one of the greatest human and political scandals of all time: the organization of a police state that deceived humanity and plunged it into slavery under the pretext of emancipating it—though, nothing being completely bad, one is grateful to that government for having saved us from Hitler's tyranny, in January 1943, at Stalingrad.

4

The greatness of André Gide's commitment cannot be disregarded. This pure, classic artist crowned his literary oeuvre by acting in an unprecedented and threefold way: he acted with sincerity, in *Corydon;* with charity, in the *Voyage au Congo;* and with lucidity, in the *Retour de l'U.R.S.S.* It is through this commitment that Gide becomes the equal of Paul Valéry, author of the *Cahiers.* These two great writers wanted to create works of art that were dense with humanity; they did this by increasing the beauty of their works of art with a quasi-scientific richness, a richness imparted through reflection and through an "orphic" exploration of the human condition. Their wager was that the artist is perhaps more qualified than the philosopher to help us understand more deeply the mystery of being human. Is this pretense or truth? It is up to each individual to judge by rereading Valéry's *Cahiers,* that Everest of the human intellect comprising twenty-eight thousand pages, and Gide's *Journal 1889–1939, Corydon, Voyage au Congo,* and *Retour de l'U.R.S.S.:* a meditation, over the course of more than fifty years, on one man's contacts with existence and Western culture, followed by three major analyses, first of a human being's innermost sensibility, then of true charity, and finally of the politics within which we must live. By deepening his works of art in this way, through his own special means, this artist fully plays out his role among humankind, his role of guide and master.

Translated by Virginia M. Marino and Stephen Westergan

Notes

1. This essay was written in French in 1997 and was entitled "Sens et portée de l'engagement d'André Gide."
2. "André Gide, ou le courage de s'engager."
3. "[C]e qui s'oppose à son intégrité, à son intégration" (995).
4. "Je ne suis pas pareil aux autres."
5. "[S]ecrets orphiques de l'univers."
6. "Amour et moi. J'aurais pu apporter à l'Amour si le destin l'eût voulu, une contribu-

tion : une cruauté envers moi-même, et une conscience rigoureuse, qui jointes à mon sens naturel de la physique humaine et à ce mysticisme sans objet, qui est en moi, eussent peut-être, si quelque femme s'était rencontrée ayant du corps et de l'esprit un sens analogue, une fureur intelligente et expérimentale, un pressentiment de la volupté comme *moyen* — c'est là le neuf — eussent, dis-je, (et je le disais à P[ierre] L[ouÿs] avant-hier) peut-être pu faire de l'Amour quelque chose . . . Je dis de même que la Musique pourrait devenir un moyen, etc." (401; ellipsis Valéry's).

7. "[U]ne musique malsaine."
8. "Familles, je vous hais."
9. "[N]i dans le ligne, ni dans la note."
10. "Tant de ruse entre-t-il en l'âme d'un dévot . . . de la vérité!" (ellipsis Gide's).

Works Cited

Gide, André. *Journal 1889–1939*. Paris: Gallimard, Bibliothèque de la Pléiade, 1939.

Moutote, Daniel. *André Gide : L'Engagement (1926–1939)*. Paris: SEDES, 1991.

Valéry, Paul. *Cahiers*. Ed. Judith Robinson-Valéry. Vol. 2. Paris: Gallimard, Bibliothèque de la Pléiade, 1974.

CHAPTER 2

The Unrepentant Prodigal: Gide's Classical Politics and Republican Nationalism, 1897–1909

M. Martin Guiney

At the turn of the century, Maurice Barrès, well-established mentor of young writers, and André Gide, known then only to a small circle of readers, engaged in a polemic over Barrès's novel *Les Déracinés* (1897).[1] Nationalism was the ostensible issue, or whether or not *déracinement* [uprooting], understood as the alienation from one's geographic and genetic origins, caused the decline of culture; the issue of literary influence (Barrès's abundance, Gide's lack thereof) lurks as an ulterior concern on Gide's part, although it will not be the focus of my analysis. The question that Gide's polemic with Barrès, his texts on nationalism and literature, and his story *Le Retour de l'enfant prodigue* (1907) can answer is the following: where did Gide stand in regard to the nationalist issue, and how is his stance different from Barrès's absolute belief in the authority of *"la terre et les morts,"* land and authority?

The debate, on the surface, is clear. One is for or against nationalism, just as, at the time, one was *dreyfusard* or *antidreyfusard*. As in the Dreyfus affair, however, in which Gide managed to avoid adopting a clear position for much of the duration of the debate, his relation to the nationalist issue is, predictably, an ambiguous one. Gide's arguments are undoubtedly anti-Barrèsian; it is less certain, however, that they are antinationalistic. During the Third Republic, there was a tendency of the political opposition (culminating first in the *boulangisme* movement, and again, a few years later, with the *antidreyfusards*) to monopolize the issue of nationalism, with the purpose of portraying the Republic as a fundamentally unpatriotic institution. The supporters of the Republic were quick to reclaim the patriotic mantle by making more explicit a nationalist ideology of a quasi-revolutionary sort that was in stark contrast to the reactionary, populist version put forth by Barrès and other members of the right-wing opposition. I argue that Gide, in his attack on Barrès, made himself the voice of this new, abstract, and republican nationalism, going so far as to allegorize it in his literary adaptation of the parable of the Prodigal Son. The texts I discuss were written during a twelve-year period that predates Gide's open commitment to political causes. Although the "political Gide" takes the stage most obviously in episodes such as his sympathy with Charles Maurras's Action française in the years up to and including World War I, and his subsequent involvement with leftist politics and colonial issues, I argue that the debate with Barrès represents the first example in his writing, albeit a cryptic one, of a political agenda. What makes this agenda hard to recognize is Gide's insistence on adhering to literary concerns. On the surface, it appears that he is attacking Barrès purely in his capacity as a literary critic and novelist. After all, his first volley takes the form of a review of a novel, and aesthetic concerns are always paramount. Hilary Hutchinson argues that the fifty-year polemic with Barrès had no other purpose than to motivate Gide's creative output, as Gide put it: *"influence par protestation"* [influence by protesting [against the source]] (quoted in Hutchinson 856). Indeed, he may well have used Barrès as a means of defining his own identity as a writer, which is the point I make above about their relative positions in the literary pantheon of the day. I believe there is more at stake than matters of style related to literary hierarchy, however: the polemic is one of the few instances in which Gide articulated a political position to which he remained faithful throughout his life; in most other instances, he merely kept "trying out" various political guises, switching from one to another in order to subvert the demand, built into every ideology, that one commit oneself to it (as Daniel Moutote points out earlier in this book, for example, Gide had already gone beyond Communism *before* his trip to the U.S.S.R.). Gide's political stance in the texts relating to Barrès is allegorized: it is encoded in the discourse on literary style that he develops here and in later essays, and finds its highest expression in a literary work that is itself the retelling of a Christian parable: *Le Retour de l'enfant prodigue,* which I turn to later in this essay. As such, the debate on nationalism and literature is one of the more solid bases upon which his later identity as an *écrivain engagé* [committed writer] depends.

Since Gide, unlike Barrès, cannot be said to have been interested in influencing the course of republican politics, the question arises of why he found it necessary to take on Barrès, and by doing so, to participate in the Republic's reconquest of the nationalist cause, which had been monopolized by the far Right. I suggest that the answer can be found in the juxtaposition of *Les Déracinés* and *Le Retour de l'enfant prodigue.* In part, I believe that the political debate was a matter of "literary politics," a power play by Gide to challenge Barrès's position at the center of the literary world. Ultimately, however, the congruence of Gide's aesthetics and republican ideology reveals that much more was at stake than the rivalry between two authors. The extent to which Gide was aware of the long-range political consequences of this debate may come to light through the sort of broad overview and reevaluation of his political persona that this collection of essays attempts.

Let me return to the argument with which I began: Gide's position on the issue of nationalism and national identity is in fact an attack on Barrès the literary authority-figure, a statement of literary aesthetics, and not a direct attack on nationalism per se. The clearest evidence of this is that Gide's arguments define the role of French culture in relation to other cultures, and therefore present a type of (republican) nationalist agenda in the guise of an attack on nationalism as defined by the antirepublican Barrès. Gide directly attacks Barrès's central metaphor by turning *déracinement,* or uprooting, into a positive value, and not the spiritual and psychological disaster that the novel recounts. The question is: what does this difference imply? My purpose is not to paint Gide as just another turn-of-the-century nationalist ideologue, but rather to differentiate between him and Barrès in a manner that fully illustrates the complexity of their rivalry, and that associates Gide with a nationalist strain which was essential to the establishment of republican values in France. In brief: Gide's classicism is tied to nation-building. Barrès sees nationalism as a federation of regions, a model that does not allow for a parallel with classical aesthetics, in which the general dominates over the particular. As we shall see, Gide recognizes this by calling Barrès's style (and not his politics) "Asian" *[asiatique],* which is, in a historical as well as aesthetic sense, the opposite of "classical." Peter Schnyder, one of the other critics besides Hutchinson to have recently examined the polemic from a literary standpoint,[2] accurately describes the manner in which the debate about nationalism is really aesthetic, not political: "Barrès, therefore, is a traitor—to literature."[3] At the end of the present essay, I hope I will have suggested two new directions for an analysis of the polemic: first, that Gide's aesthetic objections to Barrès constitute a deeply thought-through reinvention of classicism; and secondly, that his particular classicism is in turn fraught with political meaning. In fact, I wish to say that Gide's classicism *is* his politics and, surprisingly, his politics turn out to be extraordinarily compatible with the ideology of the Third Republic under which he lived most of his life, without ever explicitly involving himself in most of its political debates.

The disagreement over the relationship between nationalism and *déracinement* began in 1897, the year Maurice Barrès published the first volume of his trilogy *Le Roman de l'énergie nationale.*[4] In response, Gide wrote "A propos des *Déracinés*" in the journal *L'Ermitage,* whence comes the famous sentence that could serve as a slogan for the universalist cause of the French Revolution: "Born in Paris of a father from Uzès and a mother from Normandy, where, M. Barrès, would you have me take root?"[5] The article continues in the same spirit, vigorously opposing Barrès's assertion that principled action, as well as art, must derive from the worship of *la terre et les morts,* the land and the dead.

Barrès's novel very clearly allegorizes such ancestor-worship, and the dangers of apostasy. *Les Déracinés* is a *roman à thèse* in which seven natives of Lorraine leave their homes for Paris, inspired by the philosophy professor of their *lycée* in Metz. The professor and surrogate father, Bouteiller, is the incarnation of the Third Republic, the all-unifying principle which he serves by abandoning his teaching career later in the novel in order to run for a seat in the Chamber of Deputies. Furthermore, he is a Kantian: doubly suspect since his philosophy is both foreign-born and overly abstract, unconnected to France and, what is worse, unconnected (according to Barrès) to *any* particular time or place.[6] As such, he can only be a corrupting influence—a Republican, a parliamentarian, a believer in the inherent universality of culture. He seduces the seven young men, from different social backgrounds, into abandoning their bastion at the literal and figurative frontier of French civilization for the sake of literary fame in Paris. Using the inheritance of one of their members (one of several echoes of the Prodigal Son parable in the novel), they found a politico-philosophical journal called *La Vraie République,* putting into practice their acquired notions of a purely abstract, transregionalist French spirit, represented alternately in the novel by two contrasting cultural icons: Napoleon I and Victor Hugo. As the title of their journal suggests, they are proselytizers for the Republic, and hence straw men for Barrès. It is not enough for them to be cut off from the wisdom of their ancestors: they fall prey to evil powers, most notably the Jewish Baron de Reinach, who involves them in the Panama Canal scandal, during which many deputies finally reveal themselves as corrupt, self-serving opportunists, leading to a parliamentary crisis which, in Barrès's opinion, is also a crisis of parliamentarism. In fact, it is essential to Barrès's argument that the dream of national unity be the all-encompassing lie behind which hide the forces of speculative capital, the front for an international Jewish conspiracy; to be a republican patriot, in other words, is to be a traitor. The Republic and the Nation are simply incompatible, an antiparliamentarian argument that reveals Barrès as a precursor to modern Fascism much more clearly than his anti-Semitism or his cult of *la terre et les morts.*[7]

The final downfall of five of the seven young men[8] is played out against the backdrop of Hugo's death and state funeral in 1885, allegorically signaling the end of the Republican dream of national unity with the passing of its greatest advocate. The governing moral of the story affirms the legitimacy of the ancestral father-figure, whom one can replace only at great peril. The strategy of the cosmopolitan forces of idealism and democracy is not only to replace the Church with a secular religion, but to replace the biological father with a more seductive and powerful father-figure, who will divert the natural devotion of the sons to the completion of his mission.

In "A propos des *Déracinés,*" Gide refuses to acquiesce to the failure of French national culture to replace regional diversity. He begins by saying that even Barrès, himself a native of Lorraine who emigrated to Paris early in his career, cannot avoid a fundamental contradiction in his narrative and even in his own life: "if the seven natives of Lorraine whose story you tell had not come to Paris, you would not have written *Les Déracinés; . . .* you would not have written this book yourself had you not come to Paris. . . ."[9] Paris, distinct both geographically and in its essence from the provinces,[10] is the catalyst for the work of artistic production, but not in the trite sense that it is the cultural capital of France, or of the world (though Gide certainly believed so). A movement that takes the form of an uprooting is the necessary precondition to narrative; and it is in the elevation of *déracinement* to the status of artistic necessity that Gide most clearly prefigures the argument for a type of "licensed freedom" later put forth in his Prodigal Son parable, to which I will return. It is in such a (literally) *radical* movement of uprooting that the text itself finds its origin, not simply in the particular case of *Les Déracinés,* but as a defining feature of the novel as a genre.[11]

Gide's opposition to Barrès leads one to conclude that he provides a counterweight to some of the more reactionary nationalist sentiments of the time,

sentiments that laid the institutional groundwork and imparted intellectual legitimacy to Fascism and collaboration.[12] Gide as a moderate of French literature,
working against the contemporary current of nationalist and anti-Semitic culture, is an image further reinforced by the fact that his influence over contemporary literature was about to exceed that of Barrès. When seeking a palliative
to the literary underpinnings of French Fascism to which Barrès contributed so
heavily, the powerful figure of Gide comes to hand, and it is hard to resist the
claim that his voice of reason and humaneness is in fact much more representative of authentic French culture than the passionate appeals of Barrès to raw sentiment and instinct: witness the following statement by Jean-Pierre Cap (taken
from the pages of *Laurels,* the French Legion of Honor's journal promoting
"French-American friendship"), which is perhaps an extreme version of the
hagiographic image of Gide as ideological savior that has prevailed during most
of this century: "no periodical contributed as much as the *NRF* [under Gide's
direction] to the breakdown of nationalism. . . . [I]t contributed to the elimina-
tion in our times of nationalism as a dominant ideological commitment for most
artists" (109). Gide's writings often serve such an appeasing purpose, and there
is plenty of evidence to support the emancipatory image associated with the
author of *Les Nourritures terrestres* (1897), a work that had an immense appeal for
the youth of the early part of the century.[13] At the same time, one has to accommodate statements such as the following, with its strong suggestion of French
cultural superiority:

> For too long I have thought, out of love for exoticism, out of wariness
> against chauvinist infatuation, perhaps out of modesty, for too long I have
> thought that there was more than one civilization, more than one culture
> that could claim our love and deserve that we should love it. . . . Now I
> know that our Western civilization (I was about to say: our French one) is
> not only the most beautiful; I believe, I know that it is the *only* one—indeed,
> the very same as the Greek one, of which we are the only inheritors.[14]

Even factoring in the date of the above entry (1914, when Gide was influenced
most strongly by wartime nationalist propaganda and the Action française), it is
hard to reconcile it with the cosmopolitanism that still attaches to Gide's persona as the champion of Shakespeare, Goethe, and Dostoevsky. Gide's nationalism, however, was not fundamentally different in 1914 than at other periods of
his life, and I argue that his cosmopolitanism must be understood as a logical
extension of his nationalism, and not as a contradiction.

The very rhetoric of reason and moderation in Gide's article in itself constitutes something quite different from the ideological neutrality he explicitly
claims to adopt. To take at face value the rhetoric of classicism, hence reason and
objectivity, which Gide invokes, is to overlook covert implications that are at
odds with the benign character often ascribed to his politics. Both the article on
Les Déracinés and the 1907 text *Le Retour de l'enfant prodigue,* as well as other
pieces I will examine, reveal that by opposing sentimental nationalism based on
the sacredness of the land and the dead, Gide in fact promoted a transcendental

doctrine of French cultural hegemony, all the stronger because it was not tied to specific coordinates of time and place. Whereas Barrès fortifies the boundaries surrounding the mythical fatherland, Gide violates them. But the fatherland itself is not dissolved when its outer limits are violated and made to disappear: on the contrary, it is simply extended indefinitely so that it occupies a temporarily limited, yet potentially infinite expanse. The dialectic of universal and particular displayed by Gide's imprecise and moving borders has powerful implications for a theory of French national identity that is more like a charter of manifest destiny than a simple claim to cultural particularity.

Gide's valorization of *déracinement* as a putative argument against integral nationalism is therefore the rhetorical equivalent of a wolf in sheep's clothing. He goes further than simply saying that such a process is not the spiritual catastrophe that Barrès warns against, for he claims that uprooting describes the necessary process by which humanity passes from a state of barbarity to one of civilization, or (agri)culture. A moral hierarchy arises precisely from man's ability to uproot himself, to sustain the condition of passing from the familiar to the unfamiliar. Observe, in the following passage from the *Déracinés* article, the militaristic, colonialist, and Nietzschean overtones: "perhaps one could measure a man's worth by the degree of disorientation[15] (physical or intellectual) that he is able to overcome. . . . [T]hat is the education required by the strong man— dangerous, it is true, and trying; it is a struggle against the *foreign;* but there is no education until instruction changes the individual. – As for the weak: take root! take root!"[16] In nationalist terms *("dépaysement")* and images of geographic conquest ("struggle against the *foreign[er]*"), Gide establishes criteria of value according to which human achievement may be measured. To remain stationary is to be tied to the lowest common denominator. The familiar, or local, according to Gide, is the moral equivalent of what the transregional/republican/cosmopolitan claims of Parisian culture imply for Barrès: both result from conformity to an arbitrary norm, dictated in Gide's case by local authority, and in Barrès's case, by the illegitimate power of the state: one man's meat is the other's poison. If one does not take the regionalist versus centralist opposition into account, however, the two demons are difficult to distinguish.

The comparison of the creation of literature to the expansionist impulse to acquire territory is the rhetorical means by which Gide's own position becomes overtly nationalistic. The term "nationalism" itself acquires a very specific meaning in the context of Gide's attack, more as a figure for textual power than as a reference to a series of social and political phenomena. In discussing the link between text and nationalism, one approaches one of the most important concerns in Gide's work: the continuing relevance of classicism to French culture. Both in the *Déracinés* article and elsewhere, classicism appears under the guise of several metaphors for the act of writing: the domestication of nature through agriculture, sexual activity liberated from its procreative function, and the waging of war against foreign enemies. I will examine these metaphors, beginning with agriculture, as they appear in certain of Gide's texts that speak most directly to the nationalist issue.

During the polemic surrounding *Les Déracinés,* Gide went on to literalize the image of *déracinement* by focusing on the nature of trees, such as the poplars that line so many French roads, especially in Alsace and Lorraine (the *peuplier*, in fact, is practically the botanical equivalent of the Alsatian national symbol of the stork). Trees, Gide maintained, were automatically transplanted by their growers in order to help them thrive, thereby refuting the claim that ties to the native soil are necessary or even positive for future development. Though Barrès himself remained regally aloof from the debate, other authors such as Charles Maurras carried the torch, became involved, and criticized Gide's interpretation of "poplar" culture.[17] The unexpected response of the nationalist contingent apparently took Gide by surprise; perhaps recoiling from the force of his opening shot in the debate, Gide published in the same journal, in 1903, "La Querelle du peuplier," a retreat from his earlier, polemical position: "my articles are most moderate, against a thesis whose only fault I can find is its excess."[18] His position is not radically different from, nor even "foreign" to that of Barrès, but simply more *reasonable:* "most moderate." Barrès is literally *outré* in his irrational attachment to the land, beyond the French pale in presenting a thesis that in other ways is legitimate. The problem with Barrès's *enracinement* [rootedness] is the way it is presented: their difference is primarily one of style. But for Gide, as we will see, style is precisely the crux of the entire debate.

"Reason" is, after all, the characteristic of French style that enables it to overcome all obstacles to meaning; it is the characteristic of the language and culture that is paradoxically most abstract and also most culturally specific, at least according to the established paradox that the classical flame burns in only one place at a time while nevertheless maintaining universal validity. In his response, in 1903, to a survey on the influence of Germany on French literature and thought, he stated that "French Cartesianism (i.e., French classicism) is the only discipline neutral and broad enough to be submitted to the widest range of mentalities. . . ."[19] The neutrality of French is not to be confused with that of an abstract code, such as mathematics: it is not a universal language. A universal language is, by definition, everywhere and nowhere at the same time, its ubiquitous validity undermined by its lack of identity. French, by contrast, is both everywhere and *somewhere,* anchored to a place from which it derives its potentially hegemonic energies.[20]

The post–1871 revanchist movement, which made the return of Alsace-Lorraine the main issue of political debate, as well as the populist, militaristic support for General Boulanger in the 1880s, constitutes the political subtext of Barrès's novel. Regionalism versus federalism, authoritarianism versus parliamentarism are the principal dichotomies according to which *Le Roman de l'énergie nationale* is organized. Though he was notoriously aloof from the political concerns of the era, one can legitimately ask whether Gide's opposition to Barrès can also be inscribed within these same dichotomies, coming down finally on the side of the Third Republic. His article on *Les Déracinés,* unlike its subject, is conspicuously devoid of references to the current political situation in France, despite the importance in the novel of Barrès's critique of the Republic and of parliamentarism in general. Instead, Gide restricts himself to the agricultural image of rootedness, and reads it as signifying culture in the broader sense. He takes the high road in the argument, choosing an aesthetic rather than social definition of civilization, thereby sidestepping Barrès's grounding of the nationalist position in actual political events.

Gide's apparently ahistorical decision to emphasize style as the means by which to overcome regional idiosyncrasies becomes increasingly apparent as one follows the course of the nationalist question in his subsequent work. In June 1909, the *Nouvelle Revue Française* published the first of his three "Nationalisme et littérature" essays, inspired by a survey in the journal *La Phalange* that asked whether "high" literature was inherently national. Gide wrote an ambiguous response in which he said that "high" culture of any kind can have absolutely no inherent, unchanging characteristic, save its very capacity to change. To be artistic is to be original; the ability to assimilate and to convey what had been previously unknown is the precondition to artistic success, which echoes the description of the Nietzschean *homme fort* from the article on Barrès. Gide's position becomes complicated, however, by the assertion that no national literature is better able to fulfill this precondition to artistic success than French literature (6: 1–20).

In an important article on Gide's flirtation with the integral nationalism of Charles Maurras and the Action française shortly before the War, Martha Hanna discusses the "Nationalisme et littérature" essays as a reaction against the right-wing belief that the seventeenth century provides the only great flowering of French culture, and rejecting the prevalent nationalist belief that "the purity of the French race was a necessary precondition of cultural grandeur" (Hanna 10). What is important to remember, however, as Hanna points out, is that Gide does not propose to abandon the classical aesthetic in order to confer national status on modernist (romantic and symbolist) literature, but rather to claim a direct family relation between these incompatible literary aesthetics: the romantic and symbolist are the direct descendants of the classical, and derive their characteristics from this lineage. The paradox of the genealogy that links classicism to the literary avant-garde of the nineteenth century is the same, I believe, as the one whereby the "cosmopolitan" Gide is a direct offshoot of the "nationalist" one. Classical nationalism, therefore, allows for the subsumption of its apparent opposite, the valorization of the non-native, and of the non- or even anti-classical.

Gide developed this contradictory stance when his original essay on nationalism was criticized shortly after its appearance by Jean-Marc Bernard, the editor of a small right-wing journal called *Les Guêpes*. Bernard and his associates, in a reactionary return to the quarrel of the ancients and moderns, argued that the seventeenth century was French literature's only moment of glory, and that the most contemporary authors could aspire to was a pale imitation of the great century. Such a nostalgic idealization of the officially sanctioned classical era in the history of French culture, combined with a refusal to grant any status to originality in the modern period, compelled Gide to expand considerably on his position in his rebuttal.[21]

The response to *Les Guêpes* provides an intriguing example of literary polemics, as well as a continuation and consolidation of the position he took twelve years earlier in the Barrès article. He again uses the image of agriculture as culture, radicalizing it so as to counteract the claim to artistic primacy on behalf of seventeenth-century classicism. Classical style, precisely by virtue of being the *first* great mature phase of culture (either of Western culture in the case of Greece, or of French culture in the case of the seventeenth century), cannot be the *greatest:* "The first lands to be cultivated are the easiest . . . not the richest, but the poorest . . . [T]he richest land, the lowest, will only be considered later. It will remain a long time in the margins of culture, 'barbaric' and unknown. Civilized man will slowly become aware of its promise. . . ."[22] "High" classical style is akin to the agriculture of the highlands, and the stylus of the poet to the farmer's plow. The barbaric lowlands, unfamiliar and foreign, will ultimately yield the finest fruit once they have been conquered by civilized man and brought into the boundary of the nation, that is to say, have lost their foreign status. One might be tempted to read Gide's response as an avant-garde manifesto (which is indeed how *Les Guêpes* chose to understand it); instead, it is a plea for the continued relevance of classicism to the idea of an infinitely expandable national identity. Through the organic metaphor of culture, the classical past of French literature becomes the progenitor, as opposed to the antithesis, of French literary modernity.

Le Retour de l'enfant prodigue was published in 1907, and it constitutes an important stage in the debate to which the Barrès article and the two ulterior pieces on nationalism, "La Querelle du peuplier" and "De l'influence allemande," belong. Martha Hanna recognized that the story is another version of the reconciliation of opposites that Gide was later to attempt in "Nationalisme et littérature" (13). I would go even further and say that it is the clearest statement of Gide's own brand of nationalism, in which the classical is not the irretrievable golden age of the reactionary Right, but rather the source for the ability of the literary tradition to assimilate increasing degrees of otherness. *Le Retour de l'enfant prodigue* allegorizes the nationalism that is put forth in the 1909 articles; and Martha Hanna was absolutely correct in seeing the texts as being thematically and ideologically connected. Classicism is no longer a style so much as it is a mandate: the right to conquer new territories in the name of the father(land). In fact, Gide indicates in his secular rewriting of the New Testament parable precisely how the agricultural images of the earlier texts translate into the human sphere. Man's point of origin or homeland, the precisely demarcated territory of the familiar, finds its representation in the domain of the father. But there is another, nonspatial dimension to the authority of the father which is essential to Gide's particular deviation from the Biblical myth: the notion of heredity, not as the ritualized transmission of ownership of the land, but rather the ability—and social obligation—to make use of one's inherited potential by becoming a father in turn. Heredity involves here the preservation of a single identity over the course of generations, the preservation of individuality in the midst of multiplicity, as well as the respect for the status of fatherhood which makes such preservation possible. After Gide's prodigal returns to the household, he enters into dialogue with each member of the family. In the

section entitled "La Réprimande du frère aîné," he discusses with the older
brother their respective relationships to the father:

> "My big brother," he began, "we scarcely look alike. My brother, we do
> not look alike."
> The older brother:
> "It's your fault."
> "Why mine?"
> "Because I dwell in order; all that distinguishes itself from order is the fruit
> or the seed of pride."
> "Can't I have anything distinctive besides faults?"
> "Give the name 'quality' only to whatever brings you back into order, and
> curtail everything else."
> "That is the mutilation I fear. The qualities in me that you intend to sup-
> press also come from our father."[23]

Genetic continuity through the determining influence of the father is at first
denied by the protagonist, and then paradoxically reaffirmed. The prodigal's "we
do not look alike" is a denial of the father's power to be a determining factor
in the identity of the individual from a strictly hereditary standpoint: the difference between the two brothers is a sign of the radical difference between father
and son on the physical, or biological plane, liberating sexuality from procreation
by challenging the laws of heredity.[24]

There is much more at work, however, than the opposition between individual freedom and biological determinism in the service of social conservatism
("order"). The prodigal claims that his "fault," or crime against society, while it
distinguishes him from his brother and all others, also derives from the father
who embodies two contrasting (but not, as we shall see, incompatible) principles: the freedom to leave the household as well as the obligation to remain.
Gide does not entirely reject heredity, just as earlier, in his polemic with Barrès,
he did not reject nationality: both terms are simply taken from their narrow, sec-
tarian context in order to arrive at a more appropriate, universal meaning. After
all, Gide's prodigal, upon his return, was recognized neither by the servants nor
even by his own dog,[25] yet he was unhesitatingly recognized and welcomed by
the father. This scene of anagnoresis, in which the father acknowledges the per-
manence of the filial relationship despite the son's disobedience, is to be read, so
to speak, in the Gidean sense: as granting legitimacy to the desire to escape, and
to the exercise of freedom that it represents, much like the final admonition to
Nathanaël in Les Nourritures terrestres, "Jette mon livre" (248) [Throw away my
book [which you have just read]].

Gide's version emphasizes the possibility, denied in the evangelical interpretation of the parable, that the father has approved of, albeit tacitly, the actions of
the prodigal. The older son narrows the role of the father to the point where it
is supplanted, completely contained in his own authority ("Je suis dans l'ordre"
[I dwell in order]). This is more than a suppression or "mutilation" of the prodigal: it is a usurpation, in the form of mutilation, of the father's power. Accord-

ing to this highly unorthodox retelling of the parable, the older son, as a figure for the Church, is actually responsible for the castration of the father; and the prodigal is elevated to the status of redeemer: he is authorized to find the suppressed/mutilated will of the father out in the wilderness, especially as the father himself admits that "here it is he [the older brother] who makes the law. . . ."[26] Since the older son has taken over authority in the household in a manner inconsistent with the father's legitimate exercise of power, the prodigal is morally obligated to go elsewhere to recover the father's true will.

It is this same transcending of geographical boundaries in the name of paternal, national, and cultural authority that will eventually enable Gide to posit a "French identity" that is not constricted by the borders of the Republic, much less by those of Barrès's mythical regions.[27] The transgression of a particular, social law (enacted by the older son) is redeemed by adhering to a higher, spiritual law (of the father). Traditional readings that limit *Le Retour de l'enfant prodigue* to an attack on institutionalized religion, such as the following passage by Aldyth Tain, miss the mark: "to Gide [artistic] freedom exists only beyond the boundaries of all religious and intellectual systems, in the world of the unknown to which one must go forth alone" (21). To reduce the entire parable to a critique of the Catholic Church, which it undoubtedly provides, is to overlook its consequences, not just for Gide's attitude toward Christianity, but for his peculiarly hegemonic conception of French culture as well. Gidean freedom (which he famously termed *disponibilité* [availability]) is valid, not in reaction against the father, but rather by virtue of the father, whose negative authority (insisting on conservation and reproduction) can blossom into a positive force (promoting expenditure and assimilation).

The term "mutilation," which occurs in the dialogue between the two sons, suggests primarily disfigurement and castration, both of which are extremely relevant in the context both of individual and collective identity-formation. Their language evokes the father's reproductive function as both a creative force (the production of life) and a conservative one (continuation of the species and of society through its microcosm, the family). "That is the mutilation that I fear," spoken by the prodigal, suggests fear of castration, no matter how much the older brother insists that he merely demands a curtailing, not a suppression (*réduire* instead of *supprimer*), of his desire to wander away from home. If remaining at home is a form of castration, however symbolic, then the prodigal's departure can be construed as an affirmation, rather than negation, of the sexual potency, hence the potential for fatherhood, with which he is endowed. But fatherhood within a socially sanctioned environment is by itself not the sole guarantor of the legitimate use of such potency, according to the sexual ethic that *Le Retour de l'enfant prodigue* advances.

In the original parable, when it is said that the prodigal "wasted his substance on riotous living" (Luke 15:13), we know that the text refers to his allotted portion of his father's wealth; with Gide, we must also ask whether the son's inheritance does not also refer to his sperm, with the implication that he wasted his seed by forsaking the social conventions of marriage and fatherhood which control the male reproductive function.[28] Abandoning the family and (presumably)

consorting with harlots opens up the space for a type of "free play" of sexuality
that is a more enriching, because more adventurous, manner of making use of
God's gift.[29] The adventurousness of the sexual pioneer parallels that of the
farmer who claims ever more distant "lowlands" in the name of civilization,
taming them with his plow, which becomes the pen (or stylus) and derives from
the phallus. Sexual practices that customarily belong to the category of the
unnatural and antisocial are stripped of their offensiveness by their integration
into the civilizing process. No degree of deviation from a norm of any kind,
such as homosexuality,[30] will marginalize the subject to such an extent that he
is excluded from the father's auspices. The reconciliation of the parable is meaningless for Gide: in his patriarchy, the fatted calf is always already slaughtered.

The sexual motif reappears in one of Gide's last written passages on Barrès,
from the *Journal* in 1932, in which he describes his impression upon rereading
decadent authors from the late nineteenth century, in particular Barrès: "Flaccidity. Sentences without muscles. . . . Slackened, wilted grace. . . . Faced with
this Asiatic style, how Dorian I feel!"[31] To call the anti-Semitic Barrès "Asiatic"
is Gidean wit at its most subtle;[32] no less ironic (though less subtle) are the insistent images of impotence he uses to describe his former father-figure. Most
important, however, is the word "Dorian," which not only connotes the phal-
lic authority and beautiful simplicity of "high" (i.e., most ancient) classical style,
but also reverberates with the reputation of the Dorian people as great military
conquerors. Furthermore, the Ionic mode, in contrast to the Doric, not only is
more recent, hence more decadent, but is also the more fluid (flaccid) and "Asiatic," hence impotent, of ancient styles. Gide could not more clearly challenge
Barrès's role as the "inseminator" of youth, or more strongly stake his own claim
to power well outside the domain of the Barrèsian father-figure.

If I point out the irony in Gide's description of Barrès's style as "Asiatic,"
hence Jewish, it is for a reason. Gide's own anti-Semitism (which I mentioned
in note 13), like his nationalism, needs to be confronted with the much more
explicit, and therefore more widely recognized, anti-Semitism of Barrès, and
Jocelyn Van Tuyl's essay in this book is another foray into this particularly
marshy lowland.

The opposition of Asiatic "flaccidity" and Doric "firmness" does more than
perpetuate the conventional image of West versus East as a male-female, or
potent-impotent opposition; it also enlists sexual imagery within the ideology of
cultural hegemony, according to which the phallus is not so much an instrument
of (pro)creation as, in effect, a sort of banner rallying the conquering forces, and
a scepter to maintain power over the assimilated masses. Such is precisely the
function served by the imagery of the phallus in Gide's rewriting of the parable
of the Prodigal Son. In the quarrel of the ancients and the moderns that was
revived by the editors of *Les Guêpes,* Gide at first seems to come down in favor
of the latter: as with Barrès, he explicitly takes the opposite position from his
adversary. Yet he comes to define classicism in a way that makes the ancient-
modern distinction untenable, since it is in the nature of the classical constantly
to seek out the new and to colonize it. In another parallel study of Gide and
Barrès, Peter Schnyder elegantly resolves the contradictions in Gide on a per-

sonal, psychological level: "[Gide] sees the human subject as divided, in part defending itself from itself, in part rejecting the other in itself in the name of an imagined identity."[33] Gide's view of classicism and nationalism, however, ranges far beyond the literary construction of the self that is so fundamental to most of his work: "the human subject" is not the symbolic subject but the existential one, the social and political entity who is profoundly implicated in the never-ending creation of civilization.

The dynamism of the civilizing process in the congruence of "fatherhood" and "territoriality" (terms also present in Barrès's cult of the land and the dead) is illustrated in another passage from the dialogue of the two sons in *Le Retour de l'enfant prodigue,* beginning with the older son:

"What wealth do you seek elsewhere that you cannot find here in abundance? Or rather: only here is your wealth to be found."
"I know you have kept riches for me."
"That part of your wealth that you did not squander, which is to say that part which we all own in common: the landed property."
"Don't I own anything myself anymore?"
"Yes; those gifts which our father might still consent to bestow on you."
"That is all I want; I consent to own only those."[34]

The father's material legacy is divided into two parts: the personal wealth bestowed upon the individual, equated with "substance" in the New Testament, and collectively owned wealth in the form of real estate *["biens fonciers"].* The distinction is crucial: real estate necessarily carries certain obligations that money does not, beginning with the obligation, or physical necessity, to remain in one and the same place: in fact, real estate is self-possession, the grounding of identity-as-action in appropriation, read literally as the appropriate relationship between action and space. It represents an absolute value that is protected from the vagaries of free exchange, if only figuratively, since it cannot move. The myth of personal identity derived from the land requires that the "family farm" never be sold, just as Alsace-Lorraine cannot simply and unproblematically transfer to German rule, which was Barrès's argument in his national trilogy. Gide's brilliant but problematic improvement on Barrès's nationalism was to make the homeland potentially present wherever the prodigal decides to go: a mandate for conquest, colonial or otherwise, if ever there was one.[35]

The prodigal wants only that part of the father's wealth which can be gambled or spent, for which he alone is responsible. The question now arises whether his capacity to reproduce, his sexuality, is his own property or belongs to the collective. In the brief dialogue with the mother, he tells her to select a wife for him without regard to his preferences. Such a sacrifice shows his determination that the role he will play in the household not be tainted by his own desire. Rather than trade freedom for responsibility, he has foregone both alternatives. The gesture of contrition accomplished by his return implies that he has stolen from the family trust, but that his betrayal can be redeemed. The restitution, however, is meaningless as long as the prodigal refuses to take possession of the land and all it implies, and thereby protects himself from the ultimate consequences of his return.

The distinction between liquid and solid assets, in reference to the father's wealth, like the distinction between Doric firmness and Ionic fluidity, is crucial to an understanding of Gide's nationalist argument. *Le Retour de l'enfant prodigue* emphasizes their difference by showing the son's willing acceptance of the money, and his refusal of the land. Yet it is the unexplained, continuous relation between the two types of wealth that is important. While having currency in the world at large, the father's gold nevertheless originates in the estate, in the sense that it is representative of the wealth contained in, or rather produced by, the land. It is the inalienable characteristic of currency that it be exchanged, which in turn implies that it can always find its equivalent on the open market. With his "substance"–his inherited money and his (also inherited) seed–the prodigal acquired knowledge of the foreign, also in the form of sexual experience. When he ran out (of money, that is), he was reduced to serving a foreign lord. It was his wealth, derived directly from the land of his father, that gave him dominion, albeit temporarily, over the world outside the walls of the estate. The preservation of a connection between a currency and its particular place of origin prevents Gide from merely advocating financial and cultural relativism, which would be in diametric opposition to the essentialism of Barrès.

The financial metaphor becomes more apparent if one remembers that the Gide-Barrès polemic is primarily about literature, and only indirectly about national politics, i.e., revanchism and republicanism. *Les Déracinés* proposes a regionalist, hence federationist concept of nationalism, according to which France is divided into discrete territories with separate claims to cultural identity; in turn, the cultural specificity of each region gives it the right to political independence from the centralist institutions of the Republic. Gide illustrates a very different theory, according to which France is the country of synthesis, moderation, and dialectic; therefore, it is ideally suited to the assimilation and integration of that which is foreign. Because of its unique nature, it is absurd to think of it as a territory defined by strict boundaries, since the name "France" has meaning only in reference to an ability to dissolve the borders separating native from foreign: "To what does France owe this extraordinary privilege? Probably, as with Greece, to a fortunate congruence of races, to a mixture that is precisely what nationalists today deplore."[36] The specificity of French identity relies on the notion of synthesis rather than purity, the melting pot rather than the mosaic.[37]

A passage from the "Nationalisme et littérature" articles raises this transnationalist French nationalism to the level of an actual call to arms: "A long time man will shrink before the dangers and miasmas of the lowlands; a long time, the uncertain shores of more than one Stymphalus lake will await their hero in vain."[38] By attacking the "lowlands" of culture, the French language and its herculean heroes (Gide included) enable the Greek classical heritage to continue to fulfill its epic destiny, moving from the language of agriculture to that of militarism.[39]

The lowlands in their primitive state are *inculte,* both literally (uncultivated) and figuratively (uncultured); one thinks of the swamps of *Paludes* (1896) and especially, if antonymically, of the culturally barren (according to Gide) North African desert in which he found so much to challenge his stylus/plow, as several essays in this book attest. More than simple foreignness, it is this dimension of savagery that makes them preferable to the land already under cultivation. It is their capacity to resist as strongly as possible the inroads of the plow or stylus which ensures that the pioneer wielding the instrument will produce exceptional results. Two important assumptions are implicit in this image: first, that the unfamiliar "culture" actually is not a culture at all until it has been thoroughly assimilated by the civilizing action of the plow; secondly, that the characteristics, or identity of the land itself are ultimately irrelevant, since they are only a pretext for exercising and improving the skills of the writer, making manifest what was already latently present in *himself* rather than in the land. This idea is echoed in Gide's recurring statements that his pleasure in reading Goethe and other foreign authors was finding confirmation of his own ideas, such as this passage from the *Nouvelle Revue Française* written in 1903: "The best of what Goethe, Heine, Schopenhauer, Nietzsche have taught me is perhaps their admiration for France."[40]

The "Dialogue avec le frère puîné," in which the prodigal's younger brother resumes his abortive quest, shows how the foreign is at first highly valued, and then dismissed as merely a means toward the development of the potential already contained in the individual. Pointing to a wild pomegranate that the swinekeeper brought back from the desert, the younger brother says:

"[I]ts bitterness is almost unbearable; yet I feel that if I were thirsty enough, I would bite into it."
"Ah! now I can tell you: that is the thirst I was seeking in the desert."
"A thirst that only this bitter fruit is able to quench . . ."
"No; but one must love this thirst."[41]

The wild fruit is, in and of itself, worthless: it cannot quench the thirst which compelled the prodigal to go search for it. The foreign, nondomesticated object of desire is valuable, not for what it might be, or do, or say, but only as an outlet for the individual's compulsion to break out of the confines of the home while bringing his wealth along with him, so that the home itself will be seen as encompassing a potentially infinite space. Such radical devaluation of the foreign accounts for the prodigal's response to the younger brother's hopeful affirmation that only the wild fruit is capable of assuaging the thirst that drives one into the desert. No, it does not, says the prodigal; but the thirst or desire itself is its own purpose, the fruit only a pretext for the exile that it induces. The tension between domesticity and wildness results at first in a preference for the latter: there are always new lands to conquer, and unknown objects of desire to attain. Such conquest inevitably leads to domestication, which invariably implies an *extension* rather than a repudiation of the boundaries of the patrimonial territory.

Gide places himself at the margins of culture. Yet, as he admits in a passage that tells of his own experience with ownership of the land, it is a mistake to view the margins as always fixed in their relation to that which they demarcate. In "Jeunesse," a text published in the *Nouvelle Revue Française* in 1931 as a sort of addendum to his memoirs *Si le grain ne meurt* (1926), he discusses his role as the proprietor of La Roque, the estate in Normandy that he inherited from his mother:

> This domain I inherited as a young man from my mother—I could not bear to know its boundaries. Or rather: I refused to know them, not so that I could imagine myself owning more than I did, but on the contrary, in order to prevent myself from thinking that any of what I loved here was personally and exclusively my *own*. . . . I . . . did not feel more obligations towards the land than the land had towards me.[42]

If "the land and the dead" have no hold over Gide, it is at least partly due to his ability to think of national identity as an abstraction, an intellectual process rather than an unconscious atavism. Inherited wealth in all its forms, from genetic determinism to the cultural legacy of the collective, provides the strength with which to create a space for originality. The notion that this space is gained through conquest, itself a throwback to a certain classical conception of native versus foreign, is in the nature of the inheritance.

It is possible to read Gide's critique of the doctrine of the land and the dead simply as a political move within the literary hierarchy of the late nineteenth century. After all, one earns a name for oneself by entering the fray and challenging those whose laurels one covets. What supports this reading is the peculiar manner in which Gide later retreated from his confrontational stance, as if to admit that his motives were more self-interested than he at first had allowed. But the relevance of the Prodigal Son story to his position on nationalism carries the deception one step further. Gide and Barrès, far from being adversaries in any conventional sense, are members of the same family: at most, perhaps, they can be represented by a prodigal who attempts to justify his creative actions to a stern, reactionary older brother, so as to wrest from him the authority to influence the younger generation. In the particular internecine dynamic that they embody, the causes of the family and of the nation both ultimately triumph.

Notes

1. To call this episode a "polemic" or even a "debate" is misleading, because Barrès himself never responded directly to Gide's attacks. Charles Maurras and Léon Blum were two among those who championed Barrès's point of view in what was called the *querelle du peuplier* (which I mention again later), thereby serving as surrogate opponents. Given, however, that one of the issues at stake may not have been about ideology but, rather, about literary prominence, it is likely that for Barrès the best defense against Gide's claim to fame was simply to ignore him—which, by and large, he did.
2. Hutchinson and Schnyder approach the polemic from the point of view of literature, while Martha Hanna looks at it purely from a political standpoint, beginning with

Gide's relationship to the Action française. In this essay, I hope to reconcile these two opposing ways of analyzing Gide's writings on Barrès and on nationalism, including one of his major statements on those subjects, *Le Retour de l'enfant prodigue*.

3. "Barrès, donc, a trahi – la littérature" (37).

4. Barrès's trilogy also includes *L'Appel au soldat* (1900), centering on the Boulanger affair, and *Leurs Figures* (1902), which again takes up the Panama Canal scandal and attempts to discredit once and for all the parliamentary system.

5. "Né à Paris, d'un père uzétien et d'une mère normande, où voulez-vous, Monsieur Barrès, que je m'enracine?" (2: 437). This and all other citations from Gide refer to the edition of the *Œuvres complètes* published between 1932 and 1939, and will henceforth be identified by volume number and page. Few of these nonliterary works by Gide have been published in English.

6. The Barrèsian cult of the nation has much in common with his brand of Catholicism. *La Colline inspirée,* his 1913 novel on the subject of religion, proposes that religious faith also needs to be anchored in a specific place. It is in some ways a heretical work, in that it undermines the authority of Rome in order to place the true seat of the Church in the specific environment of the believer: *la colline* takes over from the Vatican as the source of divine inspiration.

7. The role of Barrès as a forerunner of twentieth-century Fascism is well documented. From a political point of view, see Soucy or, for a slightly more nuanced analysis of the complicated politics of the period, Sonn. These works clearly show not only the nature of Barrès's legacy but also how much further engaged in the political arena he was than Gide in the decades immediately preceding World War I. Suleiman is helpful in exploring the political dimensions of Barrès's literary work, as opposed to his speeches and articles.

8. Two of the heroes of Barrès's novel survive their Parisian ordeal, Roemerspacher and Saint Phlin. The reasons they are spared the effects of *déracinement* are interesting in themselves. First of all, they are close to being autobiographical figures for the author, in particular Saint Phlin, thereby giving Barrès's own career a fictional exculpation from the very sins he attacks. Furthermore, as Suleiman points out, those two are the only members of the group who are wealthy, and whose ties to the land are therefore all the more solid: "in order not to suffer from *déracinement,* one has to *own* the ground as well as live on it" (122). The role of land ownership comes up in Gide's *Le Retour de l'enfant prodigue,* which I discuss later on.

9. "[S]i les sept Lorrains dont vous donnez l'histoire n'étaient pas venus à Paris, vous n'eussiez pas écrit les *Déracinés; . . .* vous n'eussiez pas écrit ce livre si vous-même n'étiez pas venu à Paris . . ." (2: 444).

10. Both Gide and Barrès agree on the essential difference between Paris and the rest of the country, thus carrying on the tradition, exemplified in Balzac, that Paris cannot be treated as just another region: in fact, its nature is to be the *opposite* of a region, whatever that might be.

11. By calling attention to the necessity of a disruptive event, such as the departure from the fatherland, as a characteristic starting point for the novel, Gide in fact establishes an affinity between Barrès and himself. "Leaving home" is a thematic constant in Gide's narratives, and constitutes virtually the entire plot of his one proclaimed novel, *Les Faux-Monnayeurs.* But it is a two-way street: by showing that Barrès is unwittingly in agreement with him on the fundamental nature of narrative, Gide erases the distinction he so explicitly asserts between Barrès's ideology and his own. This is one of several ways in which the article accomplishes the opposite of its purported aims.

12. The clearest link between Barrès and the subsequent generation of right-wing nationalists is his son Philippe, who was a champion of the writings of Brasillach, Drieu la Rochelle, and others. The precise role of Barrèsian nationalism in the

history of French Fascism has been partly explored (see, for example, Soucy). There is a good deal more to be done in this area, however, as it seems that connections between literary works and political movements are seldom made, except when they are even more blatant than in the case of Barrès. It is certain that Philippe gained influence in certain intellectual *and* political circles based solely on his father's reputation; as Jean-Marie Domenach points out, Barrès's influence on nationalist movements was far greater than that of the "vicious ghetto" *["ghetto hargneux"]* of organized proto-Fascist groups such as the Action française (52).

13. In *Legacies of Anti-Semitism in France,* Mehlman reads the hidden anti-Semitic codes of *Les Caves du Vatican.* His strategy is far more effective than if he had simply taken the explicit anti-Semitic statements to be found in Gide, because it suggests that such a phenomenon cannot be isolated and then in some way surgically excised from an author's work so that it is otherwise pure, free of any ideological taint. By using as an example a text that contains no explicit anti-Semitism, Mehlman demonstrates convincingly that one cannot isolate the work as a whole from any of its specific characteristics.

As far as Gide's explicit anti-Semitism is concerned, the definitive statement is the following, dated 1914:

It suffices for me that the qualities of the Jewish race are not French ones; even if [the French] are less intelligent, less resistant, less valorous in every way than the Jews, it is still true that what they have to say can only be said by them, and that the contribution of Jewish qualities to literature, where only the personal has value, does not so much bring new or enriching elements, as it interrupts the explanation slowly being given by the French race and seriously, intolerably distorts its meaning. . . .

I certainly don't deny the great merit of some Jewish works of literature. . . . But how much more easily I would admire them if they came to us only as translations! For what do I care that the literature of my country is becoming richer if that happens at the cost of its significance? The day the French language will no longer have enough strength, it would be better for it to disappear than to let an uncouth [*malappris,* literally "poorly taught"] person take its place and play its part, in its name.

[Il me suffit que les qualités de la race juive ne soient pas des qualités françaises; et lorsque [les Français] seraient moins intelligents, moins endurants, moins valeureux de tous points que les Juifs, encore est-il que ce qu'ils ont à dire ne peut être dit que par eux, et que l'apport des qualités juives dans la littérature, ou rien ne vaut que ce qui est personnel, apporte moins d'éléments nouveaux, c'est-à-dire un enrichissement, qu'elle ne coupe la parole à la lente explication d'une race et n'en fausse gravement, intolérablement, la signification. . . .

Je ne nie point, certes, le grand mérite de quelques œuvres juives. . . . Mais combien les admirerais-je de cœur plus léger si elles ne venaient à nous que traduites! Car que m'importe que la littérature de mon pays s'enrichisse si c'est au détriment de sa signification. Mieux vaudrait, le jour où le français n'aurait plus de force suffisante, disparaître, plutôt que de laisser un malappris jouer son rôle à sa place, en son nom.] (*Journal* 397–398)

14. "Trop longtemps j'ai pensé, par amour de l'exotisme, par méfiance de l'infatuation chauvine et peut-être par modestie, trop longtemps j'ai cru qu'il y avait plus d'une civilisation, plus d'une culture qui pût prétendre à notre amour et méritât qu'on s'en éprît . . . A présent je sais que notre civilisation occidentale (j'allais dire : française)

est non point seulement la plus belle; je crois, je sais qu'elle est *la seule* – oui, celle même de la Grèce, dont nous sommes les seuls héritiers" [*Journal* 416; ellipsis Gide's].

15. *Dépaysement* contains the word *pays* [country] and therefore means more than "disorientation." The term "alienation," taken literally to mean "making foreign," would perhaps come closer to the original.

16. "[P]eut-être pourrait-on mesurer la valeur d'un homme au degré de dépaysement (physique ou intellectuel) qu'il est capable de maîtriser. . . . [V]oilà l'éducation que réclame l'homme fort, – dangereuse, il est vrai, éprouvante; c'est une lutte contre l'*étranger;* mais il n'y a éducation que dès que l'instruction modifie. – Quant aux faibles : enracinez! enracinez!" (2: 442).

17. The *querelle du peuplier* evolved roughly as follows: Gide wrote his article partly in response to Léon Blum's favorable review of *Les Déracinés* in *La Revue blanche*. Charles Maurras, taking the position of Barrès in the polemic, criticized the concept of *déracinement* as a positive process, defended in another review of Barrès's novel; Gide learned of these other contributions upon reading Barrès's *Scènes et doctrines du nationalisme* (1902), which prompted a second piece by Gide in *L'Ermitage,* dated November 1903. In his "Réponse à M. Maurras," Gide retreats from his stark confrontational stance against nationalist doctrine but clings to his theory of the positive effects of uprooting. In order to prove that regular uprooting and transplanting are standard procedure in raising poplars, he quotes from the catalogue of a tree nursery, obviously delighted to find concrete evidence for his thesis, as well as an echo of Montaigne: "Our trees have been TRANSPLANTED (the word is in bold type in the text) 2, 3, 4 times or more, depending on their strength. THIS OPERATION HELPS THEM TAKE ROOT MORE STRONGLY; THEY ARE SPACED APART APPROPRIATELY SO AS TO OBTAIN WELL-FORMED HEADS (here, the emphasis is mine)" [Nos arbres ont été TRANSPLANTÉS (le mot est en gros caractères dans le texte), 2, 3, 4 fois et plus, suivant leur force, opération qui favorise la reprise; ILS SONT DISTANCÉS CONVENABLEMENT AFIN D'OBTENIR DES TÊTES BIEN FAITES (ici, c'est moi qui soulignais)] (4: 402). The part of the sentence Gide capitalizes echoes Montaigne's desire for "well-formed," rather than "well-filled," heads (i.e., minds) in his essay on the education of children. Echoes of the *querelle* will still be heard as late as 1948, when Henri Massis defends Barrès against Gide in his book *D'André Gide à Marcel Proust*.

18. "[M]es articles sont des plus modérés contre une thèse dont je ne blâme que l'outrance" (4: 403).

19. "[L]e cartésianisme français (i. e. le classicisme français) est la seule discipline assez neutre, assez générale, pour être proposée à des esprits les plus divers . . ." (4: 413).

20. The use of the word "place" in this context requires some clarification. If indeed the French classical spirit can be said to reside somewhere specific (let us say Paris), it must also be pointed out that this is not a "place" in the traditional sense of the word. Paris is distinct from the provinces, for example, in that all provinces have something in common (regionalism, *terroir* [native soil] cultural practices that deviate from the ideal, etc.), whereas Paris does not. But it must also be noted that I am speaking here of an idealized–Gidean–Paris. The real city, of course, has its social, geographic, cultural particularities . . . but these have nothing to do with the notion of French national identity in the abstract, which also resides in Paris, but on an elevated plane that is removed from the populations that inhabit the various *quartiers*.

21. Several qualifications need to be made if one is to present Gide's position on nationalism as consistent with republican ideology. First, as I have already mentioned, there is Gide's own detachment from the entire arena of historical debate; in his ahistoricity, however, Gide does nothing different from what the Republic was also accomplishing: presenting its political agenda in a way that appears motivated solely by the disinterested search for truth. More problematic is the conflict over the seventeenth

century as the high point of French culture: by maintaining, as I am about to show, that the modern era is in fact *superior* to the period of "high" classicism, Gide goes directly counter to the process by which the Republic, through its schools, would institutionalize the seventeenth-century canon as the apex of national culture (a process very well portrayed by Albanese).

22. "Les premières terres cultivées, ce sont les plus faciles . . . non les plus riches, mais les plus pauvres. . . . [Les] terres riches, les terres basses, [on] ne les considérera que plus tard. Longtemps, elles resteront en marge de la culture, « barbares » et méconnues. Le civilisé ne s'avisera que lentement de leurs promesses . . ." (6: 15–16).

The passage on agriculture represents the clearest example in Gide's work of the considerable influence of his uncle, the well-known economist Charles Gide (1847–1932). Gide is paraphrasing his uncle's interpretation of the work of the American economist Henry Charles Carey (1793–1879). The theory that the best land is the last to be colonized seems to derive partly from Carey's analysis of the domestication of the American frontier. The way in which this and other economic theories are put to use in Gide's text has yet to be fully explored.

23. "– Mon grand frère, commence-t-il, nous ne nous ressemblons guère. Mon frère nous ne nous ressemblons pas.
Le frère aîné :
– C'est ta faute.
– Pourquoi la mienne?
– Parce que je suis dans l'ordre; tout ce qui s'en distingue est fruit ou semence d'orgueil.
– Ne puis-je avoir de distinctif que des défauts?
– N'appelle qualité que ce qui te ramène à l'ordre, et tout le reste, réduis-le.
– C'est cette mutilation que je crains. Ceci aussi que tu vas supprimer, vient du père." (5: 11)

24. Although the mother does make an appearance in the story, there is no allusion whatever to her input in the genetic makeup of her offspring, nor does she play a role as a distributor of the wealth of the estate. In light of this, it is interesting to note that the family estate of La Roque, with which Gide claimed to identify, belonged to his mother. The emphasis on the father is so consistent throughout his work that one can discern an attempt to invert the principle of matrilinearity. The purpose of such an inversion might be to cast doubt on the entire principle of genetic transmission by accentuating the arbitrary and doubtful nature of fatherhood, and perhaps even to alienate further Judaism, and its matrilinear transmission of racial identity, from a discussion of French culture.

25. The mention of the dog would appear to be an ironic allusion to Odysseus's return, in which his blind, decrepit dog "sees" immediately who he is, while others must rely on clues such as his scar and his athletic prowess. In Gide, the basis for recognition is precisely *not* the natural physical affinity that a dog can instinctively perceive. That is not to say that there is no basis for recognition whatsoever, but rather that it derives from a more abstract conception of kinship than mere physical resemblance.

26. "[I]ci c'est lui [le frère aîné] qui fait la loi . . ." (5: 10).

27. Georges Poulet was one of the first to identify the conspicuous lack of any connection between Gide's writing and a real or imagined locus in space and time: "It is immediately apparent in Gide that space, in its most general and crudest form, does not exist" [Il apparaît tout de suite que, chez Gide, l'espace, pris sous sa forme la plus générale et la plus nue, n'existe pas] (232).

28. The French version of the Gospel according to Luke admittedly does not lend itself as well to the sexual interpretation: "He dissipated his wealth in a prodigal's lifestyle"; "[il] dissipa son bien dans une vie de prodigue." The French word *"bien"* can refer

only to his wealth, while the English word "substance" has broader connotations of anything that is material, of this world rather than other-worldly. But "riotous living" or *"vie de prodigue"* can include sexual license, with which the Bible is rife, and which allows that particular Gidean twist on the parable to manifest itself.

29. It is impossible on this subject to ignore Gide's attempts in *Corydon* (1911) and elsewhere to defend male homosexuality as not only legal in practice, but socially acceptable as well. The fact that homosexuality and pederasty were social practices in ancient Greece serves as his basic argument for purging the "deviant" sexual act of its transgressive character. It has been noted, for example in Richard Howard's introduction to his translation of *Corydon,* how unusual Gide's position was, especially his refusal to admit to any kind of guilt as a result of his homosexual practice. This is in strong contrast to Proust, to name just one contemporary example.

30. In *Corydon* Gide chooses to defend homosexuality in one of its most marginal manifestations, the relationship between older men and adolescent boys; yet he places his defense within the classical culture of pederasty, thereby reconciling the transgressive with the traditional. The most extreme form of homosexuality from the point of view of conservative bourgeois culture, the seduction of young boys, just happens to be also one form of homosexuality for which he can easily find classical antecedents. The consequences of this strategy are explored in Patrick Pollard's recent work *André Gide: Homosexual Moralist.* Where Pollard looks at Gide and the issue of homosexuality as it was understood in the late nineteenth and early twentieth centuries, Michael Lucey's *Gide's Bent* specifically confronts the question of homosexual writing as an exegetical tool in Gide's work.

31. "Flaccidité. Phrases sans muscles. . . . Grâce détendue, retombée. . . . En face de cet asiatisme, combien je me sens dorien!" (*Journal* 1134).

32. For an analysis of Barrès's own terror at the Orient and the Jewish threat it contains, see Reid.

33. "L'homme, [Gide] le voit double, se défendant d'une part de lui-même, rejetant l'autre en lui au nom d'une identité imaginaire" (41).

34. "– Quel bien peux-tu chercher ailleurs, qu'ici tu ne trouves en abondance? ou mieux : c'est ici seulement que sont tes biens.
– Je sais que tu m'as gardé des richesses.
– Ceux de tes biens que tu n'as pas dilapidés, c'est-à-dire cette part qui nous est commune, à nous tous : les biens fonciers.
– Ne possédé-je donc plus rien en propre?
– Si; cette part de dons que notre père consentira peut-être encore à t'accorder.
– C'est à cela seul que je tiens; je consens à ne posséder que cela." (5: 14)

35. The issue of colonialism is visible like a watermark throughout this discussion of nationalism. Without going into detail concerning Gide's views on the subject (of which *Voyage au Congo* is but one small indication), it is interesting to point out that the integral nationalists like Barrès and Maurras were opposed to the colonial enterprise, arguing that France first had to regain its lost territories before conquering new ones, and condemning colonial expansion as "adventurism." The Third Republic, on the other hand, placed colonialism at the center of its international policy. Gide's nationalism is once again very much a republican nationalism, in that it provides an ideological argument in favor precisely of "adventurism."

36. "A quoi la France doit-elle cette extraordinaire faveur? – Sans doute, ainsi que la Grèce, à un heureux confluent de races, à un mélange que précisément les nationalistes déplorent aujourd'hui" (6: 7).

37. Discussions of nationalism always bring to mind concerns of the day, particularly when national myths are being constructed and destroyed at the pace we are currently witnessing. For many years, it seems, France, among other nations, criticized

the United States for believing in the myth of the melting pot, and hiding its social, racial, and sexual conflicts behind a star-spangled veil. Now, with French society under attack by the forces of immigration (Giscard d'Estaing, for example, has spoken of an "invasion"), the United States is paradoxically seen as having *failed* to sustain the assimilationist principle of the melting pot and having surrendered to the atomizing pressures of multiculturalism. The debate is raging in the French press: for one example, see Julliard.

38. "Longtemps l'homme reculera devant les dangers et les fièvres des terres basses; longtemps, de plus d'un lac Stymphale, les rives incertaines attendront en vain leur héros" (6: 15–16).

39. Although Gide speaks of "high" culture as the easily tilled plateaus that man's ingenuity first overcame, he does not seem to imply that the purpose of contemporary authors is to deal with "low" or popular culture. The term *"terres basses"* is nevertheless ambiguous. At times, he appears to refer to the subject matter of literature: the obvious problems have all been dealt with, leaving the modern author with the difficult task of thinking of something to say. It would also be accurate to read the term as referring literally to foreign literature, on which the French language must exercise itself. This literalizes the native-foreign distinction that is made throughout Gide's argument, and also is consistent with the traditional idea that foreign authors (Shakespeare, Dostoevsky) are somehow "wild" and need to be tamed by translation before they attain their potential. This would put Gide in the tradition of Voltaire's ambivalent relationship to Shakespeare, and somewhat in opposition to Stendhal's argument in *Racine et Shakespeare,* in which he defends the "barbarian" component of the foreign text.

40. "[C]e que Goethe, Heine, Schopenhauer, Nietzsche, m'ont appris de meilleur, c'est peut-être leur admiration pour la France" (4: 413).

41. "– [E]lle est d'une âcreté presque affreuse; je sens pourtant que, si j'avais suffisamment soif, j'y mordrais.

– Ah! je peux te le dire à présent : c'est cette soif que dans le désert je cherchais.

– Une soif dont seul ce fruit non-sucré désaltère . . .

– Non; mais il faut aimer cette soif." (5: 25–26; ellipsis Gide's)

42. "Ce domaine que j'héritai, fort jeune encore, de ma mère, je souffrais d'en connaître les limites; ou plutôt : je me refusais à les connaître; non pour pouvoir m'imaginer que je possédais davantage, mais au contraire pour me retenir de penser que rien de tout ce que j'aimais ici fût personnellement et exclusivement *mon* bien. . . . Je . . . ne me sentais pas plus d'obligations envers le pays que le pays n'en avait envers moi" (15: 71–72).

Works Cited

Albanese, Ralph, Jr. *Molière à l'école républicaine : de la critique universitaire aux manuels scolaires (1870–1914)*. Saratoga, CA: Anma Libri, 1992.

Barrès, Maurice. *L'Appel au soldat*. Paris: F. Juven, 1900.

———. *Leurs Figures*. Paris: F. Juven, 1902.

———. *La Colline inspirée*. Paris: Émile-Paul Frères, 1913.

———. *Les Déracinés*. Paris: Fasquelle, 1897.

———. *Scènes et doctrines du nationalisme*. Paris: Plon-Nourrit, 1925.

Cap, Jean-Pierre. "André Gide's *Nouvelle Revue Française* and Cosmopolitanism." *Laurels* 51.2 (Fall 1980): 101–109.

Domenach, Jean-Marie. *Barrès par lui-même*. Paris: Éditions du Seuil, 1954.

Gide, André. "A propos des *Déracinés*." *Œuvres complètes*. Vol. 2. Ed. Louis Martin-

Chauffier. Paris: Gallimard, 1932. 435–444.

———. *Corydon.* Trans. Richard Howard. New York: Hippocrene Books-Octagon, 1983.

———. "De l'influence allemande." *Œuvres complètes.* Vol. 4. Ed. Louis Martin-Chauffier. Paris: Gallimard, 1933. 411–414.

———. "Jeunesse." *Œuvres complètes.* Vol. 15. Ed. Louis Martin-Chauffier. Paris: Gallimard, 1939. 69–89.

———. *Journal 1889–1939.* Paris: Gallimard, Bibliothèque de la Pléiade, 1939.

———. "Nationalisme et littérature." *Œuvres complètes.* Vol. 6. Ed. Louis Martin-Chauffier. Paris: Gallimard, 1934. 1–20.

———. *Les Nourritures terrestres. Romans, récits et soties, œuvres lyriques.* Ed. Yvonne Davet and Jean-Jacques Thierry. Paris: Gallimard, Bibliothèque de la Pléiade, 1958. 151–250.

———. "La Querelle du peuplier." *Œuvres complètes.* Vol. 4. Ed. Louis Martin-Chauffier. Paris: Gallimard, 1933. 399–410.

———. "Le Retour de l'enfant prodigue." *Œuvres complètes.* Vol. 5. Ed. Louis Martin-Chauffier. Paris: Gallimard, 1933. 1–28.

Hanna, Martha. "What Did André Gide See in the Action française?" *Historical Reflections / Réflexions Historiques* 17.1 (Winter 1991): 1–22.

Hutchinson, Hilary. "Gide and Barrès: Fifty Years of Protest." *Modern Language Review* 89.4 (October 1994): 856–864.

Julliard, Jacques. "Les États désunis d'Amérique." *Le Nouvel Observateur* 1383 (May 9–15, 1991): 23.

Lucey, Michael. *Gide's Bent: Sexuality, Politics, Writing.* New York: Oxford University Press, 1995.

Massis, Henri. *D'André Gide à Marcel Proust.* Lyon: Lardanchet, 1948.

Mehlman, Jeffrey. *Legacies of Anti-Semitism in France.* Minneapolis: University of Minnesota Press, 1983.

Pollard, Patrick. *André Gide: Homosexual Moralist.* New Haven: Yale University Press, 1991.

Poulet, Georges. *La Pensée indéterminée II : du romantisme au début du XXe siècle.* Paris: Presses Universitaires de France, 1987.

Reid, Martine. "L'Orient liquidé (Barrès, *Les Déracinés*)." *Romanic Review* 83.3 (May 1992): 379–388.

Schnyder, Peter. "Gide face à Barrès." *Orbis Litterarum* 40.1 (Winter 1985): 33–43.

Sonn, Richard. "The Early Political Career of Maurice Barrès: Anarchist, Socialist, or Protofascist?" *Clio* 21.1 (Fall 1991): 41–60.

Soucy, Robert. *French Fascism: The Case of Maurice Barrès.* Berkeley: University of California Press, 1972.

Suleiman, Susan Rubin. *Authoritarian Fictions: The Ideological Novel as a Literary Genre.* Princeton: Princeton University Press, 1993.

Tain, Aldyth. *Gide's Le Retour de l'enfant prodigue.* Logan: Utah State University Press, Monograph Series VII: 4, 1960.

CHAPTER 3

Practices of Posterity: Gide and the Cultural Politics of Sexuality[1]

Michael Lucey

In a passage from *Les Nouvelles Nourritures* that Gide apparently composed during the early 1920s, he imagines a figure of posterity:

> You who will come when I no longer hear the noises of the earth and my lips no longer drink of its dew—you who will perhaps read me later—it is for you that I write these pages; for you are perhaps not astonished enough with living; you do not properly admire this stunning miracle that is your life. It seems to me sometimes that you will drink with my thirst, and that what inclines you toward this other being whom you caress is already my own desire.[2]

This anchoring of the drive to write in the possibility of being read posthumously by the arguably young and male figure, who takes time out from caressing his arguably young and male friend in order to cast his eyes over Gide's words, represents an intriguing moment in Gide's way of figuring posterity to himself. Compare, for instance, what he says in his journal entry of December 22, 1918, about the loss of his correspondence with his wife, Madeleine:[3]

> Certain days, above all certain nights, I feel crushed by regret for these destroyed letters. In them especially I had hoped to survive.[4]

Gide—like many, though not all, writers—experiments obsessively with figures of posterity, as if those figures were totemic ones that guaranteed the possibility of any literary writing. The years encompassing the writing of the two passages just cited are years in which Gide's diverse representations of posterity come into acute conflict, and his journal entries for the last months of 1918, as he mourns the loss of his correspondence with Madeleine, are rich in traces of that conflict.

If the imagined future reader of Gide's correspondence with his wife seems hardly likely to be the same reader he imagines as he composes *Les Nouvelles Nourritures,* it's not as if there's a clean change of regime from one image of posterity to the next. The rhythm according to which one or the other assumes primacy at any given moment is complex. Consider, for instance, the following passage from Gide's *Journal,* from November 24, 1918:

> To her alone would I write with abandon.
>
> Not a cloud, never the least disturbance between us. *Possibly there was never a more beautiful correspondence*—for it does not suffice to say that my best was to be found there, but hers as well, for I never wrote for myself alone. Ah! Next to those letters, of what value are my *Porte étroite,* my *Nourritures,* fragile sparks escaped from an immense hearth.
>
> At least now nothing prevents me any longer from publishing in my lifetime both *Corydon* and the Memoirs.[5]

It's the abrupt switch from the despairing, melodramatic rhetoric around the loss of his letters to his wife, to the flatter, almost cold statement of the last sentence, "at least now nothing prevents me," that catches the ear, indicating some kind of split voice, some kind of rhythmic to and fro between different agencies. The "any longer" of "nothing prevents me any longer" lets us know that the difficult negotiation between the different versions of posterity, as well as between the different voices that correspond to those differing versions, has been long on-going. Likewise, the question of what to do with his treatise on male love, *Corydon,* and his memoirs, *Si le grain ne meurt,* has been in the air for a long time.

Corydon had already been privately published at this point. And Gide was thinking of the same course for *Si le grain ne meurt,* a fair amount of which he had already finished composing. Indeed, it's worth noting that Gide's discovery that his wife had burnt his letters happened because he asked her for access to the correspondence to verify a date for his memoirs. As he mourns the loss of the correspondence, he spends his time putting the final touches on *Si le grain ne meurt,* and, still hesitant as to whether he'll send the manuscript to his publisher or not, he nonetheless makes sure he keeps an extra copy, of his own, perhaps for posterity's sake:

> I occupy myself with going over and updating the rough copy of my *Mémoires,* so that I will retain a complete text for myself even if I also provide one to Verbeke [his publisher]. I am not very satisfied with this revisiting of the text: the sentences are weak; it's too self-conscious, too precious, too literary . . . [6]

Si le grain ne meurt—how to write it, what to do with it—seems to represent for Gide a new relation to posterity (conceivably a new relation to literature itself), as well as a new stylistic effort. All of these considerations (of style, of literature, whether or not to publish, what relation to posterity to hope for) become related, as we shall see in what follows, to a concern with the odd question of how most appropriately to say what Gide will refer to as "everything" *[tout dire]*—where "everything" means not exactly everything, but, more specifically, how to tell of homosexual sex. Gide's dealings with his friend and fellow writer Roger Martin du Gard are an optimal place for observing the interrelation of Gide's concerns about homosexual explicitness, its relation to style and genre, and his general relation to literature and "literary posterity."

Martin du Gard's association in Gide's mind with these questions is indicated clearly enough in his mischievous way of inscribing his friend into the very text of his memoirs. At the end of the first part of *Si le grain ne meurt,* Gide writes:

> Roger Martin du Gard, to whom I have shown these Memoirs, finds fault with me for never saying enough in them, and for leaving the reader unsatisfied. And yet I have meant all along to say everything. But in making confidences, there is a limit which cannot be overstepped without artifice, without strain; and what I aim at above all is to be natural. (232)[7]

Gide thus turns Martin du Gard into a voice encouraging him on his new path, seconding Gide's efforts to renovate his literary profile, to pursue a kind of avant-garde openness about his sexuality. And indeed, reading Martin du Gard's October 7, 1920 letter to Gide, one is inclined to think that Gide, in *Si le grain ne meurt,* has understated Martin du Gard's position:

> The more I think of your memoirs the less I am satisfied with them. . . . I have read 300 pages, and I have yet to have encountered you. . . . Now is the time to open fully the secret door, to enter there, and to lead us there with you, in a stream of light. . . . *What child were you, for yourself, in your solitude?* What sort of affection did you have for those around you? What dreams of the future? What precise and successive troubles assailed you from age 12 to age 16? And afterwards? How was your literary vocation born? What were your childhood vanities, your infatuations, your particular weaknesses? Your curiosities? Your initiations? Your nocturnal reveries? And on awakening, what remained of them that you then combined with your waking life?[8]

"Now is the time to open fully the secret door . . . and to lead us there with you," announces Gide's seemingly daring friend, demanding precision in a way that, despite a flimsy veil of seemingly sociologically informed curiosity ("from age 12 to age 16"), seems rather more prurient. Further, as we shall see, Martin du Gard's "us" is not particularly inclusive, and the temporality of "now is the time" is not as based in the "present" as it might at first seem. Or rather, it turns out to be the present of posterity. In Martin du Gard's journal entry from the previous day, October 6, he says of his conversation with Gide (he both wrote to and spoke in person with him about this), "I made him recognize that he had here the opportunity to write *the immortal book about his true interior life,* and that it was necessary not to shy away from any secret, but to descend to the absolute depths, to the most troubled abyss, and to unfold the truth in its integrity. Such

was the price of the work's beauty" (my italics).[9] Martin du Gard thus understands his advice to increase the explicitness of the text as crucial to Gide's literary posterity—conceived, we shall see, in a way that Gide cannily chooses not
to accept. He further characterizes his advice as *aesthetic* advice, and it seems
worth trying to comprehend how, for both Gide and Martin du Gard, there
were important questions of aesthetics residing in the choice both to portray
homosexual sex in some detail and to find the appropriate style, genre, and publication strategy through which to do so.

But to return to Martin du Gard's "now is the time" for a moment: in point
of fact, Martin du Gard, for all his eagerness to give advice, and for all his happiness at being one of Gide's readers, also claims not to have wanted Gide to
publish his memoirs. We might therefore surmise that he would be unhappy to
be mentioned in the published version of *Si le grain ne meurt* as a person asking
for more explicitness. And, indeed, he wrote a reply to Gide's invocation of his
name, which he inserted into his own copy of *Si le grain ne meurt,* imagining,
correctly, that it would find its way to posterity's eyes:

> I don't deny having encouraged André Gide, with all of my affection, to
> write his life's confession, nor do I deny having pushed him to stay as close
> as possible to the truth, to multiply authentic details, no matter how unin-
> hibited they were; in a word, *to say everything.* But, on the other hand, no
> one was more opposed than I to the *publication* of these Mémoirs; and I
> persist in thinking that they should not have appeared during the author's
> lifetime (nor even soon after his death).
>
>   I even believe that my indiscreet insistence on this point was not unre-
> lated to Gide's long hesitation, for, after having 6000 copies of a first edi-
> tion printed, and after ordering and then canceling their delivery to
> bookstores twenty times, he kept this stock for nearly two years in his cel-
> lar (from 1921 to 1923), before resolving to put it into circulation.[10]

Martin du Gard's qualifications encourage us to consider how the version of
posterity one chooses to use as a guide is crucial to the shaping of one's literary
career. What would have been the shape of Gide's literary career had he chosen
to leave *Si le grain ne meurt* in his basement, awaiting posthumous publication?
One is reminded of a comment Gide makes in *Si le grain ne meurt,* regarding his
mother's attempt to dissuade him from bringing Athman to Paris: "It has not
often happened to me to renounce a thing on which I have set my heart; a post-
ponement is the utmost that obstacles wring from me" (294).[11] The statement
works fairly well as a version of Gide's publication strategies as well, and it's clear
that his delays were in fact never so long as to jeopardize the establishment and
maintenance of the particular literary profile he came to imagine for himself.
(Martin du Gard's delays were quite a bit longer, and to telling effect.)

Quite early on in their friendship, Gide shows a full awareness of the significance of Martin du Gard's differing relation to posterity. Consider the following interesting reflections from Gide's journal entry for October 5, 1920, just

after the conversation with Martin du Gard regarding the desirable level of explicitness for *Si le grain ne meurt*:

> He lets me know of his profound disappointment: I have avoided my subject; fear, shame, worry over the public reaction, I have dared to say nothing truly intimate, I've only succeeded in provoking questions . . . [These reflections would disturb me more if I did not begin to comprehend that it is in the character of M du G always to dream of a chimerical beyond, yet in such a way that any realization of it would leave him unaffected. One of the most curious characters that I have ever encountered.]
>
> Since coming here, received from him a long, excellent letter in which he returns to all of the points on which our conversation had touched. I am, however, conscious of having told everything about my childhood that I remembered, and of having told it as indiscreetly as possible. It would be artificial to introduce there more shadow, more secrecy, more misdirection.[12]

The variant sentences from the manuscript, bracketed in this quotation, show Gide already having understood that posterity functions for Martin du Gard in a way inappropriate to Gide's own project. Martin du Gard's call to explicitness is enabled by his belief in a posterior moment at which that explicitness carries no price—but therefore, Gide must realize, also no gain. Also interesting in this passage is Gide's careful effort to calculate the appropriate level of explicitness for his memoirs: "I am, however, conscious of having told everything about my childhood that I remembered, and of having told it as indiscreetly as possible." One might well take the first claim of the sentence (to have recounted everything he remembers) with a grain of salt. The second claim is more interesting: to have been as indiscreet as "possible"—where "possible" clearly doesn't mean "as indiscreetly as *anyone else* might have done." As the whole interaction with Martin du Gard makes clear, the calculus as to what is possible, how much of a risk one can take, in the field of indiscretion is a complex one, involving questions of style, reputation, and literary and social prestige, as well as any number of interrelated personal and psychological struggles.

Tellingly, Gide makes an odd slip between the last two sentences in the passage I've just cited. Having claimed to have been as indiscreet as possible, he then adds: "It would be artificial to introduce there more shadow, more secrecy, more misdirection." The superficial logic is hard to follow: "I've been as indiscreet as possible; it would be artificial to add further devices of discretion." Perhaps Gide is hearing in Martin du Gard's call for more information about "your curiosities," "your particular weaknesses," "your initiations," or "your nocturnal reveries" a request for some additional, overly gothic, and melodramatic material. Perhaps Gide has the sense that adding more information would distort his style, ruin his carefully calculated position vis-à-vis discretion. He admits a sentence or two later that perhaps Jacques Raverat was correct in suggesting that "my story, often, in wanting to be clear, simplifies a bit much my gestures, or at the

very least the moving forces behind them."[13] In any case, consciously or unconsciously, Gide, in *Si le grain ne meurt,* is clearly working out an approach that is
stylistic (a careful balancing act of *"l'artifice"* and *"le naturel,"* of indiscretion and
discretion) and strategic—in relation to both his future reputation (posterity)
and his contemporary literary profile. Martin du Gard here seems to play a useful role by embodying the arrière-garde to Gide's avant-garde. He is one of the
many forces within Gide's contemporary literary field to serve as an important
counterexample both in terms of stylistic choices and strategic literary positioning. We might almost say that he (unwittingly?) helps Gide to experience his
own more productive, more successful relation to posterity.

In thinking about Gide's relation to Martin du Gard in these terms, in using
concepts such as "strategy," in comparing different trajectories of literary
careers, I rely on some of Pierre Bourdieu's useful thinking about both biography and literature itself. In a short essay entitled "L'illusion biographique," for
instance, Bourdieu suggests:

> To try to understand a life as a unique and self-sufficient series of succes-
> sive events without any connection other than their association with a
> "subject" whose consistency is undoubtedly only that of a proper name, is
> just as absurd as attempting to make sense of a subway ride without taking
> into account the structure of the system, that is to say, the matrix of objec-
> tive relations among the different stations. Biographical events take shape as
> so many *placements* and *displacements* in social space, that is, more precisely,
> in the different and successive states of the structure governing the distri-
> bution of different kinds of capital which are at stake in the given field.[14]

To outline a few episodes in the relationship between Gide and Martin du Gard
is to begin to outline the social space in which Gide is making complicated
decisions about what it means to be an openly homosexual literary figure. Such
decisions are heavily mediated by all sorts of forces within the social field as well
as the specifically literary field. Establishing a productive relation to "literary
posterity" involves bringing to a successful conclusion a set of negotiations with
some of these forces. A relation to "posterity" is not solely a psychological fantasy. It's a complicated, historically and socially sedimented structure that helps
form a particular practice of literature. That practice will involve numerous literary choices, choices having to do with style, genre, plot, publication strategies,
establishment of archives, etc.[15] Those choices and the relation to "posterity"
that looms behind them will be crucial in determining what Bourdieu would
call one's trajectory through the literary field. Influencing those choices will be
not only one's background and the various kinds of "capital" one begins with
or accumulates, but also one's perception of the choices made by one's competitors and predecessors, and the forms taken by one's own literary ambitions.
To cite Bourdieu again,

> This means that one may only understand a trajectory on condition of
> having first constructed the successive states of the field in which it

unfolds, the ensemble of objective relations that have tied the given agent—at least in a certain number of pertinent states—to the ensemble of other agents engaged in the same field and confronted with the same space of possibilities.[16]

Martin du Gard is clearly one important interlocutor for Gide, in relation to whom Gide imagines what is possible for him, what risks are appropriate. It would be worth noting here some of the other figures to whom Gide has a relation in this regard—sometimes, perhaps, by virtue of their literary or intellectual weight, a more consequential relation than the one with Martin du Gard, even if they are more distant from Gide's daily life: Wilde, Proust, Freud, and Dostoevsky.[17]

As regards Dostoevsky, whose presence in this list might seem at first glance the least self-evident, consider a journal entry of Martin du Gard's from March 11, 1922, just as Gide apparently makes the decision to forsake Martin du Gard's advice and bring the copies of *Si le grain ne meurt* up out of the basement:

> Gide has told me that he feels the need to publish as soon as possible *Corydon* . . . and *Si le grain ne meurt*. . . .
>
> I am in a state of desperation over it. I am certain that nothing can damage the full flowering of his maturity more than this useless scandal, whose wound he will feel intensely, and which will create around him a new atmosphere of suspicion, of indignation, and of contemptuous slander. This will not serve but to strongly arm his enemies, who are legion, and to drive from him the two thirds of his current friends who accept a situation that is dissimulated, discreet, but who will have to take a position once Gide has cynically declared to the public the nature of his private life. . . .
>
> In reality, he is above all the victim of a Russian intoxication. It's Dostoevsky who eggs him on. He has now spent several months engaged with Dostoevsky in order to prepare his lectures and his book on Dostoevsky. And he has been infected. He feels the need to make public confession. . . .[18]

This telling passage shows Martin du Gard miscalculating the possibilities of the literary field, and of Gide's position in it; yet the passage also reveals Martin du Gard's clear sense that what is under discussion here is a strategic decision about a literary career. His use of the word "cynically" is quite telling in this regard (*"lorsque Gide aura cyniquement avoué en public"*): it implies that what we might otherwise take as Gide's confessional *impulse* is hardly impulsive, that it's rather carefully timed, as if Gide has known how to wait sufficiently long to put his friends into an awkward position, knowing that at present they would have too much to lose in turning away from him.

Martin du Gard persists in imagining that Gide, through this timely or untimely publication, will damage his relation to posterity ("the full flowering of his maturity"), and that this long-term damage will arise from the more immediate damage he unquestionably will do (in Martin du Gard's estimation) to his relations with his contemporaries. Gide's calculation would appear to be different: that his relation to posterity now depends on the putting at risk of certain relations with his contemporaries. Yet that risk, as Martin du Gard's "cynically" clearly suggests, is one that Gide has managed carefully. His closest literary friends already have copies of both *Corydon* and *Si le grain ne meurt.* The very ethos of his group of friends and associates at the *Nouvelle Revue Française,*[19] the friendships and professional relations that constitute that group, and the credibility and literary prestige that it has accumulated since its establishment all serve to limit Gide's risk.

Gide's *"intoxication russe,"* portrayed by Martin du Gard as a dangerous attraction to certain forms of self-revelation and confession, could just as profitably be seen as part and parcel of the aesthetic and literary preoccupations that he shares with his associates. His preoccupation with Dostoevsky intermingles in a complex way the aesthetic and literary concerns of the *NRF* group with his own morally conceived project of sexual self-revelation; through this intermingling, Gide's work on Dostoevsky may well contribute to his effort to legitimize a variety of tasks in which he is engaged: explicit self-representation *(Si le grain ne meurt),* public advocacy of same-sex relations *(Corydon),* and the insertion of openly homosexual characters and themes into the novel *(Les Faux-Monnayeurs).* Martin du Gard wasn't yet closely attached to the *NRF* group in 1913–1914 when, in an earlier moment, the groundwork for this productive confusion of agendas was laid. In March 1914, the *NRF* published the third installment of Gide's *Les Caves du Vatican,* which included a paragraph of homoerotically inclined reminiscences on the part of its protagonist, Lafcadio Wluiki. Paul Claudel, a *NRF* contributor, read the paragraph with consternation, and wrote to Gide demanding a confession as to whether Gide shared Lafcadio's inclinations, and also demanding suppression of the offending paragraph. In the end Claudel would obtain something like a confession, though perhaps not one as repentant as he would have liked. As for the excision of the passage, here is how Auguste Anglès recounts Gide's response:

> As for the invitation to suppress out of "prudence" the incriminating sentence—really a paragraph—he regretted not being able to give in there. The "reassuring" prophecy—"little by little one will forget"—appeared "shameful" to him: "No, do not demand from me either cover-up or compromise; or it is I who will have less esteem for you."[20]

Claudel had suggested that if Gide eliminated the paragraph in question from future publications of the novel, people would gradually forget that Gide had ever written it. That his clumsy invocation of an appropriately cleansed relation to the future was strategically the least adroit tactic he could have chosen is made clear by the moralizing tone of Gide's response.

Interesting for our purposes is the strategic positioning of the offending paragraph in the novel just prior to one of the plot's most crucial moments—indeed, one of its most Dostoevskian moments: Lafcadio, Gide's most Dostoevskian character, is about to kill, for no apparent reason, the person with whom he is sharing a train compartment. When Anglès is analyzing the preoccupations in the *NRF* group with the form of the novel in the years surrounding the publication of Gide's *Caves du Vatican* (1913–1914), he describes the group as "at the confluence of the waters of the Russian novel and of the English novel," and notes that Gide, in particular, "strove to capture and unite in his *Caves du Vatican* the two currents of *Tom Jones* and the *Brothers Karamazov*."[21] A reading of Anglès's account of the writings in which various members of the *NRF* group grapple with the form of the novel[22] reveals many parallels between those formulations and Gide's ideas in his lectures on Dostoevsky from nearly a decade later. As Gide has it in those lectures, "In the work of Dostoevsky . . . children abound; moreover, it is worth noting that most of his characters, and some of the most important, are creatures who are still young, hardly formed. . . . He is particularly attached to disconcerting cases, to people who rise up as challenges to accepted morality and psychology."[23] Anglès points to Jacques Copeau's[24] reasons for prefering H. G. Wells's *Ann Veronica* to the novelistic production of a typical French writer like Paul Bourget: "Copeau dedicates himself to justifying an adolescence that breaks with conformity. But it is not by chance that an ethos complicit with youth orients its adherents towards a particular type and tone of novel. The novel runs the risk of calcifying in a 'learned and sterile thesis,' or it risks drying out 'on the steppes of theory': but here [in *Ann Veronica*], we have a book that is 'human, spontaneous, direct, and probing' without being 'systematic or premeditated.'"[25] The terms of the discussion as to the nature of the novel are both aesthetic and generational, Bourget being cast in the role of the old generation. For the *NRF*, it is a question of renovating the French novel, and in this they try to fashion themselves as an avant-garde, claiming to find friendly examples in the contemporary English novel, and profound precursors in the Russian novel.

Gide, in his lectures, contrasts Dostoevsky with Balzac, and ends up finding in favor of Dostoevsky's method for constructing characters (one Gide was clearly working with in both *Les Caves du Vatican* and *Les Faux-Monnayeurs*):

> I would also say that not only the characters of the *Comédie humaine,* but those of the real comedy that we live as well, form themselves—that all of us French, such as we are, we, too, form ourselves—after a Balzacian ideal. The inconsistencies of our nature, should there indeed be any, appear embarrassing, ridiculous, to us. We deny them. . . .What does Dostoevsky present us with in this regard? Characters who, without any concern about remaining consistent, yield obligingly to all of the contradictions, all of the negations which their own nature is capable of. It seems as if that is precisely what interests Dostoevsky the most: inconsistency. Far from hiding it, he continually makes it stand out; he illuminates it.[26]

Proust, in fact, will think of both Balzac and Dostoevsky when he reads *Les Caves du Vatican*. In one letter to Gide, he writes in praise, it seems, of the portrayal of Lafcadio, and in particular of his sexuality: "But in the creation of Cadio, no one has been objective with that much perversity since Balzac and *Splendeurs et misères*. All the more so, it seems to me, since Balzac was aided in inventing Lucien de Rubempré, by a certain personal vulgarity."[27] In a letter a month or so later, Proust speculates (with arch wickedness) as to whether Gide wouldn't be seen as a mere imitator of Dostoevsky in his way of portraying Lafcadio's criminality, but then decides that Gide needn't fear the comparison; his originality is secure, for Dostoevsky would never have given one of his ambiguous criminals Lafcadio's seductiveness and "immorality" (Proust 34). Proust's speculations, whatever invidious undercurrents they may contain, reveal the imbrication both he and Gide perceived, relied on, sought to legitimate, between their aesthetic projects and their portrayals of same-sex sexuality. That is, both Proust and Gide saw their struggles to bring representation of same-sex sexualities into the novel as a crucial part of their claim to be doing something new with the novel and with literature more generally. Their claims on literary posterity, their claims to be working within and to be advancing the tradition of the European novel rely in part on their innovative use of sexuality, and reciprocally, they intend their aesthetic success to legitimize their representation of that sexuality.

As Gide and Proust would have it, then, the sexual and the aesthetic advances they were striving for should be construed as inextricable. *Les Caves du Vatican* is evidently one of the better, more prestigious examples that the *NRF* group has of the kind of avant-garde or renovated French novel it is trying to encourage.[28] The protagonist is an adolescent in revolt, and one who illustrates a practice of "inconsistency" *[inconséquence],* in part through a passage that includes reflections on his sexually adventurous past and leads up to his rather Dostoevskian crime.[29] Gide would, of course, claim that his novel was not an illustration of the aesthetic theories of his associates at the *NRF,* and Jacques Rivière, who had written the most coherent statement of the group on their hopes for the novel,[30] would find *Les Caves du Vatican* "imperfect," and its subject matter insufficiently mastered (see Anglès 3: 300, 322). Even so, it is clear that an aesthetic interest in Dostoevsky and the psychology of his characters, a preoccupation with novels about rebellious adolescents, and an effort to transform the French novel are all in the air at the *NRF,* and that in combination they create a set of circumstances in which Gide successfully publishes a novel whose "pederastic" passages catch many eyes, threaten a number of friendships, and yet ultimately constitute a step along a career path he will feel able to pursue even further in the years ahead.

We have seen Roger Martin du Gard refer to part of Gide's pursuit of this literary cutting edge as "cynical." How cynical, or how impulsive, are the calculations that lead Gide to decide to publish *Corydon* and *Si le grain ne meurt?* Examining the complex compulsions that work through the relation to "posterity" in figures like Gide and Martin du Gard inevitably raises such difficult questions. Martin du Gard's vocabulary in the passage cited earlier reveals his own indecisiveness in this regard: on the one hand, Gide is making certain careerist decisions "cynically"; on the other hand, "it's Dostoevsky who eggs him on . . . he has been infected." Consider the same indecisiveness reflected in two passages from Martin du Gard's journal entry three days later:

Why throw off the mask at this very moment? Above all because the times are changing; the books of Proust, the movement of ideas in Germany and in Italy, where one claims freedom for love, the theories of Freud will all bring about very quickly a moment when one will regard with a completely different eye sexual deviance; there will no longer be anything courageous about throwing off the mask.[31]

There is more than simply courage in him, and desire for truth; there is more than merely a desire for mortification and opprobrium. There is also the ambition to perform a gesture that he finds noble, and the hope that this sincere gesture, disinterested, courageous, will secure for him, in the eyes of certain others, *in the eyes of posterity,* a particular veneration, a renewal of grandeur, of influence. (my emphasis)[32]

The ethical and temporal quandaries, the quandaries about sincerity, that arise out of these passages are all linked to the odd structure of the relation to posterity. Posterity can be thought of as an introject, an internalized model that comes to form part of oneself. Like other introjects, it is anachronistic. Many introjects are figures or voices internalized in the past and carried forward within the self into the present. Posterity is an introject of—an image of—the future carried *back* into the present. Introjected figures or agencies tend, if they evolve at all, to evolve at a slower rate than their referents in the external world—thus the anachronism. Introjects tend to be behind the times, to lag behind the cutting edge, to provide resistance to complete contemporaneity. The lack of coincidence between introject and external referent applies in the case of figures of posterity as well—for the future obviously has no obligation to produce referents for images of posterity previously imagined, and as time passes, figures of posterity may need updating as well.

Introjects of posterity have perhaps a less self-evidently close relation to particular persons than do the more familiar past-anchored introjects. From an analytic point of view, then, it can be easier, in the case of posterity, to avoid personalizing the introject, and to notice the social forces that work through it. At the outset of this essay, I contrasted Gide's internalized image of posterity with his internalized image of his wife. In the case of what Madeleine came to represent, we can see how difficult it is *not* to personalize past-anchored introjects: it would be quite a task to disentangle "Madeleine Gide" from Gide's internalized image of her, to understand the social and psychological forces at work through the agency of the introject. Jean Schlumberger's book *Madeleine et André Gide* is interesting in this regard. One way of understanding Schlumberger's project in that book is to say that he meant simply to show the distance between Madeleine Gide and Gide's image of her—the anachronism of the introject, we might say. Gide's introject couldn't evolve quickly enough to keep up with the evolution within his wife's life. Another slightly divergent way of thinking about this would be to wonder (and Schlumberger's book, so biographically inclined, doesn't move in this direction) what *social* forces were at work in the internalized representation of the person for whose eyes Gide apparently wrote until the crisis of 1918. That the internalized representation of those social forces continued to be a productive motor for Gide's writing is clear from his ongoing commentary on his relation to his wife (*Et nunc manet in te*[33] being

the capital instance). But hearing talk of Dostoevsky, and of "a desire for mortification and opprobrium," we might hesitate, and choose to revise an overly
hasty, overly complete or absolute identification between this introject and
"Madeleine." Simply to identify this introject, and the psychic agency within
which it is situated, with Madeleine would be to overlook the wider social forces
it obviously represents.[34] Gide would frequently look for common ground
between this agency and the more socially radical agency representing future
sexualities. His work on and relation to Dostoevsky could be thought of as an
effort at compromise. Yet it may be precisely his search for compromise that creates the odd sense of his work—for some of his contemporaries and for many
readers today—as being simultaneously forward-looking and behind the times.

Up to this point, I have suggested that Gide and Martin du Gard relate to posterity differently, and that this difference provides one measure of the ongoing
difference in their reputations. Nonetheless, while I will be detailing their differences a bit further, it is also worth insisting that from a slightly more removed
perspective, their relation to a particular set of practices of posterity is part of their
shared literary ethos—one that dates and socially positions both of them.

Consider for a brief moment further Schlumberger's *Madeleine et André Gide*.
Its major preoccupation tends to be corrective—the version of Madeleine Gide
that André Gide used was not the real woman. This preoccupation is legitimated
by reference to a certain posterity: a truer image of Madeleine Gide should be
available to the future. Yet if the book is undertaken out of devotion to
Madeleine, then at the very end of it, Schlumberger sabotages his own project.
In its last several pages Schlumberger turns from his task of rescuing Madeleine,
and, orthodox man-of-letters of his moment that he is, he provides us with a
wonderfully clear, wonderfully banal personification of "posterity" itself:

> Posterity cares little for what occurred in the hearts of those who are now
> dead. It is interested in the works of theirs that remain vital. The question
> posterity will pose will be the following: Did this love serve Gide's oeu-
> vre, or did it rein it in?
>   Posterity will place side by side all of the passages where Gide interro-
> gates himself on this point . . .[35]

The innate value of Madeleine Gide's particularity is effaced in this imagined
scene of future literary scholarship. Having imagined here how some scholar in
the future will be spending his or her time, Schlumberger then ends his book by
being of some help to that scholar, looking for a moment or two at passages in
which André Gide tries to answer what is imagined to be posterity's question;
and Schlumberger more or less decides that Gide's work did indeed benefit from
Madeleine's influence. Schlumberger thus seems not to have noticed the cruel
irony in his book: through his devotion to this cult of literary posterity, he has
sabotaged his own project of rescuing the figure of Madeleine from André's final
picture of her in *Et nunc manet in te*. For Schlumberger, too, is trapped in the
gaze of an imagined posterity (formed mainly, from what we can tell, of literary
scholars with an archival and historico-biographical bent). That his devotion to

Madeleine should be thus deflected indicates how powerful this fantasy of literary posterity was in Gide's circle. For obviously a first step towards revaluing her would have been to avoid giving way to this particular fantasy.

Gide, Martin du Gard, and Schlumberger, then, are all engaged in a set of practices that constitute a cult around this figure of posterity (a cult that includes the preservation of letters, journals, testamentary dispositions of archives, intensely felt obligations to write down memories of literary friends, various publication strategies, etc.). It is worth characterizing specifically, however, the practical insight Gide had that some others lacked. Schlumberger and Martin du Gard anachronistically depend on future people to conform to their own figure of posterity and to invest in the critical and literary procedures that they are presently encouraging and foresee being continued. Gide, more practically, understands that many things shift with time, that what is courageous and innovative—and of critical interest—today may not be so tomorrow. So all the while indulging in the same archival practices that to a large extent constitute the cult of posterity current in his circle, Gide nonetheless *publishes* texts like *Si le grain ne meurt* shortly after having written them. If the ghostly figure of posterity for this group often seems to be that strange future literary archivist, the archivist, in Gide's case, has a strong competitor in the figure of the young man entwined with his lover, some kind of general reader, it would seem (if, indeed, he reads!), who calls Gide to immediate publication.

Consider Gide reading Martin du Gard's own childhood memoir. Martin du Gard had offered him a few chapters in exchange for *Si le grain ne meurt,* and Gide notes in his *Journal,* in a passage from October 3, 1920 (first published in the 1996 edition):

> Read last night, in bed, the pages of reminiscences that Roger Martin du Gard had delivered to me that very morning. They interested me more than he could have believed and seemed excellent to me. I do not see how *Si le grain ne meurt* is any better, except perhaps for the strangeness of my case, if in fact it is more strange. But my story is not better, nor more honest, nor more emotional. The abominable discomfort that he describes persuades me once again that nothing can be more desirable in the life of a child than the love of an older boy who instructs him and initiates him.[36]

The sentence "I do not see how *Si le grain ne meurt* is any better, except perhaps for the strangeness of my case, if in fact it is more strange" catches the eye. Is Gide suggesting that the only factor that makes *Si le grain ne meurt* more compelling than Martin du Gard's memoirs—or at least the chapters in question here—is that Gide is portraying a child developing a set of same-sex erotic practices and Martin du Gard doesn't? As for the "if it is in fact more strange," those few words were to ensure that, a decade and a half after the entire passage was written, it would become a fabulous bone of contention between the two friends. At first glance, Gide is apparently merely wondering if there is anything that greatly differentiates the childhood troubles that were the forerunners of his *homosexuality* from the childhood troubles that were the forerunners of Martin du Gard's *sexuality.* But Martin du Gard will apparently have a more paranoid reading of the phrase, imagining it to suggest that there wasn't much difference between Gide's sexuality (childhood or adult) and his own.

Gide writes to Martin du Gard on July 5, 1934, about the journal passage from October 3, 1920, which is ready to go to press as part of volume 9 of Gide's *Œuvres complètes.* He asks Martin du Gard if he'd prefer to be identified by the initial X, or if he'd prefer the passage be cut altogether. This provokes a lively correspondence, not all of which Martin du Gard chose to publish. The following passage, at least, he let past his censor. It is from a letter of July 12, 1934:

> If tomorrow I were to burn this chapter of my "Souvenirs d'enfance" and nothing was left of it except what is in your *Journal,* the impression would nevertheless remain that my childhood was troubled by sexual disorders *analogous to your own,* and that I wrote (later destroyed) a confession concerning *homosexual* tendencies. But, as you well know, this is a flagrant imprecision, since, in these memories of troubled childhood, it is only a matter of the disturbance provoked by the revelation of the phenomena of *procreation!* . . . The idea did not come to you to write: "M. du G. has written some memoirs of childhood in which he relates such and such kind of sexual disturbance. And, *even though his troubles were very different from and even almost the opposite of my own,* I note, *in spite of that,* that they confirm me in my conviction that the initiation of an older homosexual is of benefit, etc., etc." If all of the documents about our age were to disappear and there were to remain only your testimony, the future historian would conclude: "Gide lived in a curious time when all of the calves were born with five feet . . ."[37]

Note the persistence of this odd fantasy of the future historian, of figures of posterity in the archives, of destruction and misreading. Note in particular how the fantasy of a misinformed posterity occurs in tandem with concerns about being thought to have shared Gide's sexual inclination.[38] Martin du Gard took out a further insurance policy regarding posterity's relation to this episode: the editor of the 1996 edition of Gide's *Journal* (which restores unpublished passages and reveals the names behind the initials) provides the text of a "rectification" that Martin du Gard wrote, dated November 29, 1951, nine or so months after Gide's death, and inserted into the manuscript of Gide's *Journal* at the place of the unpublished 1920 entry. Martin du Gard's rectification seems to show him becoming an ever more inexact reader of that original entry:

> The way in which Gide, a victim of his private obsessions, insists on the "strangeness" of my "case" [Martin du Gard's misreading is quite astonishing]; the complacent comparison he makes between my banal adventure and his first sexual stirrings, as he analyzes them in *Si le grain ne meurt* . . . , allow one to suppose quite another thing from what my story contains.

My two chapters of *Mémoires* are still in my archives; and the exactness of what I advance today will be easy to verify.

However, as I have taken steps so that my papers should remain sealed for at least 30 years after my death, and as the unpublished material from Gide's *Journal* will very likely be known well before this delay is over, it seemed to me useful to append the present rectification to the *Carnet* of 1920.[39]

In point of fact, Martin du Gard's childhood memoirs (published in the first volume of his *Journal*)[40] beat Gide's *inédits* to posthumous publication by about four years.

An entry in Gide's journal from 1920 about a text Martin du Gard wrote for his friends and for "posterity" is the subject of an exchange in 1934. Gide excises the passage from his published *Journal*. But the passage, and the threat it represents, remain active in Martin du Gard's mind for several decades, provoking him to concoct a carefully placed rectification and affecting the publication strategy he lays out in his will for various posthumous texts.[41]

"Posterity" is closely tied to sexual revelation for these writers, just as it is tied to a certain set of literary practices, and a certain understanding of the kind of institution literature is and the kinds of work that support that institution. Indeed, part of what distinguishes this group of writers and their place in this moment in literary and social history is the manner in which the figure of posterity under which they operate enables or even helps produce not only a set of practices and beliefs as to the private/public nature of sexual experience but, further, a set of practices and beliefs that for them anchor the very institution of literature in which they see themselves participating.

It is interesting, in this light, to read of Martin du Gard's consternation, in 1947, upon reading in *Les Temps Modernes* the essays that would become Sartre's *Qu'est-ce que la littérature?* One of those essays was called "Pour qui écrit-on?" [For whom does one write?]. Sartre's answer was definitely not "posterity." Martin du Gard expresses his consternation as a fear that a new generation has somehow rejected the older generation's conception of literature and literary value. In his introduction to the Gide-Martin du Gard correspondence, Jean Delay cites a letter from Martin du Gard to Maria Van Rysselberghe on this subject:

Sartre's manifesto did me in . . . [It gave me] the impression that a tombstone, icy and heavy, implacable, definitive, had just fallen on . . . everything that had been furnishing us some reason to continuing living and exercising our wills.[42]

He takes a more philosophical tone in his letter to Gide on the subject, praising Sartre's essay as being full of startling new insights, and instructive as to the difference between the generations. He speaks of being *dépassé* [outdated], and even claims there might be an advantage to that position: "These are the products of a different climate; but they are not degenerate products. Very instructive for us! . . . The sole consolation of decrepitude is that it is not incompatible with an increase in lucidity."[43] Gide replies in a similar vein:

> We are "outdated" (I take up your word) by those who follow; just as they will be outdated by those who will come later. It is painful to remark that the values with which one had made one's fortune, those one considered "money in the bank," no longer have currency; it is painful for oneself and one's work no longer to have anything to offer except historical interest. . . .[44]

Gide's economic metaphor—his literary values being compared to the safest, surest of investments—seems oddly appropriate in the context of Sartre's criticism of those who rely too easily on "eternal" values. On the very first page of "Pour qui écrit-on?" he writes: "It is dangerously easy to speak too quickly of eternal values: eternal values are seriously lacking in substance."[45] Gide was not, we might note, of merely historical interest to Sartre. In "Pour qui écrit-on?", for instance, Gide provides an example of how a writer necessarily imagines and therefore necessarily writes for a certain class of readers. Sartre, writing of the reader addressed in Gide's *Les Nourritures terrestres,* is at his invidious best:

> Thus do all works of genius contain in themselves an image of the reader to whom they are addressed. I could, having read *Les Nourritures terrestres,* paint a portrait of Nathanaël [the person to whom the book is addressed]: as for the alienation that he is invited to overcome, I see that it has to do with the family, the fine properties that he possesses or will possess through inheritance, the utilitarian project, a received moralism, a narrow theism; I also see that he possesses a certain amount of culture, as well as leisure time. After all, it would be absurd to propose Ménalque [the exemplar of nonconformity offered to Nathanaël] as an example to a manual laborer, or to someone unemployed, or to a Black from the United States. I know that he is menaced by no exterior peril . . . the unique danger that he runs is that of being the victim of his own milieu. Thus he is a White, an Aryan, rich, the beneficiary of a great bourgeois family that still lives in a relatively stable and comfortable epoch, in which the ideology of the property-owning class has scarcely begun to recede. He is precisely the Daniel de Fontanin [a character in Roger Martin du Gard's *Les Thibault* who reads *Les Nourritures terrestres* at an important point in the novel] whom Martin du Gard presented to us later as an enthusiastic admirer of André Gide.[46]

The terms of Sartre's class analysis seem hard to deny. One might see him as posterity's revenge on Gide, Martin du Gard, and their circle—except that Sartre has an almost thoughtlessly narrow idea of who might find profit, solace, or inspiration in reading about a person from a different social position who struggles with alienation. And in the case of Gide, it would seem reasonable to take more seriously the future reader that Gide imagined in a sexual embrace with his friend in the *"Toi qui viendras"* [You who will come] passage with which I began. That is to say, it is not without effect that Gide allowed his literary career to be inflected by the agency of posterity represented by that *"toi,"* not without effect on what he ended up writing, not without effect on his readership. (Similarly, it is not without consequence that Martin du Gard was never effectively able to envision and write for another posterity than the dominant one in his group.) For, in fact, Gide immediately had, and has always had since, readers—certainly sometimes hostile and vengeful—whose allegiances have been primarily to a queer posterity. Such readers might indeed include Sartre in other contexts, as they have included Proust. They would include, thinking only of French writers, such names as Marguerite Yourcenar, Jean Genet, Roland Barthes, Christiane Rochefort, Hervé Guibert, and many others.[47] In short, *pace* Sartre, they would fit no easy profile. If Sartre gives voice to a certain revenge of "posterity" on Gide and his friends, it might equally be said that the motley group that makes up Gide's readers represents a certain revenge (sexuality's this time) on Sartre.

Notes

1. Thanks to David Copenhafer for research help and for providing most of the translations.
2. "Toi qui viendras lorsque je n'entendrai plus les bruits de la terre et que mes lèvres ne boiront plus sa rosée — toi qui, plus tard, peut-être me liras — c'est pour toi que j'écris ces pages; car tu ne t'étonnes peut-être pas assez de vivre; tu n'admires pas comme il faudrait ce miracle étourdissant qu'est ta vie. Il me semble parfois que c'est avec ma soif que tu vas boire, et que ce qui te penche sur cet autre être que tu caresses, c'est déjà mon propre désir" (253).

   On the date of composition of this passage, see the "Notice" on *Les Nouvelles Nourritures,* pp. 1492–1502.
3. Gide's wife Madeleine burned the correspondence in 1918 upon learning that Gide was taking an extended trip to Cambridge with the young Marc Allégret, to whom he had formed a deep and abiding attachment. André and Madeleine had married in 1895. André evidently considered the marriage (apparently never consummated) a deep spiritual commitment that did not preclude sexual adventures elsewhere. For the most part his sexual adventures were brief encounters. The liaison with Marc was much more serious, and Madeleine, faced with this new departure of Gide's, apparently reread the entire correspondence and then burned it. Gide gives one account of this crisis in *Et nunc manet in te.* Another point of view is given in Jean Schlumberger, *Madeleine et André Gide.*
4. "Certains jours, certaines nuits surtout, je me sens broyé par le regret de ces lettres anéanties. C'est en elles surtout que j'espérais survivre" (1080).
5. "A elle seule j'écrivais avec abandon.

   Pas un nuage, jamais le moindre souffle entre nous. *Peut-être n'y eut-il jamais plus belle correspondance* — car il ne suffit pas de dire que le meilleur de moi s'y trouvait, mais d'elle également, car je n'écrivais jamais pour moi-même. Ah! que valent près de cela ma *Porte étroite,* mes *Nourritures,* étincelles fragiles échappées d'un immense foyer.

   Du moins à présent rien ne me retient plus de publier durant ma vie et *Corydon* et les Mémoires" (1077).
6. "Je m'occupe à revoir et mettre au point le brouillon de mes *Mémoires,* de manière à garder un texte complet si j'en confie un à Verbecke. Je ne suis pas très satisfait de cette relecture : les phrases sont molles; cela est trop conscient, trop surveillé, trop littéraire . . ." (*Journal* 1079; Gide's ellipsis).

7. English versions of passages in *Si le grain ne meurt* come from Dorothy Bussy's translation, *If It Die* . . . "Roger Martin du Gard, à qui je donne à lire ces Mémoires, leur reproche de ne jamais dire assez, et de laisser le lecteur sur sa soif. Mon intention pourtant a toujours été de tout dire. Mais il est un degré dans la confidence que l'on ne peut dépasser sans artifice, sans se forcer; et je cherche surtout le naturel" (280).

8. "Plus je songe à vos souvenirs et moins j'en suis satisfait. . . . J'ai lu 300 pages, et je ne vous ai pas encore connu. . . . Il est temps d'ouvrir carrément la porte secrète, d'y entrer, et de nous y conduire avec vous, dans un flot de lumière. . . . *Quel enfant étiez-vous, pour vous-même, dans la solitude?* Quelle sorte d'affection aviez-vous pour votre entourage? Quels rêves d'avenir? Quels troubles précis et successifs vous ont assailli de 12 à 16 ans? Et ensuite? Comment est née votre vocation littéraire? Quelles étaient vos vanités d'enfant, vos engouements, vos sottises particulières? Vos curiosités? Vos initiations? Vos songeries nocturnes? Et qu'en subsistait-il au réveil, que vous amalgamiez à votre vie du jour?" (Gide and Martin du Gard 1: 157–158).

9. "Je lui ai fait remarquer qu'il avait là l'occasion d'écrire *le livre immortel de sa véritable vie intérieure,* et qu'il ne fallait reculer devant aucun secret, mais descendre jusqu'au plus profond, jusqu'au plus trouble abîme, et étaler la vérité dans toute son intégrité. A ce prix était la beauté de l'œuvre" (*Journal* 2: 171–172).

10. "Je ne me défends d'ailleurs pas d'avoir encouragé de toute mon amitié André Gide à écrire cette confession de sa vie, ni de l'avoir poussé à serrer d'aussi près que possible la vérité, à multiplier les détails authentiques, fût-ce les plus libres; enfin à *dire tout.* Mais, en revanche, nul n'a été plus opposé à la *publication* de ces Mémoires; et je persiste à penser qu'ils n'auraient pas dû paraître du vivant de l'auteur (ni même aussitôt après sa mort).

    Je crois même que mon indiscrète insistance sur ce point n'a pas été étrangère à la longue hésitation de Gide, qui, après avoir fait tirer 6000 exemplaires d'une première édition et après avoir vingt fois ordonné puis décommandé la mise en librairie, a gardé ce stock près de deux années (1921 à 1923) dans sa cave, avant de se résoudre à le mettre en circulation" (*Journal* 2: 172n).

11. "Il ne m'est pas arrivé souvent de renoncer. Un délai, c'est tout ce qu'obtient de moi la traverse" (355).

12. "Il me fait part de sa déception profonde : j'ai escamoté mon sujet; crainte, pudeur, souci du public, je n'ai rien osé dire de vraiment intime, ni réussi qu'à soulever des interrogations . . . [Ces réflexions m'ébranleraient plus si je ne commençais à comprendre qu'il est dans le caractère de M du G de rêver toujours un au-delà chimérique, de sorte que toute réalisation le laissera loin du compte. Un des plus curieux caractères que j'aie rencontrés.]

    Depuis que je suis ici, reçu de lui une longue, excellente lettre où il revient sur tous les points que notre conversation avait touchés. J'ai pourtant conscience d'avoir raconté de mon enfance tout ce dont j'avais gardé souvenance et le plus indiscrètement possible. Il y aurait artifice à y mettre plus d'ombre, plus de secret, plus de détour" (*Journal* 1110–1111, with Gide's ellipsis; the bracketed sentences are listed in the notes to this edition, 1688–1689).

13. "[M]on récit, souvent, pour vouloir être clair, simplifie un peu trop mes gestes, ou du moins les ressorts de ceux-ci" (*Journal* 1111).

14. "Essayer de comprendre une vie comme une série unique et à soi suffisante d'événements successifs sans autre lien que l'association à un « sujet » dont la constance n'est sans doute que celle d'un nom propre, est à peu près aussi absurde que d'essayer de rendre raison d'un trajet dans le métro sans prendre en compte la structure du réseau, c'est-à-dire la matrice des relations objectives entre les différentes stations. Les événements biographiques se définissent comme autant de *placements* et de *déplacements* dans l'espace social, c'est-à-dire, plus précisément, dans les différents états successifs de la

structure de la distribution des différentes espèces de capital qui sont en jeu dans le champ considéré" (71).

15. Consider, in this light, some "aesthetic" (although it is clearly not just aesthetic) advice that Martin du Gard offered Gide, in a letter of December 16, 1921, about narrative choices and choices of characterization in *Les Faux-Monnayeurs:* "The more I think about it, the more I would want to remove from this work, which truly seems destined to become something great, any unnecessary occasion for personal scandal. I suspect that at times you have too much courage, a useless temerity. Do not be angry if I tell you that, all things considered, I do not see what the character of Édouard gains from a too clear exposition of his private inclinations. (I even find myself wondering this morning if it truly is more profitable than harmful to make a novelist of him, and if this is not a means, and a most dangerous one, to reintroduce the "subjective" into a work that would otherwise do quite well without it.) I would prefer, should you insist on Édouard having those inclinations, that his life remain mysterious, and that the reader have *as many* reasons for doubting as for believing things about it" [Plus j'y songe aussi et plus je voudrais éloigner de cette œuvre, qui semble vraiment partie pour être la grande chose, tout sujet inutile de scandale personnel. Je soupçonne que vous avez par instants trop de courage, une inutile témérité. Ne vous fâcherez-vous pas si je vous avoue que, tout bien pesé, je ne vois pas ce que le caractère d'Édouard gagne à une exposition trop claire de ses goûts privés? (Je me demande même ce matin s'il est plus profitable que nuisible d'en faire un romancier, et si ce n'est pas un moyen, dont l'emploi est plein de danger, de réintroduire le « subjectif » dans une œuvre que s'en passerait fort bien.) J'aimerais assez, si vous persistez à placer Édouard de ce côté-là du fossé, que sa vie reste mystérieuse, et que le lecteur ait *autant* de raisons d'en douter que d'y croire] (Gide and Martin du Gard 1: 177–178).

One can begin to appreciate how complicated and multilayered Martin du Gard's "aesthetic" obsessions with novelistic "objectivity" or "subjectivity" must, in fact, have been.

16. "C'est dire qu'on ne peut comprendre une trajectoire . . . qu'à condition d'avoir préalablement construit les états successifs du champ dans lequel elle s'est déroulée, donc l'ensemble des relations objectives qui ont uni l'agent considéré — au moins, dans un certain nombre d'états pertinents — à l'ensemble des autres agents engagés dans le même champ et affrontés au même espace des possibles" (72).

17. I have written a bit about Gide's relation to Proust and Wilde in this regard in the introduction to *Gide's Bent* (8–16). As for Dostoevsky, Gide's lectures on him (published in 1923) make it clear not only how important his thinking about Dostoevsky was in conceptualizing his own novelistic project in *Les Faux-Monnayeurs,* but also how fruitful reflection on Dostoevsky was in conceptualizing his own personal practice of and investment in literature. To show the complex interrelations between his thoughts on Dostoevsky and everything else that was going on in his personal and his literary life would take an essay in its own right, but several passages from his lectures show reasonably clearly some of the forms of identification at work: "He is particularly attached to disconcerting cases, to people who rise up as challenges to accepted morality and psychology. Obviously, he himself does not feel at ease with the morality and psychology current in his day" [Il s'attache particulièrement aux cas déconcertants, à ceux qui se dressent comme des défis, en face de la morale et la psychologie admises. Évidemment dans cette morale courante et dans cette psychologie, il ne se sent pas lui-même à l'aise] (146). Or, in a section on Dostoevsky's epilepsy: "At the origin of every great moral reform, if we seek carefully, we will always find a small psychological mystery, a dissatisfaction of the flesh, a disquietude, an anomaly. . . . I do not believe that one could find, among those who would propose new values to

humanity, a single reformer in whom one could not discover a . . . flaw" [A l'origine de chaque grande réforme morale, si nous cherchons bien, nous trouverons toujours un petit mystère physiologique, une insatisfaction de la chair, une inquiétude, une anomalie. . . . Je ne sache pas qu'on puisse trouver un seul réformateur, de ceux qui proposèrent à l'humanité de nouvelles évaluations, en qui l'on ne puisse découvrir . . . une tare] (209–210).

18. "Gide m'a confié qu'il sentait le besoin de publier le plus tôt possible *Corydon* . . . et *Si le grain ne meurt* . . .

    J'en suis désespéré. J'ai la certitude que rien ne peut nuire davantage au plein épanouissement de sa maturité que cet inutile scandale, dont il ressentira très intensément la blessure, et qui créera autour de lui une atmosphère nouvelle, de méfiance, d'indignation, de méprisantes calomnies. Cela ne servira qu'à armer solidement ses ennemis, qui sont légion, et à écarter de lui les deux tiers de ses amis actuels, lesquels acceptent une situation qui est dissimulée, discrète, mais qui devront prendre parti lorsque Gide aura cyniquement avoué en public ce qu'est sa vie privée. . . .

    En réalité, il est surtout victime d'une intoxication russe. C'est Dostoïevski qui le pousse. Voilà plusieurs mois qu'il vit avec Dostoïevski pour préparer ses conférences et son livre sur Dostoïevski. Et il a pris la contagion. Il éprouve le besoin de la confession publique . . ." (2: 294).

19. I am using "ethos" in a way suggested by Bourdieu, in a passage from *Les Règles de l'art* where he is, in fact, discussing Gide and his group: "The gathering together of the authors and, secondarily, of the texts which make up a literary review has as its genuine principle, as we see, social strategies close to those governing the constitution of a salon or a movement—even though they take into account, among other criteria, the strictly literary capital of the assembled authors. And what these strategies themselves have as a unifying and generative principle is not something akin to the cynical calculation of a banker with symbolic capital (even if André Gide is also that, objectively . . .) but rather a common habitus, or, better still, an ethos which is one dimension of it and which unites the members of what one calls the 'nucleus'" [Le rassemblement d'auteurs et, secondairement, de textes qui fait une revue littéraire a, on le voit, pour principe véritable, des stratégies sociales proches de celles qui président à la constitution d'un salon ou d'un mouvement — même si elles prennent en compte, parmi d'autres critères, le capital proprement littéraire des écrivains réunis. Et ces stratégies elles-mêmes ont pour principe unificateur et générateur non quelque chose comme le calcul cynique d'un banquier en capital symbolique (même si André Gide est aussi cela, objectivement . . .), mais un habitus commun ou, mieux, l'éthos qui en est une dimension et qui unit les membres de ce que l'on appelle « le noyau »] (*The Rules of Art* 273; *Les Règles d'art* 379).

20. "Quant à l'invite à supprimer par « prudence » la phrase, — en réalité un paragraphe, — incriminée, il était au regret de n'y pouvoir déférer. La « rassurante » prophétie, — « peu à peu on oubliera », — lui paraissait « honteuse » : « Non; ne me demandez ni maquillages ni compromis; ou c'est moi qui vous estimerais moins »" (Anglès 3: 312).

21 "[A]u confluent des eaux du roman russe et du roman anglais . . . Gide ambitionne de capter et d'unir dans ses *Caves du Vatican* le courant de *Tom Jones* et celui des *Frères Karamazov*" (2: 480).

22. Anglès's chapter entitled "Vers le vrai roman" (2: 456–485) is especially interesting in this regard. Gide's confrontation with Claudel is recounted in the chapter "Orage sur Sodom" (3: 302–352).

23. "Dans l'œuvre de Dostoïevsky . . . les enfants abondent; même il est à remarquer que la plupart de ses personnages, et des plus importants, sont des êtres encore jeunes, à peine formés. . . . Il s'attache particulièrement aux cas déconcertants, à ceux qui se dressent comme des défis, en face de la morale et la psychologie admises" (146).

24. *Les Caves du Vatican* is dedicated to Copeau.

25. "C'est à justifier l'adolescence en rupture de conformisme que s'attache Copeau. Mais ce n'est pas par hasard qu'une éthique complice de la jeunesse oriente ses partisans vers un type et un ton de roman. Celui-ci risquait de s'ossifier en une « thèse inféconde et savante » ou de se dessécher « dans les steppes de la théorie » : or nous avons un livre « humain, spontané, direct et probant », sans rien « de systématique et de prémédité »" (2: 462).

26. "Aussi bien dirai-je que, non seulement les personnages de sa *Comédie humaine,* mais ceux aussi de la comédie réelle que nous vivons, se dessinent — que nous tous Français, tant que nous sommes, nous nous dessinons nous-mêmes — selon un idéal balzacien. Les inconséquences de notre nature, si tant est qu'il y en ait, nous apparaissent gênantes, ridicules. Nous les renions. . . . En regard de cela, que nous présente Dostoïevsky? Des personnages qui, sans aucun souci de demeurer conséquents avec eux-mêmes, cèdent complaisamment à toutes les contradictions, toutes les négations dont leur nature propre est capable. Il semble que ce soit là ce qui intéresse le plus Dostoïevsky : l'inconséquence. Bien loin de la cacher, il la fait sans cesse ressortir; il l'éclaire" (135–136).

27. "Mais dans la création de Cadio, personne ne fut objectif avec autant de perversité depuis Balzac et *Splendeurs et misères.* Encore, je pense, que Balzac était aidé, pour inventer Lucien de Rubempré, par une certaine vulgarité personnelle" (Proust 24–25).

28. Not that Gide is without noteworthy competitors. In 1913, the *NRF* publishes Valery Larbaud's *A. O. Barnabooth,* Alain-Fournier's *Le Grand Meaulnes,* and part of Roger Martin du Gard's *Jean Barois.* In April 1914, it publishes the final installment of *Les Caves du Vatican.* In June and July of 1914, it publishes two sets of excerpts from Proust's *A la recherche du temps perdu.* The *NRF* had earlier turned down a chance to publish *Du côté de chez Swann,* and had been smarting from its mistake ever since the group read the volume when it was published by Grasset. Various members of the group worked to convince Proust to forgive them, and to agree to have subsequent volumes published by the *NRF.* Also, given what the *NRF* was publishing at that moment, given their efforts to think about the future of the French novel, and given that they would publish a novel including a character like Lafcadio, it's likely that there was no place where Proust would rather have been published. He switched over to the *NRF* in 1914. (See Anglès 3: 226–229, 266–270, 289–290, 310–331, 336–338, 369–379, 421–432.)

29. In *Gide's Bent* (117–142), I argue that *inconséquence* is crucial to the implicit theorization of sexuality in Gide's *Les Faux-Monnayeurs* as well. I argue at length in that chapter, and throughout the rest of the book, what I am able only to suggest here: that it is in fact the case that Gide's sexual concerns are not isolatable to this or that excisable paragraph, are not incidental and effaceable components of this or that character, are not a part of his personal life that can be overlooked (even if many critics have preferred to treat them as such) but in fact constitute a crucial part of his aesthetic, intellectual, and political endeavors.

30. See Rivière's essay "Le roman d'aventure," published in the *NRF* in May, June, and July 1913.

31. "Pourquoi jeter le masque dès maintenant? D'abord parce que les temps pressent; les livres de Proust, le mouvement des idées en Allemagne et en Italie où l'on proclame la liberté de l'amour, les théories de Freud vont amener très vite un moment où l'on regardera d'un tout autre œil les écarts sexuels; il n'y aura plus aucun courage à jeter le masque" (2: 295–296).

32. "Il n'y a pas que courage en lui, et désir de vérité; il n'y a pas non plus qu'un désir de macération et d'opprobre. Il y a aussi l'ambition d'accomplir un geste qu'il trouve noble, et l'espoir que ce geste sincère, désintéressé, courageux, lui vaudra, aux yeux de

certains, *aux yeux de la posterité,* une vénération particulière, un regain de grandeur, d'influence" (2: 296).

33. *Et nunc manet in te* is a set of reflections on Gide's relation to his wife written in the years following her death, as well as a collection of journal passages about her that he had not previously allowed to be published. He collected his reflections and the journal passages, along with some commentary on them, and published them together in a limited edition shortly before his death. A general edition followed a few years later. The journal passages have been reincorporated into the latest (1996) publication of his *Journal.*

34. I won't pursue this topic any further here, except to suggest that this writing agency is in fact shared by many members of the *NRF* group, and is usually linked to their varied forms of preoccupation with religion (a preoccupation with possible conversions to Catholicism on the part of the Protestants in the group, for instance). This agency, furthermore, is one of the social markers that distinguishes the literary avant-garde the *NRF* group is aiming to create from other early twentieth-century potential avant-gardes that might include people such as Jarry, Apollinaire, Artaud, the Surrealists, etc.

35. "La posterité se soucie peu de ce qui s'est passé dans le cœur des défunts; ce qui l'intéresse, c'est leurs œuvres demeurées vivantes. La question qu'elle posera sera celle-ci : Cet amour a-t-il servi l'œuvre de Gide ou l'a-t-il bridée? Elle mettra côte à côte tous les passages où il s'est interrogé sur ce point . . ." (250).

36. "Lu hier soir, dans mon lit, les pages de souvenirs que Roger Martin du Gard m'avait remises le matin même. Elles m'ont intéressé plus qu'il ne pouvait croire et m'ont paru excellentes. Je ne vois pas en quoi *Si le grain ne meurt* l'emporte sur elles, sinon peut-être par l'étrangeté de mon cas si tant est qu'il soit plus étrange. Mais mon récit n'est pas meilleur, ni plus honnête, ni plus ému. Le trouble abominable qu'il décrit me persuade une fois de plus que rien ne peut être plus souhaitable pour un enfant que l'amour d'un aîné qui l'instruise et qui l'initie" (1110).

37. "Si je brûlais demain ce chapitre de mes « Souvenirs d'enfance » et qu'il n'en reste d'autre trace que votre *Journal,* il resterait : que j'ai eu une enfance troublée par des désordres sexuels *analogues aux vôtres;* et que j'ai écrit, (puis détruit) une confession relative à des tendances *homosexuelles.* Or, vous le reconnaissez, c'est une flagrante inexactitude, puisque, dans ces souvenirs d'enfance troublée, il ne s'agit que du trouble provoqué par la révélation des phénomènes de *procréation!* . . . [I]l ne vous est pas venu à l'idée d'écrire d'abord : « M. du G. a écrit des souvenirs d'enfance où il relate tel et tel genre de troubles sexuels. Et, *bien que ces troubles aient été très différents et presque à l'opposé des miens,* je constate *cependant* que cela me renforce dans ma conviction que l'initiation d'un aîné homosexuel est un bienfait, etc. etc. » . . . Si tous les documents sur notre époque disparaissaient et qu'il ne reste que votre témoignage, l'historien futur conclurait : — « Gide a vécu à une époque curieuse, où tous les veaux naissaient avec cinq pattes . . . »" (Gide and Martin du Gard 1: 627; the second ellipsis is Martin du Gard's).

38. Martin du Gard's defensiveness has merely left him open to malicious gossipy books about his sexual proclivities (apparently not so different from Gide's). Posterity has thus not exactly conformed to his dreams about it. José Cabanis's *Le Diable à la NRF* is a perfect example of the genre. For Cabanis, the ideal reader of Martin du Gard is "suspicious" [soupçonneux] (84); such a reader slowly joins a group of "readers in the know" (119), all of whom would be receptive to "a tiny involuntary signal perceptible to the reader on the lookout" [un petit signe involontaire au lecteur déjà alerté] (119). And Cabanis is himself an avid member of this group, extolling the pleasures of this form of reading: "Others write, in order to unburden themselves,

confessional literature that can be passionate as well. The secretive ones are quite seductive, and they are wrong if they are upset with a society—with others—that forbids them to say everything. Often it is their double game that saves them" [D'autres écrivent pour se livrer, littérature de l'aveu qui peut être passionnante, elle aussi. Les cachottiers sont bien séduisants et ils ont tort s'ils en veulent à la société — les autres—qui leur interdit de tout dire. C'est souvent leur double jeu qui les sauve] (75). They are saved from being as boring as they truly are, apparently, because they allow others later to write books "elegantly" outing them and their friends, as if that were the primary form of attention their sexuality should deserve: "Thus we have an advantage in reading in the *Journal* and in the *Correspondance* those pages that could have been tiresome, were they not strewn with amusing riddles to decipher. Schlumberger, being more or less of the same ilk, was also of the opinion that the truth ought not to be told. Yet with him one patiently reads in vain entire works, and, however kindly one's intentions, there's no chance of amusement" [Nous y gagnons de lire dans le *Journal* et la *Correspondance* des pages qui pourraient être lassantes, si elles n'étaient parsemées de devinettes à décripter, qui amusent. Schlumberger, à peu près à la même enseigne, était d'avis, lui aussi, que la vérité n'est pas à dire. Avec lui on a beau lire patiemment des ouvrages entiers et mettre du sien, on ne s'amuse guère] (77).

39. "La façon dont Gide, victime de ses obsessions personnelles, insiste sur l'« étrangeté » de mon « cas »; la comparaison qu'il fait complaisamment entre ma banale aventure et ses premiers émois sexuels, tels qu'il les analyse dans *Si le grain ne meurt . . .* , laissent supposer tout autre chose que ce que contient mon récit.

Mes deux chapitres de *Mémoires* sont encore dans mes archives; et l'exactitude de ce que j'avance aujourd'hui pourra aisément être vérifiée.

Cependant, comme j'ai pris des dispositions pour que mes papiers restent sous scellés au moins trente ans après ma mort, et que les inédits du *Journal* de Gide seront vraisemblablement connus bien avant ce délai, il m'a paru qu'il n'était pas inutile de joindre la présente rectification au *Carnet* de 1920" (Gide, *Journal* 1690).

40. The passage about his childhood troubles is on pp. 27–28.

41. The following is from a letter he left for the friend to whom he confided the manuscript of his childhood memoirs; one sees here again the links between the obsessive figure of posterity and a certain kind of future literary critic: "It appears that these confidences concerning my childhood . . . seriously risk falsifying the judgment of critics if they are published after my death, and before—long before—my complete biography is known through the publication of my *Journal*. . . . *Their publication should thus be delayed* until such time as I have authorized the Bibliothèque Nationale to open the case that contains my *Journal* and other biographical documents. Thus I beg you to append a copy of the present interdiction to the manuscript that you have so that, if you should happen to pass away before the publication of my *Journal,* none of your heirs might commit the indiscretion of publishing the confidences of these *Souvenirs d'enfance*" [Il apparaît que ces confidences sur mon enfance . . . risquent de fausser profondément le jugement des critiques si elles sont rendues publiques après ma mort, avant — et longtemps avant — que ma biographie complète soit connue par la publication de mon *Journal*. . . . *Cette publication devra donc être différée* jusqu'au moment où j'ai autorisé la Bibliothèque nationale à ouvrir la cantine qui contient mon *Journal* et autres documents biographiques. Je vous prie donc de joindre au manuscrit que vous avez une copie de la présente interdiction pour que, si vous veniez à disparaître avant la publication de mon *Journal,* aucun de vos héritiers ne commette l'indiscrétion de rendre publiques les confidences de ces *Souvenirs d'enfance*] (see the first volume of his *Journal,* pp. 45–46).

42. "Le manifeste de Sartre m'a porté le dernier coup . . . L'impression qu'une pierre tombale, pesante et glacée, implacable, définitive, vient de tomber sur . . . tout ce qui nous apportait quelques raisons de vivre ou de vouloir" (1: 105; the first ellipsis is Martin du Gard's).

43. "Ce sont des produits d'un autre climat; mais non des produits dégénérés. Bien instructif pour nous! . . . La seule consolation de la décrépitude, c'est qu'elle n'est pas incompatible avec un surcroît de lucidité" (2: 376).

44. "Nous sommes « dépassés » (je reprends votre mot) par ceux qui viennent; comme ceux qui viennent seront dépassés par ceux qui viendront. Il est pénible de constater que n'ont plus cours les valeurs dont on avait garni son portefeuille et que l'on considérait comme « de tout repos »; de ne présenter plus, soi et son œuvre, qu'un intérêt historique . . ." (2: 377–378).

45. "Il est dangereusement facile de parler trop vite des valeurs éternelles : les valeurs éternelles sont fort décharnées" (Sartre 87).

46. "Ainsi tous les ouvrages de l'esprit contiennent en eux-mêmes l'image du lecteur auquel ils sont destinés. Je pourrais faire le portrait de Nathanaël d'après les *Nourritures terrestres* : l'aliénation dont on l'invite à se libérer, je vois que c'est la famille, les biens immeubles qu'il possède ou possédera par héritage, le projet utilitaire, un moralisme appris, un théisme étroit; je vois aussi qu'il a de la culture et des loisirs puisqu'il serait absurde de proposer Ménalque en exemple à un manœuvre, à un chômeur, à un Noir des États-Unis, je sais qu'il n'est menacé par aucun péril extérieur . . . l'unique péril qu'il court c'est d'être victime de son propre milieu, donc c'est un Blanc, un Aryen, un riche, l'héritier d'une grande famille bourgeoise qui vit à une époque relativement stable et facile encore, où l'idéologie de la classe possédante commence à peine de décliner : précisément ce Daniel de Fontanin que Martin du Gard nous a présenté plus tard comme un admirateur enthousiaste d'André Gide" (92).

47. See, for an interesting set of responses to Gide in 1968, including one by Rochefort, "Gide vu par . . ."

Works Cited

Anglès, Auguste. *André Gide et le premier groupe de La Nouvelle Revue Française*. 3 vols. Paris: Gallimard, 1978–1986.

Bourdieu, Pierre. "L'illusion biographique." *Actes de la recherche en sciences sociales* 62–63 (June 1986): 69–72.

———. *Les Règles de l'art : genèse et structure du champ littéraire*. Paris: Éditions du Seuil, 1992.

———. *The Rules of Art: Genesis and Structure of the Literary Field*. Trans. Susan Emanuel. Stanford: Stanford University Press, 1996.

Cabanis, José. *Le Diable à la NRF, 1911–1915*. Paris: Gallimard, 1996.

Gide, André. *Dostoïevsky; articles et causeries*. Paris: Plon, 1923.

———. *Et nunc manet in te, suivi de Journal intime*. Neuchâtel: Ides et Calendes, 1951.

———. *If It Die . . .* Trans. Dorothy Bussy. London: Penguin, 1977.

———. *Journal 1887–1925*. Ed. Éric Marty. Paris: Gallimard, Bibliothèque de la Pléiade, 1996.

———. *Les Nouvelles Nourritures. Romans, récits et soties, œuvres lyriques*. Ed. Yvonne Davet and Jean-Jacques Thierry. Paris: Gallimard, Bibliothèque de la Pléiade, 1958. 251–300.

———. *Si le grain ne meurt*. Paris: Gallimard, 1985.

Gide, André, and Roger Martin du Gard. *Correspondance*. Introduction by Jean Delay. 2 vols. Paris: Gallimard, 1968.

"Gide vu par . . ." *Magazine littéraire* 14 (January 1968): 23–25.

Lucey, Michael. *Gide's Bent: Sexuality, Politics, Writing.* New York: Oxford University Press, 1995.

Martin du Gard, Roger. *Journal.* Ed. Claude Sicard. 3 vols. Paris: Gallimard, 1992–1993.

Proust, Marcel. *Lettres à André Gide.* Neuchâtel: Ides et Calendes, 1949.

Sartre, Jean-Paul. *Qu'est-ce que la littérature?* Paris: Gallimard, 1978.

Schlumberger, Jean. *Madeleine et André Gide.* Paris: Gallimard, 1956.

C H A P T E R 4
_____

Gide and Justice:
The Immoralist in the Palace of Reason

John Lambeth

> *Les mœurs sont l'hypocrisie d'une nation.*
> —Honoré De Balzac

Gide's writings on the French justice system attracted little attention from critics either at the time of their publication or in the years following his death. This is unfortunate for four reasons: 1) Gide's publications on the justice system, particularly his *Souvenirs de la cour d'assises,* are a rare example of commentary on the French system for the general public written by a layman; 2) his reports on infamous crimes, *L'Affaire Redureau* and *La Séquestrée de Poitiers,* offer insight both into the judicial process and public perception of crime; 3) these texts, taken together with his "Faits divers," allow him to develop a subtle critique of rationalism and the distorted view rationalism gives of human motivations; and 4) these texts provide a better understanding of the psychological motivations of some of Gide's key fictional characters and shed light on recurrent themes, specifically hypocritical bourgeois codes of conduct.

Furthermore, one might legitimately claim that his *Souvenirs de la cour d'assises* was the first in a series of texts offering political or social commentary, to be followed by his writings on colonialism *(Voyage au Congo, Le Retour du Tchad)* and Communism *(Retour de l'U.R.S.S.). Souvenirs* marks the beginning of an active interest in social problems that would intensify during World War I and lead to a more complex vision of human society in subsequent work. His reconstruction of the *fait divers* [news item] constitutes a critique of social structures, families in particular, and at least implicitly of patriarchal legal systems, such as the Napoleonic Code, that try to force human acts into the Procrustean bed of rationalism. Léon Pierre-Quint provides an interesting perspective on Gide's confrontation with the "machine of justice" and its search for truth through an oversimplified cause-and-effect reasoning. Pierre-Quint describes the situation like this: "A crime has been committed. The community feels itself under attack and demands reparation. Certainly society must intervene.

By responding to the crime with a punishment, does one erase the crime? Does this system of compensation return the law that was broken to its original wholeness?"[1]

Gide was certainly aware of the theory of justice in the French legal system; his father, after all, was a respected jurist and professor of law in Paris, and Gide counted many jurists among his friends and family connections. But one needs to dig deep within the definitions offered by the *Petit Robert* to find the particular notion of justice that Gide encounters and exposes in his *Souvenirs*. The ideal is expressed in the first of these definitions as the "Just appreciation, recognition, and respect for the rights and the merit of individuals," illustrated by the quote from Proudhon, "Justice is respect for human dignity." The second definition characterizes justice as the principle of conformity to positive or natural law; the third goes to the power to enforce the law of the land. But it is the fourth definition that becomes the focus of Gide's critique as a juror: "Organization of judicial power; all of the agencies in charge of administering justice, in accordance with legal practice."[2] The distance between the theory (human dignity) and the practice (a class-based bureaucracy) is a recurring concern in this text.

Indeed, this is a concern to which Gide returns in the late 1920s when he opens the pages of the *Nouvelle Revue Française* to the *faits divers* and in 1930, when he publishes his aptly titled collection *Ne jugez pas*. These cases, along with extensive reports on the sensational trials of the mass murderer Redureau and of the *séquestrée* of Poitiers at the beginning of the century, are presented with practically no commentary, in a simple ordering of documents from court records and newspaper accounts. Gide's report of the turn-of-the-century scandal known as the *Séquestrée de Poitiers* is absolutely riveting. This scandal within a respected bourgeois family has at least two well-known literary descendants: François Mauriac's *Thérèse Desqueyroux,* where it is specifically mentioned in the latter part of the novel when Thérèse is essentially locked up in her house by her husband and her husband's family and indeed with the full accord of her father, in order to hide her crime from the public's prying eyes; and in Nathalie Sarraute's *Portrait d'un inconnu,* where the nonsensical phrase that the Poitiers woman repeats, "un bon fond de Malempia," recurs in the tropistic stream of consciousness of one of the characters. These cases speak for themselves as cautionary tales for those who would try to explain criminal acts by an oversimplified psychology, and Gide uses the pages of the *NRF* to persuade readers to look more deeply behind a person's acts before assigning common-sense motives (see Goulet 598–605).

In his *Souvenirs de la cour d'assises* Gide focuses on two major problems of the machine of justice in France. The first is the problem of making a crime fit into a judicial framework based on rational thought—that is to say, the difficulty of attributing and rationalizing motives for specific criminal acts based on circumstantial evidence, hearsay, and fragmentary eyewitness reports. The corollary to this first problem is a class-based perception of the criminal act that leads Gide to an implicit criticism of bourgeois foundations of the criminal justice system. The second problem is the conflict between the jury's (and for that matter, the judge's) pure notion of justice and the practical decision about a specific conviction. This conflict hinges on jury perception of attenuating circumstances and the terms governing conviction specified by the court system. The last case that Gide describes in his *Souvenirs de la cour d'assises,* in fact, focuses on a jury "revolt."

Alain Goulet, in his excellent *Fiction et vie sociale dans l'œuvre d'André Gide,* neatly places the *Souvenirs de la cour d'assises* in the context of a growing social awareness in Gide's intellectual activities. Goulet also links this social awareness, particularly of the machine of justice, to themes of revolt against bourgeois society in Gide's subsequent works, specifically *Les Caves du Vatican* and *Les Faux-Monnayeurs.* Emily Apter, whose article on the *Souvenirs* is the only one listed in the *MLA Bibliography* since 1963, sees Gide's project here as an inverted literary form in which Gide recuperates realism and explores its opposite through genres of allegory, both theological and jurisprudential. She looks particularly to *Les Caves du Vatican* and the *acte gratuit* [unmotivated action] to demonstrate that "Gide raises the question of how one 'judges' criminal acts in a deconstructivist age that radically questions the legitimacy or referential possibility of ethical foundational principles" (560). Apter's deconstructionist method eventually becomes a psychoanalytic model, and the reduction usefully sheds light both on the author and his fictional characters and themes. For my part, I will take the opportunity presented by this essay to focus primarily on the *Souvenirs* and give a more complete view of the cases themselves and the practical decisions that Gide and his fellow jurors were obliged to make within the constraints of the French court system.

Gide was called for jury duty in Rouen in May of 1912, and although he could have easily escaped what many consider an onerous task, he decided to use this experience to observe the criminal justice system—the content, the various actors, and the logic of the procedure. During the first decade of the twentieth century, Gide had become increasingly aware of society as something more than a repressive burden of banality, a position one might associate with Gide's early attitudes, even as he distanced himself from the Symbolist group. Moving away from the highly individualistic concerns and intimate perspective of turn-of-the-century works such as *Les Nourritures terrestres* and *L'Immoraliste,* Gide demonstrates a growing awareness of the literary public in lectures and articles early in the new century. Certainly his collaboration with a group of friends to create a literary journal began to broaden his perspective on the function of literature in society. Finally, the so-called crisis of the novel in France, which one might in fact date from the bitter debate over Naturalism in 1889, had Gide and others talking about a new type of novel, one full of adventures and social interaction.

Yet Gide was also facing several difficulties during these years of growing social awareness. He had been working on *Les Caves du Vatican* for a couple of years, but he had reached an impasse and was frustrated by his inability to move forward with this project. He had published a very limited edition of a first version of *Corydon,* a treatise on homosexuality, but had distributed it to only a few close friends. The *NRF* was struggling with problems of editorial identity, attacked from the outside by more traditional literary opinion and beset by internal arguments concerning editorial policy (Auguste Anglès gives a detailed account of Gide's multiple activities during these years).

Gide begins with a summary of the jury selection procedures, and after remarking only that the majority of jurors are farmers, he quickly moves on to the presentation of specific cases. As a member of the jury pool, he attends all of the proceedings even when he is not on the jury for a specific case.

The first case that Gide hears as a member of the jury is worth looking at for a moment because he touches on several points that will return constantly in the other deliberations. Our juror is appalled by the vagueness of the evidence, its lack of precision, its fragmentary quality, and its reliance on mere supposition (16). What seems to be more important, though, is the impression that the two thieves make on the jury: "The opinion of the jury is that, after all, if it isn't absolutely certain that they committed these thefts, they must have committed others or they will eventually commit some, and so they might as well be locked up."[3]

Once the jury retires for deliberations, Gide narrates the jurors' desire to render justice by punishing the criminals, but not more severely than they deserve. He slides into free indirect discourse to express the jurors' hesitation: "Well, they were certainly swindlers, but they weren't exactly *bandits;* I mean, they *took advantage* of the community, but they weren't trying to tear it apart. They were simply trying to help themselves and not really hurt others, etc. . . . This is what the jurors said to one another, searching for a severe yet thoughtful verdict."[4] This is a technique that Gide will use regularly throughout the text, either to summarize a long discussion (in this case) or to express what he believes to be the state of mind of fellow jurors, witnesses, or the accused. In this particular case, the jury finds itself in a judicial dilemma: the jurors believe the two thieves guilty, plain and simple—no attenuating circumstances, no aggravating circumstances—but they are obliged to answer the court questionnaire concerning the circumstances of the theft and end up, in all honesty, affirming a series of aggravating circumstances. The consequence is that they then feel obliged to come up with attenuating circumstances as a compensation. This is the first of several instances in which Gide expresses dismay at the structural problems that juries face. He carefully notes the confusion and the discomfort in the jury room during almost every deliberation. The judge's questions are posed in such a way that they rarely allow the juror to vote the way he would have wanted to, satisfying his sense of justice.

During the proceedings Gide is perplexed by the alibi of one of the accused and himself poses a question to a witness, as is a juror's right in France. The accused then sends Gide a message later in the day asking for his help and requesting a personal interview. Gide does go look at certain evidentiary documents, but in the absence of a strong enough doubt, decides not to pursue contact with the accused. He nevertheless expresses a great deal of frustration and uncertainty at the end of this first trial.

Gide later reflects that voting attenuating circumstances usually means that the jury does not have a clear idea of the defendant's guilt: "yes, the crime is serious, but we aren't quite sure that this is the person who committed it. Nevertheless, there must be some sort of punishment: so let's go ahead and punish him, since he is the one you offer us as victim; but, given our doubts, let's not punish him too much."[5] Another problem that juries have is gaining an accurate representation of the scene of the crime; this is particularly significant in the course of a case in which the reliability of a witness's testimony depends on how close she, the defendant, and the victim were to a street light. All those interrogated give varying accounts; yet it would have been relatively simple for the police to provide a diagram of the street showing the exact location where the crime took place and the positions of the various actors.

There are several other cases of property crimes, some involving violence, some not. Gide is amazed at the good sense of the jury when it acquits a man who stole a considerable sum of money from an office where he worked, but returned all of the cash except the 237 francs that he had used to pay for a round of drinks for everyone in a popular bar. The man turned himself in and promised to pay back the 237 francs. In his description of a burglary case, Gide is particularly struck by the defendant's passivity: "Marceau doesn't try to defend himself; he doesn't even try to excuse himself: he accepts the fact that he did what he did, as if he couldn't have done otherwise. He seems to be resigned to the fact of becoming the criminal whom they are describing."[6] When asked by the judge why he picked up a knife in the kitchen, he responds simply that he meant to stab the maid, and when asked why he grabbed Madame Prune by the throat, he says he wanted to strangle her! What puzzles Gide the most about Marceau is his obvious discomfort whenever he feels that the reconstitution of his crime in court is not precise; but he is never able to straighten things out nor profit from the imprecision of the testimony. It is as if the court has appropriated and deformed his story and he is deprived of his own narration. Marceau gets eight years of hard labor.

Even when a defendant does try to explain himself, he speaks too quickly and is constantly interrupted by the judge, so that his story remains unclear and he gives the appearance of guilt. Gide reflects, "Will the innocent man be more eloquent, less confused than the guilty one? Hardly! As soon as he feels that the prosecution doesn't *believe* him, he may be all the more confused if he is innocent. He will overstate his case; his protests will seem increasingly strident; he will fall apart."[7] Or as Alain Goulet has remarked, "The self-defense mechanism works in favor of the court which, by convicting the accused, transforms him into a scapegoat: 'the other' is not a man but a beast who bears the burden of all sins. The conviction signifies a fall from his condition as a man."[8]

In another burglary case, Gide is troubled by the judge's bullying of a defendant who is trying to explain that he is a victim of mistaken identity. Although Gide is not convinced by the story, he nevertheless wonders to what extent a judge should hinder or facilitate a witness's testimony and, furthermore, how difficult it is for a juror to make up his own mind instead of simply accepting the judge's obvious opinion. One detail of the defendant's behavior the evening of the crime remains obscure for our attentive man of letters. Immediately after the burglary, at midnight, while returning to town, the accused sees someone he knows along the road and, instead of continuing on his way, makes a point of stopping the man to ask for a cigarette and after a few minutes of conversation, takes his leave, telling the other man to be sure not to mention to anyone that he has seen him that night. It is the perverse and self-destructive logic of the criminal mind that fascinates Gide. This witness's testimony obviously ends up being a determining element of the prosecutor's case. As Emily Apter has remarked, "Gide's *faits divers* . . . illustrate the cliché that life imitates and even outstrips art in its configurations of the grotesque and the bizarre. In this respect they form a perfect counterpart to novels such as *Les Caves du Vatican* or *Les Faux-Monnayeurs* the plots of which are stamped with the imprint of deviant narrative strategies typically found in the *fait divers*" (564).

There is a particularly interesting case of an arsonist that leads Gide into what could properly be called psychoanalytic terrain. The arsonist is a forty-year-old laborer who is accused of setting four different fires in the homes of relatives and neighbors. Bernard admits to being the perpetrator of all four fires, but when the judge asks him why he set them, Bernard responds that he had no motive at all. On several other occasions, the judge insists on trying to determine the motive for the fires, but Bernard is adamant that he had no reason at all. This is obviously troubling to the court, which has difficulty fitting Bernard's crimes into a logical system of motivated acts. Pierre-Quint once again: "The apparent absence of human causality frightens people as much as the mysteries of infinite space."[9] The court doctor testifies that Bernard spoke to him of a strange sense of relief and relaxation that he felt after setting the fires. Gide wonders whether this feeling of relief is in some way related to sexual gratification, but he resists asking the question in court for fear that it would seem too bizarre. Certainly, the idea of an unmotivated crime must have been particularly interesting to Gide, as he was in the middle of writing *Les Caves du Vatican,* although Lafcadio's murder of Amédée is somewhat more complicated as a "premeditated" gratuitous act. It might be useful to quote Gide's "Première lettre sur les faits divers," which appears in *Ne jugez pas:* "A gratuitous act . . . I don't believe in gratuitous acts, i.e., actions motivated by nothing at all. That idea is inadmissible. There are no effects without causes. The words 'gratuitous act' are a *temporary* label which I used [in earlier works] to designate actions that escape ordinary psychological explanation, deeds that are not shaped by personal interest (and thus, by playing with words a bit, I spoke of *disinterested* actions)."[10]

Gide reports a number of trials concerning charges of immorality: three cases of fathers who each sexually abused their young daughter (two get hard labor and the revocation of paternal rights, the other is acquitted for lack of evidence and "attenuating" circumstances), and another case of a mentally retarded adolescent accused of raping a young girl. Gide is particularly outraged by the manner in which this last case is conducted. The accused is barely able to understand the proceedings and is unfairly humiliated by the judge, who in effect tricks him into saying that he has no regrets. Furthermore, the defendant has confessed and the doctors have submitted their reports; why (Gide asks the reader) must the little girl be forced to testify? The importance that Gide gives to the scene in which the helpless victim must submit to the questions and the gaze of the court reminds Emily Apter of another scene that Gide reports in *Si le grain ne meurt*. The vision of the helpless victim is described in similar terms in a Moroccan hotel where Gide, along with his friend, is having sex with a young Arab male prostitute (562). Apter is no doubt correct to associate this scene of victimization from Gide's personal life with the revulsion he feels when the robed figures in the courtroom place a distraught little girl on a high chair at the front of the courtroom and make her retell her story. Gide's sympathy also extends to the defendants in these morals cases, who suffer public humiliation. Indeed the general outcry against them influences the way the jurors and the court officers treat them, a point to which Gide will return in some of the more sensational cases in the *Souvenirs* and in more explicit detail in his reports fifteen years later on the *Affaire Redureau* and the *Séquestrée de Poitiers* in *Ne jugez pas*.

A case of infanticide leads Gide to question the motives of the court itself. A seventeen-year-old live-in maid named Rachel is accused of murdering her newborn child. Rachel tried to hide her pregnancy for fear of being let go, and indeed the testimony of her employer later confirms that she would have been dismissed. Rachel gave birth in her room and worried that the baby's cries would attract attention, and she ended up suffocating her. Assuring herself that the baby was dead by making a little cut on the baby's throat (!), she then put the corpse in a bucket in her room and went back to work. She later dug a shallow grave for the baby, but it was soon discovered. The trial reveals that the employer's son was the father of the baby, and although the employer herself claims that she never noticed the girl was pregnant, we are told that over the course of the past several months the family would frequently sit the maid down in the evening to listen to newspaper reports and stories about infanticides. The judge thinks that this information is totally irrelevant, and when the matter of paternity and the responsibility of the son arise, he makes it obvious, according to Gide, that he does not want the interrogation to get off track, and so he stops the witness and pursues other questions. It is not clear here whether the judge is trying to protect the bourgeois family or simply wants to keep the case from getting messy. Alain Goulet relates such scenes of curious behavior on the part of judges to Gide's portrayal of jurists in *Les Faux-Monnayeurs,* specifically Molinier. "Justice does not exist to help people know the truth, but to protect the established order."[11] Rachel is found guilty but nevertheless acquitted due to attenuating circumstances.

A sensational murder case receives Gide's very careful and sympathetic attention. Charles is accused of murdering his mistress, striking her with a knife 110 times. Charles had left his wife and children for Juliette and from all evidence was madly in love with her. Although the landlady and neighbors report occasional arguments, Charles and Juliette were a well-behaved couple. The night before the murder, according to Charles, Juliette refused to sleep with him, and when she refused again the next morning, Charles went into a rage and began hitting her with the tip of a knife blade. Gide interprets his intent as not to kill but to maim and disfigure Juliette; in his rage, however, Charles apparently cut her carotid artery, and she died almost immediately. This is certainly a crime of passion, but the judge keeps trying to get Charles to come up with a motive, a logical reason why he decided to kill this woman. Charles claims not to remember anything that happened after his first blows, though he does not deny the evidence against him. The doctor who examined Charles found that he is of sound mind but has a personality characterized by unstable judgment, indecision, and lack of self-discipline. Gide wonders whether it is these qualities that allowed such an abrupt transformation of unsatisfied sexual desire into violence (112). Gide finds the jury decision in this case deplorable. Despite ample evidence that Charles had no intent to kill his mistress and committed his crime in a fit of passion, the jury condemns him to life in prison. Gide believes that certain details during the trial unduly influenced jury opinion, specifically the vivid description of the sound of the knife blade entering the victim's shoulder and the number of wounds on the body. Furthermore, during the trial, a Rouen newspaper published an opinion piece mocking juries that are too lenient. Gide saw the article being passed around by jurors during the deliberations. "Who can say what power of persuasion—or intimidation—a page of print may have on the minds of those not well-armed in criticism and so conscientious, so anxious to do the right thing! . . ."[12]

Finally, there is the complicated case of employee theft from a large company, bringing sixteen different defendants to trial all at once. The defendants either sold merchandise stolen from their company or bought it knowing it was illegal merchandise. The details of all the petty larcenies, who stole what when and who sold to whom, are complicated. The bottom line is that the company employees had long been loyal to the original company, called La Compagnie de l'Ouest, but when it was sold and became La Compagnie de l'État they decided to steal. The jury has great difficulty deciding where to lay the blame; there does not seem to be a ringleader. They feel great sympathy with the employees and do not want to convict them for being petty thieves, but they do want to convict the fence who was getting all the merchandise to resell, feeling that she is in fact the instigator of the crimes. They decide essentially to ignore the judge's instructions and the questionnaire concerning the circumstances of the thefts—in sum, to revolt against the system. The jury votes not guilty for the theft and guilty for the resale. The judge points out the obvious, that one cannot illegally resell something that was not stolen in the first place. The jury is sent back to reconsider its judgment and realizes, in fact, how little power it has in the final analysis to break away from the rigid structure of the court questionnaire.

Gide's encounter with the *"machine-à-rendre-la-justice"* (177) [machine of justice] in Rouen was a discouraging experience, as he states in the preface to *Souvenirs:* "During twelve days of anguish I was able to feel very acutely the extent to which human justice is a murky and precarious thing."[13] As Pierre-Quint says, this anguish is produced in modern consciousness by the very nature of judicial method, since it depends on analogies, appearances, and presumption, which are all by nature inconclusive means of arriving at truth (190). Gide does, however, offer a few proposals for reform in an appendix to the *Souvenirs.* Several are of a procedural nature: he suggests that more care be taken in jury selection and in the selection of a jury foreman; he also suggests that the list of questions that juries must answer concerning the circumstances of a crime tends to force them into a restrictive decision-making process that often frustrates their sense of justice. He suggests that if the questions cannot be modified, at least the jurors might be given some initial instruction about the sentences that may result from particular answers. Finally, he worries about the ways a jury gets influenced by a prosecuting judge, who has already formed an opinion about a case. As discouraged as Gide may have been by this experience, it is evident that he nevertheless found confirmation of his belief in the nonrational nature of human action and the inability of a rational system like the French judiciary to do more than protect a certain idealized conception of bourgeois society.

Gide was well-suited to formulate a critique of the judicial system, particularly if one views it as a narrative instance that attempts to establish a coherent story line with plot, characters, and motives. In effect, this is his *métier* as a novelist, taking brute reality and transforming it so that it has internal coherence. He is careful to add physical descriptions of various witnesses and defendants and especially to look behind appearances for psychological motivations. Physical appearance is something that does not come out in the court record, but often has an overwhelming effect on jury perception.

Souvenirs de la cour d'assises is a hybrid form that presents true events, but casts them in a narrative form. One might argue that this is inevitable, but Gide does this in a very self-conscious way by using specific literary techniques, subtly weaving together a primary narrative voice and the accounts of witnesses and the accused, the suppositions of an omniscient storyteller, free indirect discourse, and a few different types of "authorial" intrusion.

Gide's first fictional work, *Les Cahiers d'André Walter,* presents itself as a *fait divers,* the diaries of a hypersensitive young man who died of "brain fever," published for the edification of the public. Similarly, Gide's *Prométhée,* in its own quirky way, deals with crimes of a metaphysical type. This fascination with the circumstances and motivations surrounding the transgressive acts of individuals and groups will become a regular feature of Gide's fictional *œuvre.* In four major works that Gide published in the early years of the twentieth century, *L'Immoraliste, La Porte étroite, Isabelle,* and *La Symphonie pastorale,* the "crimes" that he narrates are of a personal, moral nature that center on the idea of self-deception. These four books are critical works that ironically deconstruct their subjects, embodied by the four successive protagonists—Michel, Alissa, Gérard, and the pastor—each beset by the demon of self-deception. All are deluded in their attempts at lucidity concerning the motives for their own actions and those of others. They each interpret events and construct their persona by relying on a lopsided vision of the world. In the case of Michel, individualism becomes egocentrism and eventually self-indulgent narcissism. Similarly, Alissa's Protestant mysticism becomes a narcissistic martyrdom. In the case of *Isabelle* there is a real crime, but the subject of the story is "Gérard's disappointment as soon as plain reality takes the place of illusion once again."[14] In *La Symphonie pastorale,* the pastor's pretense to altruism and purity of motives, rationalized through Biblical interpretation, becomes transparently self-serving as well as destructive to those around him. All four protagonists engage in a process of rationalization in which they attempt to square actions and motivations with an accepted moral code. This process of rationalization is also at the heart of any criminal trial as the prosecution and the defense dispute the interpretation of evidence.

Certainly the protagonist of *L'Immoraliste,* Michel, having gathered a group of friends together to listen to his "confession," is struggling with the idea of justice within the context of a societal code of morality. *L'Immoraliste* also features a curious take on petty crime as the narrator observes the theft of scissors by Moktir and participates in the theft by a complicitous gaze that Moktir notices. The narrator also ends up colluding with a poacher on his own land in Normandy, in effect poaching from himself. These "criminal" acts are intimately tied to a repressed sexuality in this text, and this binarism of sexuality and criminal or antisocial behavior returns regularly in Gide's writing. Gide digs more deeply into the problems inherent in a rational moral code in works such as *Les Caves du Vatican* and *Les Faux-Monnayeurs,* which feature specifically criminal characters and others who aid and abet them, often unconsciously, for self-serving reasons. *Les Caves du Vatican,* for instance, is a variegated model of deception that undermines accepted moral codes and culminates in a dilemma of consequence and responsibility concerning the motivations (or lack thereof) behind Lafcadio's murderous *acte gratuit.*

Two weeks of jury duty opened a window for Gide, a window into a world where the form of the criminal code confronts the harsh reality of base instinct. This firm grounding in the real world of motivation and consequence pushes Gide himself toward a stronger social commitment, further reinforced by the imminent catastrophe of World War I. Subsequent to his experience in the assises court in Rouen, Gide embarks on a different tangent in his investigation of crime or, more generally, of evil in society. Certainly Protos is a representation of the devil in *Les Caves du Vatican;* and in *Les Faux-Monnayeurs* the mysterious and diabolical Strouvilhou is a character who keeps showing up in the most implausible places, who literally defies conventions of time and place by being in two places at once, and who is closely identified with another vaguely defined character—the demon, also called the devil. Yet in *Les Faux-Monnayeurs* the notion of crime and of evil in society becomes more diffuse. In the *Journal* Gide mentions a conversation with his friend Jacques Raverat in 1914 in which he expresses a belief in the devil and he says that he will certainly have a character who believes in the devil in his next novel (492). He brings up the subject again in 1916, saying this time that the devil is simply a figuration of the idea of evil (*Journal* 531). But it is in a separate text called "Feuillets," inserted into the *Journal* at the end of 1916, that he develops his thoughts more extensively and concludes that evil is our power to rationalize (*Journal* 607). Gide states that, for the first time, he has realized that evil is a positive, active, enterprising, principle, rather than simply an absence of good (608). He specifically links this realization to the War and the relief work he has been doing. This passage strongly resembles ones in both *Les Faux-Monnayeurs* and in the *Journal des Faux-Monnayeurs,* in which Gide develops the idea that evil is a part of our reasoning process, that it is imbedded within rationalism. In this passage of the "Feuillets" he goes so far as to say *"Cogito ergo Satanas"* (*Journal* 609). The existence of evil and its deceptive nature, particularly in its occurrence as self-deception and the rationalization of wrong actions, is a major theme in Gide's novel.

One of the primary characters in the *Les Faux-Monnayeurs* is an author named Édouard, who is trying to write a new novel called "Les Faux-Monnayeurs" and whose diary forms a large portion of the story. At one point Édouard even claims that everything that he is putting in the diary will become a part of his novel. Similarly, Gide was keeping a special notebook while he was writing *Les Faux-Monnayeurs,* called the *Journal des Faux-Monnayeurs,* which he published in the pages of the *NRF* soon after the novel came out. Much that is in this journal finds its way into the novel itself. Even more tellingly, however, Gide also published an appendix to this journal in which he reproduced a series of newspaper reports of *faits divers* that he used to construct some of the characters and scenes of his novel. Drawing on them helped him develop ideas about the evil that is at the heart of rationalization and self-delusion.

The first of these *faits divers* is about a gang of teenagers, originally formed as a literary society, who become involved in prostitution and the dissemination of counterfeit money. Similarly, the narrator of *Les Faux-Monnayeurs* follows several of his young characters from good upstanding families as they enter first into prostitution and then into a counterfeit ring. There seems to be no rhyme or reason for their involvement except for the thrill of the forbidden and their prestige among their friends. The narrator of the novel remains outside this group of characters, reporting their speech and actions, yet never speculating about their motivations. But the secondary narrator, Édouard, gets actively involved. Warned by a judge that his nephew Georges is part of this gang and risks imminent arrest, he decides to save his nephew from disgrace. His method, though, is a curious one.

He has spoken with Georges's mother about his delinquency and so decides to confront the young boy. Georges is disturbed during their meeting but maintains his cool. Édouard decides to give him a passage from his novel to read that is based on his conversation with the mother earlier in the week. It is a conversation between two friends about a young acquaintance of theirs who has been stealing. This third person is obviously Georges. The two friends try to decide what they could say to Eudolphe (alias Georges) to make him realize the error of his ways. It is finally decided that the best thing to do is transcribe the conversation they have just had and give it to Eudolphe to read. But contrary to Édouard's expectations, Georges's reaction to the passage is not shame but pleasure, the pleasure of being the center of attention for his uncle and of being a pretext for literature. He even says that had he not stolen, Édouard would not have been able to write those lines. At this point Édouard simply tells Georges that he knows that he has been circulating counterfeit coins and that if he does not stop he will be arrested.

Édouard, then, has misjudged his nephew by neglecting the larger context of their conversation; he wanted to convey a message through words but forgot the conditions surrounding it. He has misappropriated a *fait divers,* attempting to make it into a moral tale meant for Georges's edification. Yet this incident has an even wider significance. Because it contains an excerpt from Édouard's novel, it is also a commentary on the reader's role in the literary process and the constant dangers of misinterpretation. And the stilted language of the quoted passage reflects back on the conversation between Édouard and Georges as a caricature and forces the reader to see their conversation as a dialogue in a novel, breaking the illusion of reality. In several ways, then, Gide seems to be ironically pointing to the problems a novelist confronts by making use of the genre of the *fait divers.*

The second newspaper report Gide drew on for *Les Faux-Monnayeurs* involved a high school student who committed suicide; the report included details about the unhealthy atmosphere at his home and an unsavory group of classmates who apparently goaded and tricked him into committing suicide. This report underlies the suicide of the teenager Boris in *Les Faux-Monnayeurs.* Boris's suicide presents a dilemma of motivation, both within the text (for the other characters) and for the reader. He is introduced in the second part of the novel and is under the care of a Dr. Sophroniska, apparently a psychoanalyst, who is trying to cure him of a series of nervous disorders brought on, she says, by the factitious life of the theater—his mother is a singer. She describes his treatment in terms that closely resemble those of Freud. His symptoms include speaking nonsense and a predilection for mystical practices involving masturbation. Sophroniska soon pronounces Boris cured, to the dismay of the novelist Édouard, who believes that Boris has just repressed at a deeper level. Édouard discovers, implausibly, that Boris is the grandson of a good friend of his in Paris and offers to take Boris back to school there. Boris is desperately unhappy and falls in with the same coterie of students previously involved in prostitution and counterfeiting. Egged on by the diabolical and ubiquitous Strouvilhou, the students play upon Boris's timidity and his complexes and end up forming a rigged suicide pact that Boris loses. Boris is in fact aware that the game is rigged yet seems willing to play it and kill himself. Édouard, who is at least partially responsible for Boris's situation, cannot figure out any solid explanation for Boris's action, and so he decides to exclude this particular unpleasant event from his novel.

> Without pretending to explain anything, I would rather not offer any fact without a sufficient motivation. That is why I will not use little Boris's suicide in my *Counterfeiters:* I already have too much trouble understanding it. And I don't like *"faits divers."* There is something peremptory, undeniable, brutal, outrageously real about them . . . I accept that reality might come along to prop up my thought, as a proof—but not that it should precede it.[15]

Édouard may not like *faits divers,* but one might suppose that Gide does.

The third example of a *fait divers* incorporated into the text is the story of the shipwreck of the *Bourgogne.* That story is told by the Anglo-American Lady

Griffith to her new lover Vincent in order to convince him to abandon the woman now carrying his baby. The story is that following the shipwreck there were too few lifeboats, and each boat became so full that to allow one more person in would capsize it, thereby killing all those already on board. The sailors took the extraordinary measure of hacking off the hands of anyone who swam up and grabbed hold of the boat. This *fait divers* is presented by Lady Griffith as a parable and is meant to show Vincent that he must be willing to cut his unfortunate girl friend off so that he may get on to a better life, with his new lover. The effect, however, is chilling: Vincent does not know what to say and finds an excuse to leave, promising to make a decision by the following day. The narrator intervenes to explain Vincent's thoughts as he walks home—the satisfaction of carnal desire brings not only joy but also a sense of despair.

At this point a passage in the *Souvenirs* is illuminating. It deals with a particularly disturbing case of a robbery and mugging that pushes Gide to take independent action. One of the three defendants in the case is obviously someone of weak character who went along with the other two men who committed the crime but who bears little responsibility. He is nevertheless convicted, in part because of a previous juvenile record, to five years of hard labor and ten years of banishment. Gide and a couple of his fellow jurors argue for leniency, but other jurors are not convinced and decide to convict them all the same, to just get rid of all these low lifes. Gide is so upset by the injustice of this sentence that he cannot sleep, recalling the story of the shipwrecked *Bourgogne* that he heard from a sailor in Le Havre. In the version that Gide recounts in *Souvenirs,* he makes it quite evident that French society is like the shipwrecked *Bourgogne:* the bourgeois manning the lifeboats are letting the excluded victims of disaster drown. "Oh yes! The best thing is not to fall into the water. Afterwards, if Heaven doesn't help you, it's to the devil with you! — This evening I am ashamed of the boat and of the security that I feel there."[16] The next day Gide goes to see the defense lawyer and even the mother of the accused, to try to set the record straight. He draws up an official request to the court to lessen the sentence and convinces a majority of his fellow jurors to vote in favor of it. The young man's sentence is effectively reduced from five years to three, but Gide reflects ruefully on the young man's future—after prison he will be sent off to the colonial army in Africa and after those long years, Gide wonders, who or what will he have become? Thus Gide, with the *Bourgogne* on his mind, arrives at a complex moral position: he has saved the young man from a longer prison sentence, yet saved him for what? The effect of the same *fait divers* on Vincent is even more complicated and far darker.

Vincent is a scientist, and the primary narrator explains that his positivist education makes him easy prey for the devil precisely because he does not believe in him. The narrator explains Vincent's decision to dump his pregnant girl friend as an ethical evolution in five stages. First comes Vincent's good intention to help the girl by giving her the money his parents had saved to set him up in a medical practice. In the second stage he realizes that the sum of money is insufficient, and the demon then shows him the possibility of multiplying it by gambling; he loses it all. In the third stage he feels that he must rise above adversity—strength of character demands that he admit his gambling loss to his girl friend, and that in turn allows him to break off his relationship with her, since he can consider himself the one who has failed in his duty and thus leave her "for her own good." In the fourth stage he abandons his initial good intention, which he now perceives to be an illusion, in light of the new moral view that he has been forced to adopt in order to legitimize his behavior, save face, in sum, justify his actions. The devil whispers reasons in his mind's ear to convince him that all has turned out for the best. In the fifth stage Vincent succumbs to the triumphant disdain of the cynic, abandoning completely the ethical position. The devil has won.

Vincent goes off with Lady Griffith and soon disappears from the narrative altogether on his way to Africa with his new lover, to take part in a scientific expedition. The reader finds out much later in the novel, through an exchange between two characters who do not know Vincent, that he has gone mad, murdered Lady Griffith, and believes himself possessed by the devil. Vincent, like other characters in the story, illustrates a crisis of reason by constantly falling victim to self-justification, abandoning previously held moral positions, and acting in ways inconsistent with his stated beliefs. It is perhaps in this sense that Gide spoke of his novel as being a "perpetual upheaval" [*surgissement perpétuel*].[17]

So it is the demon who propels the story. It is he who puts the coin in Bernard's pocket at just the right moment to allow the plot to develop; it is he who provides Vincent with the self-serving rationalization to overcome his remorse for abandoning Laura; it is he who drives Vincent crazy in Africa so that he kills Lilian; and finally, it is he who, through a complex series of decisions by several different characters, pushes Boris to suicide. So one might say, in effect, that the character who believes in the devil is none other than the narrator himself. Ironic though it may seem, this is a positive quality because it indicates lucidity on the part of the primary narrator, contrary to the secondary narrator, Édouard, who continues to be deluded. The demon who appears in *Les Faux-Monnayeurs* is essentially reason at the service of self-serving delusions and desires.

This, then, is perhaps the motive behind Gide's publications on the strange cases of justice: a confrontation between rational and irrational forces in society. The trap is to think that one can find neat, logical explanations for human action; and a system of justice based on such a principle ends up being both repressive and ineffectual. As Alain Goulet has pointed out, if Gide is so interested in these cases of disturbed individuals, it is not so much from morbid curiosity as from an intuition that he will be able to understand a certain reality embedded in our world, our humanity, and ourselves, a reality that we too readily cast off as aberrant and monstrous. "He understands that all of these characters of the *faits divers,* paralleling those whom he invented for his fiction, hold out a mirror which allows us to recognize and analyze ourselves."[18]

Notes

1. "Un crime a été commis. La collectivité est heurtée dans sa conscience profonde. Elle demande réparation. Certes, il faut que la société intervienne. En répondant au crime par le châtiment, efface-t-on le crime? Ce système de compensation rend-il à la loi violée son prestige?" (188–189).

2. "Juste appréciation, reconnaissance et respect des droits et du mérite de chacun. . . . « *La justice est le respect de la dignité humaine.* » . . . Organisation du pouvoir judiciaire; ensemble des organes chargés d'administrer la justice, conformément au droit positif."

3. "L'opinion du jury est que, après tout, s'il n'est pas bien certain qu'ils aient commis ces vols-ci, ils ont dû en commettre d'autres; ou qu'ils en commettront; que, donc, ils sont bons à coffrer" (17).

4. "Enfin, pour aigrefins qu'ils fussent, ce n'étaient tout de même pas des *bandits;* je veux dire qu'ils *profitaient* de la société, mais n'étaient pas insurgés contre elle. Ils cherchaient à se faire du bien, non à faire du mal à autrui, etc. . . . Voici ce que se disaient les jurés, désireux d'une sévérité pondérée" (24–25; ellipsis Gide's).

5. "[O]ui, le crime est très grave, mais nous ne sommes pas bien certains que ce soit celui-ci qui l'ait commis. Pourtant il faut un châtiment : à tout hasard châtions celui-ci, puisque c'est lui que vous nous offrez comme victime; mais, dans le doute, ne le châtions tout de même pas par trop" (90).

6. "Marceau ne cherche pas à se défendre, pas même à s'excuser; il accepte d'avoir fait ce qu'il a fait, comme s'il ne pouvait pas ne pas le faire. On dirait qu'il est résigné d'avance à devenir ce criminel" (44).

7. "L'innocent sera-t-il plus éloquent, moins troublé que le coupable? Allons donc! Dès qu'il sent qu'on ne le *croit* pas, il pourra se troubler d'autant plus qu'il est moins coupable. Il outrera ses affirmations; ses protestations paraîtront de plus en plus déplaisantes; il perdra pied" (83).

8. "Le mécanisme d'auto-défense joue pour le tribunal qui, le condamnant, le transforme en bouc-émissaire : « l'autre » n'est pas un homme, mais une bête qu'on charge de tous les péchés. La condamnation signifie qu'on le déchoit de sa condition d'homme" (363).

9. "L'absence apparente de causalité humaine effraie l'homme autant que le mystère des espaces infinis" (195).

10. "Un acte gratuit . . . Je n'y crois pas du tout, à l'acte gratuit, c'est à dire à un acte qui ne serait motivé par rien. Cela est essentiellement inadmissible. Il n'y a pas d'effets sans causes. Les mots « acte gratuit » sont une étiquette *provisoire* qui m'a paru commode pour désigner les actes qui échappent aux explications psychologiques ordinaires, les gestes que ne détermine pas le simple intérêt personnel (et c'est dans ce sens, en jouant un peu sur les mots, que j'ai pu parler d'actes *désintéressés*)" (143; ellipsis Gide's).

11. "La justice n'est pas là pour connaître la vérité, mais pour protéger un ordre établi" (365).

12. "Qui dira la puissance de persuasion — ou d'intimidation — d'une feuille imprimée sur des cerveaux pas bien armés pour la critique, et si consciencieux pour la plupart, si désireux de bien faire! . . ." (119; ellipsis Gide's).

13. "[A] quel point la justice humaine est chose douteuse et précaire, c'est ce que, durant douze jours, j'ai pu sentir jusqu'à l'angoisse" (8).

14. "[L]a déception même de Gérard aussitôt que la plate réalité reprend la place de l'illusion" (*Œuvres complètes* 3: 1561).

15. "Sans prétendre précisément rien expliquer, je voudrais n'offrir aucun fait sans une motivation suffisante. C'est pourquoi je ne me servirai pas pour mes *Faux-Monnayeurs*

du suicide du petit Boris; j'ai déjà trop de mal à le comprendre. Et puis je n'aime pas les « faits divers ». Ils ont quelque chose de péremptoire, d'indéniable, de brutal, d'outrageusement réel . . . Je consens que la réalité vienne à l'appui de ma pensée, comme une preuve; mais non point qu'elle la précède" (*Romans* 1246; ellipsis Gide's).

16. "Oui! le mieux c'est de ne pas tomber à l'eau. Après, si le Ciel ne vous aide, c'est le diable pour s'en tirer! — Ce soir je prends en honte la barque, et de m'y sentir à l'abri" (142).

17. See *Journal des Faux-Monnayeurs* 81 and *The Counterfeiters* 409.

18. "Il comprend que tous ces personnages de faits divers, après ceux qu'il a mis en scène dans ses fictions, nous tendent un miroir qui nous permet de nous reconnaître et de nous analyser" (604–605).

Works Cited

Anglès, Auguste. *André Gide et le premier groupe de La Nouvelle Revue Française.* Vol. 2. Paris: Gallimard, 1986.

Apter, Emily. "Allegories of Reading / Allegories of Justice: The Gidean *Fait Divers.*" *Romanic Review* 80.4 (November 1989): 560–570.

Gide, André. *The Counterfeiters.* The novel translated by Dorothy Bussy, the journal by Justin O'Brien. New York: Alfred A. Knopf, 1951.

———. *Journal 1889–1939.* Paris: Gallimard, Bibliothèque de la Pléiade, 1951.

———. *Journal des Faux-Monnayeurs.* Paris: Gallimard, 1927.

———. *Œuvres complètes.* 15 vols. Ed. Louis Martin-Chauffier. Paris: Gallimard, 1932–1939.

———. *Ne jugez pas.* Paris: Gallimard, 1957.

———. *Romans, récits et soties, œuvres lyriques.* Ed. Yvonne Davet and Jean-Jacques Thierry. Paris: Gallimard, Bibliothèque de la Pléiade, 1958.

———. *Souvenirs de la cour d'assises.* Paris: Gallimard, 1924.

Goulet, Alain. *Fiction et vie sociale dans l'œuvre d'André Gide.* Paris: Publications de l'Association des Amis d'André Gide, 1984–1985.

Pierre-Quint, Léon. *André Gide : l'homme, sa vie, son œuvre.* Paris: Librairie Stock, 1952.

CHAPTER 5

Writing the Wrongs of French Colonial Africa:
Voyage au Congo and *Le Retour du Tchad*

Walter Putnam

André Gide's 1926–1927 Congo journey began as a pleasure jaunt into the exotic and the erotic: "Everything here seems to hold the promise of bliss, voluptuousness, and forgetting."[1] It survives as a text, a travel narrative addressed primarily to a European readership about the author's close encounter with the social and political reality of French colonial Africa. Gide's very decision to publish his travel writings and to take a public position based on his personal observations reveals a political strategy that he will pursue over the subsequent decade. The epistemological shift necessary for him to engage in this public debate carries with it a fundamental assumption about the writer's role in the social and political community. "What is at stake in writing is the very structure of authority itself," affirms Barbara Johnson (48). Gide had made strategic use of writing as a way to self-knowledge and revelation throughout his career. He now had to turn to the revelation of a different kind of scene of compelling dramatic importance, one that only tangentially overlapped with his personal concerns: the colonial situation in French Equatorial Africa. Political discourse exerts its power in the public sphere when it becomes visibly and tangibly connected to the author's presence. Gide's maneuvering and positioning vis-à-vis the colonial power structure, while overtly dealing with abuses witnessed during his travels in French Equatorial Africa, have a more direct bearing on his own cultural politics. His strategic opposition to colonial practices and policies underscores his desire to establish his own authority in a public debate taking place not in the Congo but in Paris, intellectual, cultural, and political capital of France's colonial empire. In a highly self-referential way, Gide inscribes his opposition to the very culture of French expansionism in which he gravitates and to which he addresses his critiques.

His influence in the French colonial debate relies on his credibility, which is directly dependent on his ability to establish his authority and sincerity. According to Koenraad Geldof, "Authority is, by its nature, a communicational and plural phenomenon— intersubjective, in other words, and social. . . . An authority is only an authority when it circulates" (22). Gide realized that his political positions would resonate most strongly if he exposed them to the public in a provocative and evocative medium. He thus resisted the writerly temptation to transform his experiences in a narrative form or to meld politics and fiction as Malraux would a few years later. Rather than textualizing Africa yet again, he chose to denounce the colonial abuses he had witnessed in a more immediate and dramatic mode. Gide's *Voyage au Congo* and *Le Retour du Tchad* do not so much represent Africa as dramatize it on the stage of French cultural politics alongside the journalistic, epistolary, and filmic versions that constitute his total involvement in the colonial debate. Although sometimes interpreted as a radical shift in Gide's trajectory, the Congo episode must be understood as a heightened example of continuity in the writer's career. If there was change, it lay in his adoption of a form appropriate to the subject, one that subordinates writerly considerations to the compelling nature of the colonial situation rather than attempting to make Africa into some raw material for his own creative purposes.

The Purloined Book: When Gallimard Stole Africa

An anecdote will help to situate the status and reputation of Gide's African writings. In 1980, the review *Peuples Noirs / Peuples Africains* planned to include an article by Odile Tobner on prominent French intellectuals who had written about sub-Saharan Africa. She immediately wished to include Gide's book, convinced as she was of its value as a cornerstone of French Africanist political discourse. Tobner declared:

> A book by André Gide dealing with Africa is not insignificant. Gide is an intellectual and spokesperson whose authority and credibility are certainly worth more than the new philosophers. At a time when Black Africa preoccupies so many people, for reasons that are varied and not always noble, the least we can say is that the posthumous voice of this great man would be a welcome addition.[2]

Like many others since its publication, Tobner assumes that Gide's scrupulous and incisive views on worldly issues will extend to his vision of the problems of sub-Saharan Africa. To her astonishment, the book was unavailable in any Parisian bookstore, and the famous Gallimard publishing house, which Gide himself had helped to found before World War I, could not provide her with a paperback copy. At that point, the noted Cameroonian novelist Mongo Beti took over the investigation and went in person to the headquarters of Gallimard, where he expressed his shock and dismay that a major work dealing with Africa by such an important author was not available to the reading public. Beti placed the case of the purloined book on the level of insidious censorship and a conspiracy of silence of the kind that so often strikes African writers themselves. In the book Gide publicly indicted abuses resulting from the concessionary companies authorized to exploit the natural resources of French Equatorial Africa.

Was it possible that his indictment might explain the discreet disappearance of his travel journals? Beti pointed out in a subsequent letter to Robert Gallimard:

> Would you not agree that this book, a particularly lucid and courageous account by one of the best and most perspicacious French writers on Africa, and dealing with the violent relationship between Whites and Blacks resulting from Western domination, deserves to be read? Would you not also agree in that case that there is no better moment than now when battalions of young French *coopérants* devoid of any spiritual grounding are once again invading the black continent armed with the same pernicious prejudices as their predecessors of the colonial era?[3]

Mongo Beti's comments might lead one to ask whether he himself had critically read Gide's account of French colonial rule in Equatorial Africa. One cannot imagine that he would endorse Gide's often reductive, condescending, and patronizing views of Africans. Suffice it to note for the moment that Gide's Congo writings have enjoyed a problematic reputation as anticolonialist texts, given their author's own close association with the colonialist machinery as well as his generalized acceptance of the fundamental principles of colonialism itself.

The case of the absent book raises the larger question of Africanist discourse. If Africa is often conceived as absence itself, as an emptied vessel waiting to be filled with Western knowledge, as "blank darkness," according to Christopher Miller's felicitous phrase, Mongo Beti's search for Gide's book becomes emblematic of the troubled and troubling relationship between Western discourse and colonialism. How might the missing book provide a link to understanding the history of that "violent relationship between Whites and Blacks resulting from Western domination" that Mongo Beti underscores? Do Gide's insights necessarily excuse his oversights? In other words, how is it that a book, any book, might at one and the same time conceal and reveal the secrets of an age-old question about what lies at the heart of that immense darkness that has come to be called Africa?

The preeminence of the written account of travels to strange and fascinating places has long surpassed the reality of the places themselves. Africa had to be emptied of its contents before it could be made to contain the stuff of myth: the *cynocephali* of antiquity, the cannibals that haunted Victorian lore, the riches of King Solomon's mines. In a by now all-too-familiar move, Western writers, historians, anthropologists, and travelers had reconstructed a mythic Africa that satisfied both their material needs and their psychological desires. "Africa is . . ." becomes both a trope of inquiry and a response to its own mystery from the moment that it *is* whatever we want it to be. The French playwright Jean Genet, when asked to write a play about *"les nègres,"* poignantly responded: "And what color might they be?"

That Gide's book has come to symbolize Africa is ironic in multiple ways, not the least of which is this episode of its disappearance, perhaps the most significant commentary it can provide on the lands it purports to describe. Its reputation owes much to the public political stances Gide took upon his return from Africa, when he led a high-profile campaign to denounce the abuses of the concessionary companies. That politicization of his journey was, in fact, a carefully planned strategy designed to make the French colonial system a more humane system of domination, but "domination" nonetheless. It was also carried out as much according to the rules and practices of Gide's Parisian literary *habitus* as it was in relation to the African reality that Gide had witnessed. "The less intelligent the White Man is, the more stupid he finds the Black"[4] still rings in the ears of readers of the *Voyage;* yet its aim is clearly to reflect on European epistemology and prejudice, rather than on African psychology. Gide's own text is traversed with comments about African stupidity. The written word could be largely ignored in favor of the quotation, the clip, the excerpt that recontextualized the knowledge of the book in such a way that it would be useful in a debate going on within the French political power structure. The text ultimately brings us back into contact with an author whom we know and whose authority we trust, one who has witnessed French colonial Africa firsthand and returned to tell what he saw, one who can speak to the issue of colonial abuse. Gide becomes our Odysseus, our Marco Polo, our Marlow who embarks on a journey into the heart of darkness only to discover that Africa is a phantom of European desires and deceits.

Bhabha in Wonder

In his seminal essay "Signs Taken for Wonders," Homi Bhabha evokes the fortuitous discovery of the book as a "scene of the cultural writings of English [substitute "French"] colonialism":

> The discovery of the book is, at once, a moment of originality and authority, as well as a process of displacement that, paradoxically, makes the presence of the book wondrous to the extent to which it is repeated, translated, misread, displaced. (quoted in Gates 163)

The European book as an "insignia of colonial authority and a signifier of colonial desire and discipline" (quoted in Gates 163) imparts the power to fill up the empty space called "Africa" in the European consciousness. Gide's Congo writings have certainly been "repeated, translated, misread, [and] displaced" numerous times since their publication. Their prominence in the public debates on government concessions points to the very real authority of Gide's account of events, situations, practices, and policies witnessed during his Congo trip. The circulation of Gide's texts and their attendant discourse on things African have held value and currency within that French debate even up to our own day. Their ostensible form as travel journal promotes their authenticity, while their displacement from the site of observation marks them with a sign of fundamental difference. Written as original and monological, their publication provides them with the possibility of achieving multiplicity and dialogue through circulation among their readers. As personal narratives, they nevertheless contain the mark of a potential readership that Gide projected even as he was writing each entry; the public accepts the pact of sincerity that underlies autobiographical writing while ignoring the facts that it cannot verify. Gide's frustration during his voyage at not being able to impose unity and coherency on his African subject will dissipate as his journals move beyond ambivalence in the hands of their readers. This slippage and the ensuing repetition within difference lead to the basic fractured quality of colonialist discourse, never providing a fixed representation of the colonized, never showing the colonizer a usable, stable identity of the Other. One must above all read Gide's discursive construction of Africa as an attempt to formulate French colonial identity against itself. This possibility did not escape the Nazi propaganda machine in its 1940 pamphlet titled *Experiences in the Congo: France's Inefficiency as a Colonial Power,* which consisted of selected excerpts from Gide's Congo writings presented as evidence that the French were unworthy allies of the British and Americans.

Constructing Authority

As a fragmented and disjointed narrative, the *Voyage au Congo* draws attention to its own gaps and to its numerous excesses. The text is indissociable from the signature of its author. It brings us back to someone we know, André Gide, who is also someone who can tell us truths we desire to hear. His travel writings mediate the desire for knowledge that has forever been associated with Africa. Indeed, its reputation as an authoritative depiction of French colonial rule in Africa relies on the fallacious notion that Gide might in some way be able to reveal Africa to a reading public desirous of such knowledge. Despite a marked sympathy and curiosity for things African, Gide clearly did not have the ethnographic bent, and he intuitively steered away from the temptation to develop it during his Congo journey. His position has nothing of the participant-observer ideal of modern ethnographic research. His party rarely stayed long enough in any one spot to focus clearly on the surroundings or to engage in any sustained cultural exchange. Paul Rabinow, considering James Clifford's studies on ethnographic authority, examines how the anthropologist establishes that he was "there" and then feigns to disappear from his text in the name of scientific objectivity (244). Rabinow goes on to tease out the ways that Clifford and Clifford Geertz, although doubtless with the best of intentions, "fail to use self-referentiality as anything more than a device for establishing authority" (244). Although Gide delivers a travel narrative with different objectives and different constraints, he nevertheless strives in similar fashion to highlight his presence in the field of French Africanist discourse as a guarantor of the truths that he reveals about the horrific abuses of the concession system. He strategically privileges the authority he will need to win his political cause over the claims of authorship he would have enjoyed in a work of creative fiction. The result of Gide's own frustrations at being largely unable to reappropriate and reread Africa in familiar, writerly terms is a travel narrative that tells us repeatedly what Africa is *not* while only rarely claiming to have seized what it is or might be. The reader who comes to the *Voyage au Congo* expecting to "see" Africa through Gide's eyes finds the author constantly blocking the view.

In the economy of Africanist writing, Gide carefully establishes the value of his textual construction in order to augment the impact of his cultural and political position. He is acutely aware that his lack of authority on African affairs will show through clearly if he attempts to discuss Africa proper in ethnographic, cultural, or historical terms. Gide lacked the expertise to undertake such a study. He therefore chose to dwell in his own area of authority: France as it relates to Africa. Contrary to a broader tendency in modernist fiction (his own included), Gide relies in his Congo writing on a greater proximity between writer and language, thus reducing the problematic nature of the telling subject that had been located in narrating figures such as the Édouard of the *Faux-Monnayeurs*.

Everything in his travel journals underscores the privileged viewpoint of Gide himself in a strategy aimed at establishing his authority. His realization that the human and political drama of the colonial Congo surpasses the literary domain proper will lead him to adopt a more "journalistic" mode of presentation.

> But how to make oneself heard? All my life I have spoken with little care as to who might be listening; I always wrote for people of tomorrow with the sole desire of lasting. I envy those journalists whose voices are heard immediately only to vanish soon after. Was I circulating up to now in a skein of lies? I want to move offstage, see behind the décor, discover what is hidden, even if it is horrible. It is that "horror" that I suspect exists and that I must see.[5]

The reference to stage performance underscores the extent to which Africa is conceived of as a spectacle, just as the events of real life for Gide always seemed to occur outside all conventional reality. The background for this position lies in the episode of the coach accident in Brittany when Gide, at the age of eighteen, obtained from his mother permission to take his first trip alone (or almost alone, since his mother was following him day by day). On an excursion one day, Gide looked up from his book to discover that the coachman had slipped off his seat and was close to falling under the wheels. Acting on instinct, Gide grabbed the reins to bring the horse to a halt. In a long *Journal* entry written some six months before his departure for the Congo (*Journal* 798–801), he recounts how he became aware that day of his sense that he lived in a spectacle detached from any common sense of reality. It was that episode that brought Gide to realize his profound division into an actor and a spectator of his own actions. He also discovered how much he could not feel fear at real or supposed dangers. This realization would later be played out in Africa first by his *insouciance* in the very project itself and then by his repeated staging of scenes from the European myth of the colonial encounter. His duality results in a capacity to observe himself from another vantage point like an actor in a performance. Speaking of the near-accident in Brittany, Gide would later tell Jean Delay that it was that episode which made him realize what irony was all about (Delay

421). He extended this Shakespearean notion of the "world as stage" to the scenes and dramas that he witnessed during his Congo journey. As we shall see in the African village scenes, Gide observes himself in performative terms before transforming each act into a written fragment of reality.

James Clifford draws a useful distinction in his reformulation of Paul Ricoeur's work on textualization: "The text, unlike discourse, can travel" (39). Gide clearly intended for his journals to travel, but he also hoped that they would travel as discourse directly traceable to his own voice. Clifford reminds us of Benveniste's classic discussion of discourse as intrinsically relying on the "presence of the speaking subject and the immediate situation of communication" (39). In a sense, the choice not to attempt an ethnographic account of what he saw in Africa spared Gide the constraints and limits of textuality as a mediated attempt at the interpretation of African cultures. The direct presence of journal entries made on the spot and ostensibly delivered intact to the reader gives his *Voyage au Congo* an immediacy that could be more readily put to political ends.

The *Voyage au Congo* places the field of truth at a premium over imagination or invention: Gide says to his readers that he has witnessed a dramatic situation, one that he will relate in a language that aims to communicate irrefutable truths. Since the facts of his account are practically unverifiable by the reader, the authority of his discourse depends on the renown and reliability of the author. In order to bolster his claims to political urgency, Gide invokes the corroborating testimony of Auguste Chevalier and Savorgnan de Brazza, whose earlier denunciations and warnings about the human abuses in the Congo had not been heeded (476). Gide's insistence on authority will endow his political message with a power that anticipates Foucault's later analysis of the reciprocal relationship between power and discourse. His discourse must circulate in the public sphere, and it must address the institutional and cultural structures that attach themselves to the colonial venture. Although Gide stops short of exploring the systems of thought that allowed colonialism to take hold, he does concentrate on a restricted, localized practice within the larger enterprise. As a social and historical phenomenon, colonialism is also a discursive construct that wields immense power and has a diffuse form of authorship which organizes the actors into fields of possible action. These agents form themselves as they are forming colonial policies and practices. This reciprocity characterizes both the power relationship and the discursive relationship that separates Gide's anticolonialist discourse from a narrative form of opposition. His discursive account of colonial abuses feeds into a system of knowledge that places him at the intersection of institutional power and intellectual opposition. Gide elaborates a powerful strategy by associating himself with Marc Allégret's film or attending public forums or following the parliamentary debate on the concessions. A discourse derives its power from its public performance. Words in a text would not have reached so far, or so deep.

The impact of Gide's account of the Congo relies directly on the author's prestige and on a model of pre-scientific reliance on authority and the primacy of belief over proof. The author here becomes an authority, having created a narrative that contains and represents "truth," still conceived as a relative, if singular notion for Gide and many of his contemporaries. As we might anticipate, the public controversy caused by Gide's account of shortcomings and abuses in colonial Africa drew vigorous rebuttals from many quarters. Much of this exchange belongs to the debate and is reproduced in an appendix to the published travel journals themselves. As might be expected, these counterdiscourses centered on the truth-value of Gide's ability to witness and comprehend events and circumstances outside of his customary realm of understanding. The argument was leveled, therefore, that he must have deformed the unseen or misunderstood truth of Africa in his written depiction. Gide ripostes in his important 1927 article "La Détresse de notre Afrique Équatoriale" by pointing out that he, André Gide, had actually crossed large parts of Africa on foot whereas M. Weber, director of the C.F.S.O., had never even visited the large concession that he controlled from his Paris office with his numerous colonial agents (480). This appeal to authoritative discourse is familiar in the religious, political, and academic spheres, as is the counterargument based on discrediting the author himself rather than the facts of his account. Interestingly enough, the attacks on Gide's Congo journals did not raise the issue of his homosexuality, by that point a matter of public knowledge, as an insidious means of undermining the impact of his narrative. In an ironic twist on the question of "truth" and "authority," the French Minister of Colonies stated proudly that he had not relied solely on Gide's written account of the Congo to form his own judgment. He had also sought out the man himself, commenting that "when one wants to know the truth, it is not enough to look for it in books" (Porra 170).

A Man with a Mission

The status of Gide's public campaign in the 1920s to expose abuses in the French colonies became even more complicated by virtue of the fact that Gide's own trip through French Equatorial Africa was undertaken with the permission and assistance of the French colonial government. Gide had requested in June 1925 an official "free" mission that was readily granted. This official seal of approval allowed him to call on French colonial administrators and officials for shelter, transportation, and native carriers. The mission was "free" in the sense that it was not financed by the French government itself. The motive that Gide gives in his official request to the Minister of Colonies is patently ethnographic in nature, suggesting that scientific inquiry was more likely to garner a favorable response than would intellectual curiosity or sexual tourism. In his request, Gide proposes to "study" in some depth four regions of the territory known as French Equatorial Africa.[6] He proposes to write a specialized monograph describing the social, religious, and racial characteristics of each territory with a view to suggesting ways of improving their condition. The first entry in his future *Voyage au Congo* points to the anomaly at the heart of the project: he and Marc are the only ones traveling "for pleasure."[7] The colonies are above all a business, something to conquer, exploit, develop, and administer but not really to enjoy. Upon returning to France, Gide will comment in his 1927 article in the *Revue de Paris:* "One does not travel in the Congo for one's pleasure."[8] This reflects the physical difficulties that Gide and Allégret encountered during the trip, especially the final stages when the sick and travel-weary pair beat a hasty retreat to France. Their focus had turned from improvement of the African Other to their own survival. The preoccupation with progress, a cornerstone of the nineteenth-century ideology that fueled colonial expansion, allied itself quite well with the prevailing attitude in France in the 1920s and 1930s: the colonizing nation had a duty toward the inferior civilizations to bring them progressively and humanely into the modern, enlightened era. Raoul Girardet's study of the French idea of colonialism underscores the progressive and humanitarian stance, often linked to socialism, that attributed a civilizing benefit to the French imperial presence around the world (216). Radical anticolonialism remained less common throughout the *entre-deux-guerres,* with most well-intentioned intellectuals content to denounce the abuses of a system that they did not fundamentally condemn.

The Minister, in granting Gide the official support of the French government, underscores his hope that this prestigious *missionnaire* will create an interest in the colonies among French youth, even if only from a tourist point of view. This propagandizing role would have found an influential spokesperson in Gide, whose fame was at its apogee and who spoke to the conscience of many young French men and women of that generation. The Ministry did not anticipate that Gide's report would turn out to be so unfavorable to the French cause in Africa. Gide's intention to spend longer periods of time in selected regions did not occur as planned; his journal reads at times as if it were relating the travels of an *homme pressé* [man in a hurry]. Gide never wrote the ethnographic study he had proposed, although one might consider Marc Allégret's extensive piece on the Massa-Mousgoum of northern Cameroon to be more in that vein (Allégret 267–289). The film shot by Gide's companion also owes a good deal to the ethnographic field that was finding its style and conventions at that time. Indeed, the *entre-deux-guerres* was the period for consolidation of the whole scientific discipline of ethnography devoted to the study of other cultures and civilizations. Gide's own interests and preoccupations, however, were elsewhere.

Traveling Through Cultures, or What Monsieur Gide Saw

Gide's initial reaction to Africa is more aesthetic and cognitive than cultural or ethnographic: he notes how new he is in the land and how difficult it is to know where to look (29). He is too new, untrained, and unfamiliar, without landmarks and vantage points from which to comprehend this new land. As he says, "one does not write well under the influence."[9] Vision has long been a powerful means of apprehending and rendering the world. It constitutes the West's most privileged marker of distance and difference between observer and observation. As a cognitive and ultimately ideological process, visualization involves recognition and familiarity. In an attempt to make sense of what he observes, Gide draws many African scenes into a familiar European field of reference: a village in ruins becomes "a sort of African Pompeii";[10] gigantic trees do not look older than oaks found in France or olive trees in Italy (403); the African woman becomes Eve, *"éternel féminin,"* albeit with sagging breasts (121). Thus visualization becomes even more critical given the many other ways in which the European visitor cannot interact with his African surroundings. Such distance has always been the cornerstone of a Western quest for objective truth and impartial witnessing of external reality. It replaces contact and protects the privileges of the observer; the superior vantage point is what allows him ultimately to wield the discourse of truth. Although the first-person narrative reinforces constantly the presence of Gide the man vis-à-vis Gide the scriptor, his writerly position is grounded more closely in a Flaubertian aesthetic of detachment. In a sense, the conflicts that lie at the heart of Gide's text might be said to come from the tension between the nineteenth-century aesthetic position inherited from Flaubert and the twentieth-century ethical stance that leads to political *engagement* à la Sartre.

Gide not only apprehends the African reality visually; he conjugates the visual as a necessary factor in understanding the strange and exotic spectacle that unfolds before him. As he begins the first leg of his trip by boat up the Congo River from Stanley Pool (what he calls in fitting literary terms the "prologue"), Gide notes that he has everything to learn and that he is "spelling" the landscape that he can only observe from a distance (33). His journey will place before him a succession of peoples and places that will provide a sense of "spectacle," sometimes magnificent, more often monotonous (32, 174). In a revealing comment dated October 18, he wonders whether his "imaginary representation" of Africa will not ultimately replace his real observations once he is back in France (87). Africa is, after all, an empty signifier waiting to be defined, an undetermined place holder with no fixed contours and no set boundaries, as much a product of Western imagination and discourse as it is an autonomous reality. Gide goes on to comment that the beauty of the outside world remains the same, while the virginity of the gaze is lost (87). He complains frequently about the indistinct, fuzzy images that correspond to nothing familiar, nothing recognizable. If reading is always at some level rereading, it is not hard to understand his frustration and the reasons why he attempts to "read" Africa like a text. Africa was for Gide first and foremost a text, although a text without an object. Without prior knowledge and experience, Gide can only rely on his own European coordinates in a world without a center where lines go off in all directions and everything seems limitless (136).

The Shape of the Land

Landscapes play an important part in the exotic quest. The European gaze over its newly discovered, newly conquered landscapes represented a clear mark of domination in colonialist discourse. With stereotypical images of the African landscape packed in his bags, Gide manifests his frequent disappointment at not finding what the "program" led him to expect. As in much colonial travel writing, the landscapes are devoid of most human content, reserved for aesthetic and naturalistic pleasure rather than for social and human contact. On the outskirts of Bosoum, Gide notes:

> Every time that the landscape takes shape, sets limits, and appears to be organized in some way, it reminds me of some part of France; but the landscapes in France are always better constructed, more distinctly drawn, and more singularly elegant.[11]

Once at Bosoum, Gide basks in the intense pleasure of the light and heat and clear air, but his gaze is drawn out over the undulating landscape that is uniformly monotonous and uninspiring. He spends the whole day there without any desire to go and see any part of this landscape any closer. Gide draws from this episode an aesthetic principle: the notion of differentiation that is critical in appreciating what is rare and exquisite, a lesson that could be the main lesson he will take away from his trip (176).

This monotony in the landscape extends to the people he encounters, people who lack individuality and individuation; the villages by and large suffer from uniformity and are like their anonymous inhabitants, who share similar tastes, values, goals, etc. (174–175). The Africans are most often depicted in terms of "herds" (36) or "swarms" (17) without any individual characteristics other than those attributed to their race. This lack of differentiation leads to a hierarchy of judgments about the African peoples that he meets. Gide reproduces some of the most deprecatory racial stereotypes, qualifying Africans as "cannibals" (18) or comparing them to squatting macaques (67). Such slurs do little to thaw out the image of a continent frozen in time and resigned to its inferior condition. There are exceptional moments when Gide admires a particular village or tribe, such as will be the case with the Massa of northern Cameroon, whose architecture, customs, music, manners, and social organization he finds "admirable," the adjective of choice to qualify all that pleases the eye (275–279). For the most part, however, Gide's characterization of the Africans is either condescending or disparaging or paternalistically optimistic. Incapable of writing an original text, Gide most often repeats the rather unoriginal stereotypes of Africans as mentally limited (130), sexually precocious (176), hypersensitive because closer to nature (176), and devoid of reason and logic (299). These abusive qualifications, while not surprising for the times, do stand out as shocking in a text by André Gide, who had earned a reputation for vigorously challenging such simplistic thinking in other realms, notably in the religious realm or as concerns homosexuality. Gide does not seem to have undertaken large quantities of serious reading about Africa before his trip, leaving that task to his young companion, Marc Allégret. The notes in Gide's text were added after the trip and include praise for such early ethnographers as Lévy-Bruhl, whose books on the primitive mentality posited an essentialist distinction between evolved, logical thinking and pre-logical, mystical thought based on a spirit of participation rather than on contradiction. Africa thus came to represent for Gide, as for many

Europeans of his day, the possibility of a simpler harmony, an authentic glimpse of human nature stripped of civilizing forces.

Colonies (nos). S'attrister quand on en parle

Flaubert's injunction to feel sadness and remorse when speaking of our colonies rings true even in our own day. Gide does not seem to have taken heed of the warning before undertaking his Congo journey, nor does he seem to have been especially aware of or concerned by the rising tide of criticism of the French colonial venture. One looks in vain for any serious discussion of Challaye, Morel, or even Brazza in his writings. His discovery of the abuses of the colonial regime relies instead on his own firsthand observation and reflects the combination of a highly emotive temperament and an evangelical, humanitarian idealism. His conscience will be touched by the troubling relationship between colonizer and colonized, which revolves around what Albert Memmi analyzes as a condition of "privilege" that separates the two groups. Gide's political and social coming of age will manifest itself along lines of class consciousness, although one might wonder if this class consciousness cannot be considered a re-encoded racial discourse resulting from his personal contact with Africans. His analyses of French colonization in Africa are no more grounded in a strict ideology, Marxist or other, than will be his political positions of the succeeding years. Gide's position remains oppositional even as he maintains close ties with the very apparatus he critiques.

His very presence in the French colony often places him in an awkward position. He knows, for example, that a score of African women, some with nursing babies, toiled in the rain all night to repair a dirt-and-rock road that only the provincial governor, and his expedition, will ever use. He is also aware that the carriers, sometimes as many as eighty men, were recruited locally to carry a 25-kilo load on their heads for 1F25 a day, food not included and with no return indemnity. As a gesture of good will, Gide's party would often feed their carriers a goat or bird in addition to the staple manioc and round up the sum of their wages. These little extras would delight the carriers so much that, instead of the customary address "Governor," they would call Gide "Government"— the irony was probably so obvious as to go unnoticed. The party did, however, make not infrequent use of the *tipoyeurs,* or chair carriers, when the weather was too hot or the march too long. Like most tourist relationships, the carriers were the natives with whom Gide came into contact most frequently and on whom he based many of his judgments about African cultures. He came to admire the people's loyalty and vigorous health, their politeness and honesty. He undertook to teach Adoum, his guide and interpreter, how to read and write French, an activity that led Gide to comment on how stupid whites are when they portray blacks as being stupid. He nonetheless goes on: "I believe, however, that [the Africans] are only capable of a limited development, their brains being dim and stagnant in the dark of night— but how often whites seem set on pushing them further down."[12] It remains nevertheless obvious that the presence of Europeans, even the most benevolent, was a direct cause of these exploitative forms of human labor, without which no such trip could have been undertaken. Like colonialism itself, like the railroad, portage was considered by Gide to be a necessary evil toward a greater good, with Africans ultimately benefiting from their cooperation with their European masters.

The African Village Scene

The village represents the basic morphological unit in the African grammar of the European traveler. Villages stand in contrast to larger towns and cities, which are products of European imperialism and which, for Gide and others, have corrupted the pure and authentic African primitive that they postulate. Villages dot the landscape, providing clusters of human presence among the vast emptiness that is synonymous with Africa. In this repetition of a classic Africanist paradigm, Gide observes: "as always in this boundless land, nothing is centered; lines go off haphazardly in all directions; everything is without limits."[13] In contrast, he notes his joy at encountering a village that is neat, proper, and clean, that has a chief dressed in European clothes who speaks French correctly, and that has a French flag hoisted in their honor (173). The village typically provides the traveler an opportunity to replenish supplies, recruit new carriers, and conduct business with the local populations. The relationship that Gide and Allégret establish with the natives is one familiar to tourists: their principal interactions with the local populations aim at obtaining food, shelter, and services or inquiring about local customs and sites to visit. They will occasionally don the masks of journalists, missionaries, explorers, *cinéastes,* doctors, scientists, or ambassadors. In typical tourist fashion, their principal challenge remains the difficult understanding of a social and cultural system that has few familiar parameters. The radical difference that is Africa defies and denies Gide's cognitive and epistemological abilities. He quickly abandons all pretense of carrying out the ethnographic observations that were supposed to constitute the aim of his official mission. He avows that he is "too new to the land"[14] and will slowly discover the true *raison d'être* of his journey in his investigation of the abuses of the concessions.

Gide will utilize the African village as the perfect décor for performing his power play. Seen in an early passage from the deck of the *Largeau* that takes them up the Congo, the villages are anything but inviting: "In the villages along the river, we meet few people who are not blemished, bruised, or hideously scarred (most often due to the yaws). And all these resigned people laugh, have fun, wallowing in a sort of precarious happiness, doubtless unable to imagine a better life."[15] A first shift in Gide's perceptions occurs about two months into the trip, following many journal entries that record his observations and, more often, his frustrations at not being able to see anything distinctly. On an automobile excursion to the waterfalls at M'Bali (admirably filmed by Marc Allégret), Gide describes the welcome scene at one of the villages. As their motor party approaches, the villagers greet their European visitors with military salutes, assuming that they play some official role. In response to their least gestures, these same villagers break out in cries of joy and peals of laughter. "If I wave toward the children as we drive through one of the numerous villages, it sets off a delirious, frenetic tremor in the crowd, a sort of joyous enthusiasm."[16] Finally, at their lunch stop, crowds of children press around their hut to observe these European visitors eat, as Gide puts it, like the crowds at the Jardin d'Acclimatation who flock to see the feeding of the seals. This is a pivotal scene in Gide's *parcours* because he realizes that he is as much the object of the Africans' curiosity as they are of his. Rather than maintaining the unidirectional gaze of ethnographic representation focused on the African object, Gide redirects their gaze toward his own person. He strategically seeks to reverse the colonial imbalance of power while performing his own Frenchness amidst France's colonized subjects.

This cultural contact leads to a reversal of the most basic relationships between colonized and colonizer, opening a space for reciprocity that Mary Louise Pratt has usefully studied. In analyzing Mungo Park's mid-nineteenth-century *Travels in the Interior of Africa,* Pratt notes that reciprocity is "the dynamic that above all organizes Park's human-centered, interactive narrative" (80). She develops the idea of reciprocity as being also one of the stories that capitalism tells itself about itself (84). The European ideal of equitable exchange, which long ago had disappeared from capitalist societies, provided one of the most seductive myths about primitive Africa and one that Gide sought to verify throughout his trip. Pratt ultimately connects these values to what she terms "the greatest non-reciprocal, non-exchange of all time: the Civilizing Mission" (85). Gide had come out to Africa to see, and now his *raison d'être* will be to be seen. This consciousness will get layered in the *Voyage au Congo* as Gide sees himself being seen, continuing the earlier spectator/actor dyad of the runaway coach episode. The monological perspective that contributes most often to the metonymic freezing associated with scientific ethnography gives way to a dynamics of reciprocal exchange and of dialogical interplay in that zone where contact is performed. The coin of strangeness and exoticism has two sides and will become the chief currency in his future exchanges around Africa.

From that point until his party reaches Islamicized Africa, Gide will note the glorious entries into each village where his cortege will attract throngs of curious observers and delirious onlookers. In anticipation of their arrival, the party begins to halt on the outskirts of certain villages to prepare their grand entry, Gide noting his amused satisfaction at playing the role of the "great white chief."[17] Runners soon precede the cortege to announce their arrival, and crowds line the roads in what Gide compares to the "entry into Jerusalem."[18] Since the men are away harvesting rubber or working on the railroad, these ceremonial greetings typically involve women, children, and elders. Gide is particularly bothered by the presence of the female element and their frenetic dances (113). The shrill voice of the elderly woman, *"la vieille folle,"* that greets them at each village is a source of much confusion and disarray. Their approach to successive villages includes throngs of women and children who line their path with cut vegetation and sand, pressing around them so hard that Gide qualifies their overwhelming greeting as being almost "cannibalism" (134). This "triumphal allure" will lead to the village chief's hut, where Gide encourages the villagers to demand two francs per kilo for their rubber and to verify the weight since the company agents are abusing their confidence and taking advantage of their ignorance of trade practices. This insertion of some suggestion of subversive or anticolonialist rhetoric admits resistance because of the very privileged status that Gide enjoys due to his nationality, race, class, and gender. Gide plays the infiltrator who tells the slave how to play the master's game although clearly, to reappropriate Audre Lorde's formula, the slave will not demolish the master's house using the master's tools.

When they find a deserted village or a cool greeting, it reminds Gide of the fear that the white man instills in the African who can be recruited as a carrier, taxed into economic servitude, or requisitioned to work on the Congo-Océan railway, which is a notorious devourer of human lives. As Gide's cortege advances, he turns these occasions into a public relations event designed, as he puts it, "to win these people back over to France."[19] This will occur, of course, by his public conduct and discourse aimed at demonstrating that all Frenchmen are not evil and cruel and that a noble, moral position on colonialism also exists. This vision of "good colonialism," in which the mutual interests of the colonizer and colonized coalesce, characterizes Gide's larger vision of the colonial question. He will perform that benevolent display at every turn while reserving the written analysis for his travel journal, official correspondence, and subsequent public campaign once back in France. Gide clearly attributes the higher function of writing to the analytical and the artistic, while the physicality of performance is reserved for his direct communication with the Africans themselves. The village scene thus becomes a site of unscripted, though ritualized improvisation that will be repeated regularly in theatrical fashion.

These contact zones become the space where power is performed and where the differential between colonizer and colonized becomes most evident. Gide's imposing cortege is regularly assumed by the Africans to be a paramilitary procession and elicits the appropriate salutes and postures proffered to the inspecting officers and dignitaries. It is his African onlookers who cast Gide in this uneasy role within the French colonial apparatus. If not a colonial agent, what else would he be doing out there? Such processions have existed, of course, since antiquity, usually to display military conquest, and Gide seems to have taken his cue from the Africans themselves, who assumed him to be their ruler. What is interesting in this realization is the manner in which Gide, in the presence of "primitive" peoples, adopts the rituals of archaic power, rather than assuming the more diffuse, internalized form of modern power described by Foucault. Based on the presumption of French superiority, both sides act out their assigned roles in a form of colonial contract. These ceremonies are strikingly reminiscent of the royal corteges of the Ancien Régime in which the monarch, in public performances and processions, became the embodiment of a higher form of power. Such theatrical, visible displays of power were important social and political rituals for the cohesion of the nation and for the assertion of the power relations between a ruler and his people. Gide likewise parades the superior colonial power before his African subjects. The writer who would be king grants audiences, distributes alms, and engages in the touching of subjects. Of course, he is operating not according to royal logic but in keeping with prevalent bourgeois paradigms consonant with his class, race, and gender. Gide is above all performing Frenchness, as he states quite clearly upon meeting the sultan of Reï Bouba: we are careful to do our best to represent "France, civilization, and the white race."[20] But the sultan is a proud leader and does not automatically assume that all white men are his superiors (390).

The Bambio Ball

The episode that will move Gide to discover his true mission in Africa takes place in late October near the village of N'Goto in the thick forest country between Bangui and Nola. The events are recounted both in the *Voyage au Congo* (92–99) and in the letter that Gide addressed to Governor General Lamblin from Nola on November 6, 1925 (451–455). A certain Samba N'Goto, mistakenly believing that Gide himself was the governor making his rounds, awakens him and Marc Allégret in the middle of the night. He has come to expose the gruesome massacre of some thirty-two men, women, and children in a neighboring village, a massacre carried out under the orders of Georges Pacha, chief administrator of the territory. In an attempt to impose the rule of law by force in one of the more contested areas of the vast French possession, Pacha was known to resort to cruel and repressive measures. The infamous "Bambio Ball" was organized to punish rubber workers who did not bring in their quotas: they were forced to carry heavy logs in the burning sun all day long and beaten if they fell off the pace. Even strong, healthy men did not survive this punishment for long. In a sense, Gide should not have been too surprised by these revelations since previous journalists and travelers had revealed similar cruel and inhumane acts, especially relating to the rubber trade. Gide, rather, analyzes the problem as resulting from insufficient personnel and insufficient funding to govern the territories in a humane, productive manner (102). He does not consider labor as exploitation, but rather as the necessary price to pay for material and social progress. In his 1927 article, Gide makes use of this interesting statement by Brazza from 1886: "Until ordered to change, our action should aim at transforming the natives into subjects who work, produce, and consume."[21] The problem stems, in large part, from the colonial relationship itself, through which France has assumed responsibility for its colonial dependencies. By the mid–1920s, this was the position taken by many socialist and leftist thinkers in France, who espoused the idea of social, economic, and cultural improvement of the colonies under government control or supervision. The "Bambio Ball," however, leads Gide to note how he had been living in a state of blissful ignorance, circulating in a maze of lies; now that he knows the terrible truth about the colonial regime, he must speak (103). The remainder of his journey, until May 1927, will include an ongoing investigation into the abuses that plague the French colony.

Gide's analysis revolves around a denunciation of the many ways that the

French possessions function poorly, yet without directly questioning the basic principle of colonialism itself. His 1927 article evokes the possibility of a "good" colonialism in which the "moral and material" interests of the colonizing and colonized peoples would converge (474). If French Equatorial Africa has not succeeded as a colony, its failures can be blamed on insufficient personnel and insufficient money (102). The skein of problems that Gide identifies includes the poor infrastructure of the French colonial regime (73), the absence of any type of stable market economy or pricing system that might encourage property and prosperity (63, 72), the incompatibility of European and African cultures (384). Worse, the concessionary companies have failed even to make any money (479–480). As we shall see, Gide's critique will focus on one of these companies, the C.F.S.O., rather than on the French colonial administration per se, which he by and large applauds for attempting to do a good job under untenable circumstances.

Making Concessions

If Gide's Congo journey can be considered political, it must be in the sense that he carefully constructed a campaign upon his return to France against a singular but visible target: the concessionary companies. Although Gide's journal entries chart his increased awareness of the deplorable situation in the African colonies, they contain few indications of the political action that he would subsequently deploy. The textual record of this political action lies, rather, in the marginalia of his travel journal and in the notes, letters, and articles consigned to the appendices, particularly in the second volume, *Le Retour du Tchad*. This position indicates not only their later addition to the main body of his travel writing but also their role as the new-found "meaning" that Gide ascribes to his trip. His journey had taken him from the geopolitical center of the French colonial empire to one of its largest but most peripheral possessions. Gide, like most other Europeans visiting Africa during the high colonial period, manifested a strong awareness of this journey into the margins of empire, of a trajectory outwards from the center, of a movement taking him from the locus of power and culture to the unmapped, undefined, and unrefined lands "out there." From a space of negativity, Gide would attempt through his political action to open up the possibility for there to emerge a positive and productive outcome to his journey. It is literally in the margins of his written record that one can discover what became Gide's truly central preoccupation within the French colonial debate.

The concession system was a perfect angle from which to attack the abusive colonial system, since it worked on the basis of long-distance exploitation and uncontrolled abuse of force and authority. In other words, Paris was the colonizing center where policies were set and directions taken that influenced millions of lives at a distance of several thousand kilometers. The timing of Gide's public offensive was determined by the fact that most of the concessions had been awarded in 1899 on a thirty-year lease basis, and their renewal would therefore be debated before Parliament soon after his return from the Congo. This government-controlled, monopolistic form of exploitation went against the basic tenet of free trade inscribed in the 1885 Berlin Conference accord that had initially divided up Africa among the European powers. The French government had subsequently conceded to forty companies the rights to exploit the natural resources in French Equatorial Africa, a territory larger than France itself. The lands were poorly mapped and largely inaccessible to Western-style development. In exchange, the companies were to pay the government a tax on all profits and respect certain general provisions about building or maintaining roads, waterways, etc. The companies generally raised capital through public stock offerings. The number of companies quickly diminished due to either bankruptcy or mergers, resulting by the 1920s in a small handful of very powerful entities within the colonial structure. Each company also had come to consider that the lease entitled it to recruit local labor, and the result was a situation tantamount to legalized slavery. The government provided armed police and even military support for the companies, whose agents acted with impunity in seeking to extract the greatest possible profit from the colony. In addition, they obtained the right by the turn of the century to tax the local population, thus creating the need for the villagers to work, usually as carriers or at collecting rubber. Some of the earliest scandals denounced by E. D. Morel, Auguste Chevalier, Albert Londres, or Brazza himself had detailed the cruel treatment of natives who were either forcibly displaced from their villages or killed outright or allowed to die from hunger or disease. The population of French Equatorial Africa is estimated to have gone from 15 million at the turn of the century to 9 million at the outbreak of World War I to as low as 2 to 3 million by the early 1920s.

Gide's particular critique was aimed at the Compagnie Forestière Sangha-Oubangui (C.F.S.O.), which held large privileges in the regions he visited. Rather than attacking the colonial administration or the French government (of which he had become an official representative), he elected to focus on a particularly blatant abuse of privilege and power that few could condone. Gide mounted a detailed, documented attack on the C.F.S.O., using official statistics and reports alongside his own firsthand observations. His accusations were even more incisive because the C.F.S.O. did not even have the redeeming virtue of turning a profit, and this despite the fact that it paid natives a lower price for rubber than in most other areas of West Africa (479–482). In addition, the company allowed or even encouraged repressive measures against the natives, such as those exposed by Samba N'Goto. Finally, the company had violated the public trust by refusing to invest in any sort of durable development of the colony, such as transportation, health, or education (80–85). This corresponds to the vision Gide lays out in his 1927 article: "If the moral and material interests of the two peoples and the two nations, the colonizing and the colonized, are not allied, then colonization will not work."[22] Gide's position is clearly stated by the framed reference to colonization, which can be good or bad, whereas colonialism as a system does not come under close scrutiny or criticism.

Through this high-profile, public campaign directed against the concessionary companies, Gide was engaging on a political level with questions that he had previously ignored. The fact that the whole polemical debate took place through articles in the Parisian press leads one to suppose that Gide considered that the cause of the abuses he had witnessed— and their ultimate solution— lay more in the French capital than in the African bush. It also allowed Gide to wield more familiar power relations and to navigate in a *habitus* he could better understand and control. It is in that sense that Gide's personal positions and investment can be considered "political." Daniel Durosay, in his valuable introduction to Marc Allégret's travel journal and in his numerous articles on the Congo journey, has argued in convincing fashion that the publications of Gide's writings and the premiere of Allégret's film were carefully orchestrated with a view to maximizing their public exposure and impact. Not surprisingly, Gide's two books and his 1927 article received great praise on the left of the political spectrum, which chose to pass over their more conservative endorsement of the basic principles of colonialism. In fact, excerpts and quotations from the books have to a large extent replaced the work itself. "The less intelligent the White Man is, the more stupid he finds the Black" still rings in readers' ears as the most durable sound bite of Gide on Africa. The colonial establishment either tried to create a blackout around his writings or attempted to discredit them on the basis of his relatively short stay in Africa or his personal agenda in demoralizing the patriotic efforts of his countrymen abroad. One contested aspect of Gide's writings persists: the belief that large excerpts of his works were read before the French Parliament during debates over the renewal of the government concessions. While it is true that his exposé was widely commented on and discussed, Véronique Porra has maintained that there is no record of official examination of his writings (169–171). The concessions were not renewed beyond their expiration in 1929 although, of course, the economics of colonialism took on other forms and practices, many of them more directly sponsored and supervised by the government itself.

Congo-Océan: *La Machine*

It is also important to point out Gide's blind spots, the most significant of which must have been his underestimation of the high human cost of building the Congo-Océan, the railroad line from Brazzaville to the coast. Begun in 1921 and not completed until 1934, the construction involved over 127,000 African laborers requisitioned from other regions and forced to abandon home and family with little or no certainty of returning alive. By conservative estimates, there were 20,000 native casualties either in transit to the construction site or due to the dangerous working conditions imposed by the French administration (Coquery-Vidrovitch 194–195). The Africans referred to the railroad as the "machine," and it proved indeed to be a "ferocious devourer of human lives," as Gide would note later.[23] In addition to the direct toll in loss of human life, one can only speculate about the disastrous economic, social, and cultural consequences of the railroad construction on local ways of life. Gide's position remains problematic and ambiguous: on the one hand, he condemns the human drama of forced recruitment of laborers, yet on the other, his subsequent remarks

either lose sight of that dramatic situation or attempt to justify the necessary sacrifices of the African people in the modernization of the colony (474). His own
personal attachment to Marcel de Coppet, charged with the recruitment of
laborers, placed Gide in an awkward moral and political position. He nevertheless seems to have passed by the "grove of death" depicted in Conrad's *Heart of
Darkness* without fully measuring the depth of destruction taking place. Gide's
condemnation stems from a humanitarian, evangelical position in the face of
extreme human suffering, yet he does not analyze the economic or political
powers that created such a situation. Because it is poorly run, the colonial enterprise is beneficial neither for the colonizers nor for the colonized. Although his
narrative alerts readers to the suffering caused by the Congo-Océan, French
readers had to await Albert Londres's 1928 *Terre d'ébène* for a detailed and
resounding condemnation of this absurd form of man's inhumanity to man.

France's Inefficiency as a Colonial Power

If discursive power can be measured to some extent by the ways it finds itself
recuperated and refracted in other settings, the final episode of Gide's Congo
writings contains a sobering lesson. In 1940, with France occupied by Hitler's
armies, the German propaganda machine wished to discredit the French in the
eyes of the British and Americans. It seized upon the idea of publishing well-
selected excerpts, in translation, of Gide's Congo journals under the title *Experiences in the Congo: France's Inefficiency as a Colonial Power*. The introduction
establishes Gide's credentials as a teller of truth, as an authoritative voice to be
heeded, as someone who "simply states facts, ever intent on getting as far as possible at the root of things" (8). While expressing reservations about the "vari-
able" character of Gide's writing as the work of a man whose "soul is tortured
by unrest" (7), this German edition nevertheless stresses his "uncompromising
love of truth" (7) and the irrefutable veracity of his account of French colonialism. It concludes: "The Congo horrors are merely another example of the
criminal inefficiency of the French as colonizers. The methods employed by
France in governing her colonies have brought disgrace upon her name. This is
the inference to be drawn from André Gide's descriptions of his travels" (39).
The recuperation of selections from Gide's writings in support of German propaganda underscores their potential use and abuse as authentic, authoritative discourse. His political writings contain many of the ambiguities of his literary
works and lend themselves to a wide range of causes and interpretations, even
those most contrary to the author's own ethical and ideological beliefs.

Notes

1. "Tout ici semble promettre le bonheur, la volupté, l'oubli" (17).
2. "Un livre d'André Gide sur l'Afrique, ce n'est pas rien. Gide, c'est un maître à penser
   dont l'autorité est tout de même plus assurée et plus crédible que celle d'un nouveau
   philosophe. En cette conjoncture où l'Afrique noire préoccupe tant de gens, pour

des raisons aussi diverses que douteuses, le moins qu'on puisse dire, c'est que la voix posthume de ce très grand bonhomme ne serait pas de trop" (R[emos] 30).

3. "Ne pensez-vous pas que si ce livre particulièrement lucide et courageux d'un des plus grands et des plus pénétrants écrivains français sur l'Afrique, c'est-à-dire sur les rapports de violence instaurés par la domination occidentale entre les Blancs et les Noirs, doit être lu, c'est, sans doute, mieux qu'à aucune autre époque, en ce moment où des bataillons de coopérants français, spirituellement démunis envahissent le continent noir, armés en définitive des mêmes préjugés pernicieux que leurs devanciers de l'époque coloniale?" (R[emos] 34).

4. "Moins le blanc est intelligent, plus le noir lui paraît bête" (26).

5. "Mais comment se faire écouter? Jusqu'à présent, j'ai toujours parlé sans aucun souci qu'on m'entende; toujours écrit pour ceux de demain, avec le seul désir de durer. J'envie ces journalistes dont la voix porte aussitôt, quitte à s'éteindre sitôt ensuite. Circulais-je jusqu'à présent entre des panneaux de mensonges? Je veux passer dans la coulisse, de l'autre côté du décor, connaître enfin ce qui se cache, cela fût-il affreux. C'est cet « affreux » que je soupçonne, que je veux voir" (103).

6. Although I use the term "Congo" in obedience to Gide's usage, the political map of Africa did not at that time contain such a nation.

7. "[P]our le plaisir" (13).

8. "On ne voyage pas au Congo pour son plaisir" (475).

9. "On n'écrit pas bien dans l'ivresse" (28).

10. "[U]ne sorte de Pompeï nègre" (157).

11. "Chaque fois que le paysage se forme, se limite et tente de s'organiser un peu, il évoque en mon esprit quelque coin de France; mais le paysage de France est toujours mieux construit, mieux dessiné et d'une plus particulière élégance" (174).

12. "Je ne les crois pourtant capables, que d'un très petit développement, le cerveau gourd et stagnant le plus souvent dans une nuit épaisse — mais combien de fois le blanc semble prendre à tâche de les y enfoncer" (130).

13. "[M]ais, comme toujours dans ce pays démesuré, rien ne fait centre; les lignes fuient éperdument dans tous les sens; tout est illimité" (136).

14. "[T]rop neuf dans le pays" (29).

15. "On rencontre, dans les villages le long du fleuve, bien peu de gens qui ne soient pas talés, tarés, marqués de plaies hideuses (dues le plus souvent au pian). Et tout ce peuple résigné rit, s'amuse, croupit dans une sorte de félicité précaire, incapable même d'imaginer sans doute un état meilleur"(51).

16. "Si j'agite ma main vers des enfants, en traversant un des nombreux villages, c'est un délire, des trépignements frénétiques, une sorte d'enthousiasme joyeux" (59).

17. "[G]rand chef blanc" (97).

18. "[E]ntrée à Jérusalem" (108).

19. "[R]egagner ce peuple à la France" (171).

20. "[L]a France, la civilisation, la race blanche" (392).

21. "Notre action, jusqu'à nouvel ordre, doit tendre surtout à préparer la transformation des indigènes en agents de travail, de production, de consommation" (476).

22. "Les intérêts moraux et matériels des deux peuples, des deux pays, j'entends le pays colonisateur et le pays colonisé, s'ils ne sont liés, la colonisation est mauvaise" (474).

23. "[U]n effroyable consommateur de vies humaines" (200).

Works Cited

Allégret, Marc. *Carnets du Congo : Voyage avec Gide.* Introduction and notes by Daniel Durosay. Paris: Presses du C.N.R.S., 1987.

Bhabha, Homi K. *The Location of Culture*. London: Routledge, 1994.

Clifford, James. *The Predicament of Culture: Twentieth-Century Ethnography, Literature, and Art*. Cambridge: Harvard University Press, 1988.

Coquery-Vidrovitch, Catherine. *Le Congo au temps des grandes compagnies concessionnaires 1898–1930*. Paris: Mouton, 1972.

Delay, Jean. *La Jeunesse d'André Gide*. Vol. I. Paris: Gallimard, 1956.

Durosay, Daniel. "Le livre et les cartes. L'espace du voyage et la conscience du livre dans le *Voyage au Congo*." *Littérales* 3 (1988): 41–75.

———. "*Le Voyage au Congo* et son livre-fantôme : la mise en question du Journal." *Littérales* 7 (1990): 121–147.

Gates, Henry Louis, Jr., ed. *"Race," Writing, and Difference*. Chicago: University of Chicago Press, 1986.

Geldof, Koenraad. "Authority, Reading, Reflexivity: Pierre Bourdieu and the Aesthetic Judgment of Kant." *Diacritics* 27.1 (Spring 1997): 20–43.

Gide, André. *Experiences in the Congo: France's Inefficiency as a Colonial Power*. Berlin, 1940.

———. *Journal 1889–1939*. Paris: Gallimard, Bibliothèque de la Pléiade, 1951.

———. *Voyage au Congo, suivi de Le Retour du Tchad*. Paris: Gallimard "Idées," 1927, 1928.

Girardet, Raoul. *L'Idée coloniale en France de 1871 à 1962*. Paris: La Table Ronde, 1972.

Johnson, Barbara. "Writing." *Critical Terms for Literary Study*. Ed. Frank Lentricchia and Thomas McLaughlin. 2nd ed. Chicago: University of Chicago Press, 1995. 39–49.

Miller, Christopher. *Blank Darkness: Africanist Discourse in French*. Chicago: University of Chicago Press, 1985.

Porra, Véronique. *L'Afrique dans les relations franco-allemandes entre les deux guerres*. Frankfurt: Verlag für Interkulturelle Kommunikation, 1995.

Pratt, Mary Louise. *Imperial Eyes: Travel Writing and Transculturation*. London: Routledge, 1992.

Rabinow, Paul. "Representations are Social Facts: Modernity and Post-Modernity in Anthropology." *Writing Culture: The Poetics and Politics of Ethnography*. Ed. James Clifford and George E. Marcus. Berkeley: University of California Press, 1986. 234–261.

R[emos], V[ince]. "Un éditeur au-delà de tout soupçon." *Peuples Noirs / Peuples Africains* 13: 29–34.

CHAPTER 6

Sightseeing: *Voyage au Congo* and the Ethnographic Spectacle

Jeffrey Geiger

Can it be that I, the elderly predecessor of those scourers of the jungle, am the only one to have brought back nothing but a handful of ashes? Is mine the only voice to bear witness to the impossibility of escapism? Like the Indian in the myth, I went as far as the earth allows one to go, and when I arrived at the world's end, I questioned the people, the creatures and things I found there and met with the same disappointment: "He stood still, weeping bitterly, praying and moaning. And yet no mysterious sound reached his ears, nor was he put to sleep in order to be transported, as he slept, to the temple of the magic animals. For him there could no longer be the slightest doubt: no power, from anyone, had been granted him . . ."

—Claude Lévi-Strauss, *Tristes Tropiques*

Contemporary readers approaching André Gide's *Voyage au Congo* and *Le Retour du Tchad* are likely to feel a certain amount of anticipation at the idea of the self-absorbed man of letters retracing the steps of Joseph Conrad's *Heart of Darkness*. We inevitably wonder whether Gide's persistent self-regard will at last find itself challenged: perhaps the precision of his prose will break down in the face of encounters with exotic locales and strange practices on the fringes of colonial control. Of course, these expectations are bound to be disappointed. For in these journals—through monotonous treks on foot, by horseback, boat, and car; through oppressive heat, bitterly cold nights, and hookworms burrowing into his flesh—Gide maintains the utmost sense of *civility*. At any given moment along the way, we might find the author uncorking a half-bottle of Cliquot, reading from Bossuet's funeral oration on Henrietta of England, "plunging" into Goethe's *Elective Affinities* after being carried for hours by bearers in a *tipoye*, or avidly writing amidst the "sickly stench" of a whale-boat (*Travels* 250), while strips of hippopotamus skin periodically rain blood—"or, more accurately, . . . sanguineous liquid"—all around (*Travels* 250).[1] It is possible to mistake such resilient civility for a form of national chauvinism during the period of "high" colonial administration in French Equatorial Africa, but the case of Gide's travels is not so simple. As a young Roland Barthes observed of the persona that often glimmers through the journals, Gide's figure has too often been perceived wholly in terms of good or evil; critics should beware of formulating overly reductive conceptions of Gide's self-projections. The journals are certainly works of egoism, but, as Barthes confirms, they are also works of perpetual self-correction, bespeaking a writer in constant fear of being misinterpreted. There are no simple critical solutions to the constantly shifting figure who appears and disappears throughout these texts, and these diaries are no exception. Thus to resolve questions of Gide's primitivism, exoticism, or colonial politics requires a sustained examination not only of his emerging conceptions of French colonial relations in the Congo, but also of his own shifting politics of self-representation as he experiences a distant and alien environment.[2]

I am first interested in examining what is likely frustrating to readers who approach Gide from a postcolonial perspective: his apparent reliance on the trappings of colonial "civility," even at what seems the most inappropriate times. In spite of his notable, and now quite famous, shades of cultural relativism, Gide's maintenance of chauvinistic control is evident not just in his actions, but in an "us and them" tone that often pervades the journals. These strategies of using the text as a vehicle for distancing and controlling his encounters might appear at odds with Gide's nonconformist ethics of *disponibilité* [openness] and his frequently stated desire to break free of a rigid, homogeneous—perhaps even colonial—French sensibility. It is tempting to view these strategies as reminiscent of the "civil" critical distance so highly regarded by traditional ethnographers performing anthropological research in the field; as Henrietta Moore notes, the relationship between self and other in modern ethnographic and travel accounts has a distinctive mark: the simultaneous desirability and fear of "going native." Going native, Moore contends, "is ultimately a fear about the erasure of difference, and in that erasure the loss of self" (115). Yet if this paradox lies at the heart of the "participant-observer" method of ethnographic research, Gide himself, though sometimes ambiguous about his motivations for traveling to the Congo, seems rarely threatened by the shadow of the west's others that might put selfhood at risk. Unlike the vivid, self-conscious explorations and tortured revelations of Michel Leiris—who in *L'Afrique fantôme* appears consumed by doubts, anxieties, and uncontrollable sexual desires in his role as part of the 1931–1933 Dakar-Djibouti ethnographic mission headed by Marcel Griaule[3]—Gide's stable identity and aesthetic integrity rarely seem endangered by his encounters. He instead takes refuge in his role *"voyageant en simple touriste"* (*Voyage* 111), a tourist who is hardly expected to "participate" or to authorize an exhaustive ethnographic or scientific account of his travels. This is clear in the opening pages of *Voyage au Congo,* where Gide seems hardly interested in ethnographic details, noting "All this not very interesting to tell . . . I leave the rest to the textbooks" (*Travels* 41),[4] but focuses instead on the merits of the landscape, on the configuration and aesthetic impact of villages and towns, and on his "scientific" mission of chasing down and cataloguing exotic butterflies. After returning to France in June 1926, Gide reworked the text and was evidently aware of the danger that its more "tragic parts, which it is important to bring out," might be "drowned under the abundance of descriptions, etc." (*Journals* 2: 380).[5] The "tragic parts" would include not only criticisms of the concessionary companies and the slavelike conditions under which Africans were laboring, but also his observations of widespread disease and neglect. Gide observes, firsthand, the ruthless exploitation of African peoples by the Compagnie Forestière, and often remarks on the generally mismanaged and badly trained colonial administration. Nonetheless his observations just as often become reduced to distant, aesthetic judgments. A description of a laboring group of Modjembo girls typifies the early pages of the *Voyage au Congo:* "their faces are ugly, but their busts admirable" (*Travels* 37).[6] Gide himself frequently comes across as an observer at a safe remove, consuming Africa as pure spectacle.

Though the journals have been seen as evidence of Gide's growing politicization, which was to culminate in his shift to Communism in the 1930s,[7] Gide did not, as Léon Pierre-Quint argued many years ago, "wish to call into question the principle of colonization itself, it is primarily the wretched horrors of its administration that he contests" (*André Gide: His Life* 264).[8] Years later, Gide would defend himself, arguing that his concern with "social problems" began long before encountering oppression in the Congo (*Journals* 3: 257).[9] More recently, Walter Putnam has again taken up this issue, aligning Gide's criticism of the French administration with Joseph Conrad's twenty-five years earlier, while pointing out that Gide never went so far as to suggest that colonialism per se be abolished but "asked himself what would be the best way to improve and 'moralize' the system already in place."[10] Consistent with the French policy of assimilation, Gide even encourages the civilizing mission of the colonial project, suggesting at one point a "flattering impression that we were winning these people over to France" (*Travels* 133).[11] The problem, in Gide's view, seems to be how to oversee the process of winning these people over at the governmental level, with access to only limited resources: "The circumscription is too vast; a single man who is without the means of rapid transport is unable to keep his eye on [*surveiller*] the whole of it" (*Travels* 72).[12] Proper surveillance of French Equatorial Africa is hindered by want of sufficient staff and sufficient money; Gide, in effect, is calling for a more extensive, panoptic version of colonial administration, and certainly not for a greater degree of indigenous self-determination.[13]

As Gide's demand for a more adequate form of surveillance suggests, his colonial politics were largely defined in oppositional terms that were occasionally, though importantly, problematized. Opposing images—west and non-west, the civilized and the primitive, those who look and those who are looked at—come to dominate his account. The second half of this essay will examine Gide's attitudes in terms of a phenomenon recently labeled the "ethnographic spectacle." As described by critics such as Fatimah Tobing Rony, the ethnographic spectacle is not precisely anthropological, but emerges at the intersections of evolving nineteenth-century discourses of anthropology, medicine, physiology, visual technology, and primitivism, which racialized the representation of "exotic" peoples and places. Rony's work focuses largely on Félix-Louis Regnault (a student of Étienne-Jules Marey, physiologist and pioneer of the early cinema), whose late-nineteenth-century chronophotographic studies of West

Africans at ethnographic expositions in France encouraged the explicit racializing of ethnographic images. By photographing, labeling, and differentiating those movements and behaviors determined to be "savage" from those assumed to be "civilized," Regnault's comparative visual studies set the stage for the chauvinistic primitivism that would dominate later ethnographic filmmaking.[14] Gide's and Marc Allégret's film of their travels, *Voyage au Congo,* is therefore not only a valuable, if partial, visual record of what they witnessed firsthand, but might also suggest other ways to situate and contextualize Gide's colonial politics, a politics clearly articulated not only in the written text but also through visual constructions of the peoples and places he encountered.

Travel and *Malaise*[15]

In the mid-1920s, encounters between what has ironically been referred to as the "West" and the "Rest" were at a transitional stage. George Stocking has observed of Boasian cultural anthropology in the United States that those who went out from the university to the field in the 1920s were beginning to develop the confidence that they could do ethnography "in a different, more efficient, more reliable, more 'scientific' way than the travelers, missionaries, and government officials whom they were pushing to the margins of the discipline" (209). At the same time in France, the disciplining of the ethnographic encounter was in fact just beginning to emerge. In 1925 Gide sold his collection of presentation copies and set sail for the Congo on an itinerary largely determined by his secretary, nephew, and traveling companion, Allégret;[16] the same year saw a nucleus of university scholars—Paul Rivet, Lucien Lévy-Bruhl, and Marcel Mauss—in the process of establishing the Institut d'Ethnologie in Paris.[17]

A number of recent critics have addressed the role of primitivism in the conceptual framework of figures such as Paul Morand, Georges Bataille, and Michel Leiris, as well as in the Dadaist and Surrealist movements.[18] Marie-Denise Shelton, for example, has usefully compared France's popular conception of the primitive in the 1920s to a "looking glass," in which the image of the European self was refracted as civilized (326). In the wake of the blunt savagery of the First World War, the call of the primitive offered itself as a respite from the fallen and self-destructive ways of the west. This movement was summed up in Louis Aragon's prophetic exclamation, *"Monde occidental, tu es condamné à mort"* (quoted in Shelton 326) [Occidental world, you are condemned to death]. But, as Marianna Torgovnick notes, the figure of the primitive also needed to stand apart, to promise and signify an experience of profound otherness, "with its aura of unchangeability, voicelessness, mystery, and difference from the west" (*Gone Primitive* 20).

It is clear that Gide sought from the primitive this sense of strangeness and estrangement from the familiar: in his journals he frequently expresses his longing for the taste of absolute difference. Observing a village near the falls of M'Bali, what moves him most is the manner in which the place signifies something absolutely other: a village "so strange and so beautiful that we felt we had found in it the very reason of our journey and its very core" (*Travels* 42).[19] Access to this strangeness is crucial to the success of the journey, yet is frustratingly ephemeral; indeed, what comes to distinguish the journals is that this promise of entering some world of absolute otherness is constantly unfulfilled. The strangeness of Africa is all too frequently lacking: the jungle is not dense enough, the landscape not wild enough. Instead, Gide often finds himself amidst a countryside "extremely monotonous and hardly at all exotic looking" (*Travels* 73).[20] He writes of Bangassou, "I am a little disappointed. The town has . . . lost much of its strangeness" (*Travels* 51).[21] In Bosoum, the people he sees remind him of "human cattle" (*Travels* 137),[22] and often he expresses the weariness of a tourist who has seen enough: "The women dance at the entrance to every village. This shameless jigging of elderly matrons is extremely painful to look at" (*Travels* 80).[23]

Ultimately, this sense of a traveler's detachment flows as a sort of undertow in the journals, Gide inscribing his *malaise,* in both senses of the word: feeling tired and also ill at ease, out of place, homeless. The opening lines of *Voyage au Congo* clearly set the tone, describing a state of "inexpressible languor; the hours slip by empty and indistinguishable" (*Travels* 3).[24] Journeying is, more often than not, about tedium: waiting for the unexpected that fails to appear. Still, it may seem odd that this tone pervades the journals, particularly as Gide was in the midst of one of the most prolific, and intensely personal, periods of his career. A month before his departure he had finished *Les Faux-Monnayeurs,* which was to appear while he was still in Africa; *Corydon* had appeared the year before, while the religious diary *Numquid et tu . . . ?* and the full public version of the confessional *Si le grain ne meurt* were soon to be ready for public sale. Perhaps more strongly than ever before, Gide's texts were to present a public figure in opposition to the social limitations of the French status quo. As Dennis Porter observes, Gide had been undertaking the investigation of what Baudelaire had called for in *Mon cœur mis à nu:* "the study of the great sickness of the horror of the home" (Porter 235). Porter, however, sees in Gide's travels not only signs of a desire for flight and displacement, but also the possibility of renewal. In essence, Gide's Congo travels were to offer the temptation of finding once again, in the exotic *there,* a sense of aesthetic vision, coherence, and the shock of the new, the farouche that French Equatorial Africa would ultimately fail to conjure up. "But in this country," he writes, "they have not the stern nobility—the kind of farouche and desperate joy that were mine in the desert" (*Travels* 59).[25]

The journey is a *de facto* act of psychic return, a fantasy "made in youth," but "realized in maturity" (*Travels* 4).[26] Barely twenty when he made up his mind to journey to the Congo, he now feels that he had not so much willed it as had it imposed upon him by a sort of "ineluctable fatality" (*Travels* 4).[27] But after more than thirty-six years his words now reflect more a sense of hesitation and uncertainty: a nagging feeling of "numbness—perhaps diminution" (*Travels* 17), where his "joy is perhaps as keen; but it penetrates less deeply . . . Oh, if only I could forget that life's promises are closing in before me!" (*Travels* 11).[28] As Putnam observes, this feeling of being perpetually out of place arises from an ongoing sensation of impossible return to a place that lives only in the imagination.

Gide began his journey by immersing himself in a textualized, Conradian dream, even wondering whether his imaginary idea of the country was so vivid that, "in the future, this false image will not be stronger than my memory of the reality and whether I shall see Bangui, for instance, in my mind's eye as it is really, or as I first of all imagined it would be" (*Travels* 60).[29]

Still, Gide clings to creating an image of the jungle that coincides with his desire, wanting to "enter *[pénétrer]* profoundly, intimately, into the heart of the country" (*Travels* 61), yet seeming all the while nascently aware that he will not find what he seeks, waiting "under a sky with no promise in it, over a landscape uninhabited by god, or dryad, or faun—an implacable landscape, with neither mystery in it nor poetry" (*Travels* 111).[30] Like the epigraph above, in which Lévi-Strauss laments not only the fallen state of an imagined primitive nature but also, curiously, the false "shadows" of ethnographic photography (41), Gide's experience of colonial Africa leaves him also feeling like a sort of "elderly predecessor" (Lévi-Strauss 41), a sightseer incapable of attaining magical vision or even escape: "the eye's virginity is lost" (*Travels* 60).[31] Sights take on the properties of mourning and loss, like western ruins: an abandoned village near Abo-Bougrima is described as "a kind of Negro Pompeii" (*Travels* 120).[32] At this point Gide expresses one of the sightseer's most mundane yet frustrating complaints: there is too little light for a photograph, leaving him unable to capture the visual splendor of a place that has moved him more than any other.

As the journey wears on, Gide finds himself chasing more than fleeting butterflies. He is frustrated at his inability to entrap and preserve brief moments of aesthetic epiphany, and the paradox of the traveler takes over: having sought escape from his existential unrest in physical adventure, he now finds himself always in thought, yet unable to pause for rest and reflection. As Harry Levin has suggested in his important survey of writers in exile, "Literature and Exile," deracination, voluntary exile, alienation, and spiritual homelessness can be seen as the hallmarks of modernist authors, where creative production often comes to depend on a state of perpetual homesickness. Gide figures largely among a group of authors who manipulate distance and displacement for aesthetic ends, Levin concluding that "detachment . . . of the one from the many . . . is the necessary precondition of all original thought" (81). Yet Caren Kaplan labels this type of critical position as distinctly modernist and essentially limited. Levin aims to define a modernist aesthetic while tending to downplay the specific historical conditions that give rise to literary activity. Exile is raised in Levin's writing to a higher level, championed as a way of "reinforcing other gifts" and highlighted as an essential step towards aesthetic gain (38–39).

Yet at moments in Gide's journals, travel comprises an exilic displacement that is anything but advantageous. Rest, reflection, and aesthetic contemplation seem unattainable, to be found neither in the metropolitan "here" *nor* in the primitive "there." Rather than supplying a sense of the author's heroic detachment of the one from the many, travel leaves Gide increasingly insecure about the adequacy of the written text to capture his fleeting experience. In a lengthy journal entry close to the journey's turning point, Gide seems to lose a sense of time and space amidst the indistinguishable islands of Lake Chad, noting the date simply as "— February" (*Travels* 178; see *Voyage* 251). He glimpses a dense forest near the shore in Cameroon, again expressing the desire to pause, "I would have given anything to penetrate beneath those mysterious shades" (*Travels* 188),[33] but passivity prevents him from stopping the party. Unable to penetrate on his own terms into the heart of the continent, Gide is left experiencing Africa as a visual spectacle, in which pleasure is marked by distance and displacement. Interestingly, Gide savors passages from Cuthbert Christy's *Big Game and Pigmies,* noting in English that they are "worth translating" (*Voyage* 383). He quotes Christy at length: "Whether in the forest or in the bush country, my experience has been that the days are not long enough to study, or even to pay attention to, a quarter of the interesting things which pass cinematograph-like before one in the twenty-four hours. One has to keep to one's subjects and leave the rest, hoping for the next occasion, which unfortunately too often never occurs" (*Travels* 280).[34] It is impossible to render adequately the experience of travel, with its constant diversions and urgent, forward movement. Traveling denies the author those moments during which he might steady his gaze and capture the lived reality of the Congo. This "cinematograph-like" sensation is essentially voyeuristic, and perhaps only adequately duplicated by the cinematic apparatus itself.

Voyage au Congo

The politics of the ethnographic spectacle suggest that the ways the west has envisioned otherness are not simply grounded in the narcissistic assumptions of colonizers, but are constructed out of intertwined discourses of colonial administration, anthropology, medicine, geography, and commerce, which are in turn inflected by issues of race, gender, nation, and temporality. Together these discourses help to reinforce the stable subjectivity of the western observer. The camera becomes a tool for framing, editing, and ultimately screening out a problematic and often irreducible reality, grasping it in a visual language comprehensible to the west's imagination. We might imagine that for Gide, who was so conspicuously concerned about negotiating the distance between exterior and interior realities,[35] the film record promised to provide visual evidence that, to utilize a phrase from Clifford Geertz, "he was there": these were sights and peoples he witnessed with his own eyes. Yet we find that Gide was in fact more skeptical: the journals indicate that he never fully embraced Allégret's methods, or the cinematic medium itself as an adequate mode of personal expression.

Daniel Durosay's in-depth work on Allégret reminds us that the film *Voyage au Congo* is—in spite of opening titles that proclaim, *"rapportées par André Gide et Marc Allégret"* [presented by André Gide and Marc Allégret]—almost wholly Allégret's vision, with participation from Gide. In his official role as Gide's "secretary," Allégret was pivotal in the initial stages of planning and designing the trip: he was a key influence on the itinerary and also performed essential geographical, ethnographic, and medical research for the journey.[36] It was Allégret's idea, in the summer of 1924, to concretize his role in the planned journey further by including photography and, soon after, cinema. Examining Allégret's photographs from the journey, Durosay finds them as revealing for what they do *not* show as for what they do: "some souvenir photos . . . some portraits of Gide, and of Dindiki, his familiar demon. Photos that are never reciprocated: one cannot find any of Marc, which suggests that Gide, considering photography the exclusive domain of his companion, hardly ever pressed the shutter release button."[37] Gide's participation seems to have extended substantially to the intertitles; he writes to Roger Martin du Gard in December of 1926: "— [w]e have followed all of your advice for the text of the film. I believe it will be quite good."[38] As the letters and journals indicate, the autumn and winter following Gide's return from Africa were characterized by feelings of lethargy and a lengthy depression that lasted well into the spring. He often claims to be doing little work (though in fact he was revising *Le Retour du Tchad* and writing *L'École des femmes* while advancing other projects), and is preoccupied with public and private reactions to the frank sexual revelations in *Si le grain ne meurt*. There is little indication that he is making a collaborative film with the object of his profound affections, Allégret. In October he notes to himself, "no desires" (*Journals* 2: 390)[39] and later to Roger Martin du Gard: "The cold numbs my thoughts, blunts my sensations, obscures my judgment. At times, for hours, I feel I am an idiot."[40] In February Gide continues to write of great fatigue, and his relationship with Allégret over the ensuing months is increasingly fraught with unfulfilled expectations and a sort of lingering torpor: "I doze while awaiting his return and waste my time as if I had a great deal to waste" (*Journals* 2: 398).[41]

Gide's published journals and letters only rarely refer to Allégret's film, leading one to conclude that he was more an observer than an active participant, preferring instead to concentrate his energies on his notebooks. It is nonetheless clear that while in Africa the idea of the cinema frequently took hold of Gide's imagination, and he even comes to see certain moments of his journey in cinematic terms. Of the oppressive heat in Lara he notes: "Life in camp is like a slow motion film" (*Travels* 299).[42] When he reflects on the filming process (often elliptically, as in the quote from Christy in the previous section), it is revealing of his attitudes towards Allégret's methods and the limitations of the cinema:

> On the whole, it seems to me that the best part of these photographs (and there will no doubt be a great deal that is excellent) will be things that have been taken by a happy accident—gestures, attitudes, which were just those one did not expect. The parts that were prepared beforehand will be, I am afraid, a little stiff, a little made-up. I feel as if I should have gone about it differently, and given up all idea of scenes and tableaux, but kept the camera in constant readiness to take the natives unawares, busy at their work or their play; for all the grace goes from anything when one tries to make them do it over again. (*Travels* 273)[43]

Gide is writing about film here, and not just photography; in the following sentence he refers to Marc's "turning" (*Travels* 273).[44] With hindsight, Gide's reflections might appear prophetic. This passage looks ahead to the more candid and spontaneous approach of *cinéma vérité,* pioneered by Jean Rouch in the 1950s, and assisted by the revolutionary theories of Dziga Vertov's *kino pravda* and the technical advances in portable sound and film equipment that occurred after the Second World War. But the confiding tone of Gide's comments also testifies to his scrupulous nonintervention in what he saw as Allégret's domain. Film might have offered Allégret a means for creative expression and a medium for carefully constructing ethnographic "evidence"; however, for Gide it was anything but an adequate negotiation of exterior reality and interior sensation, and hardly a substitute for the "thick description" and persistent self-analysis possible in the written text.

The film somewhat misleadingly came to be called *Voyage au Congo,* partly to capitalize on name recognition while acknowledging Gide's close association with the project; but like Gide's journals, it is in fact neither a straightforward travelogue, ethnographic study, nor *documentaire,* but a hybrid that encompasses a variety of approaches and observations, which follow the sequence of the journey.[45] Its subtitle, *Scènes de la vie indigène en Afrique Équatoriale,* suggests the snapshot quality of a film that brings together a number of different representational strategies commonly grouped under the term "documentary." Such strategies include the chronological mapping of the journey, "authentically" staged re-enactments of ethnographic value, scenes of local color, and exotic flora and fauna, as well as images of indigenous life captured through what would later be called direct cinema or *cinéma vérité* techniques.

At times the film seems to replicate the conventions of the early ethnographic film as envisioned by a figure like the "father" of documentary, Robert Flaherty, whose seminal romantic ethnography, *Nanook of the North* (1922), was much admired in France, and even compared to Greek classic drama.[46] According to Durosay, *Nanook* "took the natural route for documentary, that is, to witness the real-life adventures of a European and to render a report of an exotic spectacle," but Allégret consciously went against these tendencies, deliberately suppressing in the film any visual impression of effort, risk, or adventure.[47] In this sense, the dominant principles behind *Voyage au Congo* could be seen as resembling more closely Flaherty's second film, *Moana* (1926), than his earlier *Nanook.* Flaherty's Samoan film, subtitled "a romance of the Golden Age," is famous for inspiring John Grierson to use the term "documentary" (though perhaps not for the first time)[48] to describe the emerging genre of "non-fiction" filmmaking, and was intended as a complementary piece to *Nanook,* in which the heroic human spirit demonstrated in the frozen north could be explored in the tropics of the Pacific. The languor of Samoan life, however, was said to have taken over the production, and what emerged was a film that focused less on adventurous or heroic actions and more on domestic daily activities, physical sensuality, and bodily movement (reminiscent, as Rony notes, of Regnault's primitivist comparisons of the *"langage par gestes"* [language of gestures]).[49] A little more than a month after returning from his African trip, Gide wrote of watching *Moana* in Paris, noting, "I have never seen anything more voluptuous" (*Journals* 2: 382).[50]

Notwithstanding Gide's less-than-equal participation in Allégret's film, the accord between the author and his nephew in attitudes towards the primitive is striking: it is precisely this sense of an exotic, fetishized voluptuousness that stands out in *Voyage au Congo,* a tendency that can also be marked in Allégret's numerous photos where, as Durosay has observed, "The photographer shows us nothing but young bodies, firm chests and rounded breasts."[51] Allégret's fantasy of the primitive, however, also diverges from Gide's in important ways, significantly where the film fails to criticize, or even acknowledge, the colonial framework within which it operates, and the effects of that colonial system. Also less visible in the film is the insistent homoeroticism of Gide's journals, which had found open autobiographical expression in *Si le grain ne meurt.* As Gide would, with irony, recall years later in *Ainsi soit-il,* Allégret's camera was often pointed in a direction precisely opposite to that of his own gaze, manifesting his companion's "different tastes" and missing altogether such figures as "sweet little Mala," the adolescent escort "given" to Gide by a sultan at Reï-Bouba. At eighty, Gide would recall the boy with "perfect memories of sensual delight" (*So Be It* 123–124).[52] Allégret's sexualized gaze seems more clearly reflected in such images as Kaddé's torso in the sequence shot among the Saras, or in the "young Sara maidens" reclining in the photographs that accompany the published account. Allégret's primitivist fantasy, developed and heightened in French Equatorial Africa, would be transported back and incorporated into his later work in France, particularly in such projects as Josephine Baker's first sound film, *Zou Zou* (1934), which immortalized the *danse sauvage* and portrayed her, in the film's closing scenes, as a feathered bird in a golden cage.[53]

Overall, the content and style of *Voyage au Congo* suggest a spirit of investigation and innovation, gesturing to numerous modes of visual representation, but the film as a whole does not comfortably fit into any single category. Opening with scenes on the deck of the *Asie* off the coast of the Canary Islands, *Voyage au Congo* sets itself up as a spectacular travel narrative, seen through western eyes. From the start, it encodes a sense of identification with the western observer's gaze, preferably enacted at a safe remove from the observed, as the camera shows a woman (possibly the Duchesse de Trévise, notes Durosay) who playfully takes a pair of binoculars from the ship's captain and looks through them in the direction of the camera. Soon afterward the viewer is following the route of the Matadi-Kinshassa colonial railroad, and the spectator's eye is aligned with a camera perched on a moving train, which plunges through the forest. Assisted by maps of French Equatorial Africa which mark the route, the cinematic traveler is encouraged to identify with those who are about to embark on a journey into the vast and unseen reaches of the Congo. Western figures in bush helmets, clad in white, soon disappear nearly altogether, as the gaze of the traveler is established and then subsumed into the spectacle, encouraging identification with the camera as a journeying eye.[54] Soon the viewer's first glimpse of a "native," near Bangui, takes on overtones of romanticized first contact, as out on the river a young man standing in a canoe glides slowly across the water towards the spectator, arriving something like an envoy who offers the embodiment of the primitive harmoniously at one with nature.

Besides a number of more conventional travelogue scenes, Allégret includes some visually spectacular sequences, such as the falls at M'Bali and *"le spectacle"* of a dance presented by the Dakpas near Bambari (a performance that, Gide notes in his journals, was routinely done for payment). These fragments lead into the core of the film, which is made up of different sequences structured around five indigenous groups, who are announced one by one to the viewer. "To the west of Bangui," an intertitle reads, "the routes cease to be passable. The journey on foot allows us to be in the most intimate contact with the country and with five of the strangest tribes." The groups to be intimately encountered will include "the Bayas, the Saras, the Massas, the Moundangs, the Foulbés."[55] The film has now clearly established its organizing structure, and it moves on to present each of these groups in turn, all the while guiding the viewer with maps and intertitles that offer authoritative background to the images.

Each of the various groups is shown as if through a different lens, whether by intention or circumstance (Durosay suggests that both operated in surmounting the technical and scheduling difficulties of the film). Each sequence suggests a distinct stylistic and thematic approach, with an emphasis upon grand display and performance. The Bayas are shown at work, as men hunt and women dig for tubers. After exciting action shots of fires set in the brush to frighten out game for the hunt, the tone shifts, the titles noting, "nothing is more peaceful than a view of one of these villages."[56] Immediately an idyllic scene of a village appears, cutting short the action sequence and creating a bucolic mood for the rest of the segment. Opening and closing with a classic psychological technique from D. W. Griffith, the iris shot, the image helps to enclose the space as an idyll imagined in the mind's eye. The women in this group of *"anciens cannibales"* [former cannibals] are then viewed digging for cassava roots in the soil, and later preparing food, again suggesting a self-sustaining world at harmony with nature. The film then segues to the Saras (in a sequence that will be considered in more detail below), followed by the Massas, who are featured for their visually striking architecture, which for Gide combined the elements of the strange and the beautiful that he so desperately sought in Africa. Yet again the primary association is European: huts are built "in the manner of Agrippa's Pantheon," the film notes, using a phrase culled directly from the journals (*Travels* 217).[57] The following segment among the Moundangs is almost wholly given over to a performance in which they mount an extravagant ceremonial dance. Again these scenes mark the departure of Allégret's aesthetic tastes from Gide's, since Gide notes that the dance included "as usual . . . rather unpleasant jiggings right and left . . ." (*Travels* 307).[58] Still, the individual performances of the deities, captured vividly in the film, encouraged Gide to join in the proceedings. The smallest, identified in the film as Massim Biambé, "very naughty" *[très méchant],* played a Père Ubu that, Gide notes, would have enchanted Stravinsky or Cocteau (*Travels* 308; see *Voyage* 418). The final sequence, which involves a ceremony filmed at Reï-Bouba, offers a glimpse of local hierarchies, games, and the equestrian displays that Gide so admired.

The sequence involving the Saras is one of the most varied and detailed. It begins with games, including lengthy scenes of wrestling, then a *mât de cocagne* [greased pole] competition and a visually striking game with an enormous "push-ball," after which the intertitles read: "The Saras are particularly welcoming *[accueillants]*: they happily invite us into the intimacy of their lives."[59] The camera's entrance into a strange yet intimate reality, offered voluntarily and openly, no doubt corresponds to the desires of the western observer, just as the demonstration of playfulness and games helps to establish a comforting sense of familiarity with the film's subjects. This context helps to set the tone for the next sequence among the Saras: a romantic tale of a marriage proposal and negotiation, enacted by the Saras themselves. Up until this point the film has not entirely collapsed the boundary between observation and participation—a move that often happens in ethnographic texts and films—and the term *"accueillants"* here encourages viewers to identify themselves as visiting observers, present by exclusive invitation, rather than as active participants. Thus, the ensuing romantic narrative between the two young lovers, Kaddé and Djimta, shifts the rhythm and tone while still preserving the sense of voyeuristic spectacle maintained by the rest of the film. The sequence opens with a shot of Kaddé's torso, which lingers on her breasts, moves across her body and finally shows her face, where a small disc is fixed to her upper lip. The image recalls an earlier shot of Sara girls who, at the festivities shown just before the Kaddé and Djimta narrative, will "in turn prove their value,"[60] which is apparently signified by their nude bodies, clad only with strings of pearls around their torsos, each of which is examined in a slow left-to-right pan. As the viewer follows the proposal and marriage negotiation between Djimta and Kaddé's family, however, the camera rarely repeats such close-ups, maintaining its distance from the proceedings and leaving the spectator informed but always at a certain remove. Only near the end of the sequence, at a celebration of the marriage agreement, does the camera move in again to capture the sight of the rapidly moving bodies that so often offended Gide's sensibility. In the final scene, as the lovers talk, joke, and touch following the complex marriage negotiation, the camera approaches once again for a medium close-up, finally sanctioning the spectator's voyeurism by emphasizing Kaddé and Djimta's intimate relationship and their apparent ignorance of the camera's presence.

This sequence among the Saras is perhaps the most distinctive of the five tableaux. Durosay has asked, "On what basis has the director managed to effect a synthesis between the travelogue and the romantic sequence shot among the Saras?"[61] He answers the question with the help of some recently uncovered intertitles, which suggest that the tale is a sort of fantasmic detour into the daily life of the Saras, encountered along the course of the journey. Like Flaherty's *Moana,* which Fatimah Rony has seen as a form of ethnographic "taxidermy" comparable to Carl Akeley's famous taxidermic displays in the American Museum of Natural History, the Kaddé and Djimta sequence from *Voyage au Congo* suggests a romantic longing to trap and preserve a primitive past that lives in the western imagination, matched with a desire to authenticate on film what were believed to be elemental human truths. These "truths" did not always translate into accurate representations, however, as the case of Robert Flaherty has demonstrated. Flaherty's mystification of the bourgeois family is evident in his reconstruction of "native" families, as Jack C. Ellis observes:

[Flaherty] did not acknowledge the polygamy practiced in traditional Eskimo culture nor the looseness of the Samoan family arrangement. . . . The families were artificially created for the films, for the most part, with considerable care given to casting. Those selected to become father, mother, son, sister, and the rest are physically representative of the culture and also attractive—not necessarily handsome or beautiful but the best of type. (21)

The displacement and projection of an idealized western self onto an imagined other is a theme that runs throughout much of ethnographic representation. Yet recent critiques sometimes seem to forget that documentary films such as those of Flaherty or Allégret rarely made the sort of claims to truth and immediacy that later came to define the genre. Produced long before the rise of the truth-telling claims of *cinéma vérité* and direct cinema in the 1950s, and even before John Grierson's documentary movement in Britain argued for the visual inscription of social truths, these early documentaries aimed to attain something closer to the realism of the fiction film, and elaborate fabrications and simulacra were the rule rather than the exception.

Allégret's method of filming, as described (and critiqued) by Gide, demonstrates the extent to which the ground rules of documentary were axiomatically defined by the notion of reconstructing a spectacle of otherness already fixed in the western imaginary. Gide observes a telling sequence of events in the village of Yakoua, near Bol:

Marc tried to film some "documentary" scenes, but was not very successful. He wanted to get some groups of swimmers, and principally of women swimmers. In spite, however, of their being carefully chosen out, these particular ones were not very good-looking. It was impossible to get any concerted action from them. We were given to understand that it is improper for men and women to swim together. The men must start ten minutes before the women. But, as the women remained standing on the shore, the men were suddenly seized with shyness and slipped on their trousers and belts. Marc explained to me that they would no doubt undress as they got into the water; he thought it would be rather effective to see them carrying their clothes on their heads to keep them from getting wet. But their modesty was too strong; they preferred wetting their clothes—which, after all, would soon dry in the sun; and when they were pressed to undress, they gave up altogether and went off to sulk under a doum palm-tree. Marc began to lose his temper, and no wonder. (*Travels* 178–179)[62]

Allégret writes of the same scene on February 4, noting merely: "Then wanted to get some film of people swimming across the river. But failed: crisis of modesty."[63] Allégret is faced with the frustrating task of constructing an idealized image of harmonious, unspoiled native bodies and behaviors, where nudity connotes primitive nature in an Edenic state. This "crisis of modesty" suggests not only the ongoing power struggle between those who look and those who are looked at, but also unmasks the thinly veiled erotics of the encounter, and the ways that representing the other can be an explicit rendering of western—and in this case masculine—desire. Moreover, like the fiction film, the illusion of the filmmaker's invisibility is key to naturalizing the voyeuristic role of the spectator. This role is endangered by the modesty of Allégret's actors, who threaten to shatter the ideal opposition of civilized spectator and natural man by all too clearly reflecting the pedestrian desires and moral fears of western audiences.

Gide would, in his journals, explore the idea of capturing more spontaneous, "truthful" actions and expressions on film: a method more technically complicated than Allégret's approach, if not at that time practically impossible. These ideas are imprecisely linked to Gide's dissatisfaction with the inadequacies of a goal-oriented journey, and his desire for a spontaneous experience of self-recognition in a moment of rest and reflection. The hunting expedition described near the turn-around point of the journey, which marks the end of *Voyage au Congo,* metaphorically comes to represent this traveler's dilemma: "how I should have liked to stop, to sit down, there on the slope of that monumental termitary, in the dark shadows of that enormous acacia, and watch the gambols of the monkeys, and muse, and wonder! . . . The idea of killing—the very point of the chase—damps my pleasure" (*Travels* 190).[64] Gide desires the sort of rest that might lead to epiphany, the opportunity to be "motionless many minutes" during which he might disappear: "Everything would have been as if I had not existed and I should myself have forgotten my own presence and turned all vision" (*Travels* 191).[65] Yet this is not an appeal that can be realized in the frozen, voyeuristic images captured by the cinematic apparatus. Indeed, this sense of constantly deferred fulfillment, exacerbated by the demands of a full, "too well planned" itinerary (*Travels* 204),[66] extends to the act of filming itself, which always seems rushed, fragmentary, inadequate: "everything one dictates and *tries* to get appears constrained . . . we should have had to have more time and give up the idea of anything connected or continuous" (*Travels* 282).[67] More often than not leading to frustration—like the insufficient light at Abo-Bougrima—photography and film provide the theoretical promise of capturing those fleeting moments of authentic experience lost to the traveler in constant motion, but fail to deliver them. They leave the viewer still sightseeing at a distance, with images "a little stiff, a little made-up."

Ali Behdad has suggested that postcolonial travelers exploring the worlds of colonial texts might find it difficult not to demand something more of the colonial past. Our readings are conditioned by historical hindsight as well as by our sense of postcolonial and postmodern instability and emergence. If I might paraphrase Behdad, one could say that in coming to Gide's travel narratives and Marc Allégret's film, postcolonial readers perhaps look for something they unconsciously know will not be there: opposition or counterideology within a hegemonic discourse (1–3). But in the absence of this resistance, we might find in them the trace of something else: our own ambiguous familiar demon, which, if not precisely counterhegemonic, begins to help unravel the discourse of civility that guards the colonial traveler. As Maurice Blanchot has noted of Gide's work, it is the very fact of its dense paradoxes that drives it forward and, in a sense, this very forward movement that leads to its paradoxes: "Gide's boldness is a function of his prudence . . . his *inquiétude* is all the more meaningful because of his longing for rest . . ." ("Gide and the Concept of Literature" 60).[68] Perhaps it is this sense of restless self-questioning and self-doubt, this reflexive resistance to absolutes, that forms a basis for Gide's slippery and skeptical relationship to French colonial politics.

If this sense of Gidean paradox is less obvious in Allégret's film, it is perhaps, as Kirsten Hastrup has argued, that visual information inevitably remains somewhat "iconographic":

> The concreteness of visual records (which is a corollary to their metonymical relationship to reality) tends to obscure the ambiguity inherent in any instance. The visual record remains "thin," while the written record allows for "thick" description by the method of [what E. Ardener has called] "language shadows." (15)

Hastrup's argument begins to suggest certain signifying limitations of the ethnographic image. Allégret's montage, nonetheless, does incorporate a sense of ambiguity into the film's closing moments. Like Gide's journals, *Voyage au Congo* finishes by suggesting that journeying might offer sights, but cannot necessarily promise vision. After scenes at the sultanate of Reï-Bouba, images of *"la civilisation"* flash across the screen: a Protestant mission school, schoolchildren playing in uncomfortable-looking western clothing, the endless transit of boats arriving and leaving at the port of Douala, and finally the sky over the sea, fading to black.

Gide's journals also close with images that implicitly confound any pure division between the "civilized" here and the "primitive" there. He overhears a French child on the ship holding forth on numerous subjects, proclaiming among other things: "We the French detest other nations—all of us French . . . isn't it true, Georges? . . . Yes, it is a particular trait of the French, that we can't bear other nations . . ." (*Travels* 375).[69] Gide leaves us with this surreal scene of the west as embodied by the chauvinistic child, a scene reminiscent of the immense darkness that closes in upon Marlow and Kurtz's Intended near the end of *Heart of Darkness*. Both scenes suggest that to locate the horror, one need travel no further than right here.

Notes

1. "[O]deur fade" (*Voyage* 346); "ou plus exactement . . . liquide sanguinolent" (*Voyage* 346).

2. For a more sustained examination of Gide's colonial politics in light of his aesthetic and ethical concerns, see Walter Putnam's essay in this volume.

3. See Clifford, "Tell Us About Your Trip" in *The Predicament of Culture* 165–174, as well as Torgovnick, *Gone Primitive* 105–118. The African travels of Gide and Leiris have been discussed together in Dedet and Petr.

4. "Tout cela n'est pas bien intéressant à dire . . . ; j'abandonne le reste aux manuels" (*Voyage* 63).

5. "[L]es partis tragiques . . . seront noyées dans l'abondance des descriptions, etc." (*Journal* 5).

6. "Le visage est laid, mais le torse admirable" (*Voyage* 58).

7. See Porter 237–238. George D. Painter writes: "The Congo had given Gide repossession of his joy in life; it also rekindled in him a sense of social injustice which was to dominate his next decade" (101).

8. "Cependant, désirant ne pas soulever le principe de la colonisation, ce sont les funestes erreurs de son application qu'il va chercher avant tout à combattre" (*André Gide : sa vie* 306).

9. "« [P]roblèmes sociaux »" (*Journal* 395).

10. "Mais Gide ne suggère jamais l'abolition du système colonial; il s'interroge plutôt sur le moyen d'améliorer, de 'moraliser' un système déjà en place" (*L'Aventure littéraire* 158).

11. "Flatteuse impression de regagner ce peuple à la France" (*Voyage* 190).

12. "La circonscription est trop vaste; un seul homme, et sans moyens de transport rapide, ne peut suffire à tout surveiller" (*Voyage* 112).

13. Gide's view, then, was simultaneously critical of individual company policies and concessionary to the colonial project at large. It was clarified the following year in his article "La Détresse de notre Afrique Équatoriale." See also Putnam, *L'Aventure littéraire* 157.

14. See Rony 21–73.

15. A version of this section was presented at the MLA convention in 1996, as part of a panel sponsored by the Association des Amis d'André Gide. For another view of *Voyage au Congo* and *Le Retour du Tchad,* see Torgovnick, *Primitive Passions* 23–29. Torgovnick explores masculine and feminine self-projections in the context of travel writing.

16. Allégret's position as Gide's secretary and key role in the trip is outlined by Durosay in "Introduction."

17. See, for example, Clifford, "On Ethnographic Surrealism" in *The Predicament of Culture* 117–151.

18. See also works by Torgovnick and Clifford, cited above.

19. "[S]i beau, si étrange qu'il nous semblait trouver ici la raison de notre voyage, entrer au cœur de son sujet" (*Voyage* 65).

20. "Forêt des plus monotones, et très peu exotique d'aspect" (*Voyage* 114).

21. "Bangassou me déçoit un peu . . . et a beaucoup perdu de son étrangeté" (*Voyage* 77).

22. "[B]étail humain" (*Voyage* 195).

23. "Danses de femmes à l'entrée de chaque village. Extrêmement pénible, le trémoussement éhonté des matrones sur le retour" (*Voyage* 124).

24. "Indicible langueur. Heures sans contenu ni contour" (*Voyage* 13).

25. "Ils n'ont pourtant pas, dans ce pays, l'âpre noblesse et cette sorte de joie farouche et désespérée que j'ai connue dans le désert" (*Voyage* 87).

26. "[P]rojet de jeunesse réalisé dans l'âge mûr" (*Voyage* 14).

27. "[F]atalité inéluctable" (*Voyage* 14).

28. "Engourdissement, peut-être diminution" (*Voyage* 32). "La joie est peut-être aussi vive; mais elle entre en moi moins avant. . . . Ah! pouvoir ignorer que la vie rétrécit devant moi sa promesse . . ." (*Voyage* 23; second ellipsis Gide's).

29. "[Q]ue je doute si, plus tard, cette fausse image ne luttera pas contre le souvenir et si je reverrai Bangui, par exemple, comme il est vraiment, ou comme je me figurais d'abord qu'il était" (*Voyage* 95).

30. "[P]énétrer profondément, intimement, dans le pays" (*Voyage* 97); "un ciel sans promesses, un paysage que ne semble habiter aucun dieu, aucune dryade, aucun faune; un paysage implacable, sans mystère et sans poésie" (*Voyage* 163).

31. "[L]a virginité du regard s'est perdue" (*Voyage* 95).

32. "[U]ne sorte de Pompeï nègre" (*Voyage* 174).

33. "J'aurais donné je ne sais quoi pour pénétrer sous ces mystérieux ombrages . . ." (*Voyage* 265).

34. "« En forêt ou en brousse, j'ai pu connaître par expérience que les jours ne sont pas assez longs pour étudier, ou seulement porter attention au quart du spectacle qui passe devant le voyageur comme une vision cinématographique. L'on s'attache à un sujet; on laisse échapper le reste, comptant sur une occasion future, qui, hélas! ne s'offre jamais plus »" (*Voyage* 383).

35. Putnam suggests that Gide's voyage constituted, in fact, a turning point in this process: "This effort at the consolidation and construction of his being reflects a desire to integrate himself into the exterior world of reality. In this respect, Gide's voyage to the Congo served as a turning point in his evolution from living an interiorized life towards experiencing an external reality" [Cet effort de consolidation et de construction de son être reflète un désir de s'intégrer au monde extérieur, au monde réel. En cela, le voyage de Gide au Congo sert de charnière à son évolution d'une vie intérieure vers la réalité extérieure] (*L'Aventure littéraire* 143).

36. Gide wrote in July of 1924, "Marc explained a probable itinerary" [Marc explique l'itinéraire probable] (quoted in Durosay, "Introduction" 25); but a number of versions of their "elastic" itinerary were still being considered close to the date of their departure. See Durosay, "Introduction" 23–30 for a full examination of the itinerary and its many variations.

37. "[Q]uelques photos-souvenirs . . . quelques portraits de Gide, et de Dindiki, son animal fétiche. Portraits sans réciproque : on n'en trouve pas de Marc, car il semble que Gide, considérant la photographie comme le domaine réservé de son compagnon, n'ait guère pressé le déclic" ("Introduction" 46).

38. "— Nous avons suivi tous vos conseils pour les textes du film. Je crois que ça ne sera pas mal" (Gide and Martin du Gard 301).

39. "[P]as de désirs" (*Journal* 19).

40. "Le froid engourdit ma pensée, émousse mes sensations, obscurcit mon jugement. Par instants, par heures, je me crois idiot" (Gide and Martin du Gard 301).

41. "[J]e somnole en attendant son retour et perds mon temps comme s'il m'en restait beaucoup à perdre" (*Journal* 30).

42. "On vit au ralenti, dans le campement" (*Voyage* 408).

43. "Somme toute il me paraît que ce qu'il y aura de mieux dans ces vues prises (et sans doute il y aura de l'excellent), sera plutôt obtenu par un heureux hasard; des gestes, des attitudes sur lesquels précisément l'on ne comptait pas. Ce dont on convenait par avance restera, je le crains, un peu figé, retenu, factice. Il me semble que j'eusse procédé différemment, renonçant aux tableaux, aux scènes, mais gardant l'appareil tout prêt, et me contentant de prendre, par surprise et sans qu'ils s'en doutent, les indigènes occupés à leurs travaux ou à leurs jeux; car toute la grâce est perdue de ce qu'on prétend leur faire refaire" (*Voyage* 374–375).

44. "[T]ourner" (*Voyage* 375).

45. The version of *Voyage au Congo* to which I refer here is a restored copy acquired from the France 3 archives. I am very grateful to Réné Han for securing me a copy. With few exceptions, this version corresponds to the one outlined by Daniel Durosay in "Analyse synoptique." The version used for this article, however, opens with "The Film Society Presents / *Voyage au Congo* . . ." and runs for 100 minutes.

46. See Barnouw 42.

47. *Nanook* "était naturellement la voie documentaire, soit pour témoigner de l'aventure vécue par l'Européen, soit pour rendre compte du spectacle exotique" (Durosay, "Introduction" 46).

48 See Winston.

49. Frances Hubbard Flaherty, Robert Flaherty's wife, presented a detailed account of *Moana*'s lengthy gestation and emergence over two years' filming in Samoa in a series of articles published in *Asia* 25 (May–December, 1925).

50. "[J]e n'ai rien vu de plus voluptueux" (*Journal* 8).

51. "Le photographe ne donne à voir que des corps jeunes, des seins fermes, des bustes faits au tour" ("Introduction" 48).

52. "Il ne me paraît guère possible que Reï Bouba ait été avisé de mes goûts. Ceux-ci eussent-ils été différents, ainsi que l'étaient ceux de Marc . . ." (*Ainsi soit-il* 148); "Gentil Mala!" (150); "mes souvenirs de volupté les plus parfaits" (151).

53. For a reading of *Zou Zou,* see Rony.

54. Western figures will be glimpsed only a few times during the film. During scenes of the *mât de cocagne* [greased pole] competition among the Saras, a male figure in a bush helmet strides left to right across the frame, followed by a girl; Gide and Allégret are glimpsed examining a dead hippopotamus, Allégret waving his arms at the boatmen (described in *Voyage* 342–343); and in Reï-Bouba, a figure (Gide?) in western dress can be seen gesturing from a porch.

55. "A l'ouest de Bangui les routes cessent d'être praticables. Le voyage à pied nous permettra de prendre un contact plus intime avec ce pays et avec cinq des tribus les plus curieuses . . . les Bayas, les Saras, les Massas, les Moundangs, les Foulbés." The groups of this region can be found under various names: the Baya (Baja, Gbaya), the Massa (Masa), the Moundang (Mundang), the Foulbé (Foulbe, Fulani), for example. For the sake of clarity, I will largely retain the names known to Gide.

56. "[R]ien de plus paisible que la vue d'un de ces villages."

57. "[A] la manière du panthéon d'Agrippa" (*Voyage* 307).

58. "Toujours des trémoussements de droite et de gauche, assez peu plaisants . . ." (*Voyage* 417).

59. "Les Saras sont particulièrement accueillants : ils nous admettent volontiers dans l'intimité de leur vie."

60. "[V]ont à leur tour montrer leur valeur."

61. "[P]ar quel biais le réalisateur avait pu effectuer la soudure entre le documentaire de voyage et la partie romanesque tournée chez les Saras" ("Les « cartons » retrouvés" 66).

62. "Marc tâche de filmer des scènes « documentaires »; cela ne donne rien de bien fameux. Il s'agit d'obtenir certains groupements de nageurs, et principalement de nageuses. Si triées qu'elles soient, celles-ci ne sont pas bien jolies. Impossible d'obtenir un mouvement d'ensemble. On nous fait comprendre qu'il n'est pas décent que femmes et hommes nagent en même temps. Ceux-ci doivent précéder de dix minutes celles-là. Et comme celles-là restent sur la rive, les hommes, pris d'une soudaine pudeur, se couvrent, se ceinturent et enfilent des pantalons. Marc m'explique qu'ils vont se dénuder en entrant dans l'eau; il compte sur un certain effet de ces vêtements portés à l'abri de l'eau, sur la tête. Mais la pudeur est la plus forte; les hommes préfèrent mouiller ces étoffes qui sécheront vite au soleil. Si l'on insiste pour les faire se dévêtir, ils lâchent la partie et s'en vont bouder sous un palmier doum. Marc s'énerve et il y a de quoi" (*Voyage* 252–253).

63. "Puis voulu prendre un film des gens traversant à la nage. Mais raté, crise de pudeur" (*Carnets du Congo* 186).

64. "[Q]ue je voudrais m'arrêter, m'asseoir, ici, sur le flanc de cette termitière monumentale, dans l'ombre obscure de cet énorme acacia, à épier les ébats de ces singes, à

m'émerveiller longuement. L'idée de tuer, ce but à atteindre dans la chasse, étrécit mon plaisir" (*Voyage* 267).

65. "[I]mmobile depuis quelques minutes . . . comme si je n'étais pas, et j'oublierais moi-même ma présence pour ne plus être que vision" (*Voyage* 267–268).

66. "[T]rop bien préparé" (*Voyage* 291).

67. "Tout ce que l'on dicte et *veut* obtenir est contraint. . . . [I]l faudrait disposer de plus de temps, et renoncer à tout enchaînement, toute suite" (*Voyage* 386).

68. "[O]n peut bien répondre qu'il est hardi en raison de sa prudence, que son inquiétude a d'autant plus de sens qu'il souhaite ce repos . . ." ("Gide et la littérature d'expérience" 227).

69. "Nous, les Français, nous détestons les autres nations. Tous les Français . . . n'est-ce pas, Georges? . . . Oui; c'est très particulier aux Français, ça, de ne pas pouvoir souffrir les autres nations . . ." (*Voyage* 501; ellipses Gide's).

Works Cited

Allégret, Marc. *Carnets du Congo : Voyage avec Gide.* Introduction and notes by Daniel Durosay. Paris: Presses du C.N.R.S., 1987.

Barthes, Roland. "Notes sur André Gide et son journal" [*Existences,* July 1942]. Trans. Richard Howard. *A Roland Barthes Reader.* Ed. Susan Sontag. London: Vintage, 1993. 3–17.

Barnouw, Erik. *Documentary: A History of the Non-Fiction Film.* New York: Oxford University Press, 1974.

Behdad, Ali. *Belated Travelers: Orientalism in the Age of Colonial Dissolution.* Durham: Duke University Press, 1994.

Blanchot, Maurice. "Gide and the Concept of Literature as Adventure." *Gide: A Collection of Critical Essays.* Ed. David Littlejohn. Englewood Cliffs, NJ: Prentice-Hall, 1970. 49–62.

———. "Gide et la littérature d'expérience." *La Part du feu.* Paris: Gallimard, 1949. 216–228.

Clifford, James. *The Predicament of Culture: Twentieth-Century Ethnography, Literature, and Art.* Cambridge: Harvard University Press, 1988.

Dedet, André and Christian Petr. "Le Voyageur en Afrique et son regard sur l'Autre." *Journal of European Studies* 22.4 (December 1992): 323–336.

Durosay, Daniel. "Analyse synoptique du *Voyage au Congo* de Marc Allégret avec l'intégralité des inter-titres." *Bulletin des Amis d'André Gide* 22.101 (January 1994): 71–85.

———. "Les « cartons » retrouvés du *Voyage au Congo.*" *Bulletin des Amis d'André Gide* 22.101 (January 1994): 65–70.

———. "Introduction." *Carnets du Congo : Voyage avec Gide.* By Marc Allégret. Paris: Presses du C.N.R.S., 1987. 11–58.

Ellis, Jack C. *The Documentary Idea: A Critical History of English Language Documentary Film and Video.* Englewood Cliffs, NJ: Prentice-Hall, 1989.

Gide, André. *Ainsi soit-il.* Paris: Gallimard, 1952.

———. "La Détresse de notre Afrique Équatoriale." *Revue de Paris,* October 15, 1927. Reprinted in *Voyage au Congo* 531–544.

———. *Journal 1926–1950.* Ed. Martine Sagaert. Paris: Gallimard, Bibliothèque de la Pléiade, 1997.

———. *The Journals of André Gide.* Ed. and trans. Justin O'Brien. 4 vols. New York: Alfred A. Knopf, 1947–1951.

———. *So Be It, or The Chips Are Down.* Trans. Justin O'Brien. New York: Alfred A. Knopf, 1959.

———. *Travels in the Congo.* Trans. Dorothy Bussy. Hopewell, NJ: Ecco Press, 1994.

————. *Voyage au Congo, suivi de Le Retour du Tchad*. Paris: Gallimard, 1995.

Gide, André, and Roger Martin du Gard. *Correspondance 1913–1934*. Introduction by Jean Delay. Paris: Gallimard, 1968.

Hastrup, Kirsten. "Anthropological Visions: Some Notes on Visual and Textual Authority." *Film as Ethnography*. Ed. Peter Ian Crawford and David Turton. Manchester: Manchester University Press, 1992. 8–25.

Kaplan, Caren. *Questions of Travel*. Durham, NC: Duke University Press, 1996.

Levin, Harry. "Literature and Exile." *Refractions: Essays in Comparative Literature*. New York: Oxford University Press, 1966. 62–81.

Lévi-Strauss, Claude. *Tristes Tropiques*. Trans. John and Doreen Weightman. New York: Simon and Schuster, 1977.

Moore, Henrietta. *A Passion for Difference*. Bloomington: Indiana University Press, 1994.

Painter, George D. *André Gide: A Critical Biography*. London: Weidenfeld & Nicolson, 1968.

Pierre-Quint, Léon. *André Gide: His Life and Work*. Trans. Dorothy M. Richardson. New York: Alfred A. Knopf, 1934.

————. *André Gide : sa vie, son œuvre*. Paris: Librairie Stock, Delamain et Boutelleau, 1932.

Porter, Dennis. *Haunted Journeys: Desire and Transgression in European Travel Writing*. Princeton: Princeton University Press, 1991.

Putnam, Walter C. *L'Aventure littéraire de Joseph Conrad et d'André Gide*. Saratoga, CA: Anma Libri, 1990.

Rony, Fatimah Tobing. *The Third Eye: Race, Cinema, and the Ethnographic Spectacle*. Durham, NC: Duke University Press, 1996.

Shelton, Marie-Denise. "Primitive Self: Colonial Impulses in Michel Leiris's *L'Afrique fantôme*." *Prehistories of the Future: The Primitivist Project and the Culture of Modernism*. Ed. Elazar Barkan and Ronald Bush. Stanford: Stanford University Press, 1995. 326–338.

Stocking, George. "The Ethnographic Sensibility of the 1920s and the Dualism of the Anthropological Tradition." *Romantic Motives: Essays on Anthropological Sensibility*. Ed. George Stocking. Madison: University of Wisconsin Press, 1989. 208–276.

Torgovnick, Marianna. *Gone Primitive*. Chicago: University of Chicago Press, 1990.

————. *Primitive Passions: Men, Women, and the Quest for Ecstasy*. New York: Alfred A. Knopf, 1997.

Winston, Brian. "Before Grierson, Before Flaherty: The Documentary Film in 1914." *Sight and Sound* 57.4 (Autumn 1988): 277–279.

CHAPTER 7

Left-Wing Intellectuals in the
entre-deux-guerres

Jean-François Sirinelli

The 1930s, throughout which André Gide was in the thick of many of the disputes taking place on the French Left, constituted an intensive period of political engagement for intellectuals—so intensive, in fact, that this period has become a reference point, indeed, a source of nostalgia. "Where are the Gides, the Malraux, the Alains, the Langevins of today?" asked Max Gallo, writer and spokesman of Pierre Mauroy's Socialist government in July of 1983 (7). His question was a prelude to the ensuing debate among scholars that summer concerning the silence of leftist intellectuals.

But a historian's reference to intellectuals' intense engagement during the 1930s and the deep impression made by this engagement on the heart of the intellectual milieu in the late twentieth century risk becoming mere commonplaces if they are not connected to details, which provide a great many nuances compared with the impression left in our collective memory. This is all the more important because the collective memory was largely shaped by several generations of left-wing intellectuals who dominated the scene in France after World War II. The historian's first task is to move beyond all these commemorations of the 1930s and reestablish the relative strength of cultural forces during the period, as well as offer a fresh perspective on them.

Perspective and Extent

Of course, it is most important, first of all, to try to assess the boundaries of the intellectual milieu during the 1930s. Basing his work on a very general definition of the word "intellectual"—derived from the ideological struggles within the French Communist Party during the first decade of the Fifth Republic—the historian Claude Willard counted "around 450,000 intellectuals" and based his figure on the results of the 1936 census (116). Certainly, this estimate is debatable. Should all those who worked in public education, numbering

186,000 at the time, be included within the category of intellectuals? Among all educators, university professors numbered only about one thousand, compared with the more than 120,000 male and female primary- and secondary-school teachers. Certainly, the role of the latter group was pivotal in the history of the Third Republic;[1] nevertheless, should all of them be included within the category of intellectuals? Beyond the probably insoluble question of taxonomy, one senses that such an extension would lead to an inflation, and therefore also a dilution, of the category itself. Thus, if one compares the number put forward by Claude Willard for 1936 with the current estimate of the number of intellectuals at the time of the Dreyfus affair—"some thirty thousand people" (Rebérioux 186)—the number of French intellectuals would have to have increased by 1500 percent in just a third of a century, and during a period when the total population was relatively constant!

Nevertheless, even when retaining the 1936 estimate of 450,000, the world of intellectuals would represent only 2.2 percent of the work force. Its strength, therefore, is clearly not numerical. Similarly, on the parliamentary level, it would be an exaggeration to consider the Popular Front a "Republic of Professors." As was the case with the *Cartel des gauches* [Left-Wing Cartel] of 1924—a term coined by Albert Thibaudet—the political majority that won the April–May elections of 1936 included only a modest number of educators: 22 primary- and secondary-school teachers and 43 university professors—representing only slightly more than 10 percent of the whole—compared with 119 lawyers. This is far from the 34.1 percent constituted by educators elected in 1981, or even from the 17 percent in 1946.

There is more to be reconsidered beyond the demographic status and parliamentary presence of intellectuals in the 1930s. Their ideological range during the same time period also calls for clarification in contrast with what a too hasty consideration of the past sometimes suggests. According to the conventional point of view, intellectuals—like André Gide—were especially active in the great disputes on the French Left and were visible within the Popular Front as it acted on the political stage. Yet historians can at least roughly sketch what actually happened during the period, and their research shows that a large portion of the French intelligentsia of the time was leaning to the right. One could cite any number of events to justify this assertion. One of the most significant indications is the petition, from the early fall of 1935, signed by several hundred intellectuals who expressed opposition to sanctions against Italy during the Ethiopian war. The intellectuals who signed this manifesto "in defense of the West," published in the October 4, 1935 issue of *Le Temps*,[2] explicitly claimed, as did their adversaries on the Left, that they were compelled to take this step out of a duty to be "vigilant." And like their leftist adversaries, they sounded a call to "activist intellectuals," those who used their minds to fight for what was right, to rally round them.

The "activist intellectuals" who came from the Left and Right of the political landscape were, in fact, rather evenly matched. The most revealing piece of evidence in this regard, even more so than the war in Ethiopia, is the period of the Spanish Civil War. What is particularly telling is that on the domestic side during this time, opposition to the Popular Front led to a sort of Franco-French war among intellectuals. If one analyzes the battle of manifestos that took place during this period, it indeed appears that, all things considered, "activist intellectuals" in the two camps were mobilized in rather equal numbers.[3]

The Era of Intellectuals?

The above observation is unsurprising but at the same time significant: unsurprising because the history of French intellectuals since the Dreyfus affair has been marked by such binary oppositions; significant because in the 1930s these oppositions attained a magnitude that had never been seen before. And it is for this reason that the decade of the 1930s takes on particular importance in the history of intellectuals, for it was a definite turning point. Here again, the historian is compelled to offer a new perspective. Jean-Paul Sartre may have proclaimed the "duty of political engagement" in the first issue of *Les Temps Modernes* in October 1945, but his position did not really mark a new beginning. His analysis, in fact, was limited to theorizing about a process that already had largely been set in motion during the 1930s and that had broken with the preceding decade of the 1920s. Julien Benda, in 1927, had proclaimed in *La Trahison des clercs* that intellectuals should not publicly speak out or work on behalf of specific political causes, in order not to betray their nature and their role—except, he noted, when such public engagement was in defense of great universal values, such as those at stake in the Dreyfus affair. The discussions that his book provoked clearly showed that this was the opinion of numerous intellectuals at the time.

If the 1930s were a time when there was a clear and well-defined change of direction for intellectuals, then what were the causes of this shift?

The first cause is, by its nature, the most obvious. In the 1930s, History starts up again. Throughout the preceding decade, in fact, History seemed to have subsided: after the slaughter of 1914–1918 and the immense difficulties during the immediate postwar years, the stabilization of international relations and the development of real economic prosperity in industrialized countries had appeared to guarantee world peace. The formula that in France, for example, seems best to sum up the aspirations of the greatest number of people at that time is the wish that the Great War would be the "war to end all wars"—in other words, that there would never again be another war. Such a hope may seem ridiculous or pathetic in retrospect, considering what would occur less than fifteen years later. But in the context of the 1920s, this criticism would be, in a certain respect, an anachronism. In the mid-1920s, the hope that collective security and international arbitration—guaranteed by the League of Nations—would henceforth come to mediate and solve conflicts inherent within human societies was largely shared by the nations of Europe. But this hope, in fact, was only a dream, for in the 1930s History entered a new phase of turbulence. Within a few years, the new international order was subjected to increasing tension and to a growing danger of war, which—and the point must be emphasized here—would lead to vexed and difficult conflicts for pacifist intellectuals. Within the quiet atmosphere of the 1920s, such intellectuals found themselves in tune with their times. But from the 1930s on, it would be necessary for them to think about war or, at least, about the ideological conflict with Fascism. These intellectuals would find themselves torn between their attachment to preserving peace and the necessity for them to be vigilant—even at the risk of war—in the face of increasingly aggressive Fascist regimes.

More was at stake in the 1930s, however, for there was a second reason for the increasing political engagement among French intellectuals throughout this decade, a decade that, in fact, was a time of great causes which simultaneously helped not only mobilize intellectuals but also divide them. As we have seen, they rally together and confront each other in a great public battle of manifestos; Ethiopia, Spain, Hitler's designs on Central Europe, create many occasions for intellectuals to be seen and heard. The divisions among intellectuals on these issues are so great, moreover, that the emerging power of the Popular Front provokes further conflicts among them, conflicts that are less publicized, more private. This increasing number of conflicts, based on different political stances, creates a veritable system of fault lines running through French intellectual society and concentrated around one great, central rift: as one contemporary observer wrote, "Here, as in the time of the Dreyfus Affair, we are witnessing a conflict between two spirits, between two notions of justice, of political life, and of the evolution of humanity" (Simon 9–10).

Such binary oppositions, as we have already stated, occurred frequently throughout the history of French intellectuals after the Dreyfus affair. Yet, when considered carefully, the awakening of History and the increased number of great, mobilizing causes are not sufficient to explain their intensified engagement in French society. For these factors are not unique to the 1930s. On the one hand, the historian knows full well that there was no such thing as "the end of History": the Roaring Twenties did not see time stop any more than any other decade did. At most, the 1920s appear, in retrospect, as a period when time was suspended, when the course of History seemed to hesitate. On the other hand, even though the 1920s certainly contrasted with the decade that followed, a decade characterized by emergencies and great mobilizations resulting from them, we must nonetheless conclude that the 1930s did not have a monopoly on historical density. The landscape of French history as a whole is dotted with similar periods, periods likewise characterized by tension and a sense of urgency.

There is, in fact, a third factor to consider, one that clarifies what is special about the 1930s and explains the increasing engagement of intellectuals during this time. In the hundred-year history of intellectuals since the Dreyfus affair, the 1930s can be considered a turning point because during this time the ideology of both the Left and the Right paused in its course of development and got redirected. On the Left, increased engagement has to do less with defending Dreyfusian values than with battling on behalf of anti-Fascism. On the Right, anti-Communism becomes a more powerful motivation to act than the condemnation of the Republic or the exaltation of the French nation. As a result, the stakes, as far as intellectuals are concerned, change greatly. Indeed, anti-Fascism and anti-Communism are two notions that have great ideological density, which necessarily gives intellectuals the role of mentors for two camps in search of ideological identity. In the 1930s, therefore, they contribute to a number of civic debates, using their own special language, which until this time was confined to a much smaller sphere.

Nevertheless, can we conclude that these intellectuals had a definite influence on their fellow citizens? The answer, in general, varies according to the time period, the place, and the milieu. In the case of the 1930s, it is best not to unduly minimize intellectuals' influence. Certainly, as with other time periods, their engagement remained, to a great degree, endogenous: intellectuals addressed other intellectuals, and the echo of their voices resounded most strongly within their own community. However, for the reasons mentioned earlier, this echo resonated in the 1930s more than usual. Themes of anti-Communism and anti-Fascism, spread and popularized by intellectuals, profoundly permeated the political cultures of the time and left a lasting impression on them. Such moments of complete osmosis are, on the whole, rare in French history; in the 1930s, the French intellectual milieu was tinged by the political debates of the time, but to an equal extent it colored them.

Ideological Fields

Another important question remains: just what causes an intellectual to make the transition from thought to action—in other words, to engagement? Clearly, the answer has to do with a process of alchemy that definitely varies with each individual, a process that the historian cannot attempt to respond to except by analyzing the paths that lead to engagement on a case-by-case basis. At any given time, however, there are ideological influences that, like magnetic fields, exercise strong forces of attraction and thus can, as it were, direct a historian's compass along the paths intellectuals followed to engagement. Acknowledging the significance of these ideological fields, of course, does not answer the question about which personal factors made an intellectual more or less susceptible to the influence of a particular ideology. Yet, without excluding *a priori* whatever interesting information sociological research might provide, we can see that the study of ideological fields is probably as fertile an approach as work on sociological "fields," in the sense understood by, say, followers of Pierre Bourdieu.

In the decade of the 1930s, it was assuredly the ideological fields of Fascism and Communism that structured the debates among intellectuals and therefore gave rise, as we have seen, to anti-Fascism and anti-Communism as well. Many calls to action on the Left would denounce the "Fascist danger," not only beyond the borders of France but also within them. Since the 1930s, French and foreign historians alike have attempted to evaluate the exact magnitude of Fascism in France, particularly in the intellectual milieu. Certainly, the majority of historians—though there is still debate on this matter, especially concerning Zeev

Sternhell's work—have demonstrated that the Fascist threat from within France was much less clear-cut, more nuanced;[4] but they have equally stressed that intellectuals at this time perceived Fascism as a grave and imminent danger. These two observations, far from being contradictory, go to the heart of the French crisis in the 1930s. Insofar as there was a perceived Fascist threat, anti-Fascism came about as a reaction and played an essential role in French political life.

Since we are focusing just on the spread of anti-Fascism, we will set aside the question—still important, but not central to our inquiry—of the eventual exploitation of this anti-Fascism by the Soviet Union.[5] All things considered, whatever the factors were that initially led to anti-Fascism, and whatever the ulterior motives of a number of its proponents, its spread was a fundamental historical reality; and its nature, at its core, was strongly ideological.

The same is true of the attraction exerted by Communism—sometimes precisely in the name of anti-Fascism—on the French intellectual community. Here again, the 1930s introduced a significant change. Indeed, throughout the preceding decade, the attraction of Communism had remained limited: the glimmering light born in the East had been in France but a flicker that reached only a few intellectual milieux and permeated the ideological climate of only a few very small groups. Certainly, the notoriety achieved afterward by some of these milieux—such as the Surrealists—was able to make scholars and others look back and overestimate the attraction of Communism throughout the 1920s. And it would still be a mistake to think that this attraction was statistically significant. Throughout the decade that followed, on the other hand, the battles waged by intellectuals on behalf of anti-Fascism would make them more and more attracted to Communism. It is true that the degree of closeness to the Parti Communiste Français and the intensity of personal engagement with Communism vary greatly from one intellectual to another. One should therefore consider a whole palette of attitudes, from "card-carrying member" to "fellow traveler." One fact remains: even if we do not find ourselves in a situation like that of the years after 1945, which constituted the golden age in France for Communist and fellow-traveling intellectuals, there definitely was a first phase, of which André Gide was a part, during which Communism was one of the central elements of the intellectual scene.

Writers on the Front Line

During this phase, in the midst of the intellectual milieu, the writers, as at the time of the Dreyfus affair, remained in the vanguard. In 1932 one foreign observer, Ernst Robert Curtius, wrote perceptively, in his *Essai sur la France:* "In France, neither the philosopher, nor the musician, nor the scholar expresses the spirit of the nation: this role, instead, falls to the man of letters" (173). In fact, even though during the 1930s a number of scholars and professors became involved in the political field,[6] the public figure of the writer remained on the front line. This was true to such an extent that Michel Winock was able recently to propose dividing the "century of intellectuals" into periods determined by the work of great writers: the "Gide years" follow the "Barrès years" and precede the "Sartre years."

Thus, one could conclude by returning to the question that Max Gallo asked in 1983: "Where are the Gides, the Malraux, the Alains, the Langevins of today?" In one respect, the answer was given thirteen years later when it was decided that André Malraux was to be placed in the Panthéon. The transfer of the writer's ashes in November 1996 had symbolic value. As the French Republic has enacted the religious ritual of selecting its "great men"—writers among them—it has implicitly proposed a family tree of engaged intellectuals: there were the great ancestors, Voltaire, Rousseau, and Hugo; then the founding father of the Dreyfusian cycle, Zola; and then André Malraux, the archetype of the engaged intellectual. Malraux, prior to his Gaullist phase after the Second World War, embodies, along with Gide and others, the 1930s intellectual's move to the front line in the name of anti-Fascism. Political engagement by intellectuals has thus implicitly been given recognition in the most institutionalized form that the French national memory takes.

Translated by Scott Powers and Stephen Westergan

Notes

1. See Sirinelli and Rioux 150–152.
2. The first list of signatures published on this day numbered sixty-four names, of which twelve were members of the Académie française.
3. See Sirinelli, chapters 4 and 5.
4. On this complex question, see the authoritative work by Milza.
5. This thesis has been developed principally by Furet.
6. See Sirinelli, chapters 4 and 5.

Works Cited

Curtius, Ernst Robert. *Essai sur la France*. Trans. Jacques Benoist-Méchin. Paris: Éditions de l'Aube, 1995. (Original ed. Paris: Grasset, 1932.)

Furet, François. *Le Passé d'une illusion. Essai sur l'idée communiste au XXe siècle*. Paris: Robert Laffont/Calmann-Lévy, 1995.

Gallo, Max. "Les intellectuels, la politique et la modernité." *Le Monde*, July 26, 1983: 7.

Milza, Pierre. *Fascisme français. Passé et présent*. Paris: Flammarion, 1987.

Rebérioux, Madeleine. "Classe ouvrière et intellectuels devant l'Affaire : Jaurès." *Les Écrivains et l'Affaire Dreyfus*. Ed. Géraldi Leroy. Paris: Presses Universitaires de France, 1983. 185–195.

Simon, Yves. *La Campagne d'Éthiope et la pensée politique française*. Paris: Desclée de Brouwer, 1936.

Sirinelli, Jean-François. *Intellectuels et passions françaises*. Paris: Fayard, 1990. New edition Paris: Gallimard, 1996.

Sirinelli, Jean-François, and Jean-Pierre Rioux. *Le Temps des masses*. Vol. IV of *L'Histoire culturelle de la France*. Paris: Éditions du Seuil, 1998.

Sternhell, Zeev. *Ni droite ni gauche. L'idéologie fasciste en France*. Paris: Éditions du Seuil, 1983. New edition Brussels: Complexe, 1987.

Willard, Claude. "Les intellectuels français et le Front populaire." *Cahiers de l'Institut Maurice Thorez* 2.3–4 (1966–1967): 115–124.

Winock, Michel. *Le Siècle des intellectuels.* Paris: Éditions du Seuil, 1997.

CHAPTER 8

Having Congress:
The Shame of the Thirties[1]

Roger Shattuck

1

During the last two weeks of June 1935, the heat in Paris became pitiless. It was precisely the moment when scores of intellectuals from Europe and America and Asia had been summoned to that city to discuss the fate of their world. Inside the sweltering Palais de la Mutualité in the Latin Quarter, a mixed crowd of close to three thousand proletarians and mandarins, watched by muscular ushers, listened to the opening session. They anticipated excitement, portentous statements to match the turn of events. Their newspapers were still discussing a financial panic and a double cabinet crisis earlier in the month. The year had opened with the Saar plebiscite in favor of Germany and with Hitler's reestablishment of compulsory military service, followed closely by Ethiopia's second protest to the League of Nations about Mussolini's intervention in her affairs. In May Laval, now premier, had brought forth the Franco-Soviet Mutual Aid Pact, a package that confounded the French Communists, for it was accompanied by an unexpected statement from Stalin endorsing the long opposed French rearmament policy. The package also included the summary expulsion of Leon Trotsky after two years of political refuge in France. One wonders how many of the audience, most of them Soviet sympathizers, could acknowledge to themselves the murder of Kirov in Russia six months earlier and of the 105 people shot without trial to foil the "plot." Only a few days later this same auditorium in the Mutualité would house a mass meeting to celebrate the election in the Fifth Arrondissement of Paul Rivet, the first candidate in all Europe put up on a Popular Front ticket. Obviously the assembled intellectuals had multiple occasions to rise to.

It was Friday, June 21, a little after nine in the evening. When the people at the head table finally took their places, the audience could see the startlingly bald and ascetic head of the chairman behind the spider's web of microphones. He opened the session by reading in a beautifully modulated voice:

Literature has never been more alive. Never has so much been written and printed, in France and in all civilized countries. Why then do we keep hearing that our culture is in danger?

By a mixture of fate, chance, and calculation, the First International Congress of Writers for the Defense of Culture met in the very storm's eye of the thirties. The man who spoke the opening words was André Gide. His slightly Oriental face wore the patina of a half century of literary history. During the 1890s he had belonged to the group that listened to Mallarmé test the secrets and silences of poetry on Tuesday evenings. His novel about gratuitous murder and the rewards of being an imposter, *Les Caves du Vatican* (1914), had inspired the young devotees of Dada and Surrealism in the twenties; this same novel was now being revived in installments in *L'Humanité*. He had publicly proclaimed and defended his homosexuality in the twenties. For most listeners Gide, now sixty-six, had turned Communist. His bourgeois public considered him a dirty old man all over again.

At the table with Gide sat Barbusse, pacifist and leftist hero since his novel *Le Feu* (1917); Malraux, already a legend at thirty-four with his fourth novel, *Le Temps du mépris,* just out; and Aragon, convert from Surrealism to militant Communism and editor of the monthly *Commune.* After Gide's short welcome, telegrams of greeting and encouragement were read from Romain Rolland, hero of the pacifist Left, and Maxim Gorky, both in Moscow.

The first speaker was a stooped but prickly Englishman, who talked inaudibly for twenty minutes about the close connection in England between traditions and liberties, and the recent danger of censorship. With this speech E. M. Forster entered a kind of half-hearted political period that he later called *Two Cheers for Democracy.* There was more wistfulness than militancy in Forster's statement that he would perhaps be a Communist "if I was [sic] a younger and braver man, for in Communism I can see hope." He was followed by a heavyweight polemicist who brought the proceedings to life again with an impassioned simplification of Western history, and by asking in effect for a division of the house. Julien Benda, author of *La Trahison des clercs* (1927), rapped out a stinging speech affirming that, in the West, intellectual activity had traditionally stood apart from material and economic forces and inviting his Communist colleagues to answer the question: "Does Lenin form a continuity with Montaigne, or is there a fracture?" Benda had, in fact, been mousetrapped. Several speakers had their answers ready: Marx belongs to the West; Benda had ignored half the Western tradition in order to make his case; the advances of modern science are based on the very materialism Benda had scorned. They swarmed all over him.

The Congress was off, and it kept running for four more days with sessions at three in the afternoon and nine in the evening, and an extra meeting Tuesday morning, Malraux presiding, on questions of organization. The speeches poured out, ranging from one-minute greetings to a forty-five-minute harangue by Barbusse, who mistook himself for the impresario of all left-wing culture. He emptied the hall. In the heat, more and more suspenders came into sight as jackets were taken off. Speeches in foreign tongues, followed by translation, provided long intervals for beer and conversation. Yet the enthusiasm kept returning. The German poet Regler made a fiery speech about the resistance to Hitler among writers still in Germany, and dramatically handed to Gide and Barbusse token copies of underground pamphlets. "They're being circulated at this very moment." Spontaneously by all accounts, the audience rose at this point and sang the *Internationale*. Regler had in fact departed from his prepared text. Johannes Becher, later to become East German culture commissar, was outraged and hissed at Regler from the wings: "This Congress can't pretend to be neutral any longer." But Becher had nothing to fear. Efficiently organized, indulgently reported in most of the newspapers, capable of keeping its family squabbles in an inside pocket, the Congress appeared to be a great success.

But could such a congress succeed in being anything more than a mere epiphenomenon clinging to the surface of history? Could it ever constitute a nexus of real forces, a congress of *res gestae?* Of this much I feel sure: the thirties worried their way through a prolonged economic and political crisis that threw intellectuals and artists into a state of increasing tension sometimes verging on panic. The Congress is a surprisingly clear window into that decade.

The year 1935 stands centered in a triple frame of events. In 1930, Europe felt the impact of the American *Krach,* and it was the year that the Nazi Party won six and a half million votes. But the German Communist leader Thälmann refused any united front against Hitler and proclaimed that the enemy was still capitalism and the Fascism of social democracy. Until 1934 the famous "Third Period" of the Communist International called for the radicalization of the masses and no compromise with the non–Communist Left. At the other end of the decade, complementing 1930, stand Munich and all that followed.

Here is the first frame. Hitler's installation as chancellor in January 1933 and the Reichstag fire should have been enough to alert the astute to the true direction of things. But we know they were not; in May 1933 Gide was still able to write in his journal: "Excellent speech by Hitler to the Reichstag. . . . Everything remains to be seen." This date pairs off with the Proclamation of the Axis in November 1936. Here is the second frame.

In the mid-thirties, France had to assume cultural leadership of Europe by default. Writing from Moscow, Victor Serge referred to France as "an oasis . . . facing a crisis." Paris became the arena of events in great part because France was the only country in which the Communist Party emerged from the Third Period of Comintern strategy with both numbers and prestige. In Italy and Germany, the Communists had been liquidated or forced underground. But naturally in France a domestic confrontation was needed to produce a sense of urgency. Fascism in Germany and Italy could look remote and even comic until it struck in the streets of Paris. A highly complex and often contradictory sequence of events, including a financial scandal, a cabinet crisis, and a powerful prefect of police, led to what has often been interpreted as an attempted Fascist coup against the Third Republic and the parliamentary system. That was February 6, 1934. We now know better; the Fascist leagues and the Action française had planned no such coup. Nevertheless, soldiers had to be brought in to protect the Chamber of Deputies from attackers on the Place de la Concorde.

Pushed hard by demonstrators armed with iron bars and knives mounted on poles to disable the horses, the soldiers finally had to fire into the crowd. For all its confusion (there were quite a few Communists among the rioters), this single night of fighting galvanized Paris into a series of frenzied counterdemonstrations, meetings, appeals to honor and to freedom, congresses, maneuvers, and reversals of policy. Out of that activity came the victory of the Popular Front and the Blum government. Politically and intellectually, the three years from the February riots in 1934 to the triumph and decline of the Popular Front in 1936 form the heartland of the decade, the unreal interval during which it seemed still possible to save European culture from totalitarianism without war, and even to assimilate the Soviet revolution into the Western tradition without more bloodshed. Here is the third frame.

In June 1936, huddled over his shortwave radio in Norway, Trotsky wrote his fifth successive pamphlet about the crisis and called it "The French Revolution Has Begun." He was wrong; who knows what it would have taken to make him right? That was the way things felt in Paris also.

Like most crises, this one arose out of the convergence of several strands that were difficult to distinguish at the time. In each instance, there appears to be a general European development with its French counterpart. Recognized late and poorly understood even when most blatant in its methods and ambitions, Italian and German Fascism could still get away with almost anything in the mid-thirties. French Fascism lumped together militant patriots organized in *ligues,* royalist maneuvering, and anti-Semitism inherited from the Dreyfus affair.

The second strand concerns the Third Communist International. Its strategy shifted drastically in May 1934 for reasons that remain cloudy. After six years of bitter attacks on the non-Communist Left came the apparent thaw—reconciliation, the Popular Front, "the hand outstretched" to Socialists and even willing radicals, and an elaborate machinery of front organizations and cultural activities. In France, the Party seemed to have jumped the gun, primarily through Barbusse's unpredictable yet successful activities. His Amsterdam-Pleyel movement against Fascism and war in 1932 was the first of its kind. The non-Communist Vigilance Committee of Anti-Fascist Intellectuals sprang up overnight after the February riots in 1934 and set up something like an interlocking directorate with a series of Communist-sponsored groups and meetings. The most important was the Association of Revolutionary Writers and Artists (A.E.A.R.) that Vaillant-Couturier founded in 1932. The following year he assigned to Aragon the joint editorship of its monthly review, *Commune,* as well as responsibility for the Maisons de la Culture. Unlike the bleak years after 1927 when the Surrealists had tried to find nourishment in a suspicious, badly split party, in 1934 the Communists prepared to welcome the entire French Left into a huge pasture of anti-Fascism. There, the Left's fondness for revolutionary slogans, its ignorance of Marxism, and its admiration for what it thought was happening in Soviet Russia led many individuals into highly irresponsible pronouncements and actions.

Fascism and Communism were the principal ideological strands. But there were more. A genuine, vociferous opposition of militant Marxists and anti-

Stalinist Communists had existed since Trotsky's banishment—one might even say since Bertrand Russell's *The Practice and Theory of Bolshevism* (1920), in which he called the Soviet system "moribund" because the Party had taken over. But Trotsky was everybody's devil—too eloquent, too shrill, too intellectual. Russell could not be counted on: by 1932 he was endorsing Soviet policies. (In 1945 he advocated preemptive war against the Soviet Union before it developed the atom bomb.) Other writers like Panait Istrati, who produced evidence to show that the great experiment had gone sour, were quickly labeled Fascists. For those who wanted to look, magazines like *La Révolution Prolétarienne* regularly furnished reliable information about what was happening in L'URSS—a combination of letters that almost reproduces the French word for bear. But few intellectuals ever heard about the case of Victor Serge, who had been imprisoned for months and then banished to Orenburg with no means of supporting his family. The Russians had the equivalent of unlimited political and ideological credit; they alone had achieved a revolution in the twentieth century. For the French Left in 1935, "revolution" meant the republican tradition threaded from 1789 through 1848 and the Commune meant October in Russia, and also meant whatever the "Soviet experiment" had become since then. It made a heady brew. Few took the trouble to examine what had happened in twenty years, except to see that "Soviet power plus electrification" (as Lenin put it) seemed to have been a stunning success. The Big Bear had even joined the League of Nations in 1934.

The only organized group of self-professed Marxists to withdraw firmly and stridently from the Party, after having signed up, was the Surrealists. They contrived to be *plus royaliste que le roi.* Their constant protests that the Party was compromising the true revolutionary cause looked like a caricature of the Trotskyist opposition (which they later joined) and had the same kind of insistent integrity.

The last strand is pacifism. Everyone but the extreme Fascists opposed war. One of the semi-scandals of the decade was the resolution adopted by the Oxford Union in 1933, by 275 votes against 153, that its members would "not take up arms for king or country under any circumstances." Moderates, anti-Fascists, militant Communists—they all considered themselves part pacifists under the skin.

These four strands and many more coincided in the mid-thirties in the sense that they reached peak intensities at approximately the same time. But the tensions they produced in historical events and in individual lives arose because these forces worked not in one direction but in contradiction; anti-Fascism and pacifism were clearly at cross-purposes. The steady movement of intellectuals toward Soviet sympathies and Communism at the very moment when Stalin was clamping his iron control over the Party through the purges compromised the cause of anti-Fascism. A whole generation of honest men tolerated in the Soviet Union the kind of conduct they condemned in Germany and would have opposed with their lives in their own country. The pacifists and the Trotskyist opposition could do little more than call down a plague on everybody's house.

Dissent and disarray characterize any ideological crisis. But the degree of polarization in 1935 almost equaled that caused by the Dreyfus case. In April Maurice Reynal founded an independent monthly newspaper to report on art exhibits and publish little-known writers like Artaud, Queneau, Michel Leiris, and Reverdy. Its name cannot be improved upon: *La Bête Noire*. But in its four numbers the paper found very little "artistic and literary" room to turn around in. The first number devotes the front page to a *"mise au point"* by Léon Pierre-Quint. It is a revealing text. He states that all literary and artistic schools are being deserted wholesale in favor of the Fascist leagues or the Young Socialists. The young are no longer interested in Surrealism, which has now "come into its own in the university." The public has become so militant in its views that it is no longer possible to make political jokes in the music halls and cabarets. An uncommitted writer, Pierre-Quint reports, is considered either an anarchist or a *petit bourgeois*. The fourth and last number of *La Bête Noire* was almost entirely devoted, not to an exhibit or a writer, but to the proceedings of the Writers' Congress.

Bastille Day in 1935 gives the ultimate illustration to the way things were going. Organized groups had been jockeying for position since May. It turned out to be a perfect summer day. While an estimated six hundred planes flew overhead, the police for once stayed systematically out of sight. Three successive *défilés* or processions ran their course passionately yet peacefully. In the morning, the traditional military parade took care of the Unknown Soldier. In the afternoon, something approaching half a million Communists and Socialists, plus a scattering of radicals and every leftist intellectual group with any soul, trooped in a joyful mass from the Place de la Bastille to the Place de la Nation. In front of the statue of Baudin (shot during the brief uprising against Louis Napoleon's *coup d'état* in 1851) they raised their fists and renewed his oath to stand fast on the barricades. Here in the streets, the Popular Front discovered the euphoric spirit that carried it to victory a year later. Red Soviet flags mingled with the *tricolore;* apparently for the first time in such a mass meeting, both the *Internationale* and the *Marseillaise* could be sung without catcalls. Every serving participant testifies to the semi-delirium of the occasion. Fascism *must* fall back before this return to revolutionary traditions.

That evening, with torches, between thirty and forty thousand representatives of the right-wing Croix de Feu marched down the Avenue des Champs-Elysées, in step and in uniform. It was the most impressive display of force Colonel de La Rocque's semi-Fascist organization had ever staged, but from here on, its numbers dwindled.

Amid this extreme polarization of opinion that obviously left many citizens gasping, several forms of expression took on a renewed life. Every newspaper and review ran its *enquête* or opinion survey on some variation of the question: *Can we avoid a revolution?* Congresses and meetings and assemblies came so fast that the Mutualité could not handle them and the traffic overflowed to the Salle Bullier and the Cirque d'Hiver and the velodromes. Later, at the critical juncture of May 1936, while the striking workers waited for their new government to take office, this energy found a new tactic: the sit-in strike.

The only man apparently able to give some direction to these events was neither a fanatic nor a rabble-rouser. Léon Blum began as a first-rate literary and theater critic and became a courageous and honest statesman. But even his integrity failed the test of the Spanish Civil War. It is either appropriate or ironic that at this crucial moment France put itself in the hands of a literary man. Inevitably he attended the Writers' Congress and found himself face to face ("nose to nose," as the newspaper account reads) with Aragon, who had written a wildly antibourgeois poem four years earlier with the memorable line: "Shoot Léon Blum." At least one reporter was watching alertly and wrote: "But nobody flapped. The Communist poet-politico cordially shook hands with the socialist politico-poet." There is the decade in a nutshell. The pop front was a handshake in the wilderness. Today it has been romanticized by indulgent memories and documentary films (1936: *Le Grand Tournant*) into the last utopia.

Everyone I have talked to among the organizers of the Congress produces the same explanation for all that effort: anti-Fascism. Yet the invitation sent out to writers all over the world began in this bland style called "equivocal" by *La Bête Noire:* "In the face of the dangers which threaten culture in a number of countries, a group of writers are taking the initiative of bringing together a congress in order to examine and discuss means for defending that culture. They propose that the congress clarify the conditions of literary creation and the relations between the writer and his public." Nowhere in the invitation does Fascism or any political term appear.

The vagueness of the invitation was clearly a tactic to appeal to as wide a group of writers as possible. But how did the whole thing start? The explanation seems relatively simple. In August 1934 the First All-Union Congress of Soviet Writers was held in Moscow. Though a few independent voices were raised (soon to be silenced), the huge meeting served primarily as the occasion on which to promulgate the official doctrine of Socialist Realism—later called Zhadonovism after the Central Committee member who made the principal speech at that Congress. A number of foreign writers were invited to attend, including Aragon, Jean-Richard Bloch, Paul Nizan, and Malraux from France. They returned to Paris with varying degrees of enthusiasm for the new doctrine, yet all apparently eager to stage a similar mass meeting of writers in Paris. The Comintern, having just shifted a few months earlier to a new policy of alliances and popular fronts, gave support. A number of other writers were brought in to help plan the Congress, including André Chamson and Louis Guilloux. Guilloux, who was one of the secretaries and handled a large part of the correspondence, stated that the man who supplied the funds was Mikhail Kozloff, Comintern agent and commissar of the Soviet delegation. In France, of course, the Party had no official or legal control over writers. But it could now browbeat and shame them with the issue of anti-Fascism, even though the Party itself had been trying to ignore Hitler and Mussolini for five years. In an era of peace conferences and huge international assemblages, a congress could be turned into an instrument of policy.

Of the twenty-four signers of the invitation, four out of the first five in alphabetical order (Abraham, Alain, Aragon, Barbusse, Bloch) were known Communist militants—though Barbusse was allowed a very long tether. Alain, on the other hand, was the very voice of the radical party, a widely respected writer and philosopher who had taken an active part in left-wing groups after the February riots. (His name disappeared from later lists; he refused to participate in the Congress.) Other names that would be immediately recognized were those of André Gide, André Malraux, and Romain Rolland. It would be hard for leftist writers to resist this call, even though its terms were very vague. But quite a few were in fact missing. Neither Thomas Mann nor Bernard Shaw nor H. G. Wells attended, though the first two were subsequently named to the twelve-man presidium. Upton Sinclair, considered the model writer-activist because of his candidacy in California on the Socialist ticket, did not respond. Among the French, Jules Romains and Montherlant stayed away in spite of blandishments. Georges Duhamel is reported to have said, "I cannot take part in a congress along with Gide, and with men who might, one day, be responsible for the death of my three sons." One wonders if the critic Lukács, at that date in Moscow, was even invited. In addition to the organizers listed above, here are a few names from the 230 delegates from thirty-eight countries who did attend: E. M. Forster and Aldous Huxley from England; Heinrich Mann, Bertolt Brecht, Anna Seghers, Johannes Becher, and Lion Feuchtwanger from Germany—all in exile; Michael Gold and Waldo Frank fresh from the congress in New York which had organized the League of American Writers and abolished the earlier John Reed clubs; Pasternak, Babel, Ehrenburg, Alexsei Tolstoy from the U.S.S.R. Though Valle-Inclán from Spain had been put on the program, he did not appear. French writers were legion. In addition to Gide, Malraux, and Aragon, the following made speeches of some magnitude or significance: Benda, Guéhenno, Cassou, Chamson, Nizan, Jean-Richard Bloch, Tzara, and Éluard (representing Breton and the Surrealists).

The style of the Congress, judging by newspaper accounts and photographs, was that of a popular assembly prepared to honor its culture heroes, responding generously to the spoken word and impatient with any profound content. The newspapers, naturally, loved the anecdotal and sartorial side. Both Huxley and Mike Gold wore funny hats. Everyone on the platform kept his jacket on in spite of the heat. But the *Dépêche de Toulouse* reported that "Monsieur Vaillant-Couturier walked up to give his speech in a beach costume with a huge scarf tied in a bow around his neck." Delegations of children were brought up in track suits and bare feet to present flowers to foreign writers. Books were sold in the foyer, with authors to autograph them. People sketched the speakers. Photographers prowled. The talks went on and on. Enormous quantities of beer were drunk. The management of the Mutualité had to turn the lights off to drive away the knots of people arguing late into the night. The main headquarters for the celebrities and insiders was the Closerie des Lilas, floating on its fifty-year history of banquets and literary battles. Most reporters enjoyed themselves and shared the excitement. "A scene of high drama to which the modern world, hungry for enchantments, is now treating itself. . . . And what a crowd! The young and the not so young, activists, partisans, outlandish types, and girlfriends with their faces craftily painted in ocher and carmine, their fingernails tinted every color in the book."

Aragon and Nizan's monthly *Commune*—which was in a position to be considered the horse's mouth—announced that all the speeches would be collected and published in a book. Many duller and less significant works burden our shelves, but somewhere an editor showed the wisdom not to feel bound by the announcement. The principal speeches can be found scattered through various reviews and the sequence reconstructed. After Benda's rash challenge to materialism almost everyone closed ranks and found continuity and harmony in all directions. Writing in New York about what he called the "Writers' International," Malcolm Cowley had this to say in *The New Republic* after digesting the texts: "[N]obody spoke in favor of abandoning 'bourgeois culture' in favor of proletarian culture." He was generally right, but he can't have read everything.

Saturday night was the main event. It must have been worth standing in line to pay the three-franc entry fee to hear what the heavyweights would say about "the individual." Gide led off. He had made an address the previous October called "Littérature et révolution" in which he met Socialist Realism head-on by calling for something more to his liking: "Communist individualism." It must have been hard for him now to raise the ante. Nevertheless, he produced a long, carefully thought-out speech and was followed by Malraux, Ehrenburg, and Max Brod, Kafka's friend and executor, who spoke of the individual as a pure dream in a world defined by society and reason.

The next three days became very confused. The order of speakers had to be changed; squabbles arose about who should be allowed to "intervene" and for how long. On Sunday afternoon, humanism was the announced subject. Brecht got three minutes, whereas he was supposed to have had fifteen Friday night on "Cultural Heritage." Every topic began to sound the same. Sunday night was "Nation and Culture." Chamson gave a solid talk. Barbusse scuttled it with his leaden echoes. Mike Gold shook out his long hair and recited his working-class background. Except for a few tense exchanges, things sank into the doldrums until the closing session Tuesday night. Apparently, the audience never failed to fill the hall. The organizers were very efficient. On the final evening came the most vivid moment of all. Pasternak had been brought to Paris on the last day, under duress and under guard. His name was not in the program. Kozloff had insisted on his presence. His entrance into the Palais de la Mutualité produced a standing ovation. Here is the account carried in Barbusse's *Monde:* its bad faith makes one wince. "In spite of an illness from which he has been suffering for two months, the great Soviet lyric poet insisted on attending the Congress. He recited two poems, beautiful examples of the blossoming of the new Socialist Realism." No one else had the courage or the imagination to read anything but a prepared speech. Pasternak made his short preliminary remarks in French.

> I wish to speak here of poetry, and not of sickness. Poetry will always exist down in the grass; it will always be necessary to bend down to perceive it; it will always be too simple a thing to discuss in meetings. It will remain the organic function of a happy creature, overflowing with the felicity of language, tensed in the birthright of his heart, forever aware of his mission. The more happy men are, the easier it will be to find artists.

It is difficult to imagine the tone of the last sentence. One of the poems he recited (with Malraux translating) was "So It Begins," about children growing up. It ends, "So poetry sets them on their way." Without that instant of light and life, the Congress might have shriveled up and blown away.

If Pasternak gave literature back to the Congress in the form of poetry, it was the dissidents and the hotheads who gave it life. Obviously the organizers wanted to show a united front, both to the intellectuals they were trying to galvanize into action and to the forces of Fascism that were marching all over Europe. Malcontents who doubted the purposes or the integrity of the Congress were not welcome, and in general they were maneuvered into the background. Since texts of the announced speeches had to be sent to the secretariat of the Congress in advance in order to allow for preparation of press releases, summaries, and in some cases translations, the organizing committee could usually anticipate undesirable speakers. For example, the Czech delegate and poet Vítězslav Nezval waited his turn for two days in the wings and suddenly discovered the Congress was over. He had planned to greet the gathering in the name of both the left front and the literary avant-garde of Czechoslovakia, and to go on to condemn both proletarian literature and Socialist Realism. He was also one of those responsible for inviting the two Surrealists Breton and Éluard to Prague two months earlier for a series of literary-political manifestations outside Party sponsorship. This carries us into another story.

2

The political vagaries of Surrealism constitute one of the most fascinating case histories of intellectual gymnastics and conscience-searching in the thirties. The chronicle has now been filled out in considerable detail, but usually in such a way as to detach the political needle-threadings from literary activity, or to treat the politics as an inopportune and marginal pastime that merely distracted from the aesthetic concerns of the movement. Many people are involved, but only Breton remains squarely in the center of the picture. Rudely telescoped, the story runs like this.

Launched ambitiously in 1924–1925 with a manifesto and a review called *La Révolution Surréaliste,* the Surrealist movement began as an extraordinary amalgam of generalized poetics and semi-scientific experiments in altered states of consciousness. The Surrealists were also among the first French intellectuals to read Freud attentively. Almost immediately, however, a series of personal and historic circumstances carried the Surrealists toward Marxism and the Communist Party. It mattered little that the Party was in a very dry season, holding out few rewards to artists and intellectuals. Early in 1927 the five principal Surrealists joined the Party and accepted assignment to local cells. After the expulsion of Trotsky and Zinoviev in November of the same year, they had some second thoughts but did not go away. From 1927 to 1933 the Surrealists carried on a steady guerrilla war with the Party while insisting on their right to participate in events and organizations designed to give some shape and direction to artists on the Left. Supported in varying ways by Péret, Éluard, and Crevel, Breton acted in a headstrong fashion. He reaffirmed his faith in Freud. He refused to give automatic obedience to directives from Moscow. He defended Trotsky. He would not accept any policies that compromised artistic freedom and the right to experiment in new forms of expression. The Surrealists and their numerous publications represented a challenge to the steady movement of intellectuals toward the Party after 1932. That year, after a lengthy period of despicable, two-faced maneuvers, Aragon abandoned the Surrealists completely for Communism. In 1933 the Surrealists intrepidly attacked Barbusse and Romain Rolland for organizing the Amsterdam-Pleyel movement against war, calling it a betrayal of class warfare. They censured Ehrenburg and the editorial pages of *L'Humanité*. For these accumulated reasons and others, Breton and Éluard were finally expelled from the Communist-controlled Association of Revolutionary Artists and Writers. February 1934 sparked them back to life along with everyone else. Breton was one of the principal sponsors of the first major response to the riots among intellectuals. Dated February 10, "Appel à la lutte" calls for unity of action against Fascism and for a general strike. In an important lecture that June in Brussels, he reviewed the whole social evolution of Surrealism and reaffirmed its materialist position by stating: "The liberation of the spirit requires as a prior condition the liberation of man himself." At this point, Surrealism had reached the peak of its activity and its international influence. After the highly successful visit to Prague in April 1935, Breton and Éluard accepted an invitation to the Canary Islands and, in the spring of 1936, to London for a huge Surrealist exhibit with lectures and related events.

When announcements went out for the 1935 Writers' Congress, the Surrealists expressed doubt about the need to defend bourgeois culture and demanded that the agenda include a discussion of the "right to pursue, in literature and in art, new means of expression." They constituted too important a group to be excluded from the Congress. Yet not a single Surrealist appeared in the printed program, even though René Crevel was an active member of the organizing committee for the Congress. Everything was obviously up in the air when, a week before the Congress opened, André Breton recognized Ilya Ehrenburg in the street. An opponent of the Soviets in 1917, Ehrenburg had changed his mind and had spent most of the last twenty years in Paris writing for *L'Humanité* and representing Soviet literature and culture. In 1934 he published a collection of essays on the French literary scene, praising Gide and Malraux, criticizing Mauriac and Morand, and saving his most concentrated vitriol for the Surrealists.

> I don't know if they are really sick or if they are only faking their craziness. . . . These young phosphorescents, wound up in theories of onanism and the philosophy of exhibitionism, playact at being the zealots of revolutionary intransigence and proletarian honesty. . . . They have their pastimes. For example, they study pederasty and dreams.

He worked several pages out of it. Now, if there is one prejudice Breton imposed on the group around him, it was the exclusion of homosexuals. (Only

Crevel was tolerated.) Fairly early in the game the Surrealists had developed a somewhat violent strain and believed in what they called "correction." Breton, seeing their slanderer there in the street, simply raised his arm and slapped him—twice, according to some accounts. If Breton knew that Ehrenburg was head of the Soviet delegation to the Congress, it did not deter him. Ehrenburg retaliated in the organizing committee: the Surrealists must be excluded. The behind-the-scenes maneuvers were long and painful, lasting until after the Congress had opened. Crevel was both absolutely loyal to Breton and a dedicated Party worker. Jean Cassou told how Crevel persuaded him to go to the Closerie des Lilas one night after the evening session in order to convince Ehrenburg that Breton must be allowed to speak. Because the organizing committee wanted to maintain unity at all costs, Ehrenburg had a simple and totally effective answer. If Breton spoke, the Soviet delegation would walk out. Meanwhile, a kind of compromise had been reached: Éluard would read Breton's speech at the Monday evening session.[2]

Éluard was finally given the platform after midnight following a long talk on dreams by Tzara that had sent most of the audience home. Breton had written an effective and scandalous speech that trampled resolutely across all the guidelines set up by the context and the program of the Congress. He denounced the Franco-Soviet pact and any cultural rapprochement, the new patriotic face of *L'Humanité,* the Popular Front ideology, and the growing tendency to condemn all German thought. Éluard apparently read the text well, but another incident was already developing that contributed to the neglect of the strong Surrealist attack on the Congress as a sellout to the existing order.

Starting back during Tzara's talk, voices had been raised in the auditorium clamoring for a discussion of Victor Serge. For those who knew the tale, this was a more explosive situation than the Surrealist dispute. Journalists were watching alertly. The protests came from a group of non-Communist Marxists and Trotskyites, two of whom had been scheduled to speak only as the result of desperate personal appeals to Malraux and Gide. It was very late. The burly *service d'ordre* of ushers provided by the Communists left their positions and converged on the troublemakers while Éluard was reading Breton's speech. The Serge advocates had no objection to that text, but they wanted their turn. The most obstreperous of them, Henri Poulaille, finally walked out, taking the bouncers with him and ripping his photograph out of the display case on his way through the foyer. Most of the newspapers picked up these rumblings; not many of them were represented the next afternoon in a smaller hall when Magdeleine Paz was finally given the floor. Gide, Malraux, and Barbusse sat on the platform with knitted brows (as a photograph shows) while she stood to speak. Citing the printed program, she affirmed the need to discuss a specific case involving freedom of expression, direct and indirect censorship, and the dignity of the writer. Serge, French-language writer of Russian parents, Belgian birth, and revolutionary convictions, in 1919 had gone to Russia, where he was admitted to the Party and given important responsibilities in organizing and administering the Third International. His novels and historical works describing the early years of the Revolution in Russia were known to French-speaking intellectuals. In 1927 he was excluded from the Party and imprisoned without trial for several weeks on suspicion of Trotskyite sympathies. Arrested again in 1933, he was deported without trial to Orenburg in the Urals, where he was confined with no resources, material or intellectual, for three years. He could write but not send his manuscripts abroad. He and his wife were both in precarious health.

Magdeleine Paz's speech ran close to an hour, with an impassioned coda: "Right now, he's paying the price. While we sit here at a congress convoked to defend the integrity of thought, out there, on the other side of the Urals, a thinking man is trying to remain calm and hold on to his hope in the revolution." Three Russians, including Ehrenburg, answered her charges by saying Citizen Kibalchich (his family name) had bitten the hand that fed him; they knew nothing about the French writer Victor Serge. The Belgian delegate angrily retorted that they lied, that in fact Serge had translated many Russian texts of the Revolution, including the poetry of one of the Soviet delegates who had just spoken and who would otherwise be unknown in France. Unfortunately, no one made a motion or proposed any specific action. These particular speeches are the hardest of all to find. Anna Seghers provided an escape route by complaining that if the Congress was going to talk about individual cases, why didn't they bring up all the imprisoned German writers? Gide had been immensely nervous throughout the discussion, scribbling draft after draft of a closing statement. What he finally said expressed concern for the security of the Soviet Union and confidence in its actions.

3

It is no easy matter to catch the spirit and specifics of a congress that lasted five days and must have generated upward of a third of a million words, now dispersed. In order to sample those speeches, I shall reduce them to six and quote a key passage from each with a minimum of comment. Each of these six men had wide experience in polemical writing and intellectual maneuvering. In effect, they form three loose pairs of writers; each pair displays an obvious link and an equally significant contrast. It is the contrasts that I hope will make themselves clear. The first pair is the Soviet delegate Panferov and Aragon, both important and active Party members committed to the doctrine of Socialist Realism officially adopted a year earlier. Panferov spoke at the opening session and concluded his talk thus:

> Clearly, each one of our artists follows his own path, retains his own style and individuality. But all of us move toward the position of Socialist Realism, toward creating a literature such as has never existed in the history of humanity. . . .
> What then is Socialist Realism?
> Socialist Realism, according to the statutes of our writers [union] is the essential method of Soviet literary art and literary criticism. It requires of

the artist that he provide an image that conforms to truth, a concrete historic image of reality in its revolutionary development. This truth and this precision in representing reality must ally themselves with the problem of the ideological reshaping and the education of workers in the spirit of socialism.

Aragon talked on the same subject at the very last session. He was also answering Breton's speech, which had been read the previous day. His tone was fiery, almost gaudy.

Socialist Realism or revolutionary romanticism? Which shall we choose? Realism is the only way to approach the world before us. We must choose the light, and reject the dark. It is a matter of finding our way back, precisely, to the side of the light, and to neglect the shadows. . . .

Here he quoted Lautréamont's *Poésies,* stating that the passage applies perfectly to the Surrealists:

"There are debased writers, dangerous jokers, two-bit fools, solemn mystifiers, veritable lunatics, who deserve to be in an asylum. Their cretin heads, which must have a hole in them somewhere, dream up gigantic monsters which come down to earth instead of drifting away."

At the end:

Who has shouted loudest for freedom of expression? Marinetti—and look where it has led him: to Fascism. We have nothing to hide, and that is why we welcome as a joyful expression the new slogan of Soviet literature: Soviet Realism. Culture is no longer something for just a handful of people.

Aragon was a very valuable property. As time went on, he seemed to be able to get away with anything.

The next pair of speakers had no use for Socialist Realism and the Party line. Breton loved to rumble his rhetoric. He was also hopping mad as he wrote. One hopes Éluard read the text as if it were a sermon. "Beware of the perils of too great faith!" Breton said of Comintern directives backing up the Franco-Soviet pact. After an attack on those who took Rimbaud's name in vain as a political rather than a poetic revolutionary, he concludes:

We maintain that the activity of interpreting the world must go on and remain linked to the activity of transforming the world. . . . The movement of authentic contemporary poets toward a poetry of propaganda . . . signifies a negation of the very factors which historically determine the nature of poetry. To defend culture means above all to take in hand the cause of whatever stands up under serious materialist analysis, of what is viable and will continue to bear fruit. Stereotype declarations against Fascism and war will not ever succeed in liberating the spirit from its shackles, old and new. . . ."Transform the world," said Marx; "Change life," said Rimbaud. Those two watchwords are one and the same to us.

Allusions to Marx's *Theses on Feuerbach* formed one of the refrains of the Congress; Breton made it clear that there should be no compromise with bourgeois values and that Popular Front politics meant just that.

I pair Breton's intransigence with one of the most straightforward speeches in the whole five days. Gaetano Salvemini was an Italian historian and Socialist deputy whom Mussolini had exiled and stripped of his citizenship. What Salvemini said sounds very elementary. But remember: the atmosphere of the Congress was such that almost every speaker began with the symbolic greeting "Comrades." Salvemini had been fighting Fascism with word and deed probably longer than anyone else attending the Congress.

If you give the name "Fascism" to all bourgeois societies; if you close your eyes to the fact that Fascism means bourgeois society with something added, that is, a bourgeois society which has suppressed the very possibility of cultural freedom; if you apply the same treatment to two different forms of society—then you run the risk of allowing in non-Fascist societies the destruction of fragments of intellectual liberty that are not sufficient but that nevertheless have great value. We do not greatly appreciate light and air as long as we have them. To understand their value, we have to lose them. But the day we lose our freedoms, we shall not easily win them back.

Confronted by Fascist-type bourgeois societies, we Italians and Germans have had to take a position of radical negation. In non-Fascist bourgeois societies, radical nihilism is a dangerous thing. Do not scorn your freedoms; rather, defend them stubbornly, while declaring them inadequate and struggling to develop them.

The freedom to create is constrained in non-Fascist bourgeois societies. In Fascist-type bourgeois societies it is totally suppressed. It is partially suppressed in Soviet Russia. Trotsky's *History of the Russian Revolution* cannot be read in Russia. It is in Russia that Victor Serge is held prisoner. . . .

The sudden sucking in of breath at those naked words must have been audible for some distance. Anti-Fascism could take many forms, but the Congress did its best to disguise that fact. Salvemini was later appointed lecturer in history at Harvard—over President Lowell's objections.

The last pair is Gide and Malraux. Both spoke Saturday night, on the individual. Picking up a sentence out of the preface of Malraux's novel *Le Temps du mépris,* Gide developed a history of French literature in which it is Diderot and Rousseau who, after the privileged forms of classicism, brought back the turbulence and the popular feeling missing since Rabelais. Admirable as it has been, the culture handed on by bourgeois society remains artificial, something under glass.

Today in the capitalist society we still inhabit, it seems to me that the only worthwhile literature is a literature of opposition.

For the bourgeois writer, to have a true communion with his class is an impossibility. To have a communion with the people . . . Well, I'll have to say that it is equally impossible as long as the people remain what they are today, as long as they are not what they can and must become, what they will become if we do our part.[3]

. . . Only the enemies of Communism can see it as a desire for uniformity. What we expect of it, and what the Soviet Union is beginning to show us after a difficult period of struggles and temporary constraints in expectation of greater freedom, is a condition of society which would permit the fullest development of each man, the bringing forth and application of all his potentialities. In our sad Western world, as I have said, we still fall far short of the mark. For a time social questions threaten to encroach on all others—not that they strike us as more interesting than the others—but because the condition of the culture depends closely on the state of the society. It is a devotion to culture that leads us to say: As long as our society remains what it is, our first concern will be to change it.

Gide must have been in good form. He would soon regret and virtually eat his words. Deep in politics and polemic, he wrote very little during 1935 in his *Journal*. There is only one page on the Congress, which must have devoured three full weeks of his life. He tells how he greeted one dark and richly robed lady by saying he was happy to see Greece represented. *"Moi,"* she replied with annoyance, *"c'est l'Inde."*

Malraux delivered the only formal speech that did not follow a written text. Afterward the press bureau reproduced a single page of notes from which he had talked for close to an hour. He numbered eleven points, one a quotation from the preface to *Le Temps du mépris,* each a potential speech by itself. Number 8:

Fascist and Communist communions. Reply to Gide. There is a communion possible as of now with the people, not in its nature (there can never be a communion in nature) but in its finality, in this case meaning in its will to revolution. Every real communion implies a finality.

The most striking passage comes in point 3. Before him sat a vast assemblage of writers whose literary existence depended on their establishing a name and attracting readers, and who had erected for themselves the elaborate stage of an international congress. Of all of them, Malraux was the writer who most appeared to move through history as if his life were a dramatic extension of his literary work—or vice versa. Here is what he said, according to his notes:

Individualism arises out of the fact that man finds pleasure in looking upon himself as someone else *[un autre],* in living biographically. The humanism we desire to create, and which displays its earlier stages in the line of thought that connects Voltaire to Marx, requires above all a true awareness of man, a new stock-taking.

To be a man means, for each of us, to reduce to a minimum the actor within him.
[Être un homme, c'est réduire au minimum, pour chacun, sa part de comédie.]

The only proper response to that statement by one of the principal organizers would have been the immediate disbanding of the Congress. One wonders what note of irony—or bad faith—tinges the last sentence.

4

It is high time (as Aragon snorted, quoting Boileau in support of Socialist Realism) "to call a cat a cat." This was one of the most thoroughly rigged and steamrollered assemblages ever perpetrated on the face of Western literature in the name of culture and freedom. That estimate does not diminish but rather amplifies its significance as a historical and intellectual event. Only a few rightist critics and Fascist rags talked of funds from Moscow and Red writers. There sat some of Europe's most distinguished men of letters presiding over a meeting that systematically swept into a corner any dissent from the prevailing opinion that the true revolutionary spirit belonged to the Soviet government. Did they know better? Could they have known better? Must we call into question the good faith of all organizers and participants? These are sore questions. Only Alain got off the bandwagon. In exchanges I had with them thirty-five years after the fact, both Aragon and Malraux reaffirmed the genuinely anti-Fascist nature of the Congress, accepted their role in it without regret, and rejected any more ominous interpretation of these events, described by Malraux as an "impassioned confusion." Yet one wonders if Salvemini, the writer present who had suffered most for his opposition to Fascism, would have been allowed to deliver his speech had he not been a friend of Gide's. The machinery devoured Nezval, Breton, and Brecht, and kept the Serge affair almost out of sight. The two Communist publications *(Commune; Monde)* purporting to give a full account of the proceedings and to reproduce the important speeches gave only a few slanted lines to Benda, Breton, Salvemini, and Paz. The texts of the last three were too honest and too defiant of the reigning Stalinist ideology to appear anywhere except in a small left-opposition monthly called *Les Humbles*. Several sponsors in retrospect attributed the success of the Congress to the genius of Willi Münzenberg, a wealthy and powerful member of the Central Committee of the German Communist Party. He lived in France and was skilled in Popular Front tactics. He probably played a role behind the scenes, but the strains and stresses go far deeper. In Gombrowicz's crazily apt theater piece, *Operetta,* the militant revolutionary is carried into battle and on to total power on the shoulders of a willing—and obsessively vomiting—professor.

Outwardly the consequences of the Congress were pedestrian. A final declaration was adopted, an international association formed, and an executive committee with national committees appointed—all by the organizing committee, without vote or discussion. Written or at least carefully edited by Gide himself, the declaration made no waves. It asked for more translations, more travel opportunities for writers, and an international literary prize. It declared that the executive committee was prepared "to fight on its own ground, namely culture, against war, Fascism, and generally against every menace to civilization." A few days after the close of the Congress, Gide wrote the Soviet ambassador about Victor Serge and followed through with a formal visit to the embassy. Serge was finally released in 1936, thanks not to the discussion at the Congress or to Gide's appeal but (Serge writes in his memoirs) to Romain Rolland's personal intervention with Stalin. A second congress was held in Spain in the summer of 1936. Given the situation, not much could come of it. At least it provided the occasion for Malraux to meet Hemingway; they divided up the Spanish War for their private novel-writing contest.

The real effects of the Congress lie elsewhere. It was perfectly timed and designed to consolidate the formation of the intellectual Popular Front, without which the political Popular Front would have had a less euphoric reception in the Socialist and radical press. The congress called in New York one month before the French Congress had served the same purpose, apparently responding to the same directives: to politicize the independent, bourgeois *hommes des lettres* in terms of anti-Fascism and "defend the culture." Gide's case is almost classic. Benda had written ten years earlier in *La Trahison des clercs:* "Essentially ours will have been the century of the intellectual organization of political hatreds." By 1935 politics was no longer a pistol shot disrupting the literary concert; it seemed to have become the concert itself.

This development could not be traced to any spread of the idea, dear to Herzen, that the intelligentsia was part of the proletariat because it was exploited, like the working class, by traditional powers. The political drive to rediscover the people had somehow fused with the need to introduce an aesthetic attitude into daily life—a tendency almost universal in Freud, Dada, Surrealism, the Bauhaus, and the personal-journal form of writing to which Gide was dedicated. It was in 1935 that the neglected American writer Joseph Freeman explained and defended proletarian literature with this bald statement, which neatly answers Benda: "The dichotomy between poetry and politics had vanished, and art and life were fused." It begins to sound uncannily like Huysmans or Wilde stood on his head. But now there was a social cause to absorb the deep aesthetic drive toward adventure discernible in the anarchist dalliance of many artists before 1914.

The evolution of the writer can be picked out neatly in the contrast between two almost identical surveys, the one made in 1919 by the editors of the pre-Dada review, *Littérature,* the other made by the editors of the Party-controlled *Commune* in 1934. *Littérature* asked: "Why do you write?" Almost every reply was brief and facetious and implied that there probably was no purpose.

Valéry: Out of weakness.
Paulhan: I am touched that you should want my reasons, but after all, I write very little. Your reproach scarcely concerns me.

Gide: You will be able to classify writers according to whether their answers begin with "In order to," "Out of," or "Because" . . . In my case I write because I have an excellent pen and in order to be read by you . . . But I never contribute to symposia.

Gide declined to contribute to the later survey; yet it was he who had suggested rephrasing the original question to read: "For whom do you write?" Aragon was responsible for both questionnaires. In *Commune* he sifted the responses and added his own editorial comments. This time the answers were serious, long, partisan, far less quotable. Céline rants for a page on the biological impossibility of talking about the status of "writer." Romain Rolland says he writes "for those in the avant-garde of the army on the march." Maublanc wants to call himself a bourgeois revolutionary, but that way, "I run the risk of being suspect to both bourgeois and revolutionaries." No one tries to wisecrack or question the question. Aragon hectored everyone, telling them bluntly to take sides *("Prenez parti!")*. He obviously felt he could prick their bad conscience as members of an intellectual elite. His summation divided the hundred-odd replies into three categories: writing for myself, for my class, or for everyone. The true way needs no signs. He particularly denounced those who separated their political or social activity from their literary art. One of the few replies he did not try to rebut came from Roger Martin du Gard and reverts to the incisive style of the earlier survey: "I see that the world is full of partisans. Too bad: I would like to continue to write for those not yet infected with the contagion of fanaticism." For Aragon, the questionnaire produced less a sampling of attitudes than a device for manipulating or ridiculing them. He was a man of many means.

The tidal movement toward intellectual commitment was evident to the alert minds of that period. In the left-Catholic monthly, *Esprit,* Emmanuel Mounier lamented the stampede toward Communism and compared it to "finding the fountain of youth." What must have been more difficult to detect—and we have by no means freed ourselves from these pitfalls today—is a degree to which the ideological migration of the thirties, and the Writers' Congress in particular, pivoted on a set of heavily exploited confusions or equivocations. Revolution, culture, humanism, fraternity—these giddy terms were all rolled together into the great cause of the middle and late thirties: *anti-Fascism.* Unfortunately, the campaign came late and rarely found tactics more effective than committees, meetings, and tracts. (Gide's and Malraux's trip in January 1934 to Berlin to see Goebbels about the liberation of the Bulgarian Dimitrov appeared to have some effect, even though they had to write a letter because Goebbels would not receive them. Dimitrov, already acquitted by a German court of charges connecting him with the Reichstag fire, was released six weeks later.) However, it is the timing of these events that makes them both ironic and tragic. Comintern policy shifted just in time to swallow the anti-Fascist cause almost whole. The result was a fundamentally bankrupt ideology: it opposed Hitler with a kind of militant pacifism when only resolute force could have stopped him, and it gave unlimited credit to the Soviet government at the moment when the Stalinist freeze had hardened and the massive purges and trials were beginning. Possibly none of us would have shown any better judgment. But in spite of vigorous protests from some of the participants, one cannot interpret these desperate years less harshly.

Events that followed the 1935 Congress make further revelations about how literary figures recovered, or failed to recover, from the great lurch toward Popular Front politics. A year later, Gide visited Russia for six months at the invitation and expense of the Soviets. He contrived to see more than most official guests in spite of, or because of, the VIP treatment. *Retour de l'U.R.S.S.,* the book he published immediately after his return in 1936, was a bombshell. He had praise for the schools and for the gaiety of the young. His criticism was devastating: "I doubt that in any country today, even in Hitler's Germany, men's minds are . . . more constrained, more terrorized, more enslaved." And he could not bear the Soviet superiority complex. "It is the haughtiness of your bluff which made my loss of confidence, of admiration, of joy so painful and so complete." Of course, everyone snarled at Gide all over again, either for betrayal or for fickleness. This book must be read in conjunction with a later volume, published just before his death, of letters, speeches, and statements dating from 1932 to 1937. The title is perfect and wags its finger at the fashions of 1950: *Littérature engagée.* Read together, these documents form a coherent and moving record of a man's dedication and disillusionment. It is not the least of Gide's work, even though the accompanying play, *Robert, ou L'Intérêt général,* is worse than even his own low opinion of it. Gide's politics did not compromise him. But one must go over the whole course to grasp the scope of the story.

Until 1939, Aragon remained the Grand Inquisitor of the French Left, increasingly so when he became co-editor with Paul Nizan of the daily *Ce Soir.* The Moscow trials produced no noticeable turmoil in his mind. His wrigglings to explain the thunderbolt of the Hitler-Stalin pact were despicable. The Occupation forced him to retire to patriotic poetry, underground publishing, and a new literary career after the war. There was no glimmer of de-Stalinization in his politics until the Czech crisis of 1968. But his talents as a novelist died hard. His late novels must be rated among his best. The 1935 Congress came a year after he had published the first of the novel series entitled *Le Monde réel,* dedicated to his Russian wife, Elsa Triolet, "without whom I would have fallen silent." *Les Beaux Quartiers* appeared the next year. It reads like Balzac in reverse: proletarian in intent, bourgeois under the skin. His gift kept renewing itself. Communism was both a counterirritant and his private side bet. For this very reason, Aragon will be one of the most difficult of contemporary authors to insert into literary history.

After the disappointing novel *Le Temps du mépris,* written in the heat of anti-Fascism that also produced the Congress, Malraux put together a group of volunteers and went off to fight with the Loyalists in Spain. He pulled a magnificent novel out of that experience at record speed in 1937: *L'Espoir.* The film *L'Espoir* was made with the government's blessing while the war was still going on. Many of the conversations that fill the novel seem to come directly from the political wrangles and submissions that filled the period from 1934 to 1937, including Malraux's long stays in Russia. Yet politically the book conveys a profound irresoluteness beneath the sturdy anti-Fascism. Subsequently, without any dramatic episodes or major confrontations with old friends, Malraux drifted away from Communism and its outlying areas. After serving de Gaulle he died as one of the last great prophets of high humanistic culture.

Critics have generally neglected or mocked the political record of Surrealism under Breton's leadership. Yet compared to Gide, Aragon, and Malraux, he begins to look like an old walrus of intractable political sagacity. The Congress marks the period in which he was striving to reconcile Marxist materialism with the psychic insights of a whole tradition of visionaries. His best books, *Vases communicants* and *L'Amour fou,* date from 1932 and 1937 respectively. Both display his stern, even haughty resolve to come to terms with some of the problems the Congress listed hopefully in its program and never broached. Just before World War II Breton traveled to Mexico to draft and publish a joint statement on politics and culture with Trotsky. He never gave up hope for a better world. He could resist the immense intellectual suasion of the Communist Party probably because he had organized and headed his own Surrealist party. Under pressure, Breton's political naiveté took the form of an uncompromisingly principled idealism. It served him better than the conciliatory maneuverings of the literary figures who led the Congress.

5

What then was this 1935 Writers' Congress that we should pick it over for so long? Wasn't it purely and simply a flop? It could be painted very easily as a monstrous machine for grinding out worthless copy. It had no effect on history or policy, and the principal side effects worked to the benefit of a militant party subservient to a terroristic foreign state. Couldn't we forget the whole thing? Shouldn't we stick to our habits of examining individual careers and major works of art? I think not.

In the past, writers have organized themselves into different kinds of groups, from official academics to disgruntled café cliques. But unless one goes back to the great ecclesiastical councils, there have been no major attempts like the Paris Congress to mobilize all categories of writers around a political issue, however blurred, and in one convocation, however streamrolled. Even the Soviet writers' congresses that provided the precedent tended to avoid basic political discussion and to deal with the writer as the servant of the state. In their own terms, the Soviet congresses were fairly successful. Since it really had no terms, the Paris Congress neither succeeded nor failed. In a mammoth public ritual it consecrated the formation of an intellectual Popular Front. But that apparent fusion of forces and the euphoria it produced were based on a set of misunderstandings and ambiguities. "Revolution" remained as fuzzy as the "culture" they had met to defend. Since no question ever came to a vote, no terms or issues had to be clarified. The Congress probably tells us as much about the easily hoodwinked idealism, the opportunism, and the vanity of writers as about the political stresses of the era. For those who wanted to know, it was possible to find out about the terror that reigned in Soviet Russia as well as Hitler's Germany. But most people, including writers, turned their backs on at least part of the truth and accepted the dwindling options. Do you choose bourgeois–capitalist Fascism or Soviet Communism? Among the militant writers one rarely heard talk as fundamental and as illuminating as Salvemini's remarks on two kinds of bourgeoisie or Breton's refusal of any kind of political control of literature, even in the name of revolution.

The total event gives a better reading of the intellectual temperature in 1935 than, say, the Manifesto of the Intellectuals in 1898 that helped reopen the Dreyfus case. Yet ultimately the Congress makes one wonder if Valéry, who shunned politics, wasn't right after all. Gide reports something he said back in 1932: "Impossible to put together a united front to oppose the ruinous claims of the nationalists. He convinces me." But Gide was not finally convinced until five years later.

Right or wrong, many writers probably continue to believe that if they only band together, their corporate voice will be heard. The record of protest in the United States during the Vietnam War may make us feel better. But in that national conflict writers were by no means out ahead of scientists and students. The lessons of the First International Congress of Writers for the Defense of Culture will not soon fade. If the literary heroes of 1935 could not band together effectively against totalitarianism in Germany—to say nothing of Soviet Russia—what can we hope for next time?

Notes

This essay was previously published in *The Innocent Eye: On Modern Literature and the Arts* (New York: Farrar Straus Giroux, 1984) and is reprinted, with slight modifications, by permission of the author.

1. I wish to thank Pierre Abraham, Louis Aragon, Jean Cassou, Louis Guilloux, and André Malraux for the information they provided in conversation and by letter. Another valuable source of documents is an extensive file of newspaper clippings and press releases concerning the Congress collected by Rose Adler and preserved in the Fonds Doucet in Paris. Most unidentified quotations in my text come from that file. I am grateful to François Chapon, the director of the Fonds Doucet, for having brought the file to my attention at a moment when my investigations had reached an impasse.
2. This kind of personal-ideological dilemma takes its toll, particularly on the less thick-skinned. Crevel was besieged by a number of personal problems, and he had just learned that he had only a short time to live because of a pulmonary condition. Later, during the night of Cassou's useless appeal to Ehrenburg, Crevel committed suicide. His medical papers were found in his pocket. He had a speech all written out for delivery. There was a short tribute at the next day's meeting.
3. At this point the audience apparently rose and applauded for a long interval. The circumstances make it impossible to determine whether the reaction was spontaneous or induced.

CHAPTER 9

Gide and Soviet Communism

Paul Hollander

[W]hat leads me to Communism is not Marx, it is the Gospel. It is the Gospel that formed me.

—André Gide, *Journals*[1]

[T]here is something tragic about my Soviet experience. I had come as an enthusiast, as a convinced supporter, to admire the new world and to **win my affections** *I was offered all the prerogatives I abominated in the old one.*

—André Gide, *Afterthoughts* [2]

1

The political peregrinations of André Gide are emblematic of the pursuit of meaning through politics that many Western intellectuals engaged in during this century and especially during the 1930s and 1960s. More generally, as one of his biographers argues, he was "representative of the modern intellectual's contradictory longing for individualist freedom and comforting submission to authority" (Guerard viii) as well as of "the isolation . . . ; the sense of guilt, the schizoid anxiety of the modern intellectual—and his alternating impulses toward order and anarchy" (Guerard 13), to which one may add a combination of elitism and egalitarianism. Understanding Gide's politics helps us understand the period and the writer, although of course the foolish political attitudes do not illuminate his nonpolitical writings, nor do they distract from his literary contributions.

Like many of his contemporaries and the intellectuals of the generation of the 1960s, Gide hoped that radical political transformations might decisively alter the human condition, that all the corruption, irrationality, and evil he saw around him could yield to new, bold schemes of social engineering and the focused political will undergirding them. It is thus easier to explain why Gide was attracted to the Soviet Union at the time when he was than to explain why he was abruptly disaffected following his visit. Nonetheless, Gide's politics, and especially his admiration for the Soviet Union under Stalin, will strike many contemporary readers as not only implausibly dated and wrongheaded but also defying belief and common sense. How could a writer of his talents and moral sensibility revere a monstrously repressive political system such as the Soviet Union was in the 1930s? How could he perceive its intimidated and deprived citizens as joyful and liberated? To say that he was by no means alone in doing so does not fully answer the question but helps us understand these perceptions and the attitude underlying them. In the 1930s many of the most distinguished Western intellectuals and artists admired Stalin's Russia and revered Stalin; Gide's attitudes were part of a widespread phenomenon, of the *Zeitgeist*. But if Gide's veneration of the Soviet Union under Stalin was wrongheaded and grotesque, his subsequent revision of these views remains a valid and durable critique of the principal shortcomings and moral flaws of all Communist systems.

Recalling and reflecting on Gide's political beliefs also helps us to remind ourselves that being an intellectual, and even a highly distinguished one, does not provide protection or immunity against fundamentally wrongheaded political judgments, against the urge to submit to unworthy political impulses, or against confusing what is with what one would like to be. This reminder is of particular relevance at the present time when once more many Western and especially American academic intellectuals are beholden to a variety of dubious beliefs and commitments ranging from multiculturalism, deconstructionism, and radical feminism to postmodernism, all linked by an intense aversion to Western culture and ideas. If these present-day intellectuals do not go on pilgrimages similar to those of Gide and his contemporaries, it is only for want of appropriate sites in the post-Communist world; their rejection of their society and culture matches that of their estranged predecessors in the 1930s and 1960s. The currently fashionable beliefs and allegiances demonstrate (once more) that intellectuals are capable of suspending their critical faculties, and do so with ease and relish when propelled by what they consider a good cause, or lofty ideals.

There is finally the question, always intriguing, of the connections between biography and work, in this case the relationship between Gide's life and personality and his political beliefs. According to his biographers it was an unusually close one.[3]

Gide, like most prominent intellectuals of his time, was drawn to the "Soviet experiment" because he found it a promising alternative to the Western capitalist societies of the period—a new and inspiring departure in the ways of organizing society and improving human beings. As early as 1932, Gide wrote: "I admire nothing so much in the U.S.S.R. as the organization of leisure, of education, of culture" (*Journals* 547).[4] This was part of his vision of creating the "new man" of higher moral and cultural sensibilities. He believed that the Soviet Union and what it stood for represented a cause which the socially and morally conscious, engaged writer, or intellectual, was bound to support; he believed that intellectuals were obligated to take political and moral stands.

An important factor in his support for the Soviet Union, as was the case with many of his contemporaries, was his revulsion from Italian Fascism and Nazi

Germany and his perception of the U.S.S.R. as the major counterweight to Nazism; he was, for the same reason, also impressed by the Soviet support of the loyalists in the Spanish Civil War.

As early as 1931 Gide wrote: "constraint for constraint, Fascism's strikes me as a return to the past, whereas that of the Soviets seems a tremendous effort toward the future. That costly experience interests humanity as a whole and may liberate it from a frightful weight. The mere idea that it might be . . . forced to fail is insufferable to me, and that such gigantic effort toward the never-yet-attempted might remain fruitless" (*Journals* 524).[5]

In one crucial respect Gide differed from most of his contemporaries similarly disposed in political matters, as well as from the later generations of intellectuals who were admirers of the new, third-world Communist political systems: unlike most of them he was capable of radically *and publicly* changing his mind about the Soviet system, about the nature of the Soviet experiment. While Gide was by no means the only well-known Western intellectual to reassess his enthusiasm for the Soviet system over time, he stands out as quite possibly the only one who did so suddenly and dramatically under the impact of his experiences as a pampered visitor to the Soviet Union in 1936.[6] While for most Western travelers the visit to the U.S.S.R. reinforced favorable predispositions, for Gide it had the opposite effect: it compelled him to rise to intense moral indignation—to become disenchanted in spite of the immense flattery lavished upon him, in spite of the considerable efforts of his handlers.

The distinctiveness and significance of this change of attitude cannot be overestimated. The vast majority of Western intellectuals who were attracted to the Soviet Union and, later, to China, Cuba, and other third-world Communist systems had great difficulty admitting and expressing their disenchantment with these systems, if and when it set in.[7] There were many ways to rationalize such reticence, but they had in common two principal motives: one was the determination not to give any encouragement to the enemies of the Soviet Union (or other Communist systems) who were also the enemies of the Western supporters of the Soviet cause; the other reason was the great personal anguish and embarrassment intellectuals seem to experience whenever compelled to admit to flawed judgment about matters of political or moral importance. Intellectuals are people who take their own opinions very seriously and believe that others should, too. For them to admit that they were wrong or, even worse, deceived and self-deceived is almost intolerably hard.

Thus Georg Lukács said that "even the worst socialism is better than capitalism" (Tokes 469). Presumably motivated by similar sentiments, William Kunstler, the American radical lawyer, refused to "believe in public attacks on socialist countries where violations of human rights may occur" (Hentoff 25–26). Numerous authors who finally did make public their disillusionment with the Soviet system (for instance, those in the volume *The God That Failed*) dwelled on their prolonged agony in doing so in view of the encouragement their revelation would give to the enemies of the Soviet Union.

Gide himself recalled later in life (in 1945) the ways in which his critics rationalized their refusal to make any critical comment about the Soviet system:

[T]hose who became angry over my criticism of the U.S.S.R. were the very ones who had applauded when the same criticisms were directed against the by-products of "capitalism." There they admired my perspicacity, my need to disregard camouflage, my courage in denouncing. In Russia, they suddenly said, I had been incapable of understanding anything. . . . And if some admitted the justice of my observations, . . . they considered them untimely. At most a few imperfections were admitted among comrades, but the time had not yet come to speak of them. One had to realize that overall success and close one's eyes to the temporary, inevitable deficiencies . . . (*Journals* 733)[8]

He also noted in *Afterthoughts:* "You, intelligent communist, you agree to recognise this evil, but you consider it better to hide it from others less intelligent than yourself, others who might be made indignant by it . . ." (69).[9] But just about a year earlier he wrote: "It is in great part the stupidity and dishonesty of the attacks against the U.S.S.R. that today make us defend her with a certain obstinacy" (*Journals* 593).[10]

Most erstwhile admirers of the Soviet Union slowly faded away, sunk into silence or oblivion, while others took the position, much later (some only after its collapse), that they had always been aware of the flaws of the Soviet experiment. Many of them came to criticize it in public at least perfunctorily. For very few was the travel experience itself decisive, a key source of attitude change; rarely was it recognized or publicly admitted that the trips were conducted tours, that the hosts made use of favorable predispositions in devising the techniques of hospitality that were to mislead the visitors in specific, highly calculated ways. The tours were successful precisely because the visitors' critical faculties were suspended, overwhelmed by seeing what they had wished to see. It would have been especially painful and embarrassing to admit that once they stepped on the soil of the U.S.S.R. (and later, on that of China, Cuba, North Vietnam, or Nicaragua) they ceased to be critical intellectuals, ready to discern and expose sham, the gulf between appearances and reality, façade and substance.

Although Gide learned a great deal from his experiences in the U.S.S.R.— and these experiences and impressions apparently became the major determinant of his drastic change of attitude—that is not to say the *Return from the U.S.S.R.* (referred to as *Return* below) is an unambiguous document of disenchantment. Rather, it is one that still reflects a struggle between new insights and prior dispositions; nonetheless, the book was a watershed, a breakthrough, not only in Gide's life but in the emerging debate among Western intellectuals about the nature of the Soviet system.

The discussion that follows will focus on three topics. One is the specifics of the appeals the Soviet system held for Gide; the second will be the sources and process of his disillusionment with the "Soviet experiment"; and finally an attempt will be made to understand Gide's politics in the context of his personal life and attributes.

2

Gide's *Return,* the first major document of his disillusionment, still reflects the appeals of the Soviet system and the intensity of the inner conflict which the expression of his critiques created. The preface itself is apologetic:

> It is precisely because of my admiration for the Soviet Union and for the wonders it has already performed that I am going to criticize, because of what we had expected from it. . . . (*Return* xiv)[11]

> [W]ere not my convictions still firm and unshaken that, on the one hand, the Soviet Union will end by triumphing over the serious errors I point out, on the other, and this is more important, that the particular errors of one country cannot suffice to compromise a cause which is international and universal. (*Return* xvi)[12]

In the same preface he refers to the U.S.S.R. as "[an] unprecedented experiment" that he used to think of as linked to "the future of culture itself" (*Return* xi).[13] "More than a chosen land—an example, a guide. . . . A land . . . where Utopia was in the process of becoming reality" (*Return* xiv–xv).[14] "Whole regions [of it] have already taken on the smiling aspect of happiness" (*Return* xv).[15]

For Gide, as for many like-minded fellow political tourists, what mattered most in the new society was the transformation of human beings who seemed to radiate a new-found authenticity and the beneficial ways in which the political realm intersected with the personal.[16] It seemed that the Soviet system changed people for the better. This was apparent to Gide even as he was observing the crowds in the "'parks of culture'" (*Return* 5)[17] who were uniformly good-natured, behaving "with propriety, with decency" and "pervaded with a kind of joyous ardor" (*Return* 5).[18] He described in detail their wholesome recreational activities, adding: "All this . . . without the smallest vulgarity; these immense crowds behave with perfect propriety and are manifestly inspired with good feeling, dignity, and decorum . . . without any effort and as a matter of course" (*Return* 6–7)[19]—a peculiar observation in light of what we know from other sources about the public behavior of Russians especially when inebriated, a common enough part of their recreation. The Festival of Youth at the Red Square in Moscow, with its vast numbers of seemingly joyous participants marching past, was further proof of the creation of better human beings: "I had never imagined so magnificent a sight" (*Return* 9).[20] It did not occur to Gide that similar marches of similarly radiant young people in perfect formations were also performed in those years in Nazi Germany and that, generally speaking, highly regimented political systems could put on such shows at will, as they also would do in China, Cuba, and elsewhere in later years.

The sense of community and the warmth of human relations were overwhelming and implicitly contrasted with the calculating nature of personal relations in capitalist societies. Gide wrote:

Nowhere, indeed, is contact with any and everyone so easily established, and so immediately, so deeply, so warmly as in the U.S.S.R. . . . . [N]owhere is the feeling of common humanity so profoundly, so strongly felt as in the U.S.S.R. . . . I had never anywhere felt myself so fully a comrade, a brother. . . . (*Return* 13)[21]

In retrospect one may wonder how Gide reached these conclusions and in what measure these feelings were based on actual experiences, as distinct from projections of what he hoped and wished to experience. To what extent could he communicate spontaneously and unsupervised (and without an interpreter) with Soviet people? And how were those he met selected? One must also wonder how realistic his observation had been regarding "the extraordinary prolongation of youth" (*Return* 13n)[22] that he claimed to have observed in the U.S.S.R.

Children were "radiant with health and happiness" (*Return* 4) in the pioneer camps he visited;[23] "their eyes are frank and trustful; their laughter has nothing spiteful or malicious in it . . ." (*Return* 5).[24] Again the reader may wonder if children in France laughed maliciously or if many of them appeared to the casual observer as unhealthy and unhappy. As the practices of political hospitality were relatively new when Gide visited the U.S.S.R., he had no reason to reflect on the use of children as devices of political legitimization. Hitler's Germany also excelled in producing multitudes of exuberantly happy children for purposes of propaganda, as did the Communist regimes of the third world in the 1960s and 1970s.

There is more in *Return* about the simple, authentic, spontaneous humanity Gide found in the Soviet Union and the streets of Moscow: "Into this crowd I plunge; I take a bath of humanity" (*Return* 17).[25] On the same streets he also found that "[e]veryone is like everyone else. In no other place is the result of social leveling so obvious . . . a classless society of which every member seems to have the same needs as every other" (*Return* 16).[26] Even standing in line, he thought, was an activity Soviet citizens enjoyed (*Return* 18; *Retour* 37)—a particularly good illustration both of how far removed he was from Soviet reality and of the intellectual's capacity to project his own fantasies onto an unfamiliar social setting. Probably Gide felt that standing in line was some sort of agreeable communal activity, a delightful social bond that afforded further opportunity for face-to-face contact and lively exchanges of ideas.

It is of further interest, and an indication of Gide's unresolved inner conflict (regarding his attitude toward the U.S.S.R.), that at the end of *Return* (in one of the appendices) he had his publisher reprint the speech he gave in Moscow at Gorky's funeral (*Return* 65–69; *Retour* 95–99). In it he still avowed that "[t]he fate of culture is bound up in our minds with the destiny of the Soviet Union. We will defend it" (*Return* 67).[27] He also pointed out that the Soviet intellectual was no longer compelled to play an adversarial role, as intellectuals were elsewhere, but (miraculously enough) "while remaining a revolutionary, the writer is no longer a rebel" (*Return* 68).[28] In a hastily added footnote, he wrote: "This was where I fooled myself; I was obliged, alas, soon to admit it" (*Return* 68n).[29] In the same section of the book, he also reprinted a speech he gave on the same trip "to the students of Moscow" (*Return* 70–73; *Retour* 101–104).[30] In it he averred that "on the future of the U.S.S.R. depend the destinies of the rest of the world" (*Return* 73).[31]

The appendix also contains an account of his visit to Bolshevo, the model penal colony that was routinely shown to distinguished Western visitors (*Return* 89–90; *Retour* 121–122).[32] Gide, like many other visitors, was convinced that what he had seen was genuine, that the enlightened treatment of the inmates he witnessed was typical and produced reformed characters, a triumph of the Soviet penal system: "Bolshevo is one of the most remarkable successes on which the new Soviet State can plume itself" (*Return* 90).[33]

Why did he feel compelled to reprint these speeches and, more generally speaking, to publish a book that mixed praise and criticism? It is possible that at the time Gide still wished to remind readers (and himself) of his pro-Soviet credentials. Further, mixing praise and blame showed that his attitudes were not lightly taken, not shaped by unworthy motives; he came to criticize with sorrow, not with relish.

3

Let us turn now to the critiques. Gide's second book on his Soviet experiences makes clear that he was more gullible at the beginning of his journey, when, for example, he "still believed . . . that it was possible to speak seriously of culture in the U.S.S.R. and to discuss things sincerely" (*Afterthoughts* 20).[34] As Gide's narrative proceeds, one has the impression of the narrator awakening; he begins to see things the way they are: for example, the low quality of goods for sale, the tastelessness of displays in the shop windows in Moscow, the scarcities, the phony production records of Stakhanovites (workers who substantially overfulfilled production norms),[35] the untroubled enjoyment of material privileges by the new elite, the stage-managed aspects of his entire tour, and more generally the vast distance separating appearances from reality.

The visit to the "highly prosperous *kolkhoz*" (collective farm) produced a "queer and depressing impression," in particular, the homes of the workers, redolent with "complete depersonalization" (*Return* 25).[36] In Sochi, the Black Sea resort, he discovered that housing for the workers of the model *sovhoz* (state farm) that provided produce for the luxurious hotel (where he stayed) consisted of "a row of hovels" (*Return* 37).[37]

Poverty was not just a matter of backwardness, or of deprivations equally distributed and shouldered by all, as sympathetic political tourists often believed. Gide came to realize (well before Djilas, though not before Trotsky or Victor Serge) that new, politically based inequalities were emerging and growing, and that the poverty of the masses was in stark contrast to the luxuries of the privileged; "bourgeois instincts" (*Return* 39)[38] were flattered, and a new aristocracy appeared, "the aristocracy of respectability and conformism" (*Return* 39).[39] Gide recognized a most repellent feature of social inequality: "the contempt, or at any rate the indifference, which those who are . . . 'on the right side' show to 'inferiors,' to servants, to unskilled workmen, . . . to 'the poor'" (*Return* 40).[40] He wrote later:

> The new bourgeoisie . . . has all the defects of ours. . . . [I]t despises the poor. Greedy of all the satisfactions it was so long deprived of, it knows how to set about getting and keeping them. "Are these really the men who made the Revolution?" I asked in my *Return from the U.S.S.R.* And answered: "No; they are the men who profit by it." They may be members of the Party—there is nothing communist in their hearts. (*Afterthoughts* 64)[41]

Gide was also troubled by the laws against abortion and homosexuality; "non-conformism is hunted down even in sexual matters" (*Return* 38n).[42] All these developments made clear that the Soviet Union had ceased to be a revolutionary society: "the feelings which had animated the first revolutionaries began to get in the way" (*Return* 41);[43] "the revolutionary spirit (or even simply the critical spirit) is no longer the correct thing . . . [.] What is wanted now is compliance, conformism" (*Return* 41–42).[44]

Equally fundamental and penetrating were his discoveries of the lack of intellectual and political freedom. He wrote: "In the U.S.S.R. everybody knows beforehand . . . that on any and every subject there can be only one opinion. . . . Every morning the *Pravda* teaches them just what they should know and think and believe" (*Return* 27).[45] Soviet people are in "an extraordinary state of ignorance concerning foreign countries" (*Return* 30)[46] and for that reason suffer from a *"superiority complex"* (*Return* 30),[47] believing, for example, that France offers no playgrounds to children comparable to those found in the U.S.S.R., and they actually doubt that public transportation and especially subways exist in France (*Return* 31; *Retour* 54).

Even while he continued to sympathize with the ends the Soviet system supposedly pursued, he realized that they were compromised by the means. He sadly came to the conclusion that "the U.S.S.R. is not what we had hoped it would be, what it promised to be, what it still strives to appear. It has betrayed all our hopes" (*Afterthoughts* 71; see also *Return* 48).[48]

Gide does not tell the reader much about how the process of disillusionment got under way. Were there any specific and dramatic revelations or turning points that opened his eyes? Or was it a matter of slowly accumulating experiences and impressions that led at last to new insights and conclusions? Were there elements in his disenchantment that preceded the return from the U.S.S.R.? We do not know, and interestingly enough these are not questions he deals with in his *Journals*, either. It is, however, likely that experiences involving revelations on the part of Soviet citizens were particularly significant and had a major impact on him. Among them was the case of the painter who in the hall of a hotel in Sochi sought to convince him in a loud voice that Marxism—besides its other benefits—would also produce great works of art, and that Gide's defense of the autonomy of the artist was misguided. A few moments after this conversation, the painter came to his room and said, "Of course you are perfectly right . . . but there were people listening to us just now . . . and I have an exhibition opening very soon" (*Return* 54).[49]

In another incident with a similar impact, one of his Russian-speaking traveling companions asked a workman to buy him some better-quality cigarettes, which cost five rubles a pack; the price was "a day's salary," the worker informed him with a laugh (*Afterthoughts* 99–100).[50] A further, in some ways more sinister experience concerned the efforts of Bukharin to speak to Gide in private. On the first occasion these efforts were frustrated by the unexpected and unannounced arrival of "a so-called journalist"[51] who pushed his way into Gide's hotel suite and whose appearance prompted Bukharin to leave (*Afterthoughts* 77; *Retouches* 72–73). Three days later Gide met Bukharin at Gorky's funeral, and Bukharin asked him once more if he could visit him in his room at the Metropole Hotel; Gide eagerly agreed, but shortly afterwards Koltsov (an official who looked after Gide) "took him [Bukharin] aside,"[52] and Bukharin made no further attempts to talk to Gide (*Afterthoughts* 78; *Retouches* 73–74). These experiences, and similar ones, impressed on Gide that Soviet society was hardly a breeding ground of spontaneity and authenticity. By the time he wrote *Afterthoughts,* he did not flinch from concluding, "Spying is one of the civic virtues"[53] and friends are expected to betray one another to prove their loyalty to the system (*Afterthoughts* 32–33).

Despite the furious attacks *Return* provoked, it was in some ways a document of Gide's ambivalent disposition toward the Soviet Union. It was in *Afterthoughts,* a second short book devoted to the same topic, that Gide's critiques and rejection of the Soviet system found full and unconstrained expression. It was also a book in which he confronted some of his critics and reproduced some of the correspondence *Return* had occasioned. In writing *Afterthoughts,* he also benefited from the advice and work of others who did not look at the U.S.S.R. through rose-colored glasses. Once the favorable predisposition was shattered, hardly any aspect of Soviet society remained immune from his criticism. He learned, for instance, from the book of Walter Citrine that the vaunted child-care system could accommodate only one out of every eight children (*Afterthoughts* 17; *Retouches* 18), that the real wages of workers had stagnated or actually declined (*Afterthoughts* 41–42; *Retouches* 40–41), that the elections were meaningless—"the proletariat no longer possess[ed] even the possibility of electing a representative to defend its injured interests" (*Afterthoughts* 46).[54] "[A]ll real connection between the people and those who are supposed to represent it, [was] severed" (*Afterthoughts* 51).[55]

Above all Gide argued, unlike his critics, that what went wrong in the U.S.S.R. and what he reported were not minor, atypical, or temporary lapses and therefore had to be openly dissected and criticized. He also came to realize—and this is an observation of continued relevance—that it is possible to industrialize a country in a way which provides few benefits for the population at large, that the endemic shortages in the Soviet Union were directly related to the project of "'outdoing capitalism' by building gigantic factories" which had little to do with "the welfare of the workers" (*Afterthoughts* 19).[56] Another example of the hugely wasteful misuse of resources that Gide noted was the plan to build a gigantic "Palace of Soviets"[57] topped by a more than 200-foot-high statue of Lenin—a project the costs of which Gide contrasted with the under-nourished workers (*Afterthoughts* 54–55). (The palace was never built, as it turned out.) Generally speaking, Gide was most disturbed by the condition of the workers, a condition made all the more shocking because of the regime's insistence that it was "enviable" (*Afterthoughts* 29).[58]

In *Afterthoughts* Gide also comments on the influence of the handlers on the visitor's capacity to observe and register aspects of the social landscape, an obser-vation he originally made on his trip to Africa: "as long as I travelled in French Equatorial Africa accompanied by officials, everything seemed . . . little short of marvellous. I only began to see things clearly when I left the Governor's car and decided to travel on foot and alone, so as to . . . get into direct contact with the natives" (*Afterthoughts* 11–12).[59] It needs to be pointed out here that he could not have taken such liberties in the Soviet Union, that is, to travel by himself and have direct, unsupervised contact with the natives. In *Afterthoughts* there is no longer any doubt that all the factories, schools, clubs, parks, and palaces of cul-ture he was shown were exceptional specimens carefully chosen for the delec-tation of the visitor (*Afterthoughts* 12; *Retouches* 13–14). There is more information in *Afterthoughts* about experiences that had a negative effect than in *Return* and especially about the aspects of lavish hospitality that backfired. Gide wrote:

> When, after escaping with great difficulty from official receptions and offi-cial supervision, I managed to get into contact with labourers whose wages were only four or five roubles a day, what could I think of the banquet in my honour . . . ? An almost daily banquet at which the abundance of the hors-d'oeuvre alone was such that one had already eaten three times too much before beginning the actual meal; a feast of six courses which used to last two hours. . . . The expense! Never having seen a bill, I cannot exactly estimate it, but one of my companions who was well up in the prices of things calculates that each banquet, with wines and liqueurs, must have come to more than three hundred roubles a head. (*Afterthoughts* 60–61)[60]

Few Western visitors entertained similar misgivings as they were feasted and toasted by their hosts; few were made uneasy by the contrast between their material comforts and the way the ordinary natives lived. Gide also observed:

> I had never before travelled in such sumptuous style. In special railway car-riages or the best cars, always the best rooms in the best hotels, the most abundant and the choicest food. And what a welcome! What attentions! What solicitude! Everywhere acclaimed, flattered, . . . feasted. Nothing seemed too good, too exquisite to offer me. . . . But these very favours constantly brought to mind privileges, differences where I had hoped to find equality. (*Afterthoughts* 60)[61]

   What disturbed him most "was not so much to find imperfections, as to meet once again with the advantages I had wanted to escape from, the privileges I had hoped were abolished" (*Afterthoughts* 57).[62] "I did not go to the U.S.S.R. to meet with privileges over again" (*Afterthoughts* 58).[63] Unlike Gide, most of the distinguished Western intellectuals who were similarly treated had no difficulty accepting and enjoying this treatment; presumably they regarded themselves as deserving it, or they viewed it as just another manifestation of the natural hospitality of a socialist society that retained some wholesome traditional aspects. It is even possible that some of them were aware of the vast difference between their comforts and the way of life of ordinary citizens but managed to justify it along the lines suggested above.

   Gide's rejection of the Soviet system was further stimulated by his belief that "a great writer, a great artist, is essentially non-conformist . . . [and] makes head against the current" (*Return* 51)[64] and, most importantly, by his "basic mistrust of all orthodoxies" (Fowlie 101–102), which conflicted with and cut short any durable veneration of the Soviet system.

4

It is not difficult to find in Gide's life and personality factors predisposing him to the political stands he took and later abandoned. His political (as well as non-political) attitudes prior to his visit to the Soviet Union help make clear why he undertook that trip and why it had such a shattering impact. In 1932 he wrote, "Emotionally, temperamentally, intellectually I have always been a communist. But I was afraid of my own thought and in my writings strove more to hide than to express it" (*Journals* 539).[65] But if Gide fancied himself a Communist, he was the kind whose political and religious beliefs were profoundly intertwined, the kind who was led by religious impulses to political convictions. The latter were intensely moralistic and tinged with a religiosity associated with his Catholicism. As Thomas Mann observed: "There beckoned . . . two ports and comforting shelters that have served as an escape to many a contemporary: Communism and the Catholic Church. Gide, whose nature needs commitment as much as freedom from it, experimented with Communism out of sheer rebellious spirit . . ." (Guerard xxvi–xxvii). He was among many Westerners (priests and ministers included) who believed at some stage in their lives that while the religious institutions of their own societies had abandoned true Christianity, in the Soviet Union, despite the official atheism, the true values of Christianity (and especially its concern for the poor and a nonmaterialistic way of life) were being realized. As one of Gide's biographers wrote, "he had no trouble visualizing a communism which would reconcile itself with the essential teachings of Christ. The very destruction of family and orthodox church would prepare the way for a truer Christianity" (Guerard 27). In turn Gide wrote in his *Journals*:

"[M]ysticism" today is on the side of those who profess atheism and irreligion. It is as a religion that the Communist doctrine exalts and feeds the enthusiasm of the young today. . . . [T]hey transfer their ideals from heaven to earth, as I do with them. . . . (566)[66]

The mere idea of . . . having to defend Christ against Communist comrades strikes me as profoundly absurd. It is against the Russian popes, the priests etc. that I want to defend him and to restore him. . . . It is against religion that I am protesting, against the Church, dogmas, faith etc. (564)[67]

But in the same breath Gide also admitted that "Communist religion involves, it too, a dogma, an orthodoxy, texts to which reference is made, an abdication of criticism . . ." (*Journals* 566).[68] Moreover, Gide, unlike so many of his fellow intellectuals at the time (as well as in later decades), had *not* been enamored with Marxism:

> In Marx's writings I stifle. There is something lacking, some ozone or other that is essential to keep my mind breathing. Yet I have read four volumes of *Das Kapital,* patiently, assiduously, studiously; plus . . . the volume of extracts . . . chosen by Paul Nizan. . . . I have read all this with more constancy and care than I brought to any other study . . . with no other desire than to let myself be convinced. . . . And each time I came away aching all over, my intelligence bruised as by instruments of torture. . . . I think that a great deal of Marx's prestige comes from the fact that he is difficult of access. . . . When one does not understand one bows down. (*Journals* 618)[69]

Gide's reservations about Marxism are congruent with a conclusion he reached after his visit to the Soviet Union, a conclusion that has been the centerpiece of corresponding political disillusionment on the part of all those who have broken with the Soviet system and the Communist movements supporting it. Gide wrote: "Let us be aware of those who want . . . , at whatever cost, to plough straight furrows on a curving field, of those who prefer to each man the idea they have formed of humanity" (*Journals* 619).[70]

There are a number of personality traits and circumstances that help to clarify and account for Gide's political attitudes and beliefs. If a strongly felt outsider status is the point of departure for the development of moralistic, social-critical impulses, then Gide certainly had reasons for such feelings. A sickly child who lost his father at age eleven, he had a troubled childhood: "He suffered from nervous tension, from timidity, from a sense of being unattractive, from unnamed fears and nightmares, . . . from loneliness, from a feeling of inferiority with schoolmates who made his life so miserable that he invented symptoms of illness sufficient to keep him away from school. . . . Despite the many advantages of his social position and wealth, despite the attentiveness and affection of parents and relatives, Gide had . . . an unhappy childhood . . ." (Fowlie 13–14). He also had a father who was Protestant in a Catholic country, and for his Protestant background Gide suffered ridicule and worse while in school.[71]

He was also a homosexual at a time when being one was a source of shame, not pride—these are aspects of the personal background that help us to understand (though, of course, not to predict) Gide's later attitudes and world view.

Thomas Mann credited Gide's homosexual disposition with being "the root and fount of his moral dynamism, of his revolutionary disavowal of everything respectable-traditional . . ." (Guerard xxv). To such a trait, which predisposed him to question the social-moral order, one may add his privileged conditions of life, which were free from material problems, filled with leisure, allowing for reflection. Gide—like so many other Western intellectuals of comfortable means in more recent times—was apparently in the grip of guilty feelings: "Perhaps the strongest emotional force at work was class-guilt; the intolerable feeling that he was one of the favored. Only privilege had made possible his voyages, his quiet and civilized pleasures, and the prolonged self-examination which nourished his books. . . . This sense of unmerited privilege and of surrounding distress, together with the old faith in progress, pushed Gide toward communism . . ." (Guerard 26). Gide himself wrote: "What brought me to Communism . . . was the fact of the privileged position which I personally enjoy—that seemed to me preposterous and intolerable. . . . I cannot accept a place in a lifeboat in which only a limited number of people are saved" (Crossman 153).

But as was noted by a recent writer, "Along with guilt and compassion for the wretched poor, vanity beguiled him. Doubting as he often did whether his oeuvre justified his fame, he was reluctant to forego the vehement praise of young Communists everywhere. No more could he resist the opportunity to humble a society in which, despite the laurels it heaped on him, he still felt himself to be reprobate" (Brown 40).

Thus Gide's attraction to Soviet Communism, like the corresponding quests of the more recent generation of intellectuals, began with an unease with his own society, prompting a search for alternatives. In turn this unease was, in large measure, nurtured by an idealistic and moralistic disposition that conventional religion did not satisfy. Although Gide was highly successful and respected, his social status or position was rendered vulnerable by his sexuality, unconventional and deviant for his times. While there is no obvious or logical connection between sexual and political preferences, when a particular sexual disposition is ostracized, it often becomes the emotional basis of a more diffuse and deeper estrangement from the social order, an estrangement that can take political forms. At the present time, homosexual activists are also intensely critical of the social system as a whole, converting their sexual preferences into political activism and social criticism.[72] A pursuit of the unusual and exotic, a form of escape from his own constraining society, was also reflected in Gide's numerous trips to Africa preceding his journey to the Soviet Union. One in particular, his visit to the Congo in 1926, became a source of revelation and indignation about social injustice in colonial Africa. According to Enid Starkie, the trip to the Congo was pivotal in the development of his social concerns: "He now became the champion of victims and underdogs—criminal offenders for whom he demanded more sympathetic treatment; women for whom he asked equality . . . colonial natives whose causes he pleaded in the two travel books . . ." (Crossman

148; as noted above, Gide himself was well aware of certain parallels between this trip to the Congo and his trip to the U.S.S.R. in 1936). He also shared with contemporary Western and especially American intellectuals a sympathetic interest in common criminals: "His entire nature would incline him to taking the side of the outlaw . . ." (Fowlie 99).

While at the present time Gide's attraction to and rejection of Soviet Communism may be of historical interest only, the larger circumstances giving rise to these beliefs and attitudes appear remarkably contemporary. As one of his biographers wrote of Gide's times:

> The early years of the century were characterized by a fairly widespread lack of faith in rationalism. . . .
> The major supports of man which had provided him with a sense of security in the world: religion, science, a coherent psychological life, nationalism—were all being questioned and invalidated. . . . The universe again became incomprehensible. . . .
> The adolescence and young manhood of Gide coincided with a period of European civilization when the conventions that had protected and reassured men's peace of mind began to collapse. During the last decade of the nineteenth century, and well into the twentieth, individual man found himself much more alone than in earlier periods because moral and social values were being questioned more . . . the personal crisis which Gide went through in his twenties. . . was to be raised to a level of universal meaning. . . . (Fowlie 4, 6, 4)

These are conditions and problems all too familiar to present-day intellectuals and those who may read Gide at the present time. Gide's inner struggles and his short-lived attempt to find solutions to personal and moral problems in the political realm will be especially meaningful to those of our contemporaries who lived through the decade of the 1960s and emerged from it with a new understanding that the political is not and should not be personal, and that the different problems of human and social existence cannot be resolved by embracing movements or ideologies that promise radical, collective solutions.

Notes

1. *Journals* 564. "[C]e qui m'amène au communisme, ce n'est pas Marx, c'est l'Évangile. C'est l'Évangile qui m'a formé" (*Journal* 421).
2. *Afterthoughts* 62. "[I]l y a dans mon aventure soviétique quelque chose de tragique. En enthousiaste, en convaincu, j'étais venu pour admirer un nouveau monde, et l'on m'offrait, *afin de me séduire,* toutes les prérogatives que j'abominais dans l'ancien" (*Retouches* 59–60).
3. See, for example, Guerard 3–4.
4. "Aussi n'admiré-je rien tant, en l'U.R.S.S., que l'organisation du repos, de l'instruction, de la culture" (*Journal* 380).

5. "[C]ontrainte pour contrainte, celle du fascisme me paraît un retour au passé, celle des Soviets un immense effort vers l'avenir. Cette coûteuse expérience intéresse l'humanité tout entière et peut la délivrer d'un effroyable poids. L'idée seule qu'on la puisse . . . faire avorter, m'est insupportable, et qu'un si gigantesque effort vers le jamais-encore-tenté puisse demeurer vain" (*Journal* 316).

6. Perhaps the case of Malcolm Muggeridge was somewhat similar; he was certainly deeply affected by what he had seen, especially in the countryside; on the other hand, he was far less of an admirer of the system to begin with.

7. To this day it is not clear how many in fact became disenchanted with them and for what reason, given the prevailing silence on the subject. As I have noted elsewhere, there was far more public admission, delayed or not, on the part of the pro-Soviet intellectuals of the 1930s than on the part of the pro-third-world Communist intellectuals of the 1960s. I believe this can in part be explained by the massive subcultural support the later beliefs have enjoyed in what I have called enclaves of adversary culture, usually in or around academic settings. Even without such settings, social criticism (providing the basis for the idealization of distant revolutionary societies) was arguably far more widespread and influential in the 1960s than in the 1930s.

8. "[C]eux qui s'indignèrent de mes critiques au sujet de l'U.R.S.S. furent ceux-là mêmes qui avaient le plus applaudi, lorsque ces mêmes critiques portaient contre des sous-produits du « capitalisme ». Ici, l'on admirait ma perspicacité, mon besoin de passer outre les camouflages, mon courage à dénoncer. En Russie, dirent-ils soudain, je n'avais rien su comprendre. . . . Et si certains admettaient le bien-fondé de mes observations, . . . les tenaient-ils pour inopportunes. On admettait tout au plus, entre camarades, quelques imperfections, mais le temps n'était pas venu d'en parler. Il fallait comprendre la réussite de l'ensemble et fermer les yeux sur les manques provisoires, inévitables . . ." (*Journal* 1008–1009; last ellipsis Gide's).

9. "Vous, communiste intelligent, vous acceptez de le connaître, ce mal; mais vous estimez qu'il vaut mieux le cacher à ceux qui, moins intelligents que vous, pourraient s'en indigner peut-être . . ." (*Retouches* 67; ellipsis Gide's).

10. "C'est aussi, c'est beaucoup la bêtise et la malhonnêteté des attaques contre l'U.R.S.S. qui font qu'aujourd'hui nous mettons quelque obstination à la défendre" (*Journal* 509).

11. "C'est en raison même de mon admiration pour l'U.R.S.S. et pour les prodiges accomplis par elle déjà, que vont s'élever mes critiques; en raison aussi de ce que nous attendons encore d'elle . . ." (*Retour* 15).

12. "[S]i ma conviction ne restait intacte, inébranlée, que d'une part l'U.R.S.S. finira bien par triompher des graves erreurs que je signale; d'autre part, et ceci est plus important, que les erreurs particulières d'un pays ne peuvent suffire à compromettre la vérité d'une cause internationale, universelle" (*Retour* 16–17).

13. "[U]ne expérience sans précédents"; "l'avenir même de la culture" (*Retour* 11).

14. "Plus qu'une patrie d'élection : un exemple, un guide. . . . Il était . . . une terre où l'utopie était en passe de devenir réalité" (*Retour* 15).

15. "Dans des contrées entières elle présente l'aspecte déjà riant du bonheur" (*Retour* 16).

16. The theme of an inevitable and ironclad linkage between the personal and the political was revived enthusiastically and approvingly by American radical feminists in the 1960s and has remained a cornerstone of their beliefs.

17. " « [P]arcs de culture » " (*Retour* 21).

18. "[P]artout le sérieux, la décence . . . partout une sorte de ferveur joyeuse" (*Retour* 22).

19. "Tout cela . . . sans la moindre vulgarité; et toute cette foule immense, d'une tenue parfaite, respire l'honnêté, la dignité, le décence; sans contrainte aucune d'ailleurs et tout naturellement" (*Retour* 23).

20. "Je n'imaginais pas un spectacle aussi magnifique" (*Retour* 26).

21. "Aussi bien nulle part autant qu'en U.R.S.S. le contact avec tous et n'importe qui, ne s'établit plus aisément, immédiat, profond, chalereux. . . . [N]ulle part, autant qu'en U.R.S.S., l'on puisse éprouver aussi profondément et aussi fort le sentiment de l'humanité. . . . [J]e ne m'étais jamais encore et nulle part senti aussi abondamment camarade et frère . . ." (*Retour* 28).

22. "[L]'extraordinaire prolongement de la jeunesse" (*Retour* 31n).

23. "[R]ayonnants de bonheur, de santé" (*Retour* 20).

24. "Leur regard est clair, confiant; leurs rires sont sans malignité, sans malice . . ." (*Retour* 21).

25. "Dans cette foule, je me plonge; je prends un bain d'humanité" (*Retour* 37).

26. "Chacun ressemble à tous. Nulle part . . . n'est sensible le résultat du nivellement social : une société sans classes, dont chaque membre paraît avoir les mêmes besoins" (*Retour* 36–37).

27. "Le sort de la culture est lié dans nos esprits au destin même de l'U.R.S.S. Nous la défendrons" (*Retour* 97).

28. "[E]n étant révolutionnaire l'écrivain n'est plus un opposant" (*Retour* 98).

29. "C'est ici que je me blousais; je dus bientôt, hélas! le reconnaître" (*Retour* 98n).

30. "[A]ux étudiants de Moscou" (*Retour* 101).

31. "[D]e l'avenir de l'U.R.S.S. dépendront les destins du reste du monde" (*Retour* 104).

32. See Hollander 154–156.

33. "[L]a cité de Bolchevo reste une des plus extraordinaires réussites dont puisse se targuer le nouvel État soviétique" (*Retour* 122).

34. "[J]e croyais encore . . . que l'on pouvait, en l'U.R.S.S., parler sérieusement de la culture et discuter sincèrement" (*Retouches* 21).

35. A group of visiting French miners "asked to relieve a shift of Soviet miners and then and there, without putting themselves out in the least, and without even being aware of it, turned out to be Stakhanovites" [une équipe de mineurs français a demandé . . . à relayer une équipe de mineurs soviétiques et . . . aussitôt, sans autrement se fouler, sans s'en douter, ils ont fait du stakhanovisme] (*Return* 23; *Retour* 44).

36. "[K]olkhoze très prospère"; "bizarre et attristante impression"; "complète dépersonnalisation" (*Retour* 47).

37. "[U]n alignement de taudis" (*Retour* 62).

38. "[I]nstincts bourgeois" (*Retour* 63).

39. "[L]'aristocratie . . . du bien-penser, du conformisme" (*Retour* 64).

40. "[L]e mépris, ou tout au moins l'indifférence que ceux qui sont . . . « du bon côté », marquent à l'égard des « inférieurs », des domestiques, des manœuvres, . . . des pauvres" (*Retour* 64–65).

41. "[C]ette nouvelle bourgeoisie . . . a tous les défauts de la nôtre. . . . [E]lle méprise les miséreux. Avide de touts les biens dont elle fut si longtemps privée, elle sait comment il faut s'y prendre pour les acquérir et pour les garder. « Sont-ce vraiment ces gens qui ont fait la Révolution? Non, ce sont ceux qui en profitent », écrivais-je dans mon *Retour de l'U.R.S.S.* Ils peuvent bien être inscrits au parti; ils n'ont plus rien de communiste dans le cœur" (*Retouches* 61–62).

42. "[L]e *non-conformisme* est poursuivi jusque dans les questions sexuelles" (*Retour* 63n).

43. "[D]e tels sentiments, qui d'abord animaient les premiers révolutionnaires, deviennent encombrants" (*Retour* 66).

44. "[L]'esprit révolutionnaire (et même simplement : l'esprit critique) n'est plus de mise . . . [.] Ce que l'on demande à présent, c'est l'acceptation, le conformisme" (*Retour* 67).

45. "En U.R.S.S. il est admis d'avance . . . pour toutes que, sur tout et n'importe quoi, il ne saurait y avoir plus d'une opinion. . . . Chaque matin, la *Pravda* leur enseigne ce qu'il sied de savoir, de penser, de croire" (*Retour* 49).

46. "[U]ne extraordinaire ignorance de l'étranger" (*Retour* 52).

47. *"[C]omplexe de supériorité"* (*Retour* 53).

48. "L'U.R.S.S. n'est pas ce que nous espérions qu'elle serait, ce qu'elle avait promis d'être, ce qu'elle s'efforce encore de paraître; elle a trahi tous nos espoirs" (*Retouches* 68).

49. "— Oh! parbleu! je sais bien . . . Mais *on* nous écoutait tout à l'heure et . . . mon exposition doit ouvrir bientôt" (*Retour* 83; ellipses Gide's).

50. "Le salaire d'une journée" (*Retouches* 94).

51. "[U]n prétendu journaliste" (*Retouches* 73).

52. "[L]e prit aussitôt à part" (*Retouches* 73).

53. "Le mouchardage fait partie des vertus civiques" (*Retouches* 33).

54. "[L]e prolétariat n'a même plus la possibilité d'élire un représentant qui défende ses intérêts lésés" (*Retouches* 45).

55. "[E]ntre le peuple et ceux qui sont censés le représenter, tout contact réel est rompu" (*Retouches* 49).

56. "« [D]épasser le capitalisme » dans la construction d'usines géantes"; "les hommes pour la production . . . leur bien-être" (*Retouches* 20).

57. "Palais des Soviets" (*Retouches* 52).

58. "[E]nviable" (*Retouches* 29).

59. "[T]ant que, en A.E.F., j'ai voyagé « accompagné », tout . . . a paru presque merveilleux. Je n'ai commencé d'y voir clair que lorsque, quittant l'auto des Gouverneurs, je me suis décidé à parcourir le pays seul, à pied, afin de pouvoir entrer . . . en contact direct avec les indigènes" (*Retouches* 13).

60. "Quand, m'échappant à grand'peine aux officialités, aux surveillances, j'avais frayé avec des tâcherons dont le salaire n'est que de quatre ou cinq roubles par jour, le banquet en mon honneur . . . que voulait-on que j'en pense? Un banquet, presque quotidien, où déjà l'abondance des hors-d'œuvre était telle qu'on était trois fois rassasié avant qu'ait commencé le vrai repas; un festin de six plats, lequel durait plus de deux heures. . . . Quelle dépense! N'ayant jamais pu voir une note, je ne la puis préciser. Mais un de mes compagnons, fort au courant des prix, estime que chaque banquet devait revenir à plus de trois cents roubles par tête, avec les liqueurs et les vins" (*Retouches* 58).

61. "Jamais encore je n'avais voyagé dans des conditions si fastueuses. En wagon spécial ou dans les meilleures autos, toujours les meilleures chambres dans les meilleurs hôtels, la chère la plus abondante et la mieux choisie. Et quel accueil! Quels soins! Quelles prévenances! Acclamé partout, adulé, . . . fêté. Rien, pour m'être offert, ne semblait trop bon, trop exquis. . . . Mais ces faveurs mêmes rappelaient sans cesse des privilèges, des différences, où je pensais trouver l'égalité" (*Retouches* 57–58).

62. "[C]e ne fut point tant l'imparfait, que de retrouver aussitôt les avantages que je voulais fuir, les privilèges que j'espérais abolis" (*Retouches* 55).

63. "Je ne vais pas en U.R.S.S. pour retrouver des privilèges" (*Retouches* 56).

64. "[U]n grand écrivain, un grand artiste, est essentiellement anticonformiste . . . [et] navigue à contre courant" (*Retour* 79).

65. "De cœur, de tempérament, de pensée, j'ai toujours été communiste. Mais j'avais peur de ma propre pensée, et, dans mes écrits, m'efforçais plus de la cacher que de la dire" (*Journal* 353).

66. "[L]e « mysticisme », aujourd'hui, est du côté de ceux qui font profession d'athéisme et d'irréligiosité. C'est en tant que religion, que la doctrine communiste exalte et alimente les ferveurs des jeunes gens d'aujourd'hui. . . . [I]ls transfèrent leur idéal du ciel sur la terre, ainsi que je fais avec eux . . . (*Journal* 427).

67. "La seule idée de . . . devoir défendre le Christ vis-à-vis des camarades communistes me paraît profondément absurde; c'est contre les popes, les prêtres, etc., que je le veux

défendre, et . . . le restituer. C'est contre la religion que je proteste, contre l'église, les dogmes, la foi, etc." (*Journal* 424).

68. "[C]ette religion communiste comporte, elle aussi, un dogme, une orthodoxie, des textes auxquels on se réfère, une abdication de la critique . . ." (*Journal* 427; ellipsis Gide's).

69. "Dans les écrits de Marx, j'étouffe. Il y manque quelque chose, je ne sais quel ozone, indispensable à la respiration de mon esprit. J'ai pourtant lu quatre volumes du *Capital* patiemment, assidûment, studieusement; plus le volume de morceaux . . . choisis par Paul Nizan. . . . J'ai lu tout cela avec plus de constance et de soin que je n'apportai à aucune autre étude . . . sans autre désir que celui de me laisser convaincre. . . . Et je sortais de là, chaque fois, courbaturé, l'intelligence meurtrie comme par les brodequins de torture. . . . Je pense qu'une grande partie du prestige de Marx vient de ceci qu'il est difficilement abordable. . . . Où l'on ne comprend pas, l'on s'incline" (*Journal* 584–585).

70. "Défions-nous de ceux qui veulent . . . , à tout prix, tracer sur un sol courbe des sillons droits; de ceux qui préfèrent à chaque homme l'idée qu'ils se sont faite de l'humanité" (*Journal* 586). The phrase "to plough straight furrows on a curving field" ["tracer sur un sol courbe des sillons droits"] is reminiscent of "the crooked timber of humanity," which Isaiah Berlin used as a title of one of his books (New York: Knopf, 1991), and which originates in an observation made by Kant.

71. "His . . . school-fellows persecuted him for his Protestant Heresy. . . . Everyday he was chased home by a howling mob, and he reached his horrified mother covered with mud and bleeding at the nose" (Painter 5–6).

72. For example, Larry Kramer, a prominent and vocal homosexual activist and spokesman, used the AIDS epidemic to indict American society as a whole: "the AIDS pandemic is the fault of the white middle class, male majority. AIDS is here because the straight world would not grant equal rights to gay people. . . . AIDS is our holocaust and Reagan our Hitler. New York City is our Auschwitz. . . . [W]e are witnessing . . . the systematic, planned annihilation of some by others with the avowed purpose of eradicating an undesirable portion of the population" (Kramer 178, 173, 263).

Works Cited

Brown, Frederick. "The Oracle." *New Republic,* May 17, 1999: 40.

Crossman, Richard, ed. *The God That Failed.* New York: Harper, 1949.

Fowlie, Wallace. *André Gide: His Life and Art.* New York: Macmillan, 1965.

Gide, André. *Afterthoughts: A Sequel to Back from the U.S.S.R.* Trans. Dorothy Bussy. London: Secker & Warburg, n.d.

———. *Journal 1926–1950.* Ed. Martine Sagaert. Paris: Gallimard, Bibliothèque de la Pléiade, 1997.

———. *Journals, 1889–1949.* Ed. and trans. Justin O'Brien. Harmondsworth, U.K.: Penguin, 1967.

———. *Retouches à mon Retour de l'U.R.S.S.* Paris: Gallimard, 1937.

———. *Retour de l'U.R.S.S.* Paris: Gallimard, 1936.

———. *Return from the U.S.S.R.* Trans. Dorothy Bussy. New York: McGraw Hill, 1964.

Guerard, Albert J. *André Gide.* Cambridge: Harvard University Press, 1969.

Hentoff, Nat. "Joan Baez's 'Cruel and Wanton Act.'" *Village Voice,* May 28, 1979: 25–26.

Hollander, Paul. *Political Pilgrims: Travels of Western Intellectuals to the Soviet Union, China, and Cuba, 1928–1978.* New York: Oxford University Press, 1981.

Kramer, Larry. *Reports from the Holocaust: The Making of an AIDS Activist.* New York: St. Martin's, 1989.

Painter, George D. *André Gide: A Critical Biography.* London: Weidenfeld & Nicolson, 1968.

Tokes, Rudolf. *Hungary's Negotiated Revolution.* Cambridge: Cambridge University Press, 1996.

CHAPTER 10

Unfinished Business: André Gide's *Geneviève* and the Constraints of Socialist Realism

Peter F. DeDomenico

One of the most pronounced effects of the various ideological disputes that gripped the Parisian literary community in the early 1930s was the way in which polemics ultimately infiltrated that group's aesthetic production. Especially within highly influential Communist literary circles, contention focused not simply upon social and philosophical issues, but upon which literary genres and techniques were best suited for ideological communication. The growing *rapprochement* between the French intellectual establishment and the U.S.S.R. certainly had a strong effect on the outcome of these debates surrounding literary rhetoric. But even before the First Soviet Writers' Congress in Moscow in 1934, at which the doctrine of Socialist Realism was made official by the Party, many French writers had adopted defining features of that narrative genre.[1] Despite its adherents' declared commitment to the Soviet call, Surrealism was rejected by most Communists as a viable approach to literary engagement—due, in part, to its professed aim of confounding conscious meaning and its seeming preference for avant-garde forms over clearly articulated political content. Instead, a new trend in revolutionary fiction was emerging whose style, plot structure, and restricted range of possible interpretations harked back to the aesthetics of the nineteenth-century realist and naturalist traditions. Writers like André Malraux, Paul Nizan, and ex-Surrealist Louis Aragon all strove to attract the reader's sympathy to Communist values with realist narrative resembling a *roman à thèse*.[2] Their dramas often depicted human struggles against oppression; rendered in clear, descriptive prose and usually narrated from a single, omniscient perspective, such works rapidly supplanted in the consciousness of the French intelligentsia the Surrealists' disjointed, multiperspective attacks on traditional forms. For the organized Left of the early thirties, both the aesthetics and the tactics of literary *engagement* underwent profound redefinition: assaults on tradition and meaning as a means of undermining social authority gave way to the strategic manipulation of classic forms for the clear transmission of revolutionary ideology.

This dramatic shift in the practice of political aesthetics had the unfortunate effect, however, of restricting the era's committed novelists to the stylistic confines of the *roman à thèse* genre. Such constraints—the need to write without ambiguity, for example, or the use of one's fiction for the purpose of stating a thesis—at times proved inhibiting forces for writers devoted to the Soviet cause. This was the case, at least, with groundbreaking novelist and critic André Gide, who, though vocally sympathetic to Communism in the early thirties, never successfully adapted to the precise literary form promoted by it. Even before his public rupture with Soviet loyalists in 1936, the obstacles Gide faced adhering to Socialist Realism had already begun to manifest themselves. In *Geneviève,* his incomplete but nevertheless fascinating and complex psychological portrait of a young girl's rebellion against bourgeois conventions in the years just preceding the First World War, a feminist message is articulated in a distinctly Socialist Realist framework—an aesthetic that, in the end, had little in common with the one he had followed in the past. The fact that *Geneviève* could not be completed attests to the incompatibility of *roman à thèse* tactics with those traditionally associated with Gide. It also reveals the extent to which, in the thirties, the strict linking of Communist belief with a restrictive genre barred even the most sympathizing writers from the arena of literary *engagement*.

Gide in the Early Thirties: Communist Fellow Traveler and Writer of Feminist Fiction

Few writers participated more strenuously in the political debates that raged within Parisian literary circles than Gide. Although he had on many occasions addressed issues of great controversy in his writings, until the late 1920s he remained an essentially "apolitical" writer, in the sense that he had almost never openly supported a particular political entity or doctrine.[3] His career as an activist began abruptly in 1927 after the publication of *Voyage au Congo,* a travel diary chronicling the extensive, 1925-1926 journey he took through central Africa. In both this book and its continuation, *Le Retour du Tchad* (1928), Gide described in detail the brutality he witnessed against the native people by the French colonial occupiers.[4] Now embraced by the organized Left across Europe as a crusader against Western imperialism, in the thirties Gide broadened the scope of his political engagement, using his influence in the intellectual and artistic arenas to promote a variety of progressive causes.

Although he repeatedly refused to join the Parti Communiste Français, he remained a dedicated Communist "fellow traveler," lending his support throughout the period to activist writers' circles.[5] For example, he traveled to Berlin in late 1933 with Malraux as part of an international effort to secure the liberation of Dimitrov and three other men who, despite their acquittal from the crime months earlier, were still imprisoned by the Nazi authorities under suspicion of having burned down the Reichstag.[6] Secondly, at an event sponsored by L'Association des Écrivains et Artistes Révolutionnaires (A.E.A.R.) in 1933, he delivered a speech entitled "Fascisme," in which he publicly denounced Hitler's newly empowered Nazi regime and its violent repression of political dissent.[7] (Gide eventually wound up on the *comité directeur* [executive board] of *Commune,* a periodical launched by the A.E.A.R.[8]) Third, his "Message au 1er Congrès des écrivains soviétiques" was read at the 1934 convention, attended in person by fellow French novelists Aragon, Malraux, and Nizan.[9] And fourth, in 1935 Gide presided over the International Congress of Writers for the Defense of Culture, a pro-Communist event that reunited scores of major literary figures from fourteen nations.[10]

In strictly literary spheres, Gide's influence was strongly felt at the *Nouvelle Revue Française,* the popular journal he had co-founded back in 1909. In fact, it was in the *NRF's* July 1932 issue that he first proclaimed his enthusiasm for the Soviet experiment.[11] Meanwhile, behind the scenes, he encouraged favorable coverage of the U.S.S.R.: following Gide's example, from 1932 through 1935 the review maintained a neutral to friendly stance toward the Soviet Union.[12] In January 1933, the *NRF* published a series of documents honoring "The Russian Youth," and its report on the Soviet Writers' Congress was generally laudatory. The review also defended Gide in its coverage of a 1935 debate held in Paris at the Union pour la Vérité, at which he confronted a number of outspoken conservative opponents.[13]

Gide, therefore, participated most visibly in the political culture of the thirties by wielding personal influence in the literary world, in order to rally fellow intellectuals and writers to the cause of the U.S.S.R.—or more precisely, to the values it ostensibly stood for: anti-Fascism and the emancipation of workers and women from socioeconomic oppression. Moreover, his treatment of social issues as both public speaker and distinguished intellectual represents only one aspect of his involvement in literary politics of the thirties. Alongside his public activism he started addressing social issues directly in his fictional works. For example, his plays *Œdipe* (1930) and *Robert, ou L'Intérêt général* (1934), as well as the lyric prose piece *Les Nouvelles Nourritures* (1935), all have overt political themes.[14]

Yet the cause Gide promoted most loudly in his fiction of the era was feminism. At first glance, Gide's public connection to French feminist movements of the thirties appears tenuous. While both his journals and his biographers attest to the strong personal sympathy he held for women's causes at the time, his public activism centered almost exclusively upon issues concerning the U.S.S.R. and the rise of Fascism.[15] It is in his literary writing that his feminist activism is paramount.[16] Between 1929 and 1936, Gide published *L'École des femmes, Robert,* and *Geneviève,* an ambitious trilogy of *récits* that depict the bourgeois family as a primary breeding ground for male oppression. Narrated from the point of view of three characters, each providing a distinct perspective on the events recounted in the tale, this self-declared "triptych" chronicles the breakdown of a seemingly typical French nuclear household during the decades leading up to World War I. Specifically, the crisis detailed in these works revolves around Éveline and Geneviève, the mother and daughter of the family in question, as they come to grips with husband and father Robert's religious hypocrisy and controlling chauvinism.

The first book of the trilogy, *L'École des femmes* (1929), is presented in the form of a diary supposedly composed by the protagonist, Éveline; it details the initial and final stages of her ill-fated marriage to a second character, Robert. In the first section of her journal, which dates in fictional time back to October and November 1894, the young Éveline describes her brief but eventful courtship with Robert, whom she met six months earlier during a vacation in Italy with her parents. Éveline's naive perception of Robert here (though he already comes across as a bit of a louse, despite his fiancée's endless praise of him) contrasts with the portrait she gives in the later three sections of her diary, dated on the eve of the First World War. Self-righteous, posing, egotistical, and bigoted, Robert has become unbearable to Éveline, consequently driving her to escape him, and eventually lose her life, by volunteering as a nurse in the town of Châtellerault, near the front. *L'École des femmes*'s sequel, *Robert* (1930), is framed as a letter, addressed to Gide and written by the husband as a response to Éveline's diary. Here, Robert claims to take up the pen "not from a need for rehabilitation" but "solely for the sake of truth, justice, and accuracy."[17] The portrayal he gives of his marriage's collapse focuses mostly upon the years separating the beginning and final sections of *L'École des femmes;* most significantly, he associates Éveline's disillusionment with her eventual loss of religious faith. However, though superficially offering the husband's point of view on the course of events, *Robert* in fact merely reinforces the message conveyed in its precursor, as Robert's discourse bluntly betrays his hypocrisy and moral snobbery. Finally, in *Geneviève* (1936), Gide writes from the point of view of Éveline's and Robert's daughter, a declared representative of the younger, liberated generation of women. Framed as a second open letter to Gide, the protagonist/narrator Geneviève attacks her father's elitism and false piety, recounts her lesbian crush on a fellow classmate, and sharply criticizes the institution of marriage.

In the *École des femmes* trilogy, Gide's feminist ideas are not communicated directly in any expository passages, but rather are conveyed through the reader's identification with the viewpoint of a sympathetic character who belongs to the oppressed group. Framing his tales as diaries and letters, avoiding the introduction of supernatural events, he seeks to exact the reader's sympathy for characters Éveline and Geneviève at the expense of antagonist Robert. As critic Albert W. Halsall points out in his impressively detailed breakdown of Gide's feminist rhetorical techniques, *L'École des femmes* operates on the premise that the interpretation of events attributed to its heroines will appear more convincing than those of Robert.[18] Pitting in the first book the virtuous and self-effacing Éveline against her self-righteous and hypocritical husband, Gide encourages his audience to draw larger conclusions about the general condition of women—conclusions never openly articulated in the first book of his trilogy. In *Robert,* moreover, this pattern is repeated, but in reverse: under the guise of a defense narrated from the husband's perspective, Gide employs various tactics that ultimately reinforce the reader's original identification with Éveline. By burdening Robert's supposed refutation of his wife's earlier narrative with what Halsall has aptly labeled "rhetorical incompetence," the author attempts to worsen the negative image already attached to this character.[19] Finally, in the series' third

installment, Gide establishes a reliable narrative voice that stands in direct opposition to attitudes and social institutions staunchly upheld by the French Right
(patriarchy, the Church, marriage, heterosexuality, sharp class divisions, and anti-
Semitism). In doing so, *Geneviève* treats a broader range of political issues than
its precursors, and thus carries, one might assert, the heaviest ideological weight
of the trilogy.[20]

Constructing his prose to imitate "real" documents written by real people,
but calling upon his audience to identify only with particular characters in his
drama, Gide appears, superficially at least, to have modeled his tactics for his trilogy's ideological enunciation vaguely on those of a traditional *roman à thèse* (as
Susan Rubin Suleiman has defined the genre).[21] In fact, though a feminist-
rather than Communist-inspired work, the *École des femmes* trilogy nevertheless
foreshadows and reflects many aspects of the French literary trend toward doc-
trinaire realism during the early thirties: its first two installments published only
a few years before the official advent of the term "Socialist Realism," the trilogy resembles closely other examples of the Soviet-inspired literary genre, particularly in its consistent attempt to strictly limit textual ambiguity. In sharp
contrast to the playful and often cynical plurivocality of Gide's 1926 novel *Les
Faux-Monnayeurs, L'École des femmes* is designed to establish the reader's identification with particular characters in its drama, and hence to restrict its own
interpretation.

It is therefore remarkable that Gide published *Geneviève,* arguably the trilogy's
most politically charged installment, in incomplete form. In fact, the work's full
title runs as follows: *Geneviève, ou La Confidence inachevée* [Geneviève, or The
Unfinished Confidence]. As Gide himself admitted in his *Journal,* after writing
the book's first two chapters he found himself unable to complete a third.[22] The
articulation of a political message, it appears, in some way worked against the
artistic qualities of his writing. Of course, Gide made no secret of the unease he
felt toward this moment in his career. At the Union pour la Vérité debate mentioned above, for example, he repeatedly linked his political activism with artistic inaction. "I want to believe that art and Communist doctrine can be
reconciled," he stated at one point, "but I must admit that to this day I have
been unable to find their point of harmony and fusion (this problem has
resulted, as well, from long-standing habits of mine). That is why I have produced nothing in four years."[23] And later on, he declared: "To write, I have
needed that pillow of ignorance and lack of curiosity (regarding social issues).
Ever since I became concerned with social issues four years ago, I no longer
write."[24] While Gide attempted in the thirties to expand the political activism
of his public life onto the very pages of his *récits* and plays, the ideological nature
of these works interfered on a profound level with their literary value—a
conflict, he claimed, that rendered him artistically unproductive.

Unfinished as it is, *Geneviève* nevertheless remains one of Gide's most compelling narratives, as it offers a developed, psychological portrait of a hypothetical, upper-middle-class family, all the while grappling with questions of identity
politics in a way surprisingly ahead of its time. And even if one considers the
work as merely its author's personal rhetorical battleground, the *récit,* when read

with a careful regard both to style and political meaning, illustrates the challenges Gide faced in conforming to the models for politically charged fiction available to him in the thirties. On the one hand, a close reading of *Geneviève* reveals the degree to which the work stands apart from his earlier fiction, in terms of both its narrative strategy and its political message. Like the two works that precede it, *Geneviève* represents a text in which the possibility for multiple interpretations is severely restricted. Recounted from the point of view of a declared representative of the younger generation of revolutionary women, the work conveys its political message through the establishment of a reliable narrative voice that stands in direct opposition to attitudes and social institutions staunchly upheld by the French Right. On the other hand, it appears that Gide, both before and after his conversion to the social causes in the late twenties, had promoted in his novels some of the very ideological positions he seeks to undermine in *Geneviève*. With reference to his earlier writing, as well as to recent critical work by various scholars, it can be shown that the success of much of Gide's fiction has always involved a certain degree of misogyny, cultural elitism, and anti-Semitism. It is therefore understandable that Gide found *Geneviève* impossible to complete. For as a reading of this work ultimately suggests, despite the genuine sympathy he had for the plight of women and the working class in the thirties, Gide's self-imposed task of producing narrative that provides total identification with these oppressed groups entailed a repudiation of the rhetorical tactics for which he is most famous.

Geneviève: Feminism through the Socialist Realist Lens

Gide launches *Geneviève, ou La Confidence inachevée* with a brief note announcing that he received the ensuing text "in manuscript form" *[en manuscrit]*, a narrative "complementary" to the earlier writings *L'École des femmes* and *Robert*. Implying (but never specifying) the authenticity of the documents in question, he suggests that the reader consider the works "a triptych."[25] The *avant-propos* that follows is framed as a letter, addressed to Gide and dated August 1931. "The following narrative will not be to [Gide's] liking," the narrator Geneviève D. begins, for while his mind "remains on the plane of the absolute," hers exists "on the plane of the relative." While Gide attempts to resolve the vague question "what is man able to do?," Geneviève declares instead her intention to discuss the "material and precise" subject of "what today's woman can hope for."[26] Noting the great extent to which the social role of women has changed since the First World War, she adds: "And perhaps nothing less than that horrifying catastrophe was needed to allow women to make evident qualities which have seemed exceptional to this day."[27] While her mother's book addressed an earlier generation, the present text does more than simply "wish for liberty," for as Geneviève writes: "it is not a matter of wishing for liberty, but of taking it."[28] Wanting her life story to serve only as "a warning"—as "one example among many, a particular example"[29]— she concludes the introduction by suggesting *Geneviève* as the title for her tale: the pseudonym under which she appears in her mother's diary.

The first of the *récit*'s two parts begins with the narrator's reflections on her parents. Back in 1913, when Geneviève was fifteen years old and attending high school, she would do her homework with her mother, Éveline, and it was during these times that they influenced each other. Geneviève portrays her mother as industrious, self-effacing, and caring toward those less fortunate; in contrast, she describes her father, Robert, as passive-aggressive, critical of her education, ostentatious, and guilty of "attaching greater value to the appearance of virtue than to virtue itself."[30] The book's plot revolves around the narrator's expressly romantic but unrequited love for a schoolmate, Sara Keller. Daughter of a Jewish painter, of common origins and of meager means, Sara nevertheless becomes the focus of the richer, bourgeois Geneviève's obsession. Such desire is aroused on the two girls' very first day of class together. The narrator describes her almost immediate infatuation with Sara: "Seated to my right in class was, of all my peers, the one who attracted and held my gaze the most. Her brown skin, her black, curly, almost frizzy hair hid her temples and a bit of her forehead. One couldn't exactly say she was beautiful, but her strange charm was even more seductive to me than her beauty."[31] It is only a few days later, and after observing the academically uninterested but dramatically inclined Sara recite for the class the opening scene from Racine's *Britannicus,* that Gide's heroine musters the courage to ask for her neighbor's friendship. After hesitating slightly, Sara accepts Geneviève's overture and urges the latter to visit her at home the next day.

This incident provokes the *récit*'s first conflict, as Geneviève's mother is loath to permit her daughter to spend time with a school friend of lower-class, Jewish descent. Begrudgingly, however, Éveline and Robert eventually invite Sara and her parents to one of their regularly held Thursday night dinner parties. At this point the distance between the Kellers and the other guests becomes even more striking to Gide's heroine. "Ethnic" in appearance, gaudy and flamboyant, Sara's parents throw their hosts' drab attire and stiff manners into sharp relief. To make matters worse, Geneviève mentions at this point her discovery, later on, that the Kellers, though "deeply united" *[formaient un ménage profondément uni],* were in fact never legally married.[32] Such information concerning the Kellers' bohemian lifestyle, of course, does little to win Robert's approval of his daughter's friendship with Sara. As he exclaims to Geneviève the following day, "I don't like to see you spending time with people of that sort."[33] Yet despite his barely concealed anti-Semitism, social etiquette prevents Robert from forbidding his wife and daughter to attend the Kellers' own *soirée,* held soon thereafter.

A second pivotal moment occurs at the Kellers' party: a large, bustling affair, attended by numerous artists and musicians. Here, the reader gets to know in more depth Gisèle Parmentier, a fellow *lycéenne* briefly introduced earlier in the text, who eventually serves both as Geneviève's confidante and her rival for the affections of Sara. At one point secluded from the rest of the guests, the three girls embark on a candid discussion about their views toward marriage and the demeaning condition of women in modern society. Geneviève, naive in such matters, is shocked to learn of her classmates' shared distrust of the marital institution. "I don't believe I have any vocation for conjugal love," Sara boldly declares, adding: "Oh, I don't want to say that I will never fall in love. But to sacrifice my tastes, my own life for a man, to care only about pleasing him, about serving him. . . . It's a better idea not to get married at all."[34] Gisèle's feelings, though more tempered, nevertheless reveal a similar emancipatory sentiment: "I don't want to swear never to marry. I claim that, even in marriage, a woman can still maintain her freedom. . . ."[35] These sorts of revelations lead the three teenagers to found and swear their faith that evening to the *"Indépendance Féminine"*: a "secret society" devoted to, among other feminist causes, the support and protection of single mothers.[36]

Given Robert's conservatism and the intensity of Geneviève's feelings for Sara, however, the narrator's friendship with that free-thinking personality cannot succeed. The final blow falls, in large part, through the treachery of the narrator's brother Gustave who, according to Geneviève, makes a habit of winning their father's favor at her expense. A year younger than his sister and of "delicate health" *[santé délicate]*, Gustave appears to have regularly received better treatment from their father than she has. For example, while the narrator claims Robert never laid a hand on his son, she describes how her father did slap her once when she was nine, and this merely for having pointed out an evident inconsistency in his reasoning.[37] A fairly shadowy figure in Gide's tale, one who resents his sister's relationship with Sara, Gustave maliciously avenges himself, in part, by bringing to Robert's attention a newspaper review of an exhibit of paintings by Sara Keller's father. The article in question, while laudatory, divulges that the most prominent work displayed in the exposition was, in fact, a nude for which Sara was the model (the portrait, titled *L'Indolente* [The Languid Girl] depicts its subject reclining on a sofa, her face obscured by a hand mirror).[38] Such indecency on the Kellers' part provokes a violent family argument, with Geneviève steadfastly refusing to obey her father's order never to see Sara again. Now aware that the portrait she saw reproduced in the paper depicts her beloved, Geneviève becomes obsessed with the nude image of Sara. Rushing to the drawing room in an attempt to ferret out an issue of *L'Illustration* in which a reproduction of the scandalous painting appears, Gide's heroine discovers that her brother, having anticipated her move, has already cut out the photo from the magazine. Mortified, Geneviève descends upon Gustave, and a fist fight ensues between them.[39]

Now sobbing and confined to her room in self-imposed exile, Geneviève receives a visit from her mother who, having somewhat passively supported her daughter in the above dispute, comforts her by suggesting the two of them attend the Keller show together that very afternoon. Elated, Geneviève is now able to glimpse, first timidly, then with more assurance, Sara's naked image proudly exposed "in the place of honor" *[en place d'honneur]*. "I would have liked to have been alone in the room," she declares. "The gaze of other people embarrassed me. I felt they were observing me whenever I looked upon the large canvas. However, despite my suffering and embarrassment, I was drawn in by the extraordinary beauty of that *'indolente,'* who filled me with a strange unease which until that moment I had never felt before."[40] Geneviève's wish to possess the image exclusively is fulfilled, moreover, when she obtains a copy of the exhibition program. She writes:

> I was happy to keep it because of the very good reproduction of the paint-
> ing it contained and, as soon as I returned home, I locked myself in my
> bedroom to contemplate it at leisure. My imagination made an effort to
> clothe that beautiful, supple body in the dress Sara usually wore to class—
> that everyday dress in which I saw her the next day, when it was much eas-
> ier for me to imagine her stripped of it. Yes, my gaze, despite myself,
> unclothed her and I imagined her as the *"Indolente."* An unknown anguish
> gripped me, which I did not know to be desire because I did not think
> desire could be felt for someone other than of the opposite sex. . . .[41]

Geneviève becomes sick with love for her classmate, and the intensity of her passion attracts her mother's attention. In fact, the very night of the gallery exhibition, Éveline expresses her concerns in a heart-to-heart chat with her
daughter. "I am worried about your friendship for Sara," Éveline admits. "I fear
it has much suffering in store for you, and will lead further than you want to
go."[42] Indeed, the stress of this unrequited and seemingly impossible desire has
already begun to make Gide's narrator physically unwell. No longer spending
time with Sara at Éveline's request, Geneviève falls ill with scarlet fever and must
leave the *lycée* for good. It is this event that marks the transition between the two
parts of Gide's tale for, as Geneviève states in the final paragraph of the first section, illness serves to liberate her from her obsession with Sara. "The scarlet fever
in which, as Freud would say, the confusion of my entire being took refuge, res-
cued both my mother and me," she writes. "My mother told me later that during the first few days of my delirium (for I had a very high fever), Sara's image
haunted me. But when I began to recover, my ideas were taking another direction."[43]

It is precisely this "other direction" in the narrator's thinking that dominates
the second part of *Geneviève*. No longer in school and prohibited from associating with Sara, Geneviève now relies on private teachers for her education, and
it is during these lessons that she begins to hone her political convictions more
keenly. Studying English with Gisèle's mother, for example, she perfects her
debating skills by engaging Mme Parmentier in discussions of feminist literary
criticism.[44] Geneviève profits from conversations with Gisèle as well, who has
strong opinions concerning women's rights to education and work, and equality under the law.[45] Yet it is to Dr. Marchant, her science tutor, that Geneviève
makes her most daring political statement.

The reader has already encountered Dr. Marchant, for he holds a small but
pivotal role in the previous works, *L'École des femmes* and *Robert*. Though he and
Robert are friends of long standing, the doctor differs considerably from his religious, conservative peer: an atheist and a rationalist, his gruff exterior masking a
heart of gold, Marchant has become, over the years, an even closer friend of
Robert's wife Éveline. (In fact, Geneviève wonders at one point why her
mother had not married him instead of Robert.)[46] During their lessons

together, Geneviève and the doctor initially debate the merits of his pessimistic, arguably nihilistic world view against her youthful optimism. She writes: "But while Dr. Marchant resigned himself to humanity's profound misery, 'which we can at the very most only soothe a little,' he used to say, I could not concede that our hope should stop there. He called me chimerical when I spoke of a possible improvement in society's condition, and this enraged me. . . . I stuck to my 'chimera.' I held firm. This hope within me has guided my life."[47] Geneviève reveals the true vastness of her idealism, however, when a few months later she abruptly asks Dr. Marchant to help her conceive a baby out of wedlock. The doctor refuses such advances, fortunately for her; for such an extreme decision, as Geneviève articulates with hindsight, was concocted more out of a revolt against Robert than either out of love for her science teacher or out of desire for motherhood. She writes:

> To tell the truth, I had never analyzed the factors my resolution involved but, in my particular case, I think the most significant element was protest. Yes, protest against an established order I refused to recognize, against what my father called "good morals" and, more especially, against him, who symbolized these "good morals" in my eyes; a need to humiliate him, to mortify him, to make him blush on my account and disown me; a need to affirm my independence, my refusal to submit, through an act that only a woman could commit, for which I expected to assume full responsibility, the consequences of which I had not truly imagined.[48]

While Geneviève describes in the second half of her *récit* the beginnings of her radical feminist convictions, she admits that during her adolescence her immaturity limited the scope of her political activism to rash, childish rebellion.

What constitutes mature feminist activism, according to Geneviève? This question is hardly addressed in the tale, for the narrative ends abruptly here, as its heroine recounts her final, 1916 visit with Éveline at the military hospital in Châtellerault. Daughter and mother reveal secrets to each other at this melancholic encounter: while Geneviève admits that she attempted to seduce Dr. Marchant, Éveline divulges both her loss of esteem for Robert and, more surprisingly, her own hidden passion for the doctor. The two women embrace, and the narrator ends her tale by declaring: "I would never see her again."[49] Thus, like the two works preceding it, *Geneviève* concludes with Éveline, who heroically sacrifices herself by caring for the wounded near the front lines.

There exist many convincing arguments for classifying *Geneviève,* and even Gide's trilogy in general, as a feminist *roman à thèse,* a number of which having already been nicely articulated by Halsall in his rhetorical study of *L'École des femmes.* As the latter has pointed out, *Geneviève* explicitly poses itself as a "narrative *exemplum*" [exemplum *nartatif*] in its opening pages, when Gide's heroine predestines her tale to serve as a "warning" and determines that she should serve as "one example among many." Halsall goes on to illustrate various rhetorical strategies Gide puts into effect in this exemplary work, which include his demands that the reader identify with the narrator of the *récit,* Geneviève, that she be associated with another sympathetic and trustworthy narrator, Éveline, and that these two be contrasted with the unappealing and deceptive Robert.[50] Indeed, Geneviève's repeated praise of her mother's heroic qualities, combined with the evident sympathy the two seem to share throughout the narrative, serves to identify them as reliable speakers and likable protagonists. In *L'École des femmes,* the reader has already encountered the trustworthy language of Éveline's diary and admired her patriotism and self-abnegation; in *Geneviève,* such impressions are reinforced, as the narrator describes at one point her mother's "extraordinary love for the poor, the suffering. . . ."[51] The reader has also noted the profound connection Éveline claims to have with her daughter, as when she notes in her journal: "I have just had a terrible conversation with [Geneviève], where I understood that it is with her alone I might best be able to make myself understood, and at the same time why I do not want to be understood by her; it is that I fear to find in her my own thoughts but bolder, so bold that they frighten me."[52] Thus, Gide's audience is inclined to believe and respect Geneviève when, for example, she attributes her own positive qualities to Éveline's encouragement: "I take from my mother a certain taste for work, a natural diligence. . . . I also owe to my mother an ardent desire and need to make myself useful, and if this desire already existed in me naturally, dormant, she knew how to awaken it, to bring it constantly to life."[53]

In a contrary fashion, Gide uses a series of tactics in *Geneviève* to make Robert appear as despicable as possible. Having established Geneviève's narrative trustworthiness, Gide uses her to successfully undermine her father's credibility.[54] For example, she puts the value of Robert's speech in doubt, as she critiques his tendency to shape his emotions in order to fit his words. She thus depicts him as "persistently both 'behind' and indebted to himself'—that is, allowing his emotions and thoughts to be dictated by his words and gestures (rather than the other way around).[55] Likewise, she later blasts her father's endless reliance on social climbing in place of honest productivity. She writes: "[L]ike those who have no great personal worth, he liked to believe that everything is to be obtained through intrigue or cleverness. I think the lion's share of what he pompously called his 'work' consisted in giving or receiving favors, of which he kept an exact account."[56] Furthermore, Robert's laughable aspects are brought to an almost absurd level during the dramatic fight scene when, in an attempt to shock his daughter by pounding his hand against the table ("not with his fist, which would have been vulgar, but with the palm of his hand," she stresses), his coffee spoon is described as leaping up and striking him on the nose.[57]

Ultimately, Gide maneuvers this negative portrayal of Robert into a general attack against the French Right, for by associating him with various conservative and religious opinions, Gide transforms him into a sort of archetype of modern patriarchal authority. Halsall has already remarked that Robert makes his living by operating a sort of "book-of-the-month club" that caters to wealthy Catholic families, while both Halsall and Lucey have stressed as well a moment early on in the trilogy when Robert is described offering Éveline's father a copy of Édouard Drumont's anti-Semitic newspaper *La Libre Parole.*[58]

In a similar vein, in *Geneviève,* Robert is presented as subtly anti-Semitic ("without being an avowed anti-Semite, he held all Jews in suspicion"); as classist (he refers to the poor as "*nos inférieurs*" [our inferiors]); and as opposed to women's education (the narrator claims he blames her "straying of thought [and] of conduct" *[écarts de pensée [et] de conduite]* on her high-school education).[59] Robert in this way serves in the trilogy as more than just an individual figure; he constitutes as well a veritable ideological composite of the enemies Gide seeks to combat.

Gide does not rely strictly on negative rhetorical strategies to promote his feminist message in *Geneviève,* however, for he also constructs positive, though arguably vague, models of what the modern, liberated woman might look like. Such images of ideal, revolutionary subjects exist first and foremost as part of a mythic, historical continuum in the work, for at least within the fictional world of Gide's trilogy, the First World War represents a point of rupture between two distinct stages of women's political evolution. He thus sharply underscores in his tale the war's impact on gender relations in French society. For example, as Geneviève elaborates in her introduction, the horrors of the war had the positive effect of bringing women for the first time into positions of significance and authority. She writes:

> Yes, it has only been since the war, when so many women demonstrated they had a personal worth and an energy which men had hardly thought them capable of, that men have begun to recognize, and they themselves have begun to lay claim to, their right to virtues which are not simply self-abnegating, such as devotion, submission, and fidelity—devotion to man, submission to man, fidelity to man. For it seemed until today that all positive virtues had remained man's birthright and were reserved for him. I believe that no one can deny that the position of women has changed considerably since the war. And perhaps nothing less than that horrifying catastrophe was needed to allow women to make evident qualities which have seemed exceptional to this day, to allow the value of women to be taken into consideration.[60]

Subsequently, when Geneviève stresses that her mother's book addressed "an earlier generation" (and thus, implicitly, that her own tale speaks to women of a new era), she lends to her discourse a progressive, optimistic aura. In this sense as well, Éveline's disappearance at the front lines at the end of all three tales provides more than the chilling effect of a character's death, as it symbolically represents a whole generation of women heroically paving the way for the truly utopian radicalism of their daughters. While it is probably too extreme to describe *Geneviève* as fundamentally allegorical, one can trace the text's establishment of a sort of modern feminist myth, as Gide situates in his *récit* new categories of revolutionary women within a rapidly evolving historical continuum.

Gide embodies his models for new political subjects for the most part in the characters of Sara, Gisèle, and Geneviève. The first two exemplify the kind of traits the young, feminist avant-garde should possess, and serve to instill these characteristics in Gide's protagonist/narrator. Sara represents the *récit*'s central feminist figure, challenging boundaries of gender, race, and class with her iconoclasm and brash self-confidence. When the reader first encounters Sara, Geneviève draws attention to her combination of talent and rebellious lack of discipline in school. Having triumphantly impressed her schoolmates with her recitation of Racine, for example, Sara finds herself scolded by the teacher: "With your gifts, it is inexcusable that you don't work harder." The student boldly responds "with an ironic little courtesy, a sort of pirouette."[61] Moreover, along with her radical opinions on marriage, her bohemian, unmarried parents, and her Jewish background, which apparently do not make her the least bit uncomfortable before her richer, French peers, Sara exudes self-assurance when, upon entering the narrator's house, she confronts in a sentence the two girls' economic differences.[62] As Geneviève recounts the scene: "'My, aren't *you* well off,' Sara said, these being the first words she uttered, in an indefinable tone that revealed a mixture of admiring astonishment and a bit of scornful irony. . . .'"[63] In other words, free from traditional restrictions based upon race, class, morality, and gender (and thus representing the polar opposite of the obedient, Catholic, turn-of-the-century French bourgeoise), Sara operates within the narrative both as the inspiration behind Geneviève's own political awakening and as a model for a new form of enlightened, liberated subject.

One can argue as well for the ideological importance of Gisèle Parmentier in Gide's narrative, as she serves first as Geneviève's rival, and then as her intellectual double. Gisèle, on the one hand, has intimate access to Sara in a way Geneviève does not (who expresses at one point her jealousy upon discovering, for example, that Gisèle visited Sara when she posed nude for the painting of *L'Indolente*).[64] Furthermore, during the scene in which the *"Indépendance Féminine"* is founded, Gisèle demonstrates that her political savvy is superior to Geneviève's when she proclaims, with a certain degree of independence from Sara, her mature, reasoned distrust of marriage. Yet in the second part of the tale, Gisèle demonstrates her solidarity with Geneviève, first by debating the complexities of feminism with her, and later on by revealing her own sexual attraction to Sara ("if [Sara] had taken me in her arms, I would have melted like sugar," she admits to Geneviève).[65] She thus acts as a sort of double for Geneviève, only more evolved: while remarkably similar to her in terms both of social status and of a subordinate position next to Sara, Gisèle is further ahead on the path to liberty, affording Geneviève a model for what, presumably, she will become.

Yet it is through Geneviève, or more accurately through her transformation from naive character into eloquent writer, that Gide makes his political program most clear. Over the course of the text, the reader is continually asked to compare the young girl of the tale with the authoritative voice recounting it, to follow the latter's evolution away from the former. Observing Geneviève's early confrontations with a hypocritical father, the reader comes to understand the narrator's evident contempt for patriarchy; hearing both her frank disclosure of homosexual inclinations and her near-seduction of Dr. Marchant, one encounters a modern narrative speaker who, setting aside any discomfort she may feel about sexual matters in order to make her point, communicates clearly and intelligently a feminist message.

Although it would be inaccurate to classify *Geneviève* as a Socialist Realist work, its associations with the genre cannot be denied, given the *récit*'s didactic qualities and Gide's political leanings at the time of its composition. For as the above analysis demonstrates and as Emily Apter has already affirmed, *Geneviève* effectively resembles a "paradigmatic" *roman à thèse* (as Suleiman characterizes the genre), with a requisite "dialogical model of apprenticeship"; that is, a narrative based upon a well-defined, binary value system ("right" versus "wrong"), whose structure re-enacts a quasi-mythic scenario: the hero overcoming an "opponent," and through the aid of a "donor" of enlightenment.[66] Geneviève, the tale's heroine, defeats opponent Robert with the help of a progression of donors, Sara and Gisèle (and, perhaps to a lesser degree, Dr. Marchant). And while the apparent moral of the story is obviously feminist and not Leninist, the work appeared during the height of the Socialist Realist literary trend in France.

The exact nature of the feminist doctrine promoted in *Geneviève* is difficult to ascertain, however, as the work has the same unfinished quality as Geneviève's *confidence inachevée*. Specifically, the story stops prematurely, and reader never learns the narrator's precise verdict on marriage or whether she ever sees Sara again. At one point in the text, moreover, Geneviève reveals cryptically that she has a son ("I have often resorted to corporal punishment when dealing with my son," she declares in reference to Robert's having once slapped her); the identity of the child's father and the circumstances surrounding his birth are never divulged.[67] And while Halsall attempts to argue that the seeming abruptness of the tale's ending does not interfere with the work's "lack of structural unity" *[manque d'unité structurale]*—or as he also puts it, that the work does not "necessarily imply that it 'should' continue after [Éveline's disappearance]"—he nevertheless admits later on the haziness of *Geneviève*'s message, summing up in the final sentence of his critique merely what "seems to be" the thesis of Gide's work.[68] He writes: "The central idea [of *Geneviève*], hardly revolutionary in fact, . . . seems to be the following: At the beginning of the twentieth century, it was necessary to liberate women, to abolish their social inferiority to men, an inferiority institutionalized by marriage. But this institution itself, despite all its imperfections, deserves to remain the basis and support for the family, because the other solutions proposed are neither numerous nor acceptable."[69] This analysis does intelligently demonstrate that *Geneviève* is finished enough to read, and it also successfully sums up what Gide's message might have been *were he claiming that his work was complete*. Yet Halsall still leaves a number of important questions unanswered: In what way does the illusion that the tale is unfinished serve to promote Gide's supposed "central idea"? Why strive to tackle so many topics but then leave so many loose ends? Or, perhaps best phrased in biographic and psychological terms: Why would a writer like Gide publicly take a revolutionary stand but simultaneously promote in his fiction a barely articulated, centrist position? To attribute a coherent thesis to *Geneviève,* as Halsall does, is to neglect obvious signs of the work's incompleteness in favor of a clean but ultimately implausible interpretation.

A more satisfactory, and significantly less contrived, reading of the *récit* simply takes the text's pretense to being unfinished at face value, and views it as a work in progress. Indeed, while *Geneviève* attempts to encompass a wide range of social issues, the text remains cut off, leaving the questions it raises unresolved. Of course, the reader, after witnessing in the tale a series of conflicts involving sexism, spousal oppression, homophobia, anti-Semitism, and class insensitivity, easily gains in the end a rough idea of Gide's opinion on such matters. However, though a coherent doctrine is implicitly promised in the text, it is never clearly established. What is the moral of the tale? What does Geneviève ultimately learn, for instance, about her sexuality, about marriage, or about anti-Semitism in French society? Or even: Is this character on the verge of discovering class struggle at the bottom of all the social woes she depicts—a plausible ending, given Gide's intellectual and political trajectory in the early thirties? *Geneviève,* though clearly representing a left-wing *roman à thèse* (and arguably the germ of a Socialist Realist work), never delivers the ideological payoff its thematic vastness seems to promise.

Unfinished Business

One can perhaps account for Gide's inability to bring *Geneviève* to term if one considers the various ways in which the *récit* appears to be a noteworthy departure from the sorts of fiction generally associated with him. These differences do not stem from the work's superficial aspects, however, such as its structure and setting; in fact, Gide's use of the first-person, confessional form and his development of themes involving, for example, the collapse of the bourgeois household can be found in writings of his as diverse as *La Porte étroite* (1909), *La Symphonie pastorale* (1919), and *Les Faux-Monnayeurs.* Rather, the qualities relating to *Geneviève*'s political expression—its systematic reduction of textual ambiguity, its promotion of "reality" in opposition to art, and, perhaps most significantly, its somewhat heavy-handed attempt to evoke sympathy for a wide range of progressive causes—set the work apart from virtually all of Gide's previous narratives. In other words, while Socialist Realism reveals its influence repeatedly throughout *Geneviève,* the basic tactics of this literary movement seem essentially incompatible with those of the standard Gidean *récit.*

The limited possibility for multiple readings of *Geneviève,* for example, would appear to have little in common with the seemingly nonideological quality of the bulk of Gide's earlier fiction. With the possible exception of *Corydon,* his obscurely constructed defense of homosexuality written in Greek dialogue form and published in various stages between 1911 and 1924, Gide's narratives prior to *L'École des femmes* notoriously defy any reduction to a single interpretation. As David Keypour articulates in detail, it is difficult, if not impossible, to extract an authoritative message from the highly self-reflexive writings Gide produced throughout his career, whether his ironic and plurivocal *soties* or his more serious, quasi-existential reflections on the relationship of the individual to God and the self. Distinguishing between the standard *roman à thèse* and what he labels as

Gide's various *romans d'idée,* Keypour acknowledges Gide's capacity to grapple with issues, but notes as well "the persistent, interrogative tone that impregnates" Gide's writings, and how "Gidean fiction never submits to a super-system and . . . cannot be authoritative."[70] In a similar vein, Douwe W. Fokkema posits that what is probably Gide's most famous work, *Les Faux-Monnayeurs,* is emblematic of the "period code of Modernism," whose "primary organizing principle is the narrator's or the lyrical subject's awareness of the provisional, hypothetical nature of his point of view."[71] Furthermore, though Ann M. Moore and George Strauss independently have recognized a direct line between Gide's portrayal of women in *Les Faux-Monnayeurs* and the feminism of his later trilogy, both nevertheless admit the intrinsic ambiguity of the novel that distinguishes it from any *roman à thèse.*[72] And even in the case of *Corydon,* a text in which gay rights are explicitly championed, Lucey clearly points out how a certain measure of uncertainty seems to linger around Gide's actual opinion on the topic, masking at certain moments his own, subtle homophobia.[73] In other words, *Geneviève* diverges sharply from Gide's earlier, less easily interpreted literary endeavors because it expressly aims at limiting multiple textual readings; and it does this by creating a binary structure in which "good" characters are pitted against "bad" ones, and a "correct" politics is pitted against an "incorrect" one.

A related consequence of Gide's attempt to inscribe in *Geneviève* a coherent and easily recognizable level of meaning involves his repeated denigration throughout the *récit* of the imaginary, artistic realm in favor of the "real." This opposition is apparent from the very outset of the tale, when the narrator contrasts both "the relative" *[je me débats dans le relatif]* and matters of "a practical order" *[problèmes d'ordre pratique]* with the interests of the author himself, who, as she puts it, remains steadfastly on "the absolute plane" of art *[Votre esprit plane dans l'absolu].*[74] Similarly, Geneviève stresses later on the difference of purpose that separates the author's literary style from her own writing, in which "it is no longer a question of abstraction but of life." She writes: "Here we find ourselves quite far, Mr. Gide, from the considerations that dictate your books. You used to say, if I recall correctly, 'I write to be reread,' while I, in contrast, am writing this work of mine in order to help whoever reads it to move beyond it."[75] And again, still later, in response to Sara's defense of poetry as a means of abandoning the pain of terrestrial existence, Geneviève declares: "Today, I do not think it good (I was going to say 'honest') to cease living among the miseries of our world in this way, as certain mystics have done in dreams of a future life; this escape from reality seems to me a sort of desertion."[76]

Now, on the one hand, Gide's use of his own narrator's words against himself creates the sort of *mise en abyme* effect for which he is already so well known, as his character, addressing the author himself, presents her clearly fictional narrative as "truth."[77] Indeed, as David H. Walker has affirmed, Gide's writing, at least prior to 1929, uses such literary techniques to repeatedly validate the fictional realm at the expense of the supposedly "real" world situated outside his texts. As Walker quite succinctly asserts: "In Gide there is a veritable cult of writing. . . . Writing seems made to be substituted for the real, in such a way that the narrator rejoices in the defectiveness of his experience. . . . It is in the failure of the real, it seems, that the values of writing are affirmed."[78] On the other hand, it is unclear in this instance to what degree Gide intended this blurring of the line between literary and extraliterary to be ironic, particularly in a tale such as *Geneviève*—a work that, in so many other respects, he constructed to be read at face value. For when Geneviève declares the purpose of her tale "to help whoever reads it to move beyond it," Gide in fact refers fairly blatantly back to the famous appeal to his imaginary addressee in the preface of *Les Nourritures terrestres* (1897) to his imaginary addressee: "And when you have read me, throw this book away—and go out into the world."[79] Geneviève nods towards this lyric call to (sexual) liberation, a call that comes, as Paul de Man has stressed, from one of Gide's least *ironic* works; and so this intertextual reference encourages Gide's readers to take his words seriously and, ultimately, to translate the "revolution" against bourgeois morality championed by him at the turn of the century into the quite different realm of party politics.[80] In his *Journal* entries written around the time of *Geneviève*'s composition, moreover, Gide provided further, circumstantial evidence to support a most unironic reading of the *mise en abyme* effects in his tale. Resisting the temptation to rely on literary gimmicks to dazzle his audience, he stressed how the narrator of his *récit* must appear serious and rational, in order to serve as the mouthpiece for his political views. He wrote: "Something strange and bizarre, something which grabs you: this is what I was hoping for, knowing full well that only the unexpected can delight and plunge the reader into a trance-like state. But my subject (*Geneviève*) does not behave this way. I owe it to my heroine to remain reasonable, since it is through her alone that I express myself."[81] If, in *Geneviève,* Gide draws on any aspect of his earlier writings, it would be those rare moments in which satire, parody, and stylistic artifice are least apparent and the tendency toward ambiguity is subordinate to the will to persuade.

A final, but no less profound way in which *Geneviève* represents a departure from Gide's earlier writings has to do with the very heart of his political convictions. As numerous critics have pointed out, the author himself, at least up until his "conversion" to the Soviet cause in the late twenties, had both subtly and overtly promoted in his fiction a number of the ideologies he sought to undermine in his feminist *récits*. Writing from the woman's point of view, for example, was a rare occurrence in his fiction: indeed, prior to Éveline in *L'École des femmes,* one finds very few female narrators in his fiction (the character of Alissa, whose diary punctuates *La Porte étroite,* being a noteworthy exception). In *Journal* entries during this period, Gide himself admitted the discomfort he felt over what he rather dubiously labeled "writing femininely," declaring: "I achieve no satisfaction writing femininely . . . and I dislike everything I write this way."[82] Even Apter, who compliments Gide's "uncannily believable impersonation of the feminine voice" in the *École des femmes* trilogy, nevertheless underscores his recourse to descriptions of the male body in his earlier writings as a model for his depiction of Sara's body in *Geneviève*.[83] Yet beyond Gide's lack of experience in writing from the feminine perspective, a kind of underlying misogyny cannot be ignored in a number of his most important works. Naomi Segal has adeptly pointed out, for example, how Gide repeatedly kills off female characters so that the male narrator may appropriate their voice. As Segal puts it, in Gide "the figure of the woman . . . has to die so that the male narrator can tell 'his' tale [and] absorb what is the woman's, especially her voice, to destroy it in her and reproduce it as Gide's own authorship."[84]

Anti-Semitism, class insensitivity, and even homophobia, moreover, are hardly alien to the Gidean corpus. Martha Hanna has outlined Gide's decade-long association with the Royalist and racist Action française before the First World War, describing how "between 1907 and 1918 Gide was sometimes impressed, selectively enthusiastic, and . . . subtly influenced by the political and cultural arguments" articulated by this group.[85] In a similar vein, throughout the era Gide's *Journal* contains references to what Martyn Cornick has labeled his "'literary' anti-Jewish feelings," a strain of thought that, as Cornick puts it, equates "Jewish literature with second-rate, 'boulevard' or 'right-bank' literature."[86] Such sentiments have also been thought to have rubbed off on Gide's fiction, such as on his popular *sotie Les Caves du Vatican,* a work that, as Jeffrey Mehlman has attempted to prove, contains a number of anti-Semitic subtexts.[87] Finally, Lucey has detailed both Gide's frustrating lack of class consciousness during his fateful journey across Africa in the twenties and, as previously mentioned, his homophobia in *Corydon,* his supposed defense of homosexuality.[88]

How much weight should one give Gide's indifference to party politics before his sudden participation in them during the late twenties? And, especially, how significant is the sympathy he demonstrated throughout a lengthy career for the very right-wing positions that he rejected in his later fiction? Certainly, a person's political opinions are perpetually subject to change, and the degree to which people scorn this author's ideological fluctuations no doubt depends, ultimately, upon their varying world views. Born into a wealthy, upper-middle-class milieu and at times unquestionably elitist and chauvinistic, Gide revealed throughout his extensive writings a profoundly humanistic side as well, and it is precisely these two, irreconcilable aspects of his thinking that render his political respectability quite difficult to evaluate. One can certainly speak of a Gidean sort of "humanism," if one considers his persistent, quasi-Nietzschean urging of his readers to liberate themselves from the shackles of oppressive and pervasive moral systems.[89] Whether the admirable qualities of this call for liberation outweigh his numerous moments of insensitivity is a complex question that can only involve the political opinions and assumptions of each reader individually.

However one perceives Gide's muddled political thought throughout his lifetime, it does not seem unreasonable to suggest that in fiction such as *Geneviève,* he entered new literary terrain by attempting to sustain ideas which earlier had made him uncomfortable. Yet not only did the Socialist Realist approach to fiction appear to have been incompatible with his own, but it also combated the very attitudes he himself had expressed at previous times in his career. One might argue, then, that the Socialist Realism practiced by Gide in the early thirties drove him to write "against himself"—to rebel against both his previous literary tactics and his personal political instincts. Ultimately, these aesthetic and ideological conflicts rendered his Communist commitment impossible, in both the public and the literary spheres. For soon after *Geneviève*'s appearance, in

1936, Gide published *Retour de l'U.R.S.S.,* a highly critical account of his visit to the Soviet Union earlier that year.[90] Just as this harsh portrait enabled Gide to distance himself from those in sympathy with Soviet Communism, his unwillingness to finish *Geneviève* signaled his rejection of the literary doctrine they promoted.

Notes

1. For a chronicle of the 1934 Soviet Writers' Congress and detailed analysis of the origins of Socialist Realism as an official Communist Party doctrine, see Robin 9–74 and also Coombes.
2. Susan Rubin Suleiman defines the *roman à thèse* as "a novel written in the realistic mode (that is, based on an aesthetic of verisimilitude and representation), which signals itself to the reader as primarily didactic in intent, seeking to demonstrate the validity of a political, philosophical, or religious doctrine" (7).
3. For a detailed discussion of the specifically nonideological quality of Gide's fiction before 1929, see Keypour. A notable exception is Gide's brief affiliation during the First World War with the ultra-nationalist Action française; see Hanna.
4. In the chapter "*Gribouille en Afrique:* Gide's *Voyage au Congo*," Lucey discusses the ideological strengths and weaknesses of Gide's critique of French colonial Africa (143–180). See, as well, Allégret.
5. David Caute defines the fellow traveler as "an intellectual who accepts and supports the communist position in its essential points, while opting to remain outside the Party" (19).
6. See Moutote 159–160.
7. Moutote 158–159. "Fascisme" has been reprinted in Gide, *Littérature engagée.*
8. See Cornick 138.
9. See Moutote 170.
10. See Lottman 83–98.
11. *Nouvelle Revue Française* (July 1932), p. 42. Reprinted in *Pages de Journal 1929–1932.*
12. See Cornick 138–143.
13. See Cornick 144. For additional information regarding Gide's affiliation with the *NRF* in the early thirties, see Morino 187–191. A transcript of the Union pour la Vérité debate was published as *André Gide et notre temps.*
14. On *Œdipe*, see Marty 115–127 and Lévy. On *Robert, ou L'Intérêt général,* see Masson. On *Les Nouvelles Nourritures,* see Apter, "Homotextual Counter-Codes."
15. *Littérature engagée,* a thorough collection of Gide's political writings composed during the thirties, contains practically no reference to women's issues. There was, of course, an array of feminist and women's suffrage movements in France during the thirties, spanning the political spectrum but ignored by Gide. For comprehensive studies of these groups, see Bard and also Smith.
16. Also noteworthy in this respect is Gide's publication in 1930 of *La Séquestrée de Poitiers,* his journalistic documentation of the true story of Mélanie Bastian who, allegedly insane, was imprisoned in her bedroom by family members for twenty-five years. See Moutote 85–94.
17. "Si je dis tout cela, c'est pour que vos lecteurs comprennent que ce n'est nullement le besoin de réhabilitation qui me fait aujourd'hui prendre la plume, mais bien uniquement un souci de vérité, de justice et de remise au point" (*L'École des femmes* 110).
18. See Halsall, 293–317.
19. "[I]ncompétence rhétorique" (Halsall 316). Along these lines, Arthur E. Babcock has

seen an interesting link between Robert's lack of a diary and his need to police the writing of others.

20. Halsall also adds to his list of Gide's rhetorical strategies in *Geneviève* the latter's "appeals to the 'authority' of extradiagetic texts" *[des appels à l'« autorité » du texte extradiégétique]; that is, his repeated references to a sort of feminist "canon," which includes such works as *Adam Bede, Clarissa Harlowe,* and *Jane Eyre* (305). One might also consider Gide's recycling of Molière's title for the first book of his trilogy, *L'École des femmes,* as a further, more ironic example of his appeal to past literary authority.

21. See Suleiman 7.

22. Gide describes in his *Journal* how he began a third chapter of *Geneviève,* only to tear it up (1251).

23. "Que l'entente de l'art et de la doctrine communiste soit possible, je veux le croire. Mais il me faut avouer que le point d'accord et de fusion, je n'ai su jusqu'à présent l'obtenir — en raison aussi de longues habitudes prises. C'est pourquoi je n'ai plus rien produit depuis quatre ans" (*André Gide et notre temps* 11).

24. "Cet oreiller d'ignorance et d'incuriosité (des questions sociales), j'en avais besoin pour écrire. Depuis quatre ans que les questions sociales me préoccupent, je n'écris plus" (*André Gide et notre temps* 57).

25. "A short while after the publication first of *L'École des Femmes* and then of *Robert,* I received, in manuscript form, the beginning of a tale that was somewhat complementary; that is, when placed next to the other two, it could be considered the third panel of a triptych" [Peu de temps après la publication de *L'École des Femmes,* puis de *Robert,* j'ai reçu, en manuscrit, le début d'un récit en quelque sorte complémentaire, c'est-à-dire pouvant être considéré, s'ajoutant aux deux autres, comme le troisième volet d'un triptyque] (*L'École des femmes* 157).

26. "Je crains que ce livre ne soit pas du tout de nature à vous plaire. . . . Votre esprit plane dans l'absolu; je me débats dans le relatif. La question n'est point pour moi . . . d'une façon vague et générale, *que peut l'homme?* mais bien, d'une manière toute matérielle et précise : Qu'est-ce que, de nos jours, une femme est en mesure et en droit d'espérer?" (*L'École des femmes* 159-160).

27. "Et peut-être ne fallait-il pas moins que cette catastrophe effroyable pour permettre aux femmes de rendre manifestes des qualités qui semblaient jusqu'à ce jour exceptionnelles . . ." (*L'École des femmes* 160).

28. "Le livre de ma mère s'adresse à une génération passée. Du temps de la jeunesse de ma mère, une femme pouvait souhaiter sa liberté; à présent il ne s'agit plus de la souhaiter, mais de la prendre . . ." (*L'École des femmes* 160).

29. "[I]l me semble que le simple récit que je veux faire de ma vie peut avertir. . . . [C]e n'est là qu'un exemple entre maints autres, qu'un exemple particulier" (*L'École des femmes* 160).

30. "Il semblait qu'il attachât plus de prix à l'apparence de la vertu qu'à la vertu même" (*L'École des femmes* 166).

31. "En classe, ma voisine de droite était, de toutes mes camarades, celle qui attirait et retenait le plus mon regard. De peau brune, ses cheveux noirs bouclés, presque crépus, cachaient ses tempes et une partie de son front. On n'eût pu dire qu'elle était précisément belle, mais son charme étrange était pour moi beaucoup plus séduisant que la beauté" (*L'École des femmes* 166-167).

32. *L'École des femmes* 181-182.

33. "Je n'aime pas te voir fréquenter ce monde-là" (*L'École des femmes* 186).

34. "Je crois que je n'ai aucune vocation pour l'amour conjugal. . . . Oh! je ne veux pas dire que je ne m'éprendrai jamais de quelqu'un. Mais sacrifier pour lui mes goûts, ma vie propre; ne plus m'occuper qu'à lui être agréable, qu'à le servir. . . . C'est encore plus prudent de n'épouser personne" (*L'École des femmes* 189-190).

35. "Je ne veux pas m'engager à ne jamais me marier. Je prétends que, même dans le mariage, une femme peut garder sa liberté . . ." (*L'École des femmes* 192).
36. *L'École des femmes* 192.
37. "My father never laid a hand on [Gustave], but I will never forget that he slapped me once. He had just, like Solomon, advised my brother and me to follow the example of the ant . . . and I dared to answer: 'But father, you've told us many times not to act like animals'" [Jamais mon père n'avait levé la main sur lui; tandis que je n'oubliais pas qu'il m'avait une fois giflée. Il venait, comme Salomon, de nous conseiller à mon frère et moi de prendre exemple sur la fourmi . . . et j'avais osé lui répondre : « Mais, papa, tu nous dis souvent de ne pas ressembler aux animaux »] (*L'École des femmes* 196).
38. *L'École des femmes* 197.
39. *L'École des femmes* 202-204.
40. "J'aurais voulu être seule dans la salle; les regards des autres visiteurs me gênaient; il me semblait, dès que je contemplais la grande toile, qu'ils m'observaient. Pourtant j'étais attirée malgré ma souffrance et ma gêne par l'extraordinaire beauté de cette « indolente » qui m'emplissait d'un trouble étrange et tel que jusqu'alors je n'en avais jamais ressenti" (*L'École des femmes* 206).
41. "J'étais heureuse de le garder, à cause de la très bonne reproduction du tableau qui s'y trouvait, et, sitôt de retour à la maison, je m'enfermai dans ma chambre pour la contempler à loisir. Mon imagination faisait effort pour revêtir ce beau corps souple de la robe que Sara portait d'ordinaire en classe; cette robe de tous les jours dans laquelle je la revis le lendemain et dont il me fut beaucoup plus facile de l'imaginer dépouillée. Oui, mon regard, malgré moi, la dévêtait et je l'imaginais en « Indolente ». Une angoisse inconnue me décomposait, que je ne savais pas être du désir parce que je ne pensais pas que l'on pût éprouver du désir sinon pour un être de l'autre sexe . . ." (*L'École des femmes* 208-209).
42. "Ton amitié pour Sara m'inquiète. Je crains qu'elle ne te réserve pour plus tard beaucoup de souffrances et qu'elle ne t'entraîne plus loin que tu ne voudrais aller" (*L'École des femmes* 209-210).
43. "La scarlatine où, comme dirait Freud, se réfugiait le désarroi de tout mon être, secourut à la fois ma mère et moi-même. Ma mère me dit plus tard que, durant mon délire des premiers jours (car j'avais une très forte fièvre), l'image de Sara me hantait. Mais, quand je commençais de me remettre, mes idées avaient pris un autre cours" (*L'École des femmes* 213).
44. *L'École des femmes* 222-232.
45. *L'École des femmes* 233-237.
46. *L'École des femmes* 227-228.
47. "Mais, tandis que le docteur Marchant acceptait la profonde misère des hommes, « que nous pouvons tout au plus adoucir un peu », disait-il, je ne pouvais admettre que là se bornât notre espoir. Il me traitait de chimérique lorsque je parlais d'une amélioration possible de l'état social, et cela me faisait enrager . . . j'en tenais pour ma « chimère ». Je tenais ferme. Cet espoir qui m'habite a dirigé ma vie" (*L'École des femmes* 220-221).
48. "A vrai dire je n'avais jamais analysé les composantes de ma résolution mais, dans mon cas particulier, je crois qu'il entrait encore et surtout de la protestation; oui : de la protestation contre un ordre établi que je me refusais à reconnaître, contre ce que mon père appelait « les bonnes mœurs » et, plus spécialement encore, contre lui, qui les symbolisait à mes yeux, ces « bonnes mœurs »; un besoin de l'humilier, de le mortifier, de l'amener à rougir de moi, à me désavouer; un besoin d'affirmer mon indépendance, mon insoumission, par un acte que seule une femme pouvait commettre, dont je prétendais assumer la pleine responsabilité, sans trop envisager ses conséquences" (*L'École des femmes* 245).

49. "Je ne devais plus la revoir" (*L'École des femmes* 254).

50. Halsall 300–302.

51. "[U]n extraordinaire amour pour les pauvres, les souffrants . . ." (*L'École des femmes* 166).

52. "Je viens d'avoir avec elle une conversation terrible, où tout à la fois j'ai compris que c'était avec elle que je pourrais le mieux m'entendre, compris également pourquoi je ne veux pas m'entendre avec elle : c'est que je crains de retrouver en elle ma propre pensée, plus hardie, si hardie qu'elle m'épouvante" (*L'École des femmes* 79).

53. "Je tiens de ma mère un certain goût pour le travail, et une assiduité naturelle. . . . Je dois également à ma mère un ardent désir, un besoin de me rendre utile, et si déjà ce désir existait naturellement en moi, sommeillant, elle sut l'éveiller, l'aviver sans cesse" (*L'École des femmes* 165–166).

54. For a discussion of how Geneviève's decisions in her tale are dictated by her revolt against Robert, see Wynchank.

55. *L'École des femmes* 166. Halsall makes similar points about Robert's lack of rhetorical credibility in the other works of Gide's trilogy (307–317 *passim*).

56. "[C]omme ceux qui n'ont pas grande valeur personnelle, il se plaisait à croire que tout s'obtient par intrigue ou par entregent. Je crois que le plus clair de ce qu'il appelait pompeusement son « travail » consistait en courbettes à faire ou à recevoir, dont il tenait compte très exact" (*L'École des femmes* 177).

57. "[N]on du poing ce qui eût été vulgaire, mais du plat de la main" (*L'École des femmes* 198–199).

58. Halsall 311; Lucey 105.

59. "De plus, sans être antisémite déclaré, il avait en suspicion tous les juifs" (*L'École des femmes* 180). Other references: *L'École des femmes* 166, 165 respectively.

60. "Oui, ce n'est que depuis la guerre, où tant de femmes ont fait preuve d'une valeur et d'une énergie dont les hommes ne les eussent point cru capables, que l'on commence à leur reconnaître, et qu'elles-mêmes commencent à revendiquer, leurs droits à des vertus qui ne soient pas simplement privatives, de dévouement, de soumission et de fidélité; de dévouement à l'homme, de soumission à l'homme, de fidélité à l'homme; car il semblait jusqu'à présent que toutes les vertus affirmatives dussent demeurer l'apanage de l'homme et que l'homme se les fût toutes réservées. Je crois que nul ne peut contester aujourd'hui que la situation de la femme a changé considérablement depuis la guerre. Et peut-être ne fallait-il pas moins que cette catastrophe effroyable pour permettre aux femmes de rendre manifestes des qualités qui semblaient jusqu'à ce jour exceptionnelles; pour permettre à la valeur des femmes d'être prise en considération" (*L'École des femmes* 160).

61. "'Avec les dons que vous avez, vous êtes inexcusable de ne pas travailler davantage.' Sara fit une courte révérence ironique, une sorte de pirouette . . ." (*L'École des femmes* 169).

62. Sara's Montparnasse address (16, rue Campagne-Première), mentioned earlier on in Gide's tale, betrays her Left Bank, bohemian origins.

63. "— Ce que c'est cossu, chez vous! — me dit Sara; et ce furent les premières paroles qu'elle m'adressa, d'un ton indéfinissable où entrait un mélange d'étonnement admiratif et de je ne sais quelle ironie, un peu méprisante . . ." (*L'École des femmes* 182).

64. *L'École des femmes* 207.

65. "[D]ans ses bras, j'aurais fondu comme du sucre . . ." (*L'École des femmes* 248).

66. Apter, *André Gide* 140–141. Apter cites Suleiman 54–56.

67. "[J]'ai souvent usé de châtiments corporels avec mon fils" (*L'École des femmes* 196).

68. Halsall 297–298.

69. "L'idée centrale, peu révolutionnaire en fait . . . semble être la suivante : au début du XXe siècle, il a bien fallu libérer la femme, abolir son infériorité sociale à l'homme,

inferiorité institutionnalisée par le mariage. Mais cette institution elle-même, malgré toutes ses imperfections, mérite de rester comme base et support de la famille, puisque les autres solutions proposées ne sont ni très nombreuses, ni très satisfaisantes" (317).

70. "[L]e ton toujours interrogatif qui les imprègne . . . la fiction gidienne n'est point soumise à un super-système et . . . ne peut être autoritaire" (Keypour 33).

71. Fokkema 69.

72. See Moore 211 and the entire article by Strauss.

73. Lucey 68–94.

74. *L'École des femmes* 159.

75. "[I]l ne s'agit plus d'abstraction mais de vie. . . . Nous voici bien loin, M. Gide, des considérations qui dictent vos livres. Vous disiez, il m'en souvient : « J'écris pour être relu »; quant à moi, tout au contraire, j'écris ceci pour aider celui ou celle qui me lit à passer outre" (*L'École des femmes* 179).

76. "Je pense aujourd'hui qu'il n'est pas bon (j'allais dire : honnête) de déshabiter ainsi les misères de notre terre, comme certains mystiques font dans un rêve de vie future, et cet échappement au réel m'apparaît une sorte de désertion" (*L'École des femmes* 185–186).

77. Gide makes a similar maneuver in *Robert,* when his narrator makes the following suggestion: "Supreme praise: some have even been led to suppose that [Éveline's] journal had been written by you, Mr. Gide . . ." [Suprême éloge : on a même été supposer que ce journal avait été écrit par vous, M. Gide . . .] (*L'École des femmes* 113).

78. "Chez Gide il y a comme un culte de l'écriture. . . . L'écriture semble être faite pour se substituer au réel, de sorte que le narrateur se réjouit de la défectuosité de son expérience. . . . C'est au défaut du réel, paraît-il, que s'affirment les qualités de l'écrit" (Walker 121–122).

79. "Et quand tu m'auras lu, jette ce livre, — et sors" (*Les Nourritures terrestres* 15).

80. de Man 130–136. For a detailed consideration of the implications of de Man's analysis, see Lucey 183–187.

81. "Quelque chose d'étrange, de bizarre, et qui vous saisisse. C'est cela que je souhaiterais, sachant bien que seul l'inattendu peut ravir et plonger en état de transe. Mais mon sujet (*Geneviève*) ne le comporte pas. Je dois à mon héroïne de demeurer raisonnable, puisque aussi bien ce n'est qu'à travers elle que je m'exprime" (*Journal* 1195).

82. "Mais je n'éprouve aucune satisfaction à écrire, fémininement, au courant de la plume, et tout ce que j'écris ainsi me déplaît" (*Journal* 977).

83. Apter, *André Gide* 150 and 144.

84. Segal 62. Indeed, the death of principal female figures occurs in most of Gide's major works, including *L'Immoraliste, La Porte étroite, La Symphonie pastorale, Les Faux-Monnayeurs,* and *L'École des femmes.*

85. Hanna 2.

86. Cornick 151–154.

87. Mehlman 64–82.

88. See in particular the chapters "*Corydon* and *L'École des femmes:* Mimesis, the Mantis, the Gynaeceum" and "*Gribouille en Afrique:* Gide's *Voyage au Congo*" in Lucey 68–107 and 143–180. Other recent discussions dealing with the complex understanding of homosexuality Gide evokes in his fiction include Bersani 113–129 and Apter, "Homotextual Counter-Codes."

89. What constitutes "Gidean" humanism, then, and can this ethic be reconciled with the elitist aspects of his writing? In 1933, Gide wrote in his *Journal:* "What aligns me with the Communists has nothing to do with theories, which I understand poorly and have little to do with. It is simply to know that amidst them there are those for

whom the state of things is *intolerable*" [Ce qui me rapproche des communistes, ce ne sont point des théories, que je comprends mal et dont je n'ai que faire, c'est seulement de savoir que, parmi eux, il en est pour qui cet état de chose est *intolérable*] (*Journal* 1167). What is appealing to him about the proletarian movement is reflected neither in doctrine, systems of government, nor questions of social policy; the movement attracts Gide, rather, because its stated ideals are a modern embodiment of those he finds admirable in Christianity. That same year he wrote: "I must admit, what leads me towards Communism is not Marx, but the Gospel. It is the Gospel that formed me. It is the precepts of the Gospel that brought about a particular inclination in my thought, in the behavior of my whole being. They inculcated in me doubts about my own importance and taught me respect for others, for their ways of thinking, for their basic worth; and they strengthened a certain disdain within me, a certain repugnance (which no doubt already existed) toward all purely private possessions, towards all forms of monopolizing" [Mais, il faut bien que je le dise, ce qui m'amène au communisme, ce n'est pas Marx, c'est l'Évangile. C'est l'Évangile qui m'a formé. Ce sont les préceptes de l'Évangile, selon le pli qu'ils ont fait prendre à ma pensée, au comportement de tout mon être, qui m'ont inculqué le doute de ma valeur propre, le respect d'autrui, de sa pensée, de sa valeur, et qui ont, en moi, fortifié ce dédain, cette répugnance (qui déjà sans doute était native) à toute possession particulière, à tout accaparement] (*Journal* 1176). Gide saw in Marxism a modern, atheistic reworking of New Testament principles, in which abstract, humanistic values are promoted more than concrete social policies. For him, the Soviet experiment promised, on a large scale, equal worth for all individuals and mass rejection of materialistic (and hence bourgeois) attitudes. On the surface, then, Gide's moments of bigotry do seem to betray his vague, but otherwise respectable, Christian ethic.

90. For detailed analyses of Gide's break with Communist politics, see Moutote and also Maurer.

Works Cited

Allégret, Marc. *Carnets du Congo : Voyage avec Gide*. Introduction and notes by Daniel Durosay. Paris: Presses du C.N.R.S., 1987.

André Gide et notre temps. Paris: Gallimard, 1935.

Apter, Emily. *André Gide and the Codes of Homotextuality*. Saratoga, CA: Anma Libri, 1987.

————. "Homotextual Counter-Codes: André Gide and the Poetics of Engagement." *Michigan Romance Studies* 6 (1986): 75-87.

Babcock, Arthur E. "Le Journal de Robert." *Bulletin des Amis d'André Gide* 17.82-83 (April-July 1989): 243-247.

Bard, Christine. *Les Filles de Marianne. Histoire des féminismes, 1914-1940*. Paris: Éditions Fayard, 1995.

Bersani, Leo. *Homos*. Cambridge, MA, and London: Harvard University Press, 1995.

Caute, David. *Communism and the French Intellectuals*. London: André Deutsch, 1964.

Coombes, John E. "Rules of Revision: French Communist Writing in the 1930s." *Forum for Modern Language Studies* 27.3 (1991): 208-226.

Cornick, Martyn. *The Nouvelle Revue Française Under Jean Paulhan, 1925–1940*. Amsterdam: Editions Rodopi, 1995.

de Man, Paul. "Whatever Happened to André Gide?" *Critical Writings, 1953–1978*. Ed. Lindsay Waters. Minneapolis: University of Minnesota Press, 1989. 130-136.

Fokkema, Douwe W. "A Semiotic Definition of Aesthetic Experience and the Period Code of Modernism, with Reference to an Interpretation of *Les Faux-Monnayeurs*." *Poetics Today* 3.1 (Winter 1982): 61-79.

Gide, André. *Corydon*. Paris: Gallimard, 1924.

————. *L'École des femmes, suivi de Robert et Geneviève*. Paris: Gallimard, 1944.

————. *Les Faux-Monnayeurs*. Paris: Gallimard, 1925.

————. *Journal 1889–1939*. Paris: Gallimard, Bibliothèque de la Pléiade, 1951.

————. *Littérature engagée*. Textes réunis et présentés par Yvonne Davet. Paris: Gallimard, 1950.

————. *Les Nourritures terrestres et Les Nouvelles Nourritures*. Paris: Gallimard, 1935.

————. *Pages de Journal 1929–1932*. Paris: NRF, 1934.

————. *Retour de l'U.R.S.S.* Paris: Gallimard, 1936.

————. *La Séquestrée de Poitiers*. Paris: Gallimard, Collection Ne jugez pas, 1929.

————. *Voyage au Congo, suivi de Le Retour du Tchad*. Paris: Gallimard, 1927.

Halsall, Albert W. "Analyse rhétorique d'un discours gidien féministe : *L'École des femmes, Robert, Geneviève*." *Bulletin des Amis d'André Gide* 9.51 (July 1981): 293-317.

Hanna, Martha. "What Did André Gide See in the Action française?" *Historical Reflections / Réflexions Historiques* 17.1 (Winter 1991): 1-22.

Keypour, David. "Fictions Gidiennes : romans à thèse ou romans d'idées." *Bulletin des Amis d'André Gide* 15.76 (October 1987): 27-36.

Lévy, Zvi H. "André Gide entre Œdipe et Thésée." *French Studies* 44.1 (January 1990): 34-46.

Lottman, Herbert R. *The Left Bank: Writers, Artists, and Politics from the Popular Front to the Cold War*. Boston: Houghton Mifflin, 1982.

Lucey, Michael. *Gide's Bent: Sexuality, Politics, Writing*. New York: Oxford University Press, 1995.

Marty, Éric. *André Gide : Qui êtes-vous? avec les entretiens Jean Amrouche et André Gide*. Lyon: La Manufacture, 1987.

Masson, Pierre. "Gide Polémiste? Note à propos de *Robert ou l'Intérêt général*." *Bulletin des Amis d'André Gide* 11.58 (April 1983): 139-143.

Maurer, Rudolf. *André Gide et l'URSS*. Paris: Éditions Tillier, 1983.

Mehlman, Jeffrey. *Legacies of Anti-Semitism in France*. Minneapolis: University of Minnesota Press, 1983.

Moore, Ann M. "Women, Socialization, and Language in *Les Faux-monnayeurs*." *Stanford French Review* 11.2 (Summer 1987): 211-228.

Morino, Lina. *La Nouvelle Revue Française dans l'histoire des lettres*. Paris: Gallimard, 1939.

Moutote, Daniel. *André Gide : L'Engagement (1926–1939)*. Paris: SEDES, 1991.

Robin, Régine. *Socialist Realism: An Impossible Aesthetic*. Trans. Catherine Porter. Stanford: Stanford University Press, 1992.

Segal, Naomi. "'Parfois j'ai peur que ce que j'ai supprimé ne se venge'—Gide and Women." *Paragraph* 8 (October 1986): 62-74.

Smith, Paul. *Feminism and the Third Republic: Women's Political and Civil Rights in France, 1918–1945*. Oxford: Clarendon Press, 1996.

Strauss, George. "Les Personnages féminins des *Faux-monnayeurs*." *André Gide 7 : le romancier. Revue des Lettres Modernes* 688-692 (1984): 9-23.

Suleiman, Susan Rubin. *Authoritarian Fictions: The Ideological Novel as a Literary Genre*. New York: Columbia University Press, 1983.

Walker, David H. "L'Écriture et le réel dans les fictions d'André Gide." *Roman, réalités, réalismes*. Ed. Jean Bessière. Paris: Presses Universitaires de France, 1989. 121-136.

Wynchank, Anny. "Conflit et rébellion dans la trilogie d'André Gide." *Bulletin des Amis d'André Gide* 13.66 (April 1985): 229-234.

CHAPTER 11

Gide and the Feminist Voice

Naomi Segal

At the end of March 1930, while writing *Geneviève*, Gide noted in his *Journal*:

> I find it easy to escape from myself and, supplanted by a personality different from my own, I can let go with perfect abandon and no sense of opposition, and let that other personality express itself through me exactly as it should. But I get no satisfaction from writing in a feminine manner, as the pen flows, and everything I write in that way displeases me.[1]

This statement is paradoxical for a number of reasons. After all, in its most obvious vulgar Freudian significance, it puts the penis/pen where he claims to be at his most feminine, letting it all run out, exhausting himself but without the least pleasure or gratification. Is this the phenomenon we find in his own sexual practice: the fear of unstoppable flow that seems to underlie the wish to test virility to the point of the empty body?[2] What happens if that emptied body turns out, at its most entirely depleted, to be the body of a woman?

This way of writing was not always construed as unpleasant: three years earlier he had noted: "all the best things I have written have been written at once, without labour, fatigue or boredom."[3] And when he first talked about *L'École des femmes* in January 1927, he smiled as he told his friends: "'It's a new novel, which so far I'm writing as the pen flows,'" although he added three months later: "'what I've done is just written as the pen flows, so it needs some filing and all comments are welcome.'"[4] In some peculiar way, when he conceives the text as alien from himself, the very ease of production produces unease: "this book holds hardly any interest for me and my mind does not turn to it with any spontaneity,"[5] he comments in September 1928—a complaint he was to repeat endlessly over the many years he spent on the third part of the trilogy. On the other hand, masculinity may seem to be what opens the dams; when working on *Les Faux-Monnayeurs*, Gide sometimes wrote in a state of hydraulic ecstasy:

I have been known to write in a train or a metro, on benches on platforms or streets, or at the side of a road, and these are my best pages, the most truly inspired. One sentence follows the last, is born out of the last, and as it is born, swelling up in me, I feel an almost physical ecstasy. I believe this artesian out-pouring is the result of a long period of unconscious preparation. Afterwards I might make one or two revisions to that first outflow, but very few.[6]

Textuality as flow may be masculine or feminine, pregnancy or ejaculation. When a creative gestation is "artesian" enough to be sudden, irresistible and produced in incongruous places, it needs little "filing"; when it solidifies into something alien and separate, there is no pleasure in it. But for Gide creative gratification is also found in restraint: "there is scarcely one of my books that I was ready to write at the moment I would have had the most pleasure in doing so; not a single one that, at a certain moment, did not somehow pull me back-wards."[7] Desire is *also* by its very nature out of time with itself.

What is described above as "escaping from himself," what elsewhere and insistently Gide calls "sympathy" and which we find again in Édouard—"my heart beats only by sympathy: I live only through other people"[8]—is a complex process. It seems a sort of generous outpouring, but, like the similarly downward flow from senior to junior that we find in influence, fascination or the predation of sexual curiosity, it is less a gift than a demand. To the criticisms of Martin du Gard and Claudel for being too easily "had," Gide cheerfully notes: "I'm made of rubber . . . I acquiesce as much as I can, even going so far as to insincerity; but don't be taken in: once I'm alone again, I take back my old shape."[9] Like them, we should "be warned" about the seeming ease of this outflow of authorial self into feminine space.

Gide wrote two first-person fictions which are narrated in both male and female voices: *La Porte étroite* (1909) and the trilogy *L'École des femmes* (1929), *Robert* (1930) and *Geneviève* (1936). And lest it should be thought that the pain/pleasure of the flow of the pen remains simply gendered across these four texts, here are two more notations. In the first, the woman's voice is more solid, rare and satisfying:

> [*La Porte étroite*] seems to me now like a nougat in which the almonds are good (i.e., Alissa's letters and journal) but the filling is pasty, badly written; it couldn't be otherwise with the first person, since the flaccid character of my Jérôme implies a flaccid prose.[10]

In the second, with the writing of Robert's first-person narrative, there is the satisfaction at a quick job well completed:

> Read out the second part of *L'École des femmes* [i.e., *Robert*] to Pomme yes-terday. I've just finished it. Good impression. Hardly anything to redo, I think, nothing I couldn't correct on the proofs. I wrote that little book in less than a week, as the pen flows; that was exactly how it had to be writ-ten.[11]

What were, essentially, the politics of Gide's relation to women and the idea of the feminine? How possible was it for him to ventriloquize himself into the desires and fears of a female protagonist and if it was, whose substance speaks in that voice? To adopt the spatial hydraulic metaphors so crucial in thinking about Gide, shall we understand his female characters as colonised, vampirised, drained or transfused?

Klaus Mann quotes an "intimate friend" of Gide's as saying: "'women mean more to him, in a sense, than do men.'"[12] Among his real-life female acquaintances it is usual to distinguish (as he did) the saintly ladies of his Normandy childhood, among whom the shady figure of Mathilde Rondeaux stands out by unquestioned contrast,[13] and the more emancipated women he knew in his "other" life—the three generations of Van Rysselberghes, Maria, Élisabeth and Catherine, Gide's daughter.[14] In the latter category we can also find the groups or pairs of women among whom lesbianism, feminism and an Anglo-Saxon origin seem to create a cluster of aberrant femininities that both fascinated and disturbed him.[15] Among them are couples like Jane Harrison and Hope Mirrlees, who came to the Pontigny conferences, Catherine's teacher Claude Francis (to whom Gide offered a contingent second *mariage blanc* in the 1940s), Ethel Whitehorn and Enid McLeod, Élisabeth's friends—of whom already in 1918 he was remarking to the Petite Dame: "'if Élisabeth and Whity don't succeed in finding a new way of living, outside the conventions, which women will?'"[16]— and of course Dorothy Bussy.

Dorothy Bussy showed Gide her most heterosexual side, but in December 1933, she gave him the manuscript of her anonymous confessional novel *Olivia* to read—priding herself later when it was finally published that she shared with Proust the privilege of being a victim of Gide's fallible literary judgment— which is the narrative of an adolescent passion for a French schoolmistress. She was not just a point of contact through her own family the Stracheys with both Bloomsbury and psychoanalysis, she was also identified by Gide with a supposedly hardline feminism he was later to embody in the character of Geneviève. In 1931, a crisis blew up between Martin du Gard and Gide when the latter chose to disagree with his friend's fictional argument that the child of an incestuous relationship was likely to be a weakling. On the contrary, riposted Gide, he [sic] would probably be doubly healthy and robust. Martin du Gard uses a nicely hydraulic image to blame this "perversity" on the pernicious influence of "our seething friend and her even more seething daughter."[17] In the clenched-teeth smiles of conciliation that followed, he continues to accuse Dorothy and Janie of tilting at the windmills of their revolutionary-feminist moment. To Gide he shakes a wise head over the indiscipline of English women, an image with which the latter, in another context, would be the first to agree:

"I have something to confess . . . I hardly know how to tell you: I'm seventeen and still a virgin," is what a young girl from the best society of England said, blushing, to an old friend of Dorothy Bussy, who repeated these dreadful words to her in terror. And Mme Bussy, who passed them on to me in her turn, adds that this charming young woman, in whom her

family takes a most particular interest, dragged along to cocktail parties by
the young men of her circle, has been diagnosed an extreme case of alco-
holism, with absolutely no hope of a cure.[18]

England features as something of a sexual elsewhere for Gide, not a mythical
Africa in which sex is more easily available to the male traveller but as a place
where sex belongs to women in a quite unusual way. Like the real-life Sara
Breitenstein,[19] Sarah Vedel ends up going off to England to her lesbian friend
Miss Aberdeen, surely a more attractive prospect than the celibacy of Rachel or
the undesiring men whom both she and Laura seem to attract. The latter, like
Édouard, comes from or goes to England where desire is unfulfilled; Lilian Griffith (American in origin) has mislaid her husband there. Alain Goulet sees it as
"the land of liberation and radical change" where a girl might discover "the
virtues of revolt,"[20] while Pierre Masson describes the same thing from the opposite angle: a "land of sexual frustration, or rather of a scarcity that puts everything
out of balance: the male species seems curiously diminished . . . it is a land of
deficient husbands [where] the inadequacy of the men drives the women mad."[21]
Thus the dangers of feminism, lesbianism and other kinds of female excess remain
as closely associated in Gide's mind with a mythical England as they do in
Madeleine's with the bad influence of an irreligious upbringing.

Before going on to an analysis of the trilogy, I want to suggest that there are
two main positions for women in Gide's fiction: they are either *disponible,* like
his male heroes—that is, open, enquiring, available to take on experience—or
they are resigned. As these terms imply, they fall into—or move between—two
different coefficients of the feminine to the masculine, rather as if something
flowed in or out of a vessel filled with two fluids. In Freud's terms they follow
the mysterious path by which "a woman develops out of a child with a bisex-
ual disposition."[22] Of the latter, "fully feminine" position, Madeleine is the chief
example; it is surely her Gide is thinking of when he writes "the most beautiful
women's faces I have known are resigned; indeed I cannot imagine that a
woman whose happiness did not include a little resignation could appeal to me;
such a woman might even evoke a touch of hostility."[23] Resignation belongs to
(and beautifies) real women; of course by this criterion, no women are real
women, or not for long—even the good wife.

If we follow the hydraulic image through this idea, we find that resignation
is a kind of draining-out—a forced or rather accepted anorexia—of certain
energies that are construed as belonging to youth and masculinity. It is in relation to this, I think, that we can understand the metaphor of writing with which
this essay began. If Gide writes "in a feminine manner, as the pen flows," then
something is draining out of him. I will try to show how the voices of both
women and men can drain him in this way, and that it is a problem of femininity (meaning also "wrong masculinity") in either case. When, on the other hand,
spontaneous and unconstrained creativity excites him it is because it has become
an upward flow, conceived as masculine in a libidinal sense, and having a product other than emptiness.

Gide's women often start out, like Shakespeare's sister in Woolf's *A Room of*

One's Own, with all the energies and talents of a Lafcadio. Sometimes, like Woolf's heroine, they are stopped by an obstetrical trauma—Laura, Isabelle or Boris and Bernard's mothers—and thereafter have no choice except long- or short-term contrition. Alissa is an exception to this and thus the most extreme, complete example of the process of draining: she has nothing to be punished for—just like Madeleine Gide. In *Et nunc manet in te,* Gide is anxious to stress how different from Alissa his lively, smiling wife was—yet he drains her mercilessly in the course of his homage as if the fact that she became Alissa was an impudent contradiction of the line he had carefully drawn between fiction and life.[24] Why, he might want to ask, did she get all those drab housewifely habits, neglect her lovely hands, stop being interested in my interests, etc., when after all, reader, I *did* marry her? Of course he knows why, and elsewhere in the text confesses it as best he can. What he does not know, I think, caught between the well-flavoured bits of Alissa and the insipid and over-chewy paste of Jérôme, is that he did to Alissa what he has decided to do to Madeleine.

We will see in a moment that both Éveline and Geneviève refuse to submit to the same digestive process because they take the feminine trajectory and invert it, the mother by becoming *disponible,* the daughter by disobeying a number of the rules of [her] sex. Gide does well, I think, to get as far as he does in that text in biting off more than he can chew. The ways in which these two women are only partially contained and depleted are both frustrating and fascinating to observe.

The project began rather pleasantly in early 1927: "I'd left Paris in the hope of making good progress on my new novel which I'd started so joyously and easily at Cuverville, without a draft and with almost no crossings-out in the first few pages"; but a month later, he is having "great difficulty in taking my new novel seriously."[25] In December 1928, he described the plot thus to Pierre-Quint:

> I am just finishing . . . a book I've already told you about. It will be the diary of an unhappily married woman. I'll call it *The School for Wives.* Afterwards I'll probably write the companion piece, *The School for Husbands.* I am preoccupied at the moment with the idea of sympathy. How a woman may change when she falls in love; how she becomes interested in everything that interests her husband. But when her love begins to fade, the woman goes back to her original personality, which however is no longer the same, most often having become poorer, uglier than before.[26]

It is very difficult to make out here exactly what Gide is after—if this is not putting it too crudely, "whose side" he is on. The hydraulic impoverishment of the woman's character by the sympathy of love is obviously a bad thing, but is that the fault of convention (itself an ambiguous value, especially for Gide's good women) or love (generally considered an admirable motive), or of women's original weakness? Does this impoverishment depend on the worth of the female subject or the male object of a girlish enthusiasm? Is feminine naivety to be equated with the joy of innocence or the gullibility of a fool?

Everything in Éveline's girlhood voice is designed to ironize her, like Emma Bovary or Gerty MacDowell—or indeed, Joyce's character of the same name[27]—though the irony is more mitigated than Flaubert's, since Éveline will end up not so much bankrupt as capable of heroism. The first part of her narrative is a journal begun at the instigation of her fiancé Robert, who promises to write one too; it is when she discovers that he has not and never meant to that she experiences her first disappointment in him—anger and contempt would not be quite the right words, but her reaction here presages the dominance of those emotions in Part 2. Inspired to write by the artless enthusiasm of first love, she is at the same time inhibited from speaking by Robert's pedantic attitude to grammar and women's place. As Michael Lucey has pointed out, this pedantry is borrowed directly from Gide's own, in articles published in the *Figaro* during the Occupation;[28] I shall return shortly to the question of Gide's investment in certain sides of Robert. Interesting too is the fact that he himself was capable of committing the most heinous fault Éveline is accused of, using *très* to qualify a word that is not adjectival, such as *envie* or *peur*. In the *Cahiers de la Petite Dame* we find the unremarked anomaly "*très autrefois,*"once in her voice and once in his own.[29]

Éveline addresses her diary in the second person to her beloved, the person who fills what she now identifies as the empty space inside her. He will guide her "towards the beautiful and the good, towards God"[30]—in order to stop this from being too blatantly a parody of *La Porte étroite,* Gide is careful to make the couple Catholic—while she will support him and nurture his greatness: "he is modest [but] I shall be proud for him."[31] The irony of this text depends on a symbiosis of female fool and male knave exposed via her open-mouthed quotation of him while he gradually censors her pleasure in language.

> Robert has suddenly been called away to Perpignan, where his mother lives, by some bad news of her health.
> "I do hope it's nothing," I said to him.
> "That's what people always say," he replied with a solemn smile that showed how worried he was deep down. I immediately felt guilty about my absurd phrase.[32]

Clichés are, by their very nature, somehow feminine—as is underlined by Gide's frequent quotations in his journals and elsewhere of the foolishness of women. They pass for opinion while men's opinions pass for knowledge. The adolescent Éveline is positioned between two men in a conventional conflict between father and lover. Her father is a difficult husband and a freethinker in both the political and the religious sense; Robert offers the charming certainty of his certainties. Again here, though, the ironies are unclear. When at certain points she sticks to her own view of things, Part 2 will prove her wrong: Bourgweilsdorf's paintings are not "horrors" and Dr Marchant is not "an odious man."[33] Her finer qualities are those which she deposits in Robert, demonstrating by this gift a classically feminine need to make herself useful whose frustration she pities in her friend Yvonne. Hydraulically, women's energy tends towards others, Gide is saying: when Yvonne discovers her fiancé is unfaithful she seeks work as a nursing assistant. Asked if he can give her a job, Marchant scoffs, and this drives Éveline to her first rudimentary feminist reaction:

> I swear here and now that if I have a daughter, I will not teach her any of those pretty little ways Dr Marchant was so ironically contemptuous about, but I'll make sure she has a serious education so that she can do without those arbitrary concessions, kindnesses and favours.
>
> I know that what I write here is absurd, but the feeling that dictates my words is not. I find it quite natural that I should give up my independence when I marry Robert (it was an act of independence to choose to marry him against the wishes of Papa), but every woman should at least remain free to choose the servitude that suits her best.[34]

It is ironic, perhaps, that the boorish doctor, whose bark is of course worse than his bite, takes on the lovelorn Yvonne only to marry her. Their marriage seems affectionate but remains childless, so that she is strictly useless after all, denied the satisfaction Éveline has from educating her children, however timidly or frustratingly.

Part 1 ends with the notation that Robert has asked to read her diary; she gives it against her will. A day later he reveals that he has written nothing himself; it is clear thus (in another parody of Jérôme) that he provoked her text in order to see his image in it. When she says "the charm is broken,"[35] it is surely because she can no longer address herself unconsciously through him. She will marry him anyway—around the same date that Madeleine married Gide—but what has been broken is as much the innocence of writing as that of love; like the dying Alissa, this diarist has learned that there is no interlocutor.

The beginning of Part 2, set twenty years later in 1914, shows an altogether different attitude to language:

> I have brought this notebook with me as one might bring a piece of embroidery to fill the empty leisure of a rest-cure. But if I start writing in it again, it is no longer, alas, for Robert. He is sure now that he knows everything I could feel or think. I'll be writing to try and bring a little order into my thoughts, to try and see myself clearly, bearing in mind, like Corneille's Émilie,
>
> > Both all the things I risk and all the things I seek.
>
> When I was young, I saw these words as a redundancy; they seemed ridiculous, as phrases often do when one doesn't understand them properly, just as they seem redundant and ridiculous nowadays to my son and daughter, whom I made learn them by heart. No doubt one needs to have lived a little in order to understand that everything one *seeks* in life can only be achieved by *risking* precisely what one holds most dear. What I seek today is my deliverance; what I am risking is the respect of the world and of my two children.[36]

The new diary is begun, then, in a wish for clear-headedness and as a guilt-offering to the children she expects to lose. Leaving Robert seems the only way forward now that she not only sees but "*hears* through" him, finding his every utterance as hollow and fatuous as the clichés he once accused her of. Of Robert it could be said what Cocteau once said of Gide: that he is not a false token but a real token.[37] What Éveline perceives along with Dr Marchant, and what her father saw in the first place but, following her erstwhile wish, no longer sees, is that Robert is the first to be "taken in by his sonorous phrases."[38] This is, in other words, not simply the revenge of clear hard language on the feminine excess of fluency—"I am unsatisfied with what I wrote yesterday. I let my pen run on," writes Éveline in her second entry[39]—but a way of asking more complicated questions. What is the difference between the false belief in language of a young woman and a grown man? How is linguistic innocence to be gendered good or bad? Has truth simply changed sides and the wife taken on moral masculinity?

It is Pierre Herbart who identified in Gide an incapacity to "be a man," meaning by this an inability to accept or even clearly conceive the responsibility of a male adult.[40] Robert's position as the young Éveline's superior in terms of age and social visibility is revealed now as all that held this hand-puppet together, so that, far from her being given meaning by him as she supposed twenty years earlier, she filled him and kept him moving. The energies which now replace that devotion, however, cannot replenish her, since they are all negative: hatred, fear and guilt. Éveline will never be able to stop being what her daughter scathingly calls "a good woman."[41] And this is perhaps what the Gide of 1928, ten years into his own marital crisis, found so fascinating about her situation. In this first volume of the "triptych,"[42] he creates a virtuous woman frustrated by the misfortune of being married to a straw man: she has made her bed but is no longer willing to lie in it. She speaks a language her author can lend her without scruple, the language a Rondeaux might speak, and she still wants to be useful—to anyone but her husband.

The Robert of *L'École des femmes* is easier to hate than to accuse. He seems not a hypocrite but honestly self-deceived. In his exaggerated way, he is genuinely pious. He is capable of subtlety in the timing and choice of clichés. His blindness to Éveline's independence of mind is a function of indolence—"I am part of his comfort; I am his wife"[43]—rather than indifference. He is shattered when she tells him the truth, clinging as he sobs to the very possession that denies him: "'My wife doesn't love me any more! My wife doesn't love me any more!'"[44] What he lacks now that the scales have fallen from her eyes is stature. In a way that in such an old-fashioned marriage would be impossible to reverse, once he loses her esteem he forfeits her desire. Let me propose that here Gide is offering an analysis of his own marriage so chillingly clear that he hopes it will be read as comedy. He has to do this, lending Robert enough of his characteristics, if he is to let himself take the woman's dilemma seriously. She must stay virtuous.

Éveline's virtue keeps her essentially obedient to men: despite what she knows, she still seeks endorsement (however doomed to disappointment) from her priest, father or doctor. She can slough off Robert along with God, and she can even despise her son, but she cannot slough off duty—this despite knowing that her judgment is entirely rational and mature. This is what makes her, like Madeleine, the heroine of a Cornelian dilemma not exactly between love and duty but between what is true and what is right. She earns a tragic *dénouement*, but it remains a devout one. Gide chooses not to let her husband be a Racinian hero. In his volume, he will try to struggle out of his comic fustian, but only manage to stagger as far as a Romantic glade. Éveline's Racinian antagonist is her daughter.

The first two volumes, then, carefully set up two unequal protagonists in what seems to fall into two very different fictions, the male one comic, the female one tragic.[45] As soon as Geneviève comes on the scene, however—apart from in her role as the serious frame-narrator, alongside a derisory Gide—Éveline is outsized and outdistanced. The good woman's body is the Pandora's box out of which the feminism of a different generation emerges, bursting not only her but her author's intentions. When Éveline writes these lines, she is surely speaking for Gide as well:

> I have just had a terrible conversation with her, which made me realize that she is the one person I could really have an understanding with, but at the same time that I don't want her understanding. For I am afraid that I will find my own thoughts in her, only bolder—so much bolder that they horrify me. All the anxieties and doubts that touched me occasion- ally have become so many shameless negations in her. No, no, I will not consent to recognize them.[46]

The daughter is a fearful mirror to the mother, and this confrontation of alter- native femininities creates its own dynamic. In *Robert*, Éveline is accused of a conspiracy with her daughter similar to the one between the Bussy women in Martin du Gard's paranoia. In *Geneviève*, the mother is adored but extremely tame—and so indeed is the daughter, when it comes to the comparison with Gisèle and her mother or the slinkily seductive Sara. What I am suggesting here is that the trilogy is an attempt to confront and compare ways of being a woman which—especially as it coheres with the challenge of representing the genera- tion for whom Gide is pounding on open doors—grows quickly out of control. Whereas the painful loyalty of Alissa and Juliette fitted into a system of triangu- lation based on something like rivalry, these women form intellectual and pas- sional couples beyond the teacher-pupil structure that is Gide's only version of desire.

Robert takes up the pen in order to defend himself against Gide and his read- ers. All the comic-ironic devices are in place. He is surprised to find his wife capable of writing so well: "supreme praise—it has even been claimed that the journal was written by you, M. Gide, who . . . ,"[47] this followed by an asterisked footnote warning us that three lines have been omitted. Gide had fun writing this book and it seems to have caused him neither the agonies of Alissa's nor those of Jérôme's voice; this may be because he had always fancied the idea of writing comedy.[48] Robert has two good arguments for the defence: that the image Éveline came to dislike so much is one she had imposed on him herself as a girl, and that, however clumsily and inadequately, he always sincerely aspired to become a better person, a project in which his wife owed him support rather than mockery. At one point he brings these two arguments together, with a certain force: "Éveline refused to understand that I might prefer in myself the person I wanted to be and was trying to become, rather than the one I was naturally. . . . And yet the person I wanted to be was the one she had fallen in love with."[49]

He begins rather startlingly as a mixture of Gide, André Walter and Jérôme—apart from being the son of a shopkeeper in Perpignan, the rest is instantly familiar: the beloved sister with whom he shares country walks and talks, the father who dies when he is twelve, the sensitive adolescence spent in the shadow of two pious women until in one fell swoop the sister dies and an aunt leaves them a fortune; he is studious, has "a horror of the easy pleasures I saw my schoolfriends falling into,"[50] is a devout believer from infancy, remains a virgin well into his student years and he dedicates his whole heart to Éveline in a quasireligious cult. It is only after this "unhappy childhood" has been speedily established in two pages that the irony appears:[51]

> Once I had passed my exams rather brilliantly, I left Toulouse, which was no longer able to offer sufficient nourishment to my intellectual curiosity. I have already described how the notion of duty had dominated my life since my tenderest childhood. But I had to learn that, though I had duties to my mother, I had equally sacred ones to my country, which is the same as to say: to myself, for I thought only how I might serve it.[52]

Here and in the next section, where he is talking of his choice of career, the satire is simple, even heavy, focused on his vanity. When he discusses the importance of submission, especially for women but for men too—"man needs direction, a framework, domination . . . I did not demand of Éveline a submission any different from the one I imposed on my own thoughts"[53]—and more specifically when he argues straightfacedly that it would have been better for his postpartum wife to die in a state of grace than to have survived, the critique is similarly blatant, directed against all that is most grotesque in a vulgarized Catholicism. At other points, however, as in the curiously indulgent early history, we find a Robert who borrows elements of Gide's own self-image: admiring certain qualities of the Germans which his own countrymen lack, reading aloud to his wife with selfconscious diction, ignoring her modest vanity (while observing the puffiness of her features)[54] because he loves only her soul, or needing effort in order to reach a state of virtue she seems to deploy naturally. On the other hand, a slightly closer examination suggests that some of the less appealing sides of Robert derive from Madeleine: his conventional views on education, his intolerant conservatism, his habit of "looking away" from what displeases him, his insistence on aiming heavenward—even his Catholicism—are reminiscent of aspects Gide will evoke in *Et nunc manet in te* and elsewhere. The Éveline we saw as the ineluctably virtuous woman now has Gide's beliefs in pedagogic freedom, curiosity, sincerity and a freewheeling Christianity—she even has his supposed susceptibility to corruption by the young. All these characteristics are, it seems, counters to be moved around on a marital snakes-and-ladders board. The one thing that is constant and quite new in this volume is an anxious concern with the education of women. Nothing really suggested its importance in the first; indeed the two titles could be swapped without any loss of relevance. In *L'École des femmes*, Éveline's problem was that she had outgrown her husband; in *Robert*, he is determined to find out how rather than what women know.

"I could measure the decline of her love by the increasing independence of her mind," he says in exasperation, for "rebellion is always blameworthy but especially in a woman."[55] He goes on in gynaecological mode: "I do not believe in spontaneous generation, especially in the brains of women; when ideas develop there you can be sure someone has sown them."[56] Éveline's revolt must derive from Marchant or Bourgweilsdorf—or perhaps from Geneviève, who has always been "eager to learn . . . and more curious than is good for a woman."[57] In the mother-daughter pair, then, the baffled father begins to perceive the nearest thing to spontaneous generation—that is, reproduction without any evident father. Like pleasure for the infant boys on the first page of *Si le grain ne meurt*, the desire for knowledge in women is something no one learns from another, and which has somehow always been there. Between the first and second volume, it has sprung up in the female couple. Virtue in the first, irony in the second, seemed to protect the author against this female monster; in the third volume, she will begin to grow.

It is entitled *Geneviève, ou La Confidence inachevée;* the history of its production is a long tale of struggles with an intractable subject, an uncomfortable voice and an unappealing protagonist; nothing seemed to fit, or to fit properly. The incompleteness referred to in the title is the abandonment of a Part 3, set in the Foyer franco-belge years, which was to include a development of Geneviève's history into political activism and the birth of a son. Yet the text as it stands would strike most readers as rather well-rounded, finishing as it does on the death of Éveline, the framing motive of Geneviève's narrative, and pointing forward to a conception the protagonist has planned and seems well capable of bringing about; not to let us know what man helps her do so is quite consonant with her intention. The conviction of incompleteness here is surely Gide's problem—an obsession very similar to Freud's in the "Dora" case history.[58] I would go a little further and argue that by insisting that part of Geneviève is cut off her creator finds the only way to stop her spontaneously generating, for that is her *raison d'être*.

Gide began writing the novel uncomfortably "as the pen flows" in March 1930; in May 1931, he reports that it is proceeding well, emerging "just as it comes," with a subject that "may turn out terrific."[59] But by October, it is beginning to cause problems:

Up to the point where Geneviève meets Sara, everything he's reading aloud irritates him—"much too long, can't get the tone right, I still haven't found the way to write it, it's not characteristic enough" are typical remarks. I tell him I think he's tending to explain everything too much. He goes "Yes, yes, I'll chop all that, but first I have to write it all down any old how." But when it comes to the friendship of the two girls, he seems to feel better. "I need to feel there are some good things in it, so that I have the impetus to go on, telling myself it could all be of that quality. It seems such a terrific [*énorme*] undertaking to do this novel, so unlike my usual sort of thing, but on the other hand, if I put in everything I mean to, if I raise all the questions that are on my mind, I think in the end it will fit into my line after all."[60]

By June 1932, the book "no longer holds any interest for me";[61] in April 1934 he admits he is no good at realism and has been trying to write "against my natural inclination."[62] Two years later he is thinking of publishing Parts 1 and 2 on their own, and in May 1936, shortly before his visit to the USSR, he abandons Part 3 because it is "worse than bad: it's mediocre."[63]

Immediately before the lines quoted at the beginning of this chapter, Gide wrote of his new book: "I'm not sure I'll be able to complete [it] successfully. I keep telling myself that it needs to be written with no attention to style and that any attempt at formal perfection would betray my presence too much; such things could not belong to my heroine and to put them in would be a betrayal of her character."[64] This extraordinary argument has not appeared in respect of any of his earlier *récits,* including the two wholly or partly narrated in a female voice. The reason seems to be not so much a problem of gender as one of irony.

Not long ago, I mentioned Emma Bovary, Gerty MacDowell and Eveline in connexion with Gide's ironic use of the immature female voice. In *Madame Bovary,* "Nausicaa" and "Eveline," *style indirect libre* is the favoured way to represent a female character as foolish reader by ironic contradistinction to a male implied author as wise writer—God in the universe, paring his fingernails. *Style indirect libre* depends on a precisely gendered process in which the implied reader agrees to agree that a young woman addicted to romantic trash "could not" think in anything resembling high literary style. Flaubert or Joyce acquires a productive spirit presence in the text by virtue of the over-bodied, over-clichéd materialization of the girl. This (as Robert observes) is more or less what happens in *L'École des femmes.* It is not—despite the last quotation—what happens in *Geneviève.*

Gide had set himself the task of "giving a voice to the new generation,"[65] but their ideas were, he realized already in mid–1933, not really his own. Like alien creatures, those ideas had settled inside him without the "rootedness" necessary for his usual ironic method whereby an "offshoot" of his own character was fantasmatically extracted and allowed to grow to a self-destructive extreme.[66] Whereas it took the shock of the visit to the USSR to excise his desire for the communist romance, his real difficulty with the ideas of the 1930s generation appears more gradually and insidiously through the character of the young feminist. This may have much to do with the absence of libido and the necessity for respect—"can't I fall in love with my fiction any more?";[67] "I know that only the strange and bizarre can delight or induce a state of trance. But . . . I owe it to my heroine to remain reasonable, since I have to express myself through her"[68]—combined with an instinctive lack of sympathy for feminism.[69] More to the point, the new generation does not wish to borrow his voice.

So he decides eventually to "cut off" the book at the end of Part 2, where it would have "a sort of tolerable conclusion . . . though just the opposite of what I had in mind."[70] He wanted Geneviève to say, after the death of her mother, "'The way I go scarcely matters, only where I am going to'" but he cannot make her do it.[71] This sentiment—the principle of *passer outre* which exemplifies Gide's concept of young masculinity—though it appears here and there in her narrative, won't take hold in her. Instead, we must return to 1933 to see how she has taken hold in him:

> If I had been able to succeed at once with this Geneviève . . . , in which I wanted to give a voice to the new generation, I would doubtless have used up (I would have purged myself of) a whole set of cogitations that had chosen to take up residence in me and which I had found myself forced to take on. I wasn't able to upload them onto a "hero" as I had done with Nietzschean ideas in my *Immoraliste* or Christian ones in my *Porte étroite,* so I ended up caught in my own game, stuck with myself. Taking them on, I could no longer push them to the extreme, to the absurd, as I would have been able to do in a novel which could have simultaneously exposed them, gone over them critically and finally rid me of them. The trap was badly laid—I no longer had the strength to lay it well—and it closed upon me.[72]

He is unable to empty his system of Geneviève because she is not susceptible to his usual ways of driving inner problems out. At once too alien and too well implanted, like a foetus, she cannot be uprooted without tearing him apart. Far from being a bolder pendant to *Corydon,* as he suggested in 1931,[73] *Geneviève* is more accurately its refutation. For a woman could not simply take the man's place in Gide's new genealogy without upturning the whole argument. Instead of entering a triangular bind like his other women—including those occluded by the *Corydon* apologia—this heroine proposes the nearest possible thing to an exclusively female chain. No wonder he needs to believe he has left the text castrated.

With this in mind, let us enter Geneviève's narrative. Despite the firmness of the feminist principles voiced in her liminary letter, Geneviève appears surprisingly tame after the lead-in of the first two volumes. Indeed, all the women who predominate in this novel seem to metamorphose curiously, such that, while none of them is anything but excessively serious and virtuous—apart from Sara, who functions as the embodied *odor di femmina,* cut with the racial exotic—bold ideas float from mouth to mouth while Gide's rather stilted use of quasi-socratic dialogue guarantees (as it does in *Corydon*) that radical ideas are always shown up against the most dreary unenlightenment, here usually in another female voice.

What does this woman want? Three things: Sara, to have a baby without marriage, and her mother. All these are ways of engaging in an *f-f* chain.[74] I say a chain, not a pairing, because these are not couples any more than *m-f* or *m-m* pairs are couples in Gide. I want to look at each of them and try to link together the logic of desire and undesire that operates them, keeping in mind throughout that Gide really is creating something here that he has not attempted elsewhere and which, while flawed, is both acute and significantly contradictory of his usual motives.

In a number of ways, Geneviève is a typical Gidean subject: studious, virginal, incapable of knowing her own desire, which is experienced in the form of hysterical illnesses and undirected restlessness. She has a passion for Sara but does not know it or seek to know it—and is thus "innocent" of it. Her relation to her family is simple: she despises and distrusts her father and respects and admires her mother, even when they show a united front or similar attitudes—anti-semitism, snobbery, inclination to censor her, obfuscation about sexual matters. This "negative oedipus complex" flows logically enough from the family, as established in the other volumes, and the Freudian motif of the narcissism of minor differences operates very clearly in its internal politics.[75]

It is Éveline who sent her to school at the age of fifteen, one year before the confrontation of *L'École des femmes*, Part 2. She is the decisive parent, but despite this she takes the Alissa rôle vis-à-vis her daughter, piggy-backing on her education in order to get a little of her own. Mother and daughter share (with Robert, incidentally) "an ardent desire, a need to make myself useful," and the former has in addition "an extraordinary love for poor people" that she is far too retiring to show.[76]

As soon as Geneviève enters the classroom she falls passionately in love with the girl at the next desk, a sultry beauty with grubby finger-nails and a gift for recitation. Sara is a little surprised when her invitation has to be submitted to the mother's approval and she does not get it despite her courtesy and charm because, on learning she is the daughter of successful artist Alfred Keller, Éveline makes a sharp excuse. As soon as the girl has gone, she bursts out: "But you didn't tell me . . . She's a Jew!"[77] Geneviève—even though a page or two later she is quite familiar with her father's anti-semitism—is genuinely flummoxed: "I knew the history of the scriptures and what the Jews had been in the past, but I had no idea what they might be now," she confides.[78]

> "Is it because she's Jewish that you won't let me go to her house? Why did you say I wasn't free? You know quite well that's not true."
>
> "My dear child, I couldn't just say straight out that we were refusing her invitation. It's not her fault that she's Jewish and her father is an artist. I didn't want to hurt her feelings. Besides," she added, seeing the tears in my eyes, "the Jews have many fine qualities and some of them are quite remarkable people. But I prefer not to let you go into a social circle so different from our own, without having made some enquiries first."[79]

Éveline's kneejerk prejudice is never represented as out of tune with her saintly sweetness of temper and unswerving rationality, and of course Sara's parents are as caricatural as one might expect of the progenitors of *"la belle Juive."*[80] The only original aspect in this piece of grotesquery is the lesbian turn of the orientalist desire, though this too is presented as deriving from the other girl's vaguely lascivious knowingness. In the face of Jewish over-sophistication, Geneviève becomes excessively naive, tongue-tied with her school-fellows, so shocked at Sara's having posed "without any clothes on, and in front of her father" that she is forced to agree with her own hated father and falls ill of a hysterical scarlet-fever.[81]

By means of the Jewish sub-plot, the protagonist's lesbianism is exoticized and displaced in very much the same way as we find with Gide's other couples: unknown to its subject, desire is induced by something exuding from the surface of the dark-skinned other. Metamorphosed into a set of hysterical symptoms, it becomes her own and is sweated out of her. Geneviève is able then to transfer her *f-f* desire to the whole unit of Gisèle and Mme Parmentier, the model daughter-mother couple, so perfect in beauty and breeding, with a minimal touch of the exotic in the shape of the English accent and in whom emancipation as an idea combines reassuringly with respect for men, uncritical piety, love of flowers and poetry—Geneviève can rail against these quite gently while Gide uses them to support his moral decor. Of course there is inconsistency: it was while, as she later reveals, she was "crazy about Sara" that Gisèle watched her posing nude,[82] and her mother turns out to have known this when she went with her to the exhibition (though each preferred to pretend ignorance), yet when questioned about George Eliot's character Hetty Sorrel, Mme Parmentier voices the most benighted opinions about female shame—all proof of the very mixed motivation behind these rather colourless characters.

Éveline is similar: supposedly ready to answer all Geneviève's questions with reason and frankness, she tells her nothing about sexual practice and very little about reproduction. Thus both mothers leave the protagonist unsatisfied and focused on the one thing which comes to take up all her conscious thoughts in the final section: the wish to have a child without a husband. Where this motive comes from we know: it is all that is left of the coincidence of feminism with desire, the one trace of Sara that is allowed to remain after her foreign body has been excised, her obsession with *"les filles mères"* (*Romans* 1370). I have left the phrase in French because it carries a number of specific connotations absent in the English equivalent "unmarried mothers." *Fille* can mean girl, daughter or prostitute; here it stands awkwardly for unmarried woman. The phrase brings the daughter-mother relation into direct adjectival apposition, and Geneviève immediately lights on it: "the expression . . . had no precise meaning for me and it shocked me a little, though I could not have said why."[83]

This motive becomes the crux of the text and its feminist claims. Twice in the *Cahiers de la Petite Dame,* we find Gide discussing feminism with Maria Van Rysselberghe: both times the lesbian Ethel Whitehorn appears, along with Élisabeth the first time and Hélène Martin du Gard the second.[84] On each occasion it is a question of how women might invent new ways of life for themselves. Like most creative cruces, Gide's version of this invention is multiply overdetermined. In some essential way, lesbianism and maternity are co-present and productively combined.

For familiar reasons, Gide's procedure tends to deny this. Given his propensity to dispose of female characters in a triangle, we must note that this motif puts the wild card Geneviève back inside one: feminist or not, she will need the mediation of a man. She is further (and unnecessarily) reinserted into the primordial *m-f-m* triangle, for we are carefully told that—compensating the frustrated wish of Élisabeth?—she will be the mother of a son.[85] The man she chooses to become pregnant by is the good "uncle" Marchant, who refuses her in the most patronizing terms; thus again she is put back in her place by the masculine principle. For it is a truism of patriarchy's legitimization of children in marriage that behind every cultural *m-f-m* triangle there is a natural *f-m-f* one. Geneviève is trying however confusedly to create the latter when she is hoist back into the former.

That this is Gide's semi-conscious motive is clear from a conversation between him and Maria Van Rysselberghe about Dr Marchant:

> I forgot to mention that just before Martin [du Gard] arrived, I had said to Gide: "There is something I must talk to you about; it has been tormenting me ever since you read us *Geneviève*. I apologize in advance if it hurts your feelings, but I simply can't keep it to myself. Don't you realize that the answer you put in the mouth of Dr Marchand *[sic]*—'I won't do what you want because I love my wife'—is extraordinarily cruel towards Madeleine? One would think there was some sort of fatality making you always say the worst possible thing in spite of yourself."
>
> "Oh yes I know what you mean!" He looks very upset, then suddenly gives this curious answer: "But don't you think . . . that if anything it would actually reassure her?" I am staggered by his complete lack of awareness: "Yes, it would be reassuring, indeed, if you had acted in real life as Dr Marchand does; but the reason you consider valid in the mouth of that good man is exactly the one you chose to by-pass *[que vous avez passé outre]!*" "Yes," he said, "I can see that it is all bound to be misinterpreted." I did not like to pursue the matter, and yet I am really not sure that he had understood properly what I meant.[86]

As for the motives of the character Geneviève, these are initially difficult to work out because her obsession seems so little charged with ordinary desire. Under Marchant's questioning it becomes clear that she has no wish for the sensualities of pregnancy, birth, lactation or childcare; she has thought no more about these than about the sexual act that she knows must accompany impregnation. She certainly does not desire this man and loves him only in the loosest of senses. So far is this wish dissociated from the only kind of desire she has experienced that when asked whether she would have accepted a male Sara or Gisèle as the father of her child, she demurs at the one and laughs comfortably with the other.

Yet she is absolutely determined. The arguments against are given by Marchant, Gisèle and Mme Parmentier in descending order of validity. Marchant points out the practical consequences—despite his avowed longing for children, he is licensed by his profession to suggest that motherhood consists of little else but pain and dirt. Gisèle makes much the same point about unwedded partnerships, while her mother piles on the guilt and shame of Hetty Sorrel and her fatherless child until one wonders if the moral majority could find a better spokeswoman.

What is Geneviève's motive then? Surely a realization that the only way to have the mother, which is what she exclusively wants, is to become her. Her whole text with its liminal presentations is, after all, generated by the death of Éveline. Her mother is gone; she cannot have the lesbian love-object, outlawed both by an agreed anti-semitism and by the object's own failure to desire. The self-sufficient unit of Gisèle and Mme Parmentier, so enviably cemented by a dead father rather than like hers riven by a living one, is a pointer to her true object. If there could be an *f-f* couple with no trace of the masculine, that is clearly what she would wish for. But, oedipally enough, there cannot. Her mother has stayed *une honnête femme* to the last, martyred in uniform like Chateaubriand's Amélie but differing from her by being still in the service of men. The nearest Geneviève can get to her is by seeking to remake herself as mother and that is why the details do not matter. If there must be a man between them, let him carry the brief afterglow of being the one her mother should have loved.

Gide will not let Geneviève have what she wants, of course—why should he, he is the author! The best he will offer is a son conceived by unsaid means in an untold moment, for there really cannot be an all-female chain. And here we inevitably reinsert Maria Van Rysselberghe and her *"filles,"*[87] Élisabeth, Catherine and Isabelle, forming a proudly bastardizing female line, the circle closed with an identical birthday almost eighty years apart; or Dorothy and Janie Bussy, Stracheys to the last and the 54-year-old daughter and 94-year-old mother dying within the same year. As for the symmetrical arrangement of the trilogy—*f-m-f* with a derisory centre—the complex gendering of its voices and its logical wholeness disguised as incompleteness all prove the fundamental and quite hidden motive in Gide of restoring to the woman her desire for the lost mother.

Notes

This article is based on material published in my book *André Gide: Pederasty and Pedagogy*.

1. "Je m'échappe facilement à moi-même et, me laissant supplanter par une personnal-ité différente de la mienne, ce n'est qu'avec un parfait abandon de moi et sans con-tention aucune que je puis la laisser ainsi exprimer à travers moi comme il convient. Mais je n'éprouve aucune satisfaction à écrire, fémininement, au courant de la plume, et tout ce que j'écris ainsi me déplaît" (*Journal II* 194).
2. See Martin du Gard 2: 232–233.
3. "Tout ce que j'ai écrit de mieux a été bien écrit tout de suite, sans peine, fatigue ni ennui" (*Journal II* 41).
4. "'C'est un nouveau roman, dit-il avec un sourire, écrit jusqu'ici au courant de la

plume'" (Van Rysselberghe 1: 302); "'ce qui est fait est écrit au courant de la plume, ça a donc besoin d'être limé et toutes les remarques sont bienvenues'" (Van Rysselberghe 1: 322).

5. "Ce livre ne m'intéresse guère et ma pensée ne s'y reporte pas spontanément" (*Journal II* 89).

6. "Il m'arrive d'écrire en wagon, en métro, sur les bancs des quais ou des boulevards, au bord des routes, et ce sont mes meilleures pages, les plus réellement inspirées. Une phrase succède à l'autre, et j'éprouve à la sentir naître et se gonfler en moi un ravissement presque physique. Je crois que ce jaillissement artésien est le résultat d'une longue préparation inconsciente. Il m'arrive par la suite d'apporter à ce premier jet quelques retouches, mais fort peu" (*Journal I* 1245). Compare a similar description of the contrast between masculine flow and feminized unease in Flaubert's declaration to Louise Colet in a letter dated 6 April 1853: "*Saint Antoine* did not cost me a quarter of the intellectual tension that *Bovary* demands. It poured out of me; I had nothing but pleasure in the writing, and the eighteen months I spent in writing its 500 pages were the most deeply voluptuous of my whole life. Consider then, every minute I am having to get under *skins* that are antipathetic to me" [*Saint Antoine* ne m'a pas demandé le quart de la tension d'esprit que la *Bovary* me cause. C'était un déversoir. Je n'ai eu que plaisir à écrire, et les dix-huit mois que j'ai passés à en écrire les 500 pages ont été les plus profondément voluptueux de toute ma vie. Juge donc, il faut que j'entre à toute minute dans des *peaux* qui me sont antipathiques] (Flaubert 297).

7. "Il n'est presque pas un de mes livres que j'aie été à même d'écrire au moment où j'eusse pris le plus de plaisir à l'écrire; pas un qui, à un certain moment, ne m'ait quelque peu tiré en arrière" (*Journal II* 92).

8. "Mon cœur ne bat que par sympathie; je ne vis que par autrui" (*Romans* 987).

9. "Je suis de caoutchouc . . . j'acquiesce autant que je peux et vais jusqu'au bord de l'insincérité; mais ne prenez pas le change : sitôt seul, je reprends ma forme" (*Journal II* 825).

10. "Le livre à présent m'apparaît comme un nougat dont les amandes sont bonnes (*id est : Lettres et journal d'Alissa*) mais dont le mastic est pâteux, médiocrement écrit; mais il ne pouvait en être autrement avec la première personne, le flasque caractère de mon Jérôme impliquant la flasque prose" (*Journal I* 612–613). Gide was accused of having plagiarised the passages quoted from Alissa's letters and journal—lifted, perhaps from those of Madeleine, which indeed they often resemble, as we see in Schlumberger— and rebutted the accusation with some anxiety; see *Journal II* 303 and 1266.

11. "Lu hier à Pomme la *Suite de l'École des Femmes,* que je viens d'achever. Assez bonne impression. Guère rien à reprendre, je crois, que je ne puisse corriger sur épreuves. J'ai écrit ce petit livre en moins de huit jours, au courant de la plume; c'est comme cela qu'il devait être écrit" (*Journal II* 145–146). Given this, it is nice to compare the presumably ironic treatment of the same phrase in Robert's voice: "if I watch myself too closely, I may falsify the movement of my writing, and fall into the trap of affectation where I most want to avoid it . . . It is no mean task. I will solve it only, I believe, by not thinking about it—writing as the pen flows" [si je surveille trop mon écriture, je risque de fausser ma ligne et de donner dans le piège de l'apprêt au moment même et d'autant plus que je m'applique à l'éviter . . . La difficulté n'est pas mince. Je n'en triompherai, ce me semble, qu'en n'y pensant point; qu'en écrivant au courant de la plume] (*Romans* 1316, ellipses Gide's). As we shall see later in this essay, Gide's hold on irony may indeed be at its least secure in this text where it is at its most obvious. He himself uses the phrase *"au courant de la plume"* quite often in reference to his own (as well as others') writing. See *Journal I* 1141 and 1228 and *Journal II* 524.

12. Quoted without French original in Mann 103.

13. See my *André Gide: Pederasty and Pedagogy,* chapters 6 and 8.

14. In the shock caused by the birth of a daughter when he was convinced Élisabeth would have a son, he worried about her education which by a stunningly predictable logic he realised he would have preferred to see in the hands of Madeleine.

15. See Apter, "La nouvelle *Nouvelle Héloïse*" 95–99.

16. "'Si Élisabeth et Whity n'arrivent pas à trouver une nouvelle forme de vie, en dehors des conventions, quelles femmes les *[sic]* trouveront?'" (Van Rysselberghe 1: 8–9). During her time in England, Élisabeth had been associated with the "neo-Pagan" group around Rupert Brooke, with whom she had an uncomfortable love affair; see Delany. Jacques and Gwen Raverat, who never entirely forgave Gide for his sexual transgressions in Cambridge in 1918, are a common link between that group and the Stracheys.

17. "Notre bouillante amie (et peut-être de sa plus bouillante encore fille . . .)" (Gide and Martin du Gard 455, ellipses Martin du Gard's).

18. "« Il faut que je vous fasse un aveu . . . J'ose à peine vous le dire : j'ai dix-sept ans, et je suis encore vierge », disait, en rougissant, une jeune fille de la meilleure société anglaise à une vieille amie de Dorothy Bussy, qui redisait avec terreur à celle-ci ces propos horrifiants. Et Mme Bussy, qui me les rapporte à son tour, ajoute que cette jeune fille, charmante et à laquelle ceux de sa famille s'intéressent très particulièrement, entraînée aux cocktails par les jeunes gens de son entourage, vient d'être reconnue alcoolique au dernier degré, sans plus aucun espoir de guérison" (*Journal II* 134, ellipses Gide's).

19. For the story of Sara Breitenstein, beloved of both Marc and André Allégret, see Durosay.

20. "Le pays de la libération et de la rupture . . . les vertus de la révolte" (Goulet 171).

21. "Le pays de la frustration sexuelle, ou plus exactement d'une carence qui entraîne un dérèglement : il semble en effet que la gent masculine y soit curieusement diminuée . . . ce pays est celui des maris déficients [où] c'est l'insuffisance des hommes qui fait la folie des femmes" (Masson 121).

22. From "Femininity," Freud 2: 149.

23. "Les plus belles figures de femmes que j'ai connues sont résignées; et je n'imagine même pas que puisse me plaire et n'éveiller même en moi quelque pointe d'hostilité, le contentement d'une femme dont le bonheur ne comporterait pas un peu de résignation" (*Journal I* 573; see also Van Rysselberghe 1: 11).

24. It is anger at the excess and probable unintention of this "Alissa-izing" of Madeleine that surely drove Schlumberger to his counter-blow, *Madeleine et André Gide.* Unavoidably, perhaps, but still ironically, Schlumberger does just the same as the Gide of *La Porte étroite* when the nuts in the nougat of his text too turn out to be the letters and journals she would not have wanted published.

25. "J'avais quitté Paris avec l'espoir de pousser assez loin ce nouveau roman dont, à Cuverville, j'écrivais si joyeusement les premières pages" (*Journal II* 20–21); but "Grande difficulté de prendre mon nouveau roman au sérieux" (*Journal II* 26).

26. "— J'achève en ce moment, reprend Gide, un autre livre dont je vous ai déjà parlé. Ce sera le journal d'une femme mal mariée. Je l'appellerai : *L'École des Femmes.* Après, j'écrirai peut-être le pendant : *L'École des Maris.* Je suis préoccupé par l'idée de la sympathie. Combien une femme peut changer dès qu'elle éprouve un amour; combien elle s'intéresse alors à tout ce qui intéresse l'époux. Mais quand son amour commence à s'éteindre, la femme retrouve sa première personnalité, qui n'est cependant plus la même, le plus souvent appauvrie, enlaidie" (Pierre-Quint 402–403).

27. For a comparison of the *style-indirect-libre* narratives of these three characters, see my *The Adulteress's Child* 117–119.

28. See Lucey 96–107.

29. The two instances are in Van Rysselberghe 4: 30 and 3: 3. Strictly speaking, *très autre-fois* is not incorrect, since it is an adverb of degree qualifying an adverb of time—but Grévisse considers it somewhat anomalous and attributes it to "colloquial language" (1051).

30. "Vers le beau, vers le bien, vers Dieu" (*Romans* 1253).

31. "Il est modeste [mais] je suis orgueilleuse pour lui" (*Romans* 1253).

32. "Robert a été brusquement appelé à Perpignan auprès de sa mère dont il a reçu d'assez mauvaises nouvelles. / « J'espère que cela ne sera rien — lui ai-je dit. / — On dit toujours cela » a-t-il répliqué avec un grave sourire qui laissait voir combien au fond il était préoccupé. Et je m'en suis voulu tout aussitôt de ma phrase absurde" (*Romans* 1254–1255).

33. "[Des] horreurs" (*Romans* 1269); "[un] homme odieux" (1274).

34. "Et je prends ici l'engagement, si j'ai une fille, de ne lui apprendre aucun de ces petits arts d'agrément dont parlait avec tant d'ironique mépris le docteur Marchant, mais de lui faire donner une instruction sérieuse qui lui permette de se passer des acquiescements arbitraires, des complaisances et des faveurs. / Je sais bien que tout ce que j'écris ici est absurde; mais le sentiment qui me dicte ces phrases ne l'est pas. Je trouve tout naturel, en épousant Robert, de renoncer à mon indépendance (j'ai fait acte d'indépendance en l'épousant malgré papa), mais chaque femme devrait pour le moins rester libre de choisir la servitude qui lui convient" (*Romans* 1276).

35. "Le charme est rompu" (*Romans* 1277).

36. "J'ai pris avec moi ce cahier comme on emporte un ouvrage de broderie, pour occuper le désœuvrement d'une cure. Mais, si je recommence à y écrire, ce n'est hélas plus pour Robert. Il croit désormais connaître tout ce que je peux sentir ou penser. J'écrirai afin de m'aider à mettre un peu d'ordre dans ma pensée; afin de tâcher d'y voir clair en moi-même, considérant, comme l'Émilie de Corneille,

       Et ce que je hasarde et ce que je poursuis.

   Quand j'étais jeune, je ne savais voir dans ces vers que de la redondance; ils me paraissaient ridicules, comme souvent ce que l'on ne comprend pas bien; comme ils paraissent ridicules et redondants aujourd'hui à mon fils et à ma fille, à qui je les ai fait apprendre. Sans doute faut-il avoir un peu vécu pour comprendre que tout ce que l'on *poursuit* dans la vie, l'on ne peut espérer l'atteindre qu'en *hasardant* précisément ce qui parfois vous tient à cœur. Ce que je poursuis aujourd'hui, c'est ma délivrance; ce que je hasarde, c'est l'estime du monde, et celle de mes deux enfants" (*Romans* 1279).

37. "Faux jeton est un pléonasme. Gide était un vrai jeton. Un jeton de salle de jeu. Ce jeton équivalait à une vraie fortune" (Cocteau 221).

38. "Dupe des phrases sonores de Robert" (*Romans* 1280).

39. "Je reste peu satisfaite de ce que j'écrivais hier. J'ai laissé courir ma plume" (*Romans* 1281).

40. See also my discussion of this point in *André Gide: Pederasty and Pedagogy* 107.

41. "Une honnête femme" (*Romans* 1298).

42. "Triptyque" (*Romans* 1347).

43. "Je fais partie de son confort. Je suis sa femme" (*Romans* 1283).

44. "« Ma femme ne m'aime plus! Ma femme ne m'aime plus! . . . »" (*Romans* 1305).

45. See Apter, *André Gide* 140ff for a discussion of the relation of parody and gender-ventriloquism in the trilogy.

46. "Je viens d'avoir avec elle une conversation terrible, où tout à la fois j'ai compris que c'était avec elle que je pourrais le mieux m'entendre, compris également pourquoi je ne veux pas m'entendre avec elle : c'est que je crains de retrouver en elle ma propre pensée, plus hardie, si hardie qu'elle m'épouvante. Toutes les inquiétudes, tous les

doutes, qui purent m'effleurer parfois, sont devenus chez elle autant de négations effrontées. Non, non, je ne veux pas consentir à les reconnaître" (*Romans* 1295).

47. "Suprême éloge : on a même été supposer que ce journal avait été écrit par vous, M. Gide, qui . . ." (*Romans* 1316, ellipses Gide's).

48. See Gide and Martin du Gard 388.

49. "Éveline . . . se refusait à comprendre que je pusse préférer en moi celui que je voulais être et que je tâchais de devenir, à celui que naturellement j'étais. . . . Et pourtant, non de moi, mais de celui que je voulais être, c'est de celui-là qu'Éveline s'était éprise" (*Romans* 1333).

50. "Cette horreur des plaisirs faciles où je voyais mes camarades se laisser entraîner" (*Romans* 1319).

51. "Mon enfance n'a pas été très heureuse" (*Romans* 1317).

52. "Mes examens passés assez brillamment, j'avais quitté Toulouse qui n'offrait plus d'aliment suffisant à mes curiosités intellectuelles. J'ai dit que la notion du devoir, depuis ma tendre enfance, dominait ma vie. Mais il m'avait bien fallu comprendre que, si j'avais des devoirs envers ma mère, j'en avais également d'aussi sacrés envers mon pays, ce qui revient à dire : envers moi-même, qui ne songeais qu'à le bien servir" (*Romans* 1319).

53. "L'homme a besoin d'être dirigé, encadré, dominé . . . je ne souhaitais pas d'Éveline une autre soumission que celle que j'imposais moi-même à ma propre pensée" (*Romans* 1321 and 1324).

54. Cf. Gide, *Journal 1939–1949* 1153.

55. "C'est à l'indépendance de son jugement que je pouvais le mieux mesurer la décroissance de son amour. . . . L'insoumission est toujours blâmable, mais je la tiens pour particulièrement blâmable chez la femme" (*Romans* 1322).

56. "Je ne crois pas à la génération spontanée, surtout pas dans le cerveau des femmes; les idées qui s'y développent vous pouvez être sûr que quelqu'un d'autre les a semées" (*Romans* 1322).

57. "Plus avide d'instruction . . . et plus curieuse qu'il ne convient à une femme" (*Romans* 1323).

58. See Moi. Emily Apter draws a comparison between this case history and *La Porte étroite* (*André Gide* 125–126 and 129–131).

59. "Au courant de la plume" (*Journal II* 194); "tout comme cela vient . . . cela peut devenir énorme" (Van Rysselberghe 2: 145).

60. "Jusqu'au moment où Geneviève rencontre Sara, il s'impatiente contre tout ce qu'il lit : « Beaucoup trop long, le ton n'y est pas, je n'ai pas encore trouvé la façon d'écrire, pas assez particulier » sont des remarques qu'il fera tout le temps. Je lui dis qu'il me semble qu'il y a une tendance à trop expliquer. Il fait « oui, oui, sabrer dans tout ça, mais il faut d'abord que j'écrive tout n'importe comment. » Mais à propos de l'amitié des deux jeunes filles, il semble reprendre pied. « Il faudrait, dit-il, que je sente qu'il y a quelques bonnes choses pour me donner l'élan, et que je me dise que tout doit être de cette qualité! Ça me paraît énorme d'entreprendre ce roman, si peu mon genre, et d'autre part, si j'y mets tout ce que je veux, si je soulève toutes les questions auxquelles je pense, ça finira par entrer dans ma ligne tout de même »" (Van Rysselberghe 2: 161–162).

61. "Ne m'intéresse plus" (*Journal II* 365).

62. "Contre ma pente naturelle" (Van Rysselberghe 2: 371).

63. "Pire que mauvais : médiocre" (*Journal II* 522).

64. "Je ne sais si je pourrai [le] mener à bien. Je me répète que ce livre doit être écrit sans aucun souci de style et que tout effort de perfection formelle que j'y apporterais sentirait trop ma marque; mon héroïne ne les peut avoir et ce serait trahir son personnage que de les lui prêter" (*Journal II* 194).

65. "Prêter la parole à la génération nouvelle" (*Journal II* 401).

66. See the letter to Scheffer reproduced in Gide, *Œuvres complètes* 4: 615–617.

67. "Ne puis-je plus m'éprendre de ma fiction?" (*Journal II* 365).

68. "Quelque chose d'étrange, de bizarre, et qui vous saisisse. C'est cela que je souhaiterais, sachant bien que seul l'inattendu peut ravir et plonger en état de transe. Mais . . . je dois à mon héroïne de demeurer raisonnable, puisque aussi bien ce n'est qu'à travers elle que je m'exprime" (*Journal II* 450).

69. See, for example, *Journal II* 622, 738 and 842.

70. "Une sorte de conclusion supportable . . . encore qu'exactement à l'encontre de ce que je m'étais proposé" (*Journal II* 522).

71. "« Par où je passe n'importe guère, mais seulement vers où je vais »" (*Journal II* 522).

72. "Si j'avais pu mener aussitôt à bien cette *Geneviève* . . . où je me proposais de prêter la parole à la génération nouvelle, j'y aurais sans doute épuisé (je me serais expurgé de) quantité de ratiocinations qui m'ont élu pour domicile et que je me suis trouvé comme contraint d'assumer. Je n'ai pu les faire endosser par un « héros », ainsi que précédemment j'avais fait des nietzschéennes avec mon *Immoraliste,* des chrétiennes avec ma *Porte étroite,* et suis resté pris au jeu (ou au *je*). Les assumant, je ne pouvais plus les pousser à bout, à l'absurde, ainsi que j'aurais su faire dans un roman qui, tout à la fois les eût exposées, en eût fait le tour et la critique et qui m'en eût enfin délivré. Le piège, mal tendu (que je n'ai plus eu la force de bien tendre), s'est soudain refermé sur moi" (*Journal II* 401).

73. Van Rysselberghe 2: 171.

74. As I hope is obvious, *f* in these pair-, triangle-, or chain-structures stands for "female" and *m* stands for "male."

75. See Freud's discussion of this concept in "The Taboo of virginity" (1917), "Group psychology and the analysis of the ego" (1921) and "Civilisation and its discontents" ([1929], 1930), in Freud 7: 272 and 12: 131 and 305.

76. "Un ardent désir, un besoin de me rendre utile . . . un extraordinaire amour pour les pauvres" (*Romans* 1351).

77. "« Mais, tu ne m'avais pas dit . . . C'est une juive! »" (*Romans* 1356, ellipses Gide's).

78. "Je connaissais l'histoire sainte, je savais ce que les juifs avaient été autrefois mais point du tout ce qu'ils pouvaient être aujourd'hui" (*Romans* 1356–1357).

79. "« Est-ce parce qu'elle est juive que tu ne me laisses pas aller chez elle? Pourquoi lui as-tu dit que je n'étais pas libre? Tu sais bien que ça n'est pas vrai.

   — Mon enfant, je ne pouvais pas lui dire brutalement que nous refusions son invitation. Ce n'est pas sa faute si elle est juive et si son père est un artiste. Je ne voulais pas la peiner. D'ailleurs — ajouta-t-elle en voyant mes yeux pleins de larmes — les juifs ont beaucoup de qualités et certains d'entre eux sont très remarquables. Mais je préfère ne pas te laisser aller dans un milieu si différent du nôtre, avant d'avoir pris quelques renseignements" (*Romans* 1357).

80. For a sharp analysis of the anti-semitism in Gide's writing, see Mehlman 64–82. The *Journal* is, of course, studded with examples of this phobia, which was both literary and eugenic, Jews being incapable of ever being really French or writing French— this includes Proust and Montaigne, equally tainted—and thus constituting a particular threat to the line; see Van Rysselberghe 2: 146: "I would not like to let myself be infused with Jewish blood" [je n'aimerais pas me laisser infuser de sang juif]. He shared this horror with Madeleine, who went into a tragic state when their nephew Jacques Drouin brought home a Jewish fiancée, while Gide tried to protect her tender feelings as much as he could; see Gide and Martin du Gard 576–577.

81. "Sans vêtements, et devant son père" (*Romans* 1381).

82. "Folle de Sara" (*Romans* 1407).

83. "L'expression . . . n'avait aucun sens précis pour moi; et si elle me choquait un peu, je n'aurais pas su dire pourquoi" (*Romans* 1370).

84. Van Rysselberghe 1: 8–9 (1918) and 2: 231 (1932).

85. See *Romans* 1373. The father of this son was to be the Lafcadio/Bernard figure who had already stepped from one novel to another, in the course of which he carried off the virginity of a Geneviève who has certain analogies with this one (see Lambert 137) and a Sarah who is even more like this Sara (see Mehlman 78; and for the sexiness of Sara Breitenstein, Durosay 423–465).

86. "J'ai oublié de dire qu'avant l'arrivée de Martin, j'avais dit à Gide : « Il faut absolument que je vous fasse part d'une chose qui me tourmente depuis la lecture de *Geneviève*. Je m'excuse d'avance si cela doit vous être pénible, mais je ne puis garder cela pour moi : vous rendez-vous bien compte que la réponse que vous mettez dans la bouche du docteur Marchand, à la singulière requête de Geneviève : *Je ne veux pas, parce que j'aime ma femme,* est d'une singulière férocité par rapport à Madeleine? On dirait qu'il y a comme une fatalité qui vous amène malgré vous à dire toujours le pire. — Ah! je sais bien! » Il a l'air accablé, puis, brusquement, cette curieuse réponse : « Mais quoi! . . . tout de même, c'est plutôt rassurant? » Je suis démontée par son inconscience : « Oui, ce serait rassurant, en effet, si vous aviez agi dans la vie comme le docteur Marchand; mais cette raison que vous trouvez valable dans la bouche de cet honnête homme, n'oubliez pas que vous avez passé outre! — Oui, dit-il, tout cela sera fatalement interprété tout de travers. » Je n'ose pas insister, et pourtant je ne suis pas sûr [*sic*] qu'il ait bien compris la portée de ma remarque" (Van Rysselberghe 2: 526–527, ellipses the author's). He is equally careless about the obvious parallels readers will draw between Geneviève and Élisabeth, who already in November 1933 had regarded "the case of Geneviève as more interesting than Geneviève herself" [le cas de Geneviève est plus intéressant que Geneviève elle-même] (Van Rysselberghe 2: 346). To her mother three years later, the original and the character have "absolutely nothing in common: neither their personalities, nor their milieux, nor their circumstances, nor the people around them, nor the facts" [rien de commun entre Élisabeth et son héroïne! ni le caractère, ni le milieu, ni les circonstances, ni les comparses, ni les faits] (Van Rysselberghe 2: 551). She and Martin du Gard agree that it is a mercy they have both written their own version of the real-life plot.

87. Van Rysselberghe 1: 401 and 2: 20 and 369.

Works Cited

Apter, Emily. *André Gide and the Codes of Homotextuality.* Saratoga, CA: Anma Libri, 1987.

———. "La nouvelle *Nouvelle Héloïse* d'André Gide : *Geneviève* et le féminisme anglais." *André Gide et l'Angleterre.* Ed. Patrick Pollard. London: Birkbeck College, 1986.

Cocteau, Jean. *Poésie critique I.* Paris: Gallimard, 1959.

Delany, Paul. *The Neo-pagans: Friendship and Love in the Rupert Brooke Circle.* London: Macmillan, 1987.

Durosay, Daniel. "*Les Faux-monnayeurs* de A à S—et Z." *Bulletin des Amis d'André Gide* 18.88 (October 1990): 423–465.

Flaubert, Gustave. *Correspondance II.* Ed. J. Bruneau. Paris: Gallimard, 1980.

Freud, Sigmund. *The Pelican Freud Library.* Tr. James Strachey. 15 vols. Harmondsworth: Penguin, 1979–1986.

Gide, André. *Journal I, 1887–1925.* Ed. Éric Marty. Paris: Gallimard, Bibliothèque de la Pléiade, 1996.

———. *Journal II, 1926–1950.* Ed. Martine Sagaert. Paris: Gallimard, Bibliothèque de la Pléiade, 1997.

———. *Journal 1939–1949; Souvenirs.* Paris: Gallimard, Bibliothèque de la Pléiade, 1954.

————. *Œuvres complètes.* Vol. 4. Ed. Louis Martin-Chauffier. Paris: Gallimard, 1933.

————. *Romans, récits et soties, œuvres lyriques.* Ed. Yvonne Davet and Jean-Jacques Thierry. Paris: Gallimard, Bibliothèque de la Pléiade, 1958.

Gide, André, and Roger Martin du Gard. *Correspondance 1913–1934.* Paris: Gallimard, 1968.

Goulet, Alain. *Fiction et vie sociale dans l'œuvre d'André Gide.* Paris: Gallimard, 1986.

Grévisse, Maurice. *Le Bon Usage.* Paris: Duculot, 1980.

Herbart, Pierre. *A la recherche d'André Gide.* Paris: Gallimard, 1952.

Lambert, Jean. *Gide familier.* Paris: Julliard, 1958.

Lucey, Michael. *Gide's Bent.* New York: Oxford University Press, 1995.

Mann, Klaus. *André Gide and the Crisis of Modern Thought.* London: Dennis Dobson, 1948.

Martin du Gard, Roger. *Journal.* Vol. 2. Ed. Claude Sicard. Paris: Gallimard, 1993.

Masson, Pierre. *Lire les Faux-monnayeurs.* Lyon: Presses universitaires de Lyon, 1990.

Mehlman, Jeffrey. *Legacies of Anti-Semitism in France.* Minneapolis: University of Minnesota Press, 1983.

Moi, Toril. "Representations of patriarchy: sexuality and epistemology in Freud's 'Dora.'" *In Dora's Case.* Ed. Charles Bernheimer and Claire Kahane. London: Virago, 1985.

Pierre-Quint, Léon. *André Gide : l'homme, sa vie, son œuvre.* Paris: Librairie Stock, 1952.

Schlumberger, Jean. *Madeleine et André Gide.* Paris: Gallimard, 1956.

Segal, Naomi. *André Gide: Pederasty and Pedagogy.* Oxford: Oxford University Press, 1998.

————. *The Adulteress's Child.* Cambridge: Polity, 1992.

Van Rysselberghe, Maria. *Les Cahiers de la Petite Dame.* 4 vols. Paris: Gallimard, 1973–1977.

CHAPTER 12

Gide under Siege:
Domestic Conflict and Political Allegory
in the World War II *Journal*

Jocelyn Van Tuyl

Whether trapped in Nazi-occupied Tunis or enduring an onslaught of attacks in the press, André Gide spent much of the Second World War either literally or figuratively under siege. The writer spent the first two years of the war in the unoccupied south of France, but denunciations from the political Right led him to take refuge in Tunis. His account of the Allied liberation of that city served, in turn, as a pretext for attacks during the postwar purge. This essay will examine the convergence of literature, politics, and sexuality in Gide's *Journal* from the 1942–1943 siege of Tunis and in the post-armistice and post-Liberation attacks on the writer. It will focus on Gide's attempt to comprehend the war by means of a domestic allegory and François Reymond's bid to dislodge Gide's explanation in *L'Envers du Journal de Gide : Tunis 1942–43*.

Pernicious Influence: The *"Querelle des mauvais maîtres"*

As a homosexual, champion of individualism, and self-proclaimed *inquiéteur* [disturber], Gide was denounced for his "demoralizing" influence by those who sought to explain the fall of France. Many articles in the post-armistice press took up Marshal Pétain's call for intellectual and moral *redressement* [reform], suggesting that literature must be set right in order to promote the nation's recovery.[1] In the national debate about deleterious intellectual influences *("la querelle des mauvais maîtres")* following the fall of France, writers like Gide, Proust, and Valéry were blamed for the nation's "decadence" and defeat. Gide was singled out for his defense of homosexuality and his venture into Communism as well as for his literary influence (Mauclair 7). Above all, he was accused of corrupting France's youth both morally and intellectually. In a July 9, 1940 article in *Le Temps,* an anonymous attacker declared:

One cannot deny the influence of André Gide's works on contemporary literature and on the minds of our youth. It is against this considerable but disastrous influence that we must react today. The seductive author of *L'Immoraliste* and *Le Traité du Narcisse* has led a troublesome school. He has molded a proud and decadent generation; under the pretext of sincerity, he has brought them up with a perverted moral sense.[2]

Pointing out that his anonymous attacker apparently denounced him on the strength of his books' titles alone, Gide declined to defend himself publicly against such accusations (*Journals* 4: 33; *Journal II* 715). Opposing the spirit of attackers like Camille Mauclair—who would accuse him of "poisoning youth with doubt"[3]—Gide endorsed the salutary effects of doubt and questioning. Calling the education of youth the most important of tasks, Gide stressed the importance of developing children's critical faculties: "There is nothing better against 'nazism,'" he wrote on July 16, 1940 (*Journals* 4: 34).[4] Throughout the war—and particularly in his Tunis *Journal*—Gide would relate his ideas on education and child-rearing to his hopes for the nation, implicitly challenging his attackers by presenting himself as a model of positive pedagogy.

While writers and politicians debated the causes of the nation's defeat, Gide was recording his own thoughts on France's interwar "decadence" in his diary and in the *Journal* excerpts that appeared in Drieu La Rochelle's *Nouvelle Revue Française*:[5] "Softness, surrender, relaxation in grace and ease, so many charming qualities that were to lead us, blindfolded, to defeat" (*Journals* 4: 39).[6] Nevertheless, Gide rejected attempts to blame literature for the nation's defeat. Responding to *Le Figaro*'s survey on the future of literature, he declared: "I find it as absurd to incriminate our literature for our defeat as it would have been to congratulate it in 1918, when we were victorious."[7] Despite Gide's efforts to exculpate literature and his decision to keep a low profile, attacks against him continued. These offensives were not always confined to print: in May 1941, threats from the right-wing Légion française des combattants prevented the writer from delivering a purely literary lecture on the poet Henri Michaux.

At the same time, ironically, collaborationist writer Alfred Fabre-Luce had plans to co-opt Gide in support of his cause. In Fabre-Luce's 1942 *Anthologie de la nouvelle Europe,* pacifist excerpts from Gide's interwar diary appear side by side with writings by Drieu La Rochelle, Hitler, and Mussolini. One aim of Fabre-Luce's anthology was to show France and the rest of Europe that "French literature had its share of honor and responsibility in the creation of the world which we are now entering."[8] Gide's "contribution" consisted of two *Journal* excerpts considering the benefits of non-resistance and quiet compliance (Fabre-Luce 266-267). By entitling the piece "What would have happened if France had not resisted Germany?" ["Que serait-il advenu si la France n'avait pas résisté à l'Allemagne?"] and by neglecting to date the entries accurately (they were taken from Gide's *Journal* for September 19, 1938, and December 20, 1915), Fabre-Luce seemed to imply that Gide had welcomed the 1940 invasion.

By the spring of 1942, food shortages and continued attacks in the press convinced Gide to leave the south of France, where he had spent the first two years of the war. "I no longer feel safe here,"[9] he told Tunis bookstore owner Marcel Tournier, whom he had befriended during his 1923 visit to Tunis. Tournier persuaded his friend Admiral Esteva, the new Résident général, to facilitate Gide's passage to Tunis. "At least promise me that he will behave himself!" Esteva joked.[10] At first, Tournier thought that the admiral was referring to the possibility of subversive political activities on Gide's part; he soon realized, however, that Esteva had an entirely different kind of misbehavior in mind. Tournier reassured Esteva that given Gide's advanced age, there was no cause for worry; later, upon reading Gide's account of his 1942–1943 stay in Tunis, Tournier would realize that he had been mistaken (Tournier and Tournier 466–467).

Gide's Tunis *Journal:* The Historic and the Domestic

Gide arrived in Tunis on May 7, 1942. Though he wrote enthusiastically of the abundance of food, he complained of the noise and heat in letters to his friends Dorothy Bussy and Roger Martin du Gard. Gide soon left his uncomfortable hotel for a pleasant villa in nearby Sidi-Bou-Saïd, where he was the guest of the Reymond de Gentile family: architect Théo Reymond and his ophthalmologist wife, their twenty-year-old daughter Suzy, and fifteen-year-old son François. When Mme Reymond was diagnosed with a brain tumor in September 1942, her husband immediately accompanied her to Marseille for a life-saving operation. In November 1942, while Mme Reymond was convalescing, German forces invaded Tunisia and the formerly unoccupied south of France. Travel between France and North Africa became impossible, and the Reymonds were detained in France until Christmas 1944 (Derais 152). Gide would spend the six-month occupation of Tunis in the Reymonds' Tunis apartment with young François Reymond, the boy's grandmother Chacha de Gentile, and the family servant Jeanne.

Gide's diary from the six-month occupation of Tunis differs from the rest of the wartime *Journal* in that he made entries on a nearly daily basis and attempted to chronicle the progress of the war. In May 1940, Gide had vowed not to discuss current events in his diary, though this choice meant that his entries were only sporadic: "Through a sense of decency I am concerned in this notebook only with what has nothing to do with the war; and this is why I go for so many days without writing anything in it. Those are the days on which I have not been able to rid myself of the anguish, not been able to think of anything but *that*" (*Journals* 4: 18).[11] Three years later, as he looked back over his diary for the early months of 1943, Gide remarked that his most recent notebook "differs from the preceding ones, which I opened but intermittently and when the spirit moved. This last notebook became for me the buoy to which the shipwrecked man clings. There can be felt in it that daily effort to remain afloat" (*Journals* 4: 178).[12]

Daily writing was a way for the author to sustain his spirits. Yet what Gide most wanted to record in his diary—what he most needed to alleviate his anxiety—was information about the war's progress and the fate of his friends and family in France. This information was not forthcoming, however. Rumor and speculation about the North African campaign abounded, and the atmosphere was one of uncertainty. Moreover, communication with loved ones became impossible, since mail between France and Tunisia was suspended from the beginning of the Tunisian occupation until April 1943 (*Journals* 4: 197; *Journal II* 934). Despite his anxiety, Gide felt a certain excitement about being present for a crucial episode of the war:

> At times, but not always, I curse the beastly idea I had of coming here; then I think anxiously of those I left in France and shall perhaps not see again; I am worried by that increasing obscurity enveloping them, hiding them, stifling [us] . . . But at times also I congratulate myself on being at a point where a perhaps decisive contest is taking place or is about to take place . . . (*Journals* 4: 177)[13]

Though Gide appreciated the historical importance of his situation, his very presence in the occupied city meant that he had little access to meaningful news of the war. The lack of reliable information was a great source of anxiety for him: "I bend over the radio as often as six times a day with that childish illusion that my excessive attention is going somehow to hasten events," Gide wrote on January 16, 1943 (*Journals* 4: 157).[14] Though he sought news obsessively, Gide found newspapers and radio broadcasts so full of propaganda that he complained of an "atmosphere of organized falsehood" (*Journals* 4: 139).[15] Nevertheless, Gide made a point of recording what information he could obtain, even if it was scanty or specious. As Justin O'Brien has observed, the Tunis episode is the most journalistic portion of Gide's diary, yet Gide says little of substance about the events of the war: his account is "a marginal history of events recorded by an eyewitness whose vision was necessarily limited" (vii).

Lacking substantive information about events, Gide filled his notebook with a running account of his daily interactions with young François Reymond, whom he calls "Victor" in the *Journal*. According to Gide, Victor's "selfishness is manifest, resolute, cynical: he professes it" (*Journals* 4: 153).[16] The writer portrays the boy as dirty and lazy: his table manners are atrocious, and he "soil[s] the toilet seat with his dung" (*Journals* 4: 192).[17] Above all, Victor is insolent to his grandmother and to his elderly house guest: he "seems to have no other concern than to show his scorn flagrantly" (*Journals* 4: 167).[18] Gide's unsparing portrait clearly reflects the strain of sharing living quarters with near strangers under stressful wartime conditions. However, the portrait of Victor was never a wholly private matter: almost from the outset, it was charged with social symbolism.

Gide first sketched a portrait of François Reymond in a September 1942 letter to Roger Martin du Gard (Gide and Martin du Gard 269–270). His friend responded enthusiastically: "the portrait of François[19] is very well done! And it goes *far beyond* an individual case. It is one of the models . . . of the 'youth' whom all the world leaders are trying to seduce, displaying all the Machiavellisms of their propaganda."[20] Martin du Gard, who had previously encouraged Gide to devote more attention to his *Journal,* urged him to develop his portrait of the boy: "This fascinating and unpleasant specimen merits . . . a more thorough study in your *Journal*."[21] Martin du Gard's favorable reaction motivated Gide to resume writing in his diary: "your kind compliments have encouraged me and, spurred on by you, I have reopened my *Journal*."[22]

Though this exchange occurred in September and October 1942, Gide did not, in fact, write his first *Journal* entry on Victor until December 7—that is, one week after announcing the occupation of Tunis by German and Italian forces.[23] Appearing approximately once every three days from early December through the end of March, the twenty-five Victor entries are coextensive with the Tunisian occupation. This domestic chronicle is clearly a substitute for the military and political narrative to which Gide was denied access, for he made many of his Victor entries on days when power cuts, transparent propaganda, and conflicting reports left him with no war news to record.[24] Moreover, his anxiety about the war's progress and the lack of contact with friends in Europe is displaced onto and reinforced by his distress at François Reymond's hostile silence. The convergence of these two concerns is confirmed by the final Victor entry Gide made before leaving the Reymond household: "Yesterday Victor deigned to break his silence for a moment to announce to us the occupation of Gabès," Gide wrote on March 31 (*Journals* 4: 196).[25] As the boy sets aside some of his hostility to share news of an Allied victory, the domestic and historic conflicts intersect in a brief moment of détente. Thus the *Journal*'s Victor episode is closed by a momentary truce—an atypical respite that fails to resolve either the domestic or the military conflict, but that underscores their interdependence in Gide's diary.

Battles on the Home Front: The War *en abyme*

The fact that the *Journal*'s treatment of domestic conflict takes the place of a substantive historical account is an artifact of the war and of the information blackout it imposed. Yet Gide did not write about Victor *instead* of the war; rather, he wrote about the war *through* Victor. The semi-fictionalized portrait of François Reymond is Gide's attempt to comment on the causes of the war, albeit indirectly and on a small scale; it is also a reflection on the accounts of causality and influence propounded by Gide's attackers. Justin O'Brien addresses the symbolic dimension of this character sketch by describing Victor as "a portable microcosm of all that was distasteful in the world around [the author]" (vii). But Gide's portrait of Victor is far more than a social stereotype or a generalized symbol of what was wrong with the world: it is a harsh, precise allegory of pre-World War II France as the writer perceived it—an allegory in which the boy comes to represent "degenerate" interwar France.

The allegory begins with the name Gide chose for the boy. François Reymond is the only person in the Tunis diary whom Gide does not call by his real name or by the ubiquitous "X." Perhaps the name was suggested by the resemblances Gide perceived between the boy and Victor Strouvilhou, the leader of the counterfeiting band in his novel *Les Faux-Monnayeurs* (*Journals* 4: 153; *Jour-*

nal II 878). This is not the only source of the name, however. I would like to propose an alternate derivation based on history and etymology. By changing the boy's name from François [Frenchman] to Victor, Gide comments on France's decadence following World War I. The French were victors in the First World War, and according to Gide, they abused this status. Remarks to this effect abound in his *Journal* for the months after the fall of France: "We should not have won the other war. That false victory deceived us. We were not able to endure it. The relaxing that followed it brought us to our ruin"; "it would have been much better for . . . [France] had she been conquered in 1918 rather than to win that deceptive victory which put the finishing touches on her blindness and put her to sleep in decadence" (*Journals* 4: 23, 36).[26] Gide blamed France for its bad behavior when victorious: "We shall have to pay for all the absurdities of the intangible Versailles Treaty, the humiliations of those who were then the defeated, the useless vexations . . . the shameful abuse of victory," he wrote on June 24, 1940 (*Journals* 4: 25).[27] Gide portrays young François Reymond in a similar light: the boy dominates his parents, who always yield to him, and he lords it over his elderly guest: "In the absence of his parents, Victor knows that he is the master here" (*Journals* 4: 160).[28] When it comes to bad behavior, Gide depicts France and François in similar terms.

Like Victor, who was spoiled by his parents, the French people had been corrupted by excessive indulgence, in Gide's opinion. The connection between child rearing and the nation's welfare was surely present in Gide's mind as he penned his first Victor entries, for in December 1942 he was reading *Émile,* Rousseau's blueprint for educating children to be citizens (*Journals* 4: 143; *Journal II* 858). Gide began pondering this link before meeting François Reymond: "I have always thought that we raise children badly in France," he declared in April 1942, after watching a group of children ransack a public park as their parents sat idly by. What is significant about this *Journal* entry are the political conclusions Gide draws from his observations: "Is this a question of the French temperament? Or merely, as I should prefer, of upbringing? Nation unworthy of the liberty they claim" (*Journals* 4: 104–105).[29] The writer proposed rigorous discipline as the solution for both the child and the nation. Reflecting on his own attempts to correct Victor's behavior, Gide draws a political lesson from his reforming bent: "It is that constant . . . need . . . of correcting, of reforming, not only myself but others that often made me so unbearable . . . but that would make me, I think, so good a citizen of a real republic" (*Journals* 4: 195).[30] Thus, Gide uses his concerns about Victor's upbringing to promote the image of himself as a model citizen and educator—as the opposite, that is, of a *"mauvais maître"* [bad master].

The overindulgent parents were not solely to blame for Victor's behavior: according to the elderly Gide, the boy was also swayed by his classmate Lévy. On February 24, 1943, when Victor had refused to speak to him for a week, Gide wrote: "His behavior toward me, I could swear, is prompted by his friend Lévy *[le camarade Lévy],* who wanders about the apartment daily, or almost, without speaking to anyone, who is inculcating in him the principles of Marxism, confirming him in his egoism and providing solid foundations for his spontaneous caddishness" (*Journals* 4: 179).[31] If Victor stands for decadent interwar France, "comrade Lévy" represents the "corrupting" influence of Communists and Jews. Presenting Lévy as a deleterious influence brings Gide's domestic allegory very close to widespread right-wing explanations for France's decline and defeat.[32] I do not mean to suggest that Gide subscribed wholeheartedly to such explanations; rather, I propose to compare this model with the views Gide expressed elsewhere in order to elucidate the purpose of the *Journal*'s domestic allegory.

Though he deserted Communism in 1936, Gide did not vilify French Communists, nor did he blame them for France's defeat in 1940. However, the writer's own Communist sympathies were held against him by his post-armistice attackers. Indeed, the most significant aspect of Gide's domestic scenario may be precisely that it reproduces the phobic reaction of his accusers—while placing the blame elsewhere. Accused of inspiring French youth with a taste for excessive freedom and individualism, the author of *Les Nourritures terrestres* presents himself as a model disciplinarian; taxed with weakening the nation through his support of Communism, the "upper-middle-class would-be Bolshevik"[33] portrays himself as a victim shunned by hostile Marxists. In his role as Communist propagandist, Lévy clearly serves the allegory's exteriorizing function. The picture is somewhat more complex, however, if we read Lévy as a symbol of Jewish influence.

In his wartime diary, Gide does not blame his country's predicament on the Jews any more than on the Communists. On the contrary, Gide's *Journal* for the war years registers his compassion and his outrage at French and German treatment of Jews.[34] Yet the fact remains that, over the years, Gide made his share of unambiguously anti-Semitic pronouncements in his *Journal*. Many of these entries concern the influence of Jewish writers on French literature. "[T]here is today in France a Jewish literature that is not French literature," Gide states in his *Journal* entry of January 24, 1914, declaring that "the contribution of Jewish qualities to literature . . . is less likely to provide new elements . . . than it is to interrupt [*coupe[r] la parole à*] the slow explanation of a race and to falsify seriously, intolerably even, its meaning" (*Journals* 2: 4).[35] Thus, Gide's domestic drama stages the writer's long-standing fear that the Jewish influence would warp—and perhaps silence—France's "authentic" voice.

Though couched in literary terms, Gide's anti-Semitism was nevertheless political: the 1914 *Journal* entry addresses the issue in terms of race,[36] and portrays Jews as a threat to French culture. Moreover, Gide's literary remarks were later used for political ends: according to Jeffrey Mehlman, the 1914 *Journal* entry, "whose pretext, ironically, is the literary criticism of Gide's friend . . . Léon Blum, would regularly be trotted out by the French Right during the wave of anti-Semitism that greeted Blum and the Popular Front from 1936 through the Second World War. Gide, despite his embarrassment, was explicit in refusing to disavow it" (Mehlman 65).[37] A 1938 essay on Céline reflects Gide's uneasy awareness of the political ends that literary anti-Semitism could be made to serve. In "Les Juifs, Céline et Maritain," Gide disconcertingly assesses Céline's racist pamphlet *Bagatelles pour un massacre* as a literary joke.[38]

Nevertheless, he acknowledges the potentially dangerous interpretations of such a work: while many readers will derive the greatest amusement from Céline's text, which Gide interprets as a parody of anti-Semitism, "others may find unseemly a literary game which . . . risks leading to tragic consequences."[39] Although compassion dominates the wartime diary's reportage, the Victor allegory makes room for more ambivalent observations. With the introduction of Victor's Jewish mentor, Gide's domestic scenario becomes a site for reflecting on issues of literary and political influence.

Ultimately, what is being played out in Gide's domestic allegory is the writer's ambivalent relation to the ideologies of France's wartime regime. Though Gide is categorical in his criticism of Victor's lax parents and "corrupting" Jewish-Marxist friend, his own relation to notions of discipline and freedom, to Communism and to anti-Semitism was more nuanced, and the historical circumstances increased the political stakes of such positions. The familiar Gidean theme of discipline pervades the writer's wartime works, though the political message varies: in certain *Journal* passages, Gide suggests that German discipline and the rigors of occupation will be beneficial for France; in the "Interviews imaginaires," on the other hand, he presents discipline as an attribute of successful resistance.[40] Another Gidean constant, the humanitarian impulse, led to political repositionings in the 1930s and 40s. Humanitarian concerns led both to Gide's affiliation with Communism and to his disenchantment with the movement after observing the totalitarian abuses of Soviet Russia; sympathy for the plight of Jews led the writer to suspend his expressions of anti-Semitism in the *Journal* during the war years, though such observations would later resurface. Another major theme of Gidean thought and influence—and a major current in post-armistice attacks on the writer—was the question of homosexuality (and, more specifically, pederasty). This issue, significantly absent from Gide's domestic vignette, was reintroduced by François Reymond in his 1951 response to Gide's Tunis *Journal*.

Competing Stories: François Reymond's Response

Upon publication of Gide's *Journal 1942–1949* in 1950, Maria Van Rysselberghe reported that "young V., whom Gide discusses so painfully in the latest volume of the *Journal* . . . , is mad with rage and swears he will have his revenge."[41] François Reymond's "revenge" took the form of a book chronicling his side of the domestic battle. Reymond wrote his memoirs at the suggestion of Jean Amrouche, who had introduced Gide to the Reymond family, and to whom he had confided the reasons for his animosity toward Gide (Derais 145). Amrouche subsequently showed Reymond's manuscript to Gide, who took exception to a few specific points, but did not object to the substance of the text or to its publication (Derais 95, 260). Using the pseudonym François Derais,[42] Reymond published *L'Envers du Journal de Gide : Tunis 1942–43* in December 1951, several months after Gide's death.

In many respects, Reymond's unflattering portrayal of Gide is a point-by-point response to the writer's depiction of him as a boy. Many of the mutual criticisms relate to the privations of the war. Each man accuses the other of helping himself to the best of the household's meager food rations (*Journals* 4: 151,152; *Journal II* 876, 877; Derais 203), and each charges the other with hoarding food: Gide refers to the boy's "clandestine stock" *[provisions clandestines]* of chocolate (*Journals* 4: 155; *Journal II* 881), and Reymond claims Gide hid the provisions his friends brought him, indulging in "solitary daily banquets" *[festins quotidiens et . . . solitaires]* (Derais 199). Other criticisms convey the power struggle between Gide and Reymond: the man and the boy accuse each other of autocratic and inconsiderate behavior, and each refers to the other as "the master of the premises" *[maître de la place]* (*Journal II* 887; Derais 177).[43] Mutual accusations range from stinginess to bad table manners to monopolizing the affections of the family cat (*Journals* 4: 155–156, 157–158, 174; *Journal II* 881, 884, 904; Derais 174, 123, 180–182). In this game of tit for tat, Reymond's harsh and sometimes childish criticisms of the well-known author serve to highlight the pettiness of Gide's own observations about Victor in the *Journal*.

At the heart of Reymond's memoirs, however, lies an accusation which is anything but trivial: on July 25, 1942, Reymond claims, Gide sexually assaulted him. Young François, whom Gide describes as "terribly well-informed" *[terriblement averti]* (Gide and Martin du Gard 270), was aware that Gide, like many family friends, was homosexual. Though he had sometimes noticed "certain glances, certain innuendoes" from family friends which he "interpreted as discreet invitations,"[44] those acquaintances "had always behaved toward me with perfect decency," says Reymond.[45] Despite these previous advances and his knowledge of Gide's sexual orientation, Reymond initially considered the writer to be "a prestigious old man whose advanced age could only render him harmless in the field of carnal baseness."[46] François realized he had been mistaken when he repeatedly witnessed Gide's behavior with the gardener's ten-year-old son, Moktar. As the boy watered the flower beds, Reymond reminds the older man, "you stood behind him, . . . with your hand on his shoulder. . . . [Y]our hand . . . moved back and forth, sometimes kneading, sometimes pulling the child toward you abruptly, sometimes, on the contrary, relaxing so as merely to graze his nipples."[47] The boy, afraid to move, kept watering the same spot; when M. Reymond expressed his dissatisfaction with Moktar's work, the boy was relieved of his duties. Deprived of access to Moktar, Gide turned his attentions elsewhere (Derais 136). On July 25, 1942, Reymond recalls, "you found me reading, lying on the living room sofa, wearing only a short-sleeved shirt and very short shorts. . . . Under the totally phony pretext of taking an interest in what I was reading, do you remember what you did? We were almost alone then in the big house, and this time it involved more than just a shoulder."[48] Reymond writes of a second attempt a few days later, which he firmly rejected (Derais 141).[49] His fear of further advances, Reymond explains, was at the root of his hostility toward Gide: "I assiduously avoided your company"; "I was terribly frightened that you would renew your advances."[50] Feeling even more vulnerable after his parents' departure for Marseille, François bolted his bedroom door at night, avoided being alone with Gide during the day, and made himself generally disagreeable so that the elderly visitor would keep his distance (Derais 179, 202). "Little by little, I think, you came to understand that you could hope for nothing from me to satisfy your romantic whims. At that point, a treacherous spite took the place of your advances; I responded in kind, and a curious dialogue ensued," Reymond explains.[51]

The lexicon Reymond uses to describe his "curious dialogue" with Gide is that of war: he refers to their interactions as "hostilities" *[hostilités]* and "combats" *[combats],* as a "struggle" *[lutte]* and as "our battle" *[notre bataille];* he describes André Gide as "the adversary" *[l'adversaire]* and "the cunning enemy" *[l'ennemi habile]* (Derais 185; 178, 189, 205; 178, 181; 183; 205; 180). Through abundant and varied war imagery, Reymond constructs his struggle with Gide as a battle.[52] In so doing, he proposes an allegory that challenges Gide's own symbolic presentation of the domestic conflict. Reymond's memoirs recast the domestic battle as an allegory not of the interwar years but of the Occupation itself—an allegory in which his adolescent self represents the resistance, his grandmother Chacha stands for the Vichy government, and Gide, the aggressive house guest, assumes the role of the occupier. Because his aims differ from Gide's, Reymond reverses the relation of the historic and the domestic in his allegory. In his *Journal,* Gide uses the personal to understand the political, making his treatment of the domestic quarrel serve as commentary on France's social and political situation. Reymond, on the other hand, uses the historical conflict to make claims about the domestic situation, refuting Gide's portrayal of the quarrel by emphasizing the older man's role as aggressor.

In François Reymond's memoirs, Gide is portrayed not only as an attacker but as an occupier, a constant and threatening presence. Moreover, his friends are described as invaders: "your friends . . . had invaded us."[53] Gide followed his assault on François with expansionism, moving from the Reymonds' vacation home in Sidi-Bou-Saïd to their apartment on avenue Roustan in Tunis, though he had not been invited to do so (Derais 165). Young François saw Gide as an unwelcome interloper: "throughout your stay on the avenue Roustan, I never for an instant ceased to consider you an intruder and a parasite."[54] Accommodating this long-term uninvited house guest carried a financial burden like that of the Occupation: during his parents' absence, the household finances were precarious, Reymond says, and Gide contributed only "a paltry sum" *[une somme dérisoire]* (Derais 172-173). Though Gide claims to have shared household expenses with Chacha,[55] Reymond contends that his grandmother was living "entirely at my parents' expense, and you were too!"[56] If Gide represents the German occupier, François's grandmother Chacha personifies the Vichy government, an illegitimate authority that welcomed the intruder. Gide, who implies that he was Chacha's guest in Tunis, moved into the flat "knowing full well that Chacha had no right to make arrangements concerning the apartment."[57] Without the old woman's cooperation, Gide might not have installed himself so firmly in the family's territory, Reymond implies, adding: "I had difficulty forgiving my grandmother for betraying the family a little."[58]

Gide, of course, presents the situation quite differently: he justifies his presence in the Reymond apartment by portraying himself as Chacha's protector. Having heard of his plans to leave the Reymond apartment, Gide says, Chacha was "terrified at the idea of having to remain alone with her terrible grandson," and begged the writer to stay (*Journals* 4: 176).[59] If Gide should leave, Chacha threatened, both she and the family servant Jeanne would go as well, and the empty apartment would be occupied by the Germans (*Journals* 4: 176-177; *Journal II* 908). Gide's decision to remain therefore appears altruistic and patriotic. Reymond counters that the penniless Chacha had nowhere else to go, and points out that neither Jeanne nor Chacha left when Gide went into hiding in April 1943 (Derais 167, 171).[60] He suggests, moreover, that Gide might better have repaid the family's hospitality by staying in Sidi-Bou-Saïd: the villa there, which remained empty, was pillaged during the Tunisian occupation (Derais 170).

Despite the two men's opposing views on who was in the right, much of what Reymond suggests is implicit in Gide's diary. Gide's desire to discipline and improve Victor recalls the common notion that France would benefit from German discipline; his conception of himself as Chacha's protector also echoes justifications for the Occupation. Furthermore, Gide knew that the boy considered him an intruder, and realized that Chacha's cooperation irritated her grandson:

> In the absence of his parents, Victor knows that he is the master here. Is he trying to make me feel this? He is succeeding through his ungraciousness. I am becoming the intruder, and Chacha's constant attentions serve only to antagonize him the more. I doubt if I shall be able to put up much longer with his naggings. But where to go? (*Journals* 4: 160)[61]

Indeed, young François's actions were both a protest against Gide's presence and an attempt to drive him out of the Reymond home.

Implicitly relating this mission to the historical situation, Reymond describes his silence and ill-mannered conduct as *"résistance"* (Derais 253).[62] This construction is supported by Reymond's actual involvement in wartime resistance activities. Reymond's friend Lévy—the classmate whose influence Gide so deplored—introduced him to the Jeunesses communistes de Tunisie, which he joined in the spring of 1942 (Derais 215). Joining the Communist youth group represented a significant change in the boy's allegiances:

> I belonged to the Vichy youth movement "Les Compagnons de France," but I was persuaded to abandon those ideas and join the opposition to the regime then in power; a taste for danger, the appeal of the unknown, and also, whatever you may think, the noble ideas of social justice presented to me persuaded me to make this total about-face.[63]

François's resistance activities consisted mainly of drawing graffiti featuring the Communist hammer and sickle and the Gaullist Lorraine cross (Derais 219), as well as posting bills emblazoned with "incisive slogans about the occupiers and their henchmen."[64] François and his fellow group members also distributed the clandestine newspaper *L'Avenir Social* (Derais 219-220), and they tried to pro-

cure French identity cards for people with Jewish names and those sought by
the police (Derais 220). Reymond downplays the risk inherent in these activities, suggesting that he viewed the whole business as an exciting game. He
admits that he confined most of his exploits to his own home, stealing an identity card which family friends would willingly have given him (Derais 220)[65] and
drawing graffiti only in the stairwell of his own building (Derais 220, 219).

In Reymond's account, there is little difference between official resistance
activities and his boyish program of domestic "resistance." The most dramatic
aspect of his home-front maneuvers was his extensive program of household
espionage. After stating that his family was "separated into two camps" [séparée
en deux camps] and that he used to "spy on the enemy" [espionner l'adversaire]
(Derais 156), Reymond uses the lexicon of a military strategist to portray his
forays into Gide's territory. He used to go into Gide's room in the writer's
absence, Reymond admits, "in order to read your Journal in secret, and thus
obtain some information about the enemy's morale."[66] Reymond makes it clear
that his spying was of a specifically literary nature: denying the accusation that
he broke the lock of Gide's trunk (Journals 4: 192; Journal II 927), he states that:
"The only thing which interested me was your Journal, and you left that in plain
sight on your desk."[67] In addition to reading the diary, the boy actually took
notes, which he quotes in L'Envers du Journal (Derais 201-203). Using his clandestine familiarity with the manuscript diary and quoting from Gide's Journal
1942–1949, Reymond questions the author's sincerity: "you modify your diary
a bit after the fact, as I was able to ascertain by comparing the published Journal
with my memory of the passages I read furtively" during the war.[68] Claiming
that certain passages concerning himself were added after the fact and that others were deleted, Reymond asserts that the objectivity of the original diary was
marred by Gide's desire to confirm his views on Victor's character (Derais 184-
185).[69] François Reymond's clandestine reading of the Journal manuscript served
a dual function: at the time, it provided information on the "enemy"; some years
later, it provided the ammunition to attack the Journal's veracity. Ultimately,
Reymond's familiarity with the text helped to redress the power imbalance
between himself and André Gide.

The Power Of Literature:
Gide's Oeuvre and the Domestic Drama

Gide's stature as a writer was a source of power, and his fame helped him gain
access to young sexual partners. "I have no doubt that your fame and your
advanced age have accustomed you to greater docility in the young subjects which
chance delivers into your hands," writes François Reymond.[70] Reymond goes
further, declaring that Gide abused his position of power: "that you vilely deceived
my parents, abused my trust in your prestige as an old man 'wreathed in glory,' did
you even think of that . . . ?"[71] There was always an inherent power imbalance
between Gide and his young sexual partners: in addition to the difference in age,
there were often differences of race, class, and nationality, as well as economic and

educational discrepancies. Pierre Herbart attributes Gide's choice of partners to a fear of rejection: "his choice of little partners (children of the lower classes, those who do not speak his language, Blacks) with whom only a physical exchange is possible reduces the potential for disappointment."[72] Another important reason for this choice was that Gide invariably had the last word in describing—or conceal-ing—such encounters. Unlike those uneducated and non-French-speaking chil-dren, however, François Reymond was able to talk back to Gide.

At age twenty-four, this highly literate son of a bourgeois family had the power and education to respond to Gide's sexual abuse and to the harsh depic-tion of himself in the *Journal*. Ironically, one source of Reymond's ability to respond was Gide's own influence. In the afterword to *L'Envers du Journal*, Rey-mond acknowledges his intellectual debt to Gide: "Throughout the process of writing these memoirs, I have been constantly aware of everything that my thoughts and reactions owe to you, as much to yourself as to your oeuvre. Why deny it? Those whom I respected in my youth, those to whom I owe some part of my present intellectual character, were your disciples."[73] Throughout *L'En-vers du Journal,* power issues are played out around Gide's oeuvre. In fact, Rey-mond's memoirs, Gide's Tunis *Journal*—and, to a certain extent, the quarrel which those texts recount—are interwoven with Gide's fictional and autobio-graphical writings.

Upon learning that Gide would be staying with his family, says Reymond, "my first step was to carry into my room two or three of your books, . . . which I began to read or reread, in order (I originally hoped) to take full advantage of your presence."[74] One lesson the boy had clearly learned from his reading con-cerned Gide's predilection for young boys; indeed, he interpreted a family friend's allusions to Gide's works as a come-on: "Eugène K. . . . had asked me, with a curious insistence in his voice and his eyes, if I had read Gide's books, what I thought of them, etc."[75] François's knowledge gave him a degree of power over Gide, who wrote that the boy "had stayed up alone one evening, manifestly waiting for my return, after having read *Si le grain ne meurt,* but any desire to fondle him quickly gave way to a desire to box his ears once I heard his insolent remarks."[76] One pictures the teenager smirking as he let the writer know he had read the autobiographical *Si le grain ne meurt,* in which Gide recounts his first pederastic experiences during his travels in North Africa some fifty years before.

In his memoirs, as in his interactions with the author, Reymond uses Gide's writings against him. Because *L'Envers du Journal* is explicitly intended as a rebuttal to Gide's diary, Reymond includes numerous quotes from the *Journal 1942–1949,* as well as many references to it in footnotes. Furthermore, Rey-mond makes potent use of quotations from Gide's fictional oeuvre. Reymond first uses his own words to describe his reaction to Gide's assault: "Ah, you never knew how I rushed into the bathroom, soaped up, scrubbed myself with a scrub brush so hard that I bled, washing so feverishly that I repeatedly banged into the faucet and the bathtub walls."[77] He follows this explanation with a hauntingly similar quotation from Gide's *récit La Porte étroite,* in which the young Jérôme reacts violently to his aunt's unwanted caresses:

"she drew my face down to hers, passed her bare arm around my neck, put her hand into my shirt, asked me laughingly if I was ticklish—went on— further. . . . I rushed away to the other end of the kitchen-garden, and there I dipped my handkerchief into a little tank, put it to my forehead— washed, scrubbed—my cheeks, my neck, every part of me the woman had touched."[78]

One couldn't put it better, Jérôme . . . except that you were not a pretty young aunt . . . .[79]

By reading Gide's actions through his oeuvre, Reymond appropriates some of the writer's power and authority.

Gide's power as a writer was indeed considerable. As Martine Sagaert has argued, the author-protagonist of the Tunis *Journal* resembles the novelist Édouard in *Les Faux-Monnayeurs,* transforming himself and those around him into literary characters (Sagaert, "Introduction" xxii). Sagaert supports this asser- tion by demonstrating the similarities between Gide's portrait of Victor and the piggish Gnathon in La Bruyère's *Caractères* (xxiii): like Gnathon, Victor occupies more than his share of space at table, serves himself first, eats with his fingers, and picks his teeth (*Journals* 4: 157–158; *Journal II* 884; La Bruyère 329). The Tunis *Journal*'s most important intertexts, however, are drawn from Gide's own oeuvre. Afraid of the frequent bombings, François's grandmother Chacha spends every night in a tiny cloakroom. Gide compares her to Mélanie Bastian, the sequestered woman of Poitiers, who begged to return to the room where her family had kept her hidden for twenty-five years: "[Chacha] speaks of 'her little storeroom' where she takes refuge as the sequestered girl in Poitiers used to speak of her 'dear big black Malampia,'" Gide states (*Journals* 4: 155).[80] Though the comparison with the sequestered madwoman is hardly flattering, Gide is merely pointing out sim- ilarities between Chacha and Bastian—another real-life woman he described in a nonfictional text. Chacha's grandson, on the other hand, becomes fodder for Gide's fictionalizing enterprise. In an October 1942 letter to Roger Martin du Gard, Gide acknowledges that a more fully developed portrait of François would be, in part, a work of fiction: "nothing is more banal or easier to invent than the characteristics of selfish cynicism."[81] Referring to this cynical selfishness in the *Journal,* Gide explicitly considers the boy a potential source of fictional material: "Had I known him earlier, I should have enriched with his features the Strouvil- hou of my *Faux-Monnayeurs*," he declares (*Journals* 4: 153).[82] What Gide does not acknowledge is the extent to which Strouvilhou's traits and those of other fic- tional characters color his portrait of Victor, and the extent to which his literary agenda deforms his depiction of the boy.

In *L'Envers du Journal,* François Reymond exposes Gide's fictionalizing proj- ect and rewrites the Tunis episode from his own perspective: "For the first time perhaps, one of your characters, part real and part invented, has spoken up in response and told his story himself."[83] One of the elements Reymond attempts to debunk is Gide's lyrical description of a brief liaison with fifteen-year-old "F.": "This past June in Tunis, I experienced two nights of pleasure such as I thought never to encounter again at my age," Gide wrote on August 3, 1942.[84]

Gide stresses his young lover's gratitude—"[h]is entire being sang out: 'thank you'" [85]—and declares that the age difference was no impediment: "He seemed to care so little about my age that I came to forget it myself."[86] "Ah, I know of another boy who *did* care about [your age]," Reymond retorts in *L'Envers du Journal*.[87] Reymond believes that the adventure with "F." is a fabrication, and suggests that the episode is a displaced version of Gide's unsuccessful attempts to seduce him:[88] "By an unfortunate coincidence, his initial is also the initial of my first name; but is that even a coincidence?"[89] François's initial comes to designate a willing young lover, and François himself is rebaptized "Victor"—a name that links him to a despicable fictional character and makes him a symbol of a corrupt and tainted nation.[90]

Gide's fictionalization of Victor is a bid for control and an attempt to deny the real reasons for the boy's hostility. Despite his indignation, François Reymond deems the portrait a form of self-deception, not a cruel and conscious bid for revenge: "half-guessing the reasons for my attitude, you pushed those reasons aside, trying to deceive yourself."[91] Throughout the Tunis *Journal,* Gide tries to explain the boy's hostility away: "For my obnoxious attitude, for the fact that I was insolent, selfish, and deceptive toward you, you give a variety of rather fanciful explanations," writes Reymond.[92] Most of these explanations are determinist in nature. Rather than admit that the boy's rebuffs might be a form of protest, Gide dismisses his surliness as an inherent characteristic: "I convince myself that this is merely a result of his natural caddishness" (*Journals* 4: 167).[93] He even suggests that the boy's behavior is hereditary: when a neighbor mentions that he has never received a smile or greeting from Théo Reymond, Gide muses, "How can Victor, who so closely resembles his father, endure being to such a degree the prisoner of his heredity? In his stubborn silence toward me there is perhaps less resolve than surrender to his natural inclination" (*Journals* 4: 199).[94] Contemplating the boy's physical development as well as his character, Gide repeatedly states that the boy is prepubescent.[95] Though the *Journal* does not mention Gide's sexual advances or François's rejection, Reymond's memoirs make the connection explicit: "If I don't want to have sex with you, it's not, of course, because the idea doesn't appeal to me, but because I am prepubescent!"[96] Unwilling to face the true source of the boy's animosity, Gide generates alternative explanations; moreover, he deflects attention by making the household quarrel symbolize France's political troubles.

Ultimately, Gide's domestic allegory is motivated by two parallel concerns: to explain François's hostility in ways that do not implicate himself, and to propose a model for France's downfall in which his literary influence plays no part. By making the home-front battle represent the historic conflict, Gide attempts to parry both domestic aggravations and political accusations.

Hiding, Deliverance, and the Purge

The domestic battle between Gide and François Reymond ended abruptly in April 1943, when Gide left the Reymond home under dramatic circumstances.

During a raid on the home of his friends the Boutelleaus, Gide's *Journal* manuscript—which he had entrusted to Hope Boutelleau for typing—was seized by the Italian police and promptly handed over to the German authorities.[97] When the Gestapo found references to resistance activities in Gérard Boutelleau's diary, they had him deported to the Sachsenhausen-Oranienburg concentration camp (Heller and Grand 87).[98] The authorities also expressed displeasure with certain passages of Gide's *Journal* that were hostile to Germany.[99] Though it seemed unlikely that the Germans considered Gide a public enemy, the writer nevertheless feared arrest: "That my own person is sought by the German authorities is not thoroughly proved. Arrested as a suspect? Suspected of what? No, but perhaps a lawful prize as a witness likely to talk and whom they prefer not leaving to the English." The prospect of being used as a mouthpiece precipitated Gide's decision to go underground on April 13, 1943: "Even though I find it hard to convince myself that . . . my person or my voice could be of any importance, it was better not to run the risk of a forced voyage and sojourn in Germany or Italy" (*Journals* 4: 204).[100]

Gide took refuge in the apartment of Odette Duché (sister-in-law of his friend Marcel Flory), who was already concealing a M. and Mme Bigiaoui (Sagaert, "Notes" 1462). Sought by the Germans, Gide's "companions in captivity" *[compagnons de captivité]* had been in hiding for nearly six months (*Journals* 4: 204; *Journal II* 943). Gide decided to let his beard grow for the duration: "I am letting my white beard grow; I am waiting for the liberation before shaving again" (*Journals* 4: 206).[101] Living conditions were difficult: "We are living here without electricity and consequently without any news from the radio; often without water, almost without alcohol or gas or oil, on our almost exhausted remaining supplies, barely kept alive by meals that become less adequate every day" (*Journals* 4: 205).[102] Mme Duché's clandestine guests had strict orders to remain indoors and to stay away from the balcony and windows for fear of detection (*Journals* 4: 204; *Journal II* 943). Nevertheless, Gide does not appear to have taken the risk to himself very seriously: disguised as a Sicilian fisherman, he went for a walk through the neighborhood on May 1, 1943 (*Journals* 4: 208; *Journal II* 949; Sagaert, "Notes" 1462). Gide did not enjoy his stroll, however, and returned to his hiding place after half an hour: "No pleasure; pleased to return to my grotto" (*Journals* 4: 208).[103] Hirsute, undernourished, and preferring confinement, Gide himself resembles the *"Séquestrée de Poitiers"* by the end of the siege.[104]

On May 8, 1943, the day after Allied troops entered Tunis, Gide and his companions came out of their hiding place into "the wildly rejoicing city" *[la ville en délire]* (*Journals* 4: 210; *Journal II* 951). Shortly thereafter, the Beirut newspaper *La Syrie et l'Orient* published Gide's *Journal* entries chronicling the event under the title "La délivrance de Tunis." This article, comprising entries from May 7 to 14, marks the convergence of history and personal experience: as Martine Sagaert has observed, the closed world of Gide's domestic drama "opens onto a scene of deliverance, when the private and the public celebrate the same liberation."[105] After six months in the dark, Gide was finally witness to a narratable moment: he could at last piece together the story of the North African campaign, and could relate his experience of the siege to the progress of the war as a whole.[106] Gide refers to his time spent in hiding in a way that manages to be both suggestive and bravely matter-of-fact. He portrays the general euphoria and ringing cries of *"Vive la France!"* (*Journals* 4: 210; *Journal II* 952), and goes on to predict the successful conclusion of the war: "all the conquered peoples now under the German yoke will derive from this great setback to the oppressor an extraordinary encouragement to resistance. It is possible to hear in it the announcement of a general collapse" (*Journals* 4: 213).[107] He concludes with praise for the Anglo-American forces, approving of their delay in liberating Tunis—a delay he had bitterly criticized throughout the siege (*Journals* 4: 214; *Journal II* 956).

"La délivrance de Tunis" marks an important moment in the evolution of Gide's perceptions of the war. Its publication history is also of significant interest. After Gide authorized its publication in *La Syrie et l'Orient*, "La délivrance" became a popular set piece, appearing six more times between 1943 and 1944.[108] Gide was acutely aware of the irony of this success: "I have written nothing flatter; and no text of mine has ever encountered such a reception; all that remains is to serve it up in the high school anthologies!"[109] After its publication in Beirut, the article was translated into English and published in America—"with a great deal of absurd praise" *[avec force éloges absurdes]*, according to Gide (Gide and Bussy 603). The piece was then translated back into French and published without the author's knowledge or permission in the Buenos Aires weekly *La France nouvelle* and the Algiers paper *Combat*. This twice-translated article contained "atrocious mistranslations" *[d'énormes contresens]* (Gide and Bussy 603). One error was beneficial to Gide's image as a survivor of wartime hardships: whereas Gide's text briefly evokes time spent in hiding, the doubly translated version leads readers to believe Gide had been in hiding for a full six months, instead of a few weeks.[110] The original French text of "La délivrance" later appeared in a volume published by the formerly clandestine press Minuit, and was reprinted—again without Gide's knowledge or permission—on the front page of *Les Lettres françaises* in November 1944. The publication saga of "La délivrance de Tunis" exemplifies the ways in which André Gide, as a prominent intellectual, was co-opted to serve strikingly different political agendas during the Second World War. Both collaborationist editors (such as Alfred Fabre-Luce) and resistance publications (such as *La France nouvelle* and *Combat*) tried to claim the author for their cause. Even when André Gide the writer remained silent or withheld permission to publish his work, André Gide the cultural property was pressed into service.[111]

Blamed for France's defeat at the start of the war, Gide suffered during the post-Liberation purge as well. Upon moving to Algiers after the liberation of Tunis, Gide helped to found the literary journal *L'Arche*, which serialized his 1939–1942 *Journal* during the spring and summer of 1944. Scandalized by these "Pages de Journal" from the early years of the war, Communist Deputy Arthur Giovoni attacked Gide in the Provisional Consultative Assembly, demanding that the "unpatriotic" author be punished for treason: "Today literature is a weapon. That is why I demand prison for André Gide and public prosecution of the managing editor of *L'Arche*" (*Journals* 4: 309).[112] Like Giovoni, many of those who denounced Gide during the purge were Communists who came to power as members of the Resistance. The most celebrated of these was the poet Louis

Aragon, who was unable to forgive Gide for his 1936 rejection of Communism. Aragon's attack was sparked by the November 1944 publication of "La délivrance de Tunis" on the front page of *Les Lettres françaises,* the newspaper of the largely Communist Comité National des Écrivains. Aragon objected vehemently to the publication of Gide's piece by the formerly clandestine paper, and accused the editors of trying to engineer Gide's triumphant return (Aragon 1). Quoting several controversial passages from Gide's 1940 *Journal,* Aragon described Gide as "a major weapon in the hands of enemy propaganda."[113]

Though they decried Aragon's attack, Gide's friends considered the publication of "La délivrance" in *Les Lettres françaises* imprudent: "what on earth were you doing with that enemy outfit?" asked Roger Martin du Gard.[114] Gide explained that when he joined the Comité National des Écrivains, he assumed that *Les Lettres* would publish only a brief note announcing his membership (Gide and Bussy 602).[115] Upon learning that Gide had not authorized the article's publication, Roger Martin du Gard began to suspect that the entire business was "a set-up from start to finish" *[un coup monté de fond en comble]* (Gide and Martin du Gard 295); Jean Schlumberger, too, speculated that the article had been published only as a pretext for Aragon's attack (Gide and Schlumberger 964). Despite their indignation, most of Gide's friends counseled him not to reply to Aragon's vituperations. Gide refrained from responding directly to his attackers, but lamented the oppressive atmosphere of the purge. On November 25, 1944, he wrote to Roger Martin du Gard: "All freedom of opinion is compromised for a long time to come, and we are struggling and protesting against Nazi totalitarianism by becoming 'totalitarian' ourselves, in our own fashion. Whoever does not conform is suspect."[116]

In this atmosphere of threats and recriminations, Gide took certain measures to avoid further attacks. Following Giovoni's attack in the Assembly, he radically edited the volume containing his 1939-1942 *Journal* entries: "My *Pages de Journal* came out yesterday in Algiers," he wrote to Martin du Gard in October 1944, "a thin, diminished little volume, for violent Communist attacks prompted me to omit all of the pages which might fuel their accusations."[117] Gide claimed that it was a concern for decency and national unity—not fear—which prompted the changes (Gide and Martin du Gard 321, Gide and Bussy 284). Nevertheless, concerns about his personal safety significantly delayed Gide's return to France. In a letter dated January 4, 1945, General de Gaulle's secretary Claude Mauriac (son of novelist François Mauriac) declared: "in spite of the great desire I have of seeing you again, I do not advise your immediate return: passions are at their height . . ." (*Conversations with André Gide* 220).[118] Because of his vulnerable situation, Gide did not, in fact, return to Paris until May 1945, just days before Germany's capitulation.

Conclusion

Gide and his friends heard de Gaulle's proclamation of victory together, but he makes no mention of this "solemn and staggering moment" *[instant grave et bouleversant]* (Van Rysselberghe III: 354) in his diary.[119] In effect, the 1943 liberation of Tunis marks the end of the war as far as Gide's *Journal* is concerned.[120] As Martine Sagaert has remarked, the one-year Tunis interval is a cohesive unit, framed by the arrival and departure of the diarist ("Introduction" xxiv). Furthermore, the six-month occupation of the city allowed Gide to document the war in miniature. When France fell to the Germans in 1940, Gide had resolved to avoid all mention of the war in his diary (*Journals* 4: 18; *Journal II* 695). Observations on the war crept into the *Journal,* however, and by the end of 1940 some of those reflections had appeared in *La Nouvelle Revue Française.* By the time he arrived in Tunisia in 1942, Gide had revised his early opinions, and may have wished to begin anew. When the occupation of Tunis thrust him into the center of a decisive conflict, Gide seized the chance to tell his war story from the beginning—a chance he had missed in 1940.

This enterprise was hindered, however, by a lack of hard facts to record. Consequently, Gide presented the historical conflict symbolically, through the domestic allegory he constructed around François Reymond. This blending of the domestic and the historic, which arose from necessity, was also a way for Gide to rethink the divisions between private and public, between the personal and the political. Indeed, much of Gide's trouble during World War II and its aftermath arose when he—or his critics—blurred or transgressed those boundaries. Post-armistice attackers attributed political consequences to Gide's sexuality and to his literary oeuvre. Later critics focused on published excerpts from the wartime *Journal*—passages characterized by the sincerity of a personal diary, but arousing the political consequences of any text published in a time of national emergency. In the aftermath of the Liberation, many blamed Gide for remaining "above the fray," for not taking a more public and active stand against Germany and Vichy. In his writings concerning the 1942–1943 Tunis interlude, Gide creatively unsettles the boundaries between what is inherently private and what can legitimately enter the political realm, shuffling these categories to his advantage.

Gide's year in Tunis was a time of enforced passivity. Cut off from metropolitan France, physically confined during the final month of the siege, Gide had few outlets for political involvement. He therefore used his private life as a vehicle for political commentary, constructing a domestic allegory to illustrate France's problems as he understood them. This narrative is full of gaps and silences, however: it is informed by the historical conflict Gide was unable to narrate, and by the sexual violence he refused to represent.[121] In many respects, Gide's construction is a work of self-defense. Because it displaces the domestic conflict onto a historical struggle, the allegory excuses Gide from acknowledging the source of François Reymond's hostility. Because it constructs an alternative explanation for France's downfall, this scenario is an indirect response to those who blamed the writer for the nation's defeat.

Publication of Gide's private wartime experiences became a source of conflict. In the final months of the war, Maria Van Rysselberghe deemed publication of the Tunis *Journal* imprudent: "In a time still tortured with misery and catastrophe, this personal diary runs the risk of exasperating the reader," Van

Rysselberghe declared in March 1945.[122] Roger Martin du Gard had a similar reaction to the 1944 publication of "La délivrance de Tunis." Martin du Gard was struck by the discrepancy between Gide's wartime experience and that of other Frenchmen: "It is so awkward, at a time when all the 'heroes' are recounting their odysseys, and when so many of Gide's colleagues and readers have 'heroic' recollections, to publish this text on current events, this 'war diary' which can only serve to highlight the difference between Gide's wartime sufferings and those of the majority of the French people!"[123] Martin du Gard's view contrasts sharply with that of Gide's friend Jean Amrouche, who cited Gide's private hardships in the writer's defense. Amrouche stressed the similarities between Gide's experience and that of his fellow citizens in occupied France: "He submitted to the harsh discipline experienced by everyone in occupied Europe who lived outside of German laws."[124] Though Gide himself avoided such sensational language, he did emphasize the difficult conditions he experienced in hiding in a December 1944 letter to Dorothy Bussy, Jean Schlumberger, and Roger Martin du Gard. Defending his original decision to publish "La délivrance," Gide explained that he had assembled the *Journal* entries "for lack of anything better, and unable to write anything new 'ad hoc,'" adding that he was "extremely depressed by a month of confinement with barely sufficient food . . . forbidden not only to go out, but even to look out the window because of the people in the house opposite."[125] In addition to describing the hardships he had endured, Gide took this opportunity to point out that he survived the final month of the occupation thanks to "the extreme devotion of the Communist friends who housed me and brought me my daily rations."[126] At a moment when he was under attack by Communist writers and politicians, stressing this affiliation seemed crucial.[127] Thus, Gide used an account of domestic adversity to respond to political attacks.

For André Gide, the personal, the political, and the literary intersected in particularly explosive ways during the Second World War. Reflecting on this convergence and parrying his critics, Gide offers his own fusion of these elements in the Tunis *Journal,* in which he blends the historic and the domestic to figure the war *en abyme.*

Notes

1. Justifying the armistice in his radio broadcast of June 25, 1940, Marshal Pétain urged his countrymen to work toward "un redressement intellectuel et moral" (Pétain 454).
2. "On ne peut nier l'influence exercée sur la littérature contemporaine et sur l'esprit de la jeunesse par les ouvrages d'André Gide. C'est contre cette influence considérable, mais néfaste, qu'il faut aujourd'hui réagir. L'auteur séduisant de *l'Immoraliste* et du *Traité de Narcisse [sic]* a fait une fâcheuse école. Il a formé une génération orgueilleuse et déliquescente; il l'a élevée, sous prétexte de sincérité, dans la perversion du sens moral ("La Jeunesse" 1).

   Gide was accused of exerting a pernicious influence through his actions, as well as through his writings. Marshal Pétain's personal secretary, René Gillouin, claimed to have received a letter from a man whose son, "a young man of great promise, had been perverted, degraded, and finally pushed to suicide because of the influence of André Gide" [un jeune homme de grande espérance, avait été perverti, dégradé, et finalement amené au suicide par l'influence d'André Gide] (Gillouin 3). Gide's friend Roger Martin du Gard advised the writer not to respond to this accusation, for Gillouin was suggesting that the young man killed himself "not merely after having read my books, but even under my direct influence; that frequenting me perverted him, and even that I directly 'depraved' him" [non point après lecture seule de mes livres, mais bien sous mon influence directe; que c'est ma fréquentation qui l'aurait perverti, et même que je l'aurais directement « dépravé »] (*Journals* 4: 102; *Journal II* 804). Gide dismissed Gillouin's story as "pure (or impure) invention" [pure (ou impure) invention] and pointed out that his influence had saved many people from suicidal desperation (*Journals* 4: 102; *Journal II* 804). Gide argued, moreover, that sexual orientation was innate, and could not be attributed to literary or personal influences. In his 1924 treatise *Corydon,* he addressed a widespread perception that he considered erroneous: "if, despite advice, invitations, provocations of all kinds, he [the adolescent] manifests a homosexual inclination, you immediately blame certain readings, certain influences; . . . it is an acquired taste, you assert; he was taught it, to be sure; you will not admit that he could have invented it all by himself" [si, malgré conseils, invitations, provocations de toutes sortes, c'est un penchant homosexuelle qu'il [l'adolescent] manifeste, aussitôt vous incriminez telle lecture, telle influence; . . . c'est un goût acquis, affirmez-vous; on le lui a appris, c'est sûr; vous n'admettez pas qu'il ait pu l'inventer tout seul] (39).

3. "[L]'intoxication de la jeunesse par le doute" (Mauclair 7).

4. "Rien de mieux contre le « nazisme »" (*Journal II* 716). This anti-Nazi *Journal* entry was first published in the volume *Pages de Journal,* which appeared in 1944 in New York and Algiers. Gide echoed his exhortation to develop his countrymen's critical faculties in his October 1940 response to *Le Figaro*'s survey on the future of literature: "Let us hope . . . that battered France may never relinquish its principal quality: criticism. I am speaking of criticism not as a 'genre' but as a very rare quality, the quality most indispensable to all real culture, a domain in which France has no equal. . . . It . . . is criticism which, in our time, is the most endangered faculty; consequently, we must cherish our critical qualities and virtues" [Souhaitons . . . que la France meurtrie ne se dessaisisse jamais de sa qualité maîtresse : la critique. Je parle de la critique non point comme d'un « genre », mais comme d'une qualité très rare, la plus indispensable pour toute réelle culture, où la France se montre incomparable. . . . C'est . . . la critique, de nos jours, qui se trouve le plus en danger et, partant, c'est à nos qualités et vertus critiques qu'il importe de s'attacher] (Chauvet 3).

5. Under the Occupation, the direction of the influential literary journal Gide had helped found in 1909 was handed over to the Fascist writer Drieu La Rochelle. Though excerpts from Gide's 1939–1940 diary appeared in the December 1940 and February 1941 issues of *La Nouvelle Revue Française,* Gide soon had second thoughts. Citing the pro-German sentiments of *NRF* contributor Jacques Chardonne, he made a showy withdrawal from the journal in April 1941.

6. "Mollesse, abandon, relâchement dans la grâce et l'aisance, autant d'aimables qualités qui devaient nous conduire, les yeux bandés, à la défaite" ("Feuillets" 82).

7. "Il me paraît aussi absurde d'incriminer notre littérature au sujet de notre défaite, qu'il l'eût été de la féliciter en 1918, lorsque nous avions la victoire" (Chauvet 3).

8. "[L]es lettres françaises avaient leur part d'honneur et de responsabilité dans la création du monde où nous entrons" (Fabre-Luce ii).

9. "Ici . . . je ne me sens plus en sûreté" (Tournier and Tournier 466).

10. "« Vous me promettez qu'au moins il sera sage! »" (Tournier and Tournier 466).

11. "Par pudeur je ne m'occupe, dans ce carnet, que de ce qui n'a pas trait à la guerre;

et c'est pourquoi, durant tant de jours, je reste sans y rien écrire. Ce sont les jours où je n'ai pu me délivrer de l'angoisse, pu penser à rien qu'à *cela*" (*Journal II* 695).

12. "[C]e dernier carnet diffère des précédents, que je n'ouvrais que par intermittences et lorsque l'esprit m'y poussait. Ce dernier carnet devenait pour moi la bouée où le naufragé se raccroche. L'on y sent cet effort quotidien pour se maintenir à flot" (*Journal II* 909). Gide made a similar observation on February 7, 1943, when he was hard at work on the preface to his *Anthologie de la poésie française:* "I greatly need this semblance of activity to bind me to life, and this is likewise why I cling to this *Journal*" [j'ai grand besoin de ce semblant d'activité pour me rattacher à la vie; et c'est aussi pourquoi je me cramponne à ce *Journal*] (*Journals* 4: 169; *Journal II* 898).

13. "Parfois, mais pas toujours, je maudis la fichue idée que j'ai eue de venir ici; je songe alors avec angoisse à ceux que j'ai laissés en France et que je ne retrouverai peut-être pas; je m'inquiète de cette obscurité grandissante qui les enveloppe, qui les cache, qui nous étouffe . . . Mais parfois aussi je me félicite de me trouver en un point où se joue, ou va se jouer, une partie peut-être décisive . . ." (*Journal II* 908; ellipsis Gide's).

14. "Je me penche jusqu'à six fois par jour sur la radio, avec cette enfantine illusion que l'excès de mon attention va pouvoir faire avancer les événements" (*Journal II* 883). The *Journal* entry for April 10, 1943 echoes that of January 16: "On our radio set, now repaired, I anxiously listen to the news, hear it again in German, in English, in Italian, on the alert for a bit of information not given in the other language, and as if my attention could hasten the future" [Sur notre poste de radio réparé, j'écoute anxieusement les nouvelles; les réentends en allemand, en anglais, en italien, guettant un renseignement que n'aurait pas donné l'autre langue, et comme si mon attention pouvait faire avancer le futur] (*Journals* 4: 200; *Journal II* 938).

15. "Cette atmosphère de mensonge organisé" (*Journal II* 853).

16. "[S]on égoïsme est déclaré, résolu, cynique; il en fait profession" (*Journal II* 877).

17. "Victor continue à empoisser de sa fiente le siège des cabinets" (*Journal II* 927).

18. "[Il] semble n'avoir d'autre souci que de rendre flagrant son mépris" (*Journal II* 896).

19. Gide refers to the boy as "François" in his correspondence with Martin du Gard and in the *Journal* manuscript. Published versions of the diary—beginning with *Journal* excerpts published in *L'Arche* in 1946 (Derais 129)—have the pseudonym "Victor."

20. "Dites donc, il est très réussi le portrait du François! Et ça va *beaucoup plus loin* qu'un cas individuel. C'est un des types . . . de cette « jeunesse » devant laquelle tous les dirigeants du monde dansent le pas de la séduction et déploient tous les machiavélismes de leurs propagandes" (Gide and Martin du Gard 271). In a letter dated October 6, 1942, Martin du Gard again underscored the timeliness of the portrait: "This portrait could turn out to be very revealing, very timely" [Ce portrait pourrait être bien révélateur, bien actuel] (Gide and Martin du Gard 273-274).

21. "Cet attachant et antipathique spécimen mérite . . . une étude un peu poussée dans le *Journal*" (Gide and Martin du Gard 271).

22. "[V]os compliments m'ont gentiment encouragé et que j'ai rouvert (éperonné par vous) mon *Journal*" (Gide and Martin du Gard 274).

23. The Axis occupation of Tunis actually began on November 9, 1942, when German forces captured the Tunis-El Aouina airfield (Boretz 10), but many of the city's inhabitants expected speedy deliverance by Allied forces. On November 29, when fighting in the surrounding area was audible in downtown Tunis, liberation seemed imminent (Boretz 15-16). The Anglo-American offensive was unsuccessful, however. On November 30, 1942, the day after this military and psychological turning point, Gide began his *Journal* entry by stating: "The German and Italian forces are occupying Tunis" [Les forces allemandes et italiennes occupent Tunis] (*Journals* 4: 134; *Journal II* 847).

24. Five Victor entries follow days when Gide made no entry in his *Journal* (December 7, 1942, January 22, March 19, March 31, and April 10, 1943); three were made on

days when electrical outages silenced the radio (January 2 and 5 and February 3, 1943); two follow entries about propaganda and the unreliability of information (January 29 and March 27, 1943). Gide also turned his thoughts to his domestic situation when he was pessimistic about the Allies' progress, as when Allied bombing raids were temporarily suspended (January 16-17), and especially following military setbacks: after the American retreat near Tebourba, which Gide noted on January 12, 1943, there follow three days of *Journal* entries on Victor (January 13, 14, and 15).

25. "Hier, Victor a consenti à sortir un instant de son mutisme pour nous annoncer l'occupation de Gabès" (*Journal II* 933).

26. "Nous n'aurions pas dû gagner l'autre guerre. Cette fausse victoire nous a trompés. Nous n'avons pu la supporter. Le relâchement qui l'a suivie nous a perdus"; "il eût bien mieux valu pour . . . [la France] qu'elle fût vaincue en 1918, plutôt que de remporter alors ce faux triomphe qui acheva de l'aveugler et l'endormit dans la décadence" (*Journal II* 702, 718).

27. "Il nous faudra payer toutes les absurdités de l'intangible traité de Versailles, les humiliations, les vexations inutiles . . . et le peu digne abus de la victoire" (*Journal II* 704).

28. "En l'absence de ses parents, Victor se sait maître de la place" (*Journal II* 887).

29. "J'ai toujours pensé qu'en France nous élevons mal les enfants. . . . Est-ce affaire du tempérament français ou simplement (je préférerais) d'éducation? Peuple indigne de la liberté qu'il revendique . . ." (*Journal II* 807).

30. "C'est ce besoin constant . . . de redresser, de réformer aussi bien autrui que moi-même, qui m'a souvent rendu si insupportable . . . mais qui me ferait, je crois, si bon sujet d'une vraie république" (*Journal II* 931).

31. "Son comportement envers moi est, je le jurerais, dicté par le camarade Lévy, qui circule quotidiennement ou presque, dans l'appartement, sans saluer personne; qui lui inculque des principes de marxisme, l'entête dans son égoïsme et fournit des bases solides à sa goujaterie spontanée" (*Journal II* 910-911). On January 13 and 15, as well, Gide states that Lévy indoctrinates Victor in Communist thought (*Journals* 4: 154, 156; *Journal II* 880, 882).

32. In a speech to railway workers on August 21, 1941, Vichy Communications Minister Jean Berthelot "charged the Popular Front, 'monstrous alliance of Muscovite Communism, Masonic radicalism, and Jewish finance,' with having 'precipitated France into an ideological war, after having weakened her'" (Paxton 4).

33. "Ce grand bourgeois bolchevisant" (Mauclair 7).

34. Though he approved of France's decision to intern German citizens, Gide wrote in May 1940, it seemed unfair to hold that "every German Jew is German before being Jewish and remains German in spite of persecutions and massacres" [tout Juif allemand est allemand avant d'être juif, reste allemand en dépit des persécutions, des massacres] (*Journal II* 697 [my translation]). In 1942, Gide praised the Jews he had met in Tunis and decried the treatment they endured: "Certain young Jews here, whom I know, seem to be making a point of protesting by their civic virtues, their zeal and spirit of sacrifice, against the abominable ostracism to which they are subjected" [Certains juifs d'ici, que je connais, semblent prendre à cœur de protester, par leurs vertus civiques, leur zèle et leur dévouement, contre l'abominable ostracisme dont ils sont l'objet] (*Journals* 4: 141; *Journal II* 856).

35. "[I]l y a en France une littérature juive, qui n'est pas la littérature française"; "l'apport des qualités juives dans la littérature . . . apporte moins d'éléments nouveaux . . . qu'elle ne coupe la parole à la lente explication d'une race et n'en fausse gravement, intolérablement, la signification" (*Journal I* 763).

36. Gide wrote in 1938, "The [Jewish] question is not religious, but racial" [La question [juive] n'est pas confessionnelle, mais raciale] ("Les Juifs" 635).

37. In fact, Gide's revalidation of his 1914 statement came many years after the period when Blum was under attack. On January 9, 1948, Gide wrote: "I am very grateful to him [Léon Blum] for not holding against me the rather harsh passages of my *Journal* about the Jews and about him (which, by the way, I cannot disown, for I continue to think them utterly correct)" [Je lui sais grand gré de ne me tenir pas grief des passages assez durs de mon *Journal* au sujet des Juifs et de lui-même (que, du reste, je ne puis renier car je continue de les croire parfaitement exactes)] (*Journals* 4: 286; *Journal II* 1054).

38. Defending *Bagatelles pour un massacre,* Gide declared: "[Céline] does his best not to be taken seriously" [[Céline] fait de son mieux pour qu'on ne le prenne pas au sérieux] ("Les Juifs" 631).

39. "Certains autres pourront trouver malséant un jeu littéraire qui risque . . . de tirer à conséquence tragique" ("Les Juifs" 634).

40. The "Interviews imaginaires," a series of essays which ran from November 1941 to June 1942 in *Le Figaro Littéraire,* offered tacit encouragement to resist under the guise of literary criticism. Through an extended metaphor associating poetry with resistance, Gide stresses the necessity of "poetic" discipline: "Poetry was dying from strict observance of rules. It is being reborn by breaking the rules . . . [but] it is seeking new laws; it cannot do without them" [[La poésie] mourait de stricte observance. Elle renaît en rupture des règles . . . [mais] elle cherche des lois nouvelles; elle ne peut se passer de lois] (*Attendu que . . .* 155).

41. "[L]e jeune V., dont il est si fâcheusement question dans le dernier volume du *Journal* . . . est fou de rage et jure de se venger" (Van Rysselberghe IV: 175).

42. The pseudonym "Derais" evokes Gilles de Rais, the historical Bluebeard—a fifteenth-century nobleman who confessed to raping and murdering hundreds of children. Thus, the book's title page holds a suggestion of sexual violence.

43. My translation. O'Brien's version is in *Journals* 4: 160.

44. "[C]ertains regards, certaines allusions que j'interprétais comme de discrètes invites" (Derais 131).

45. "[Ils] avaient toujours eu à mon égard une attitude de parfaite correction" (Derais 131).

46. "[U]n vieillard prestigieux, que son grand âge ne pouvait que rendre inoffensif sur le terrain des bassesses charnelles" (Derais 134).

47. "[V]ous vous placiez derrière lui, . . . la main sur l'épaule. . . . [V]otre main . . . allait et venait, et tantôt pétrissait, tantôt attirait brusquement l'enfant à vous, tantôt au contraire se relâchait pour n'être plus qu'un frôlement sur la pointe de ses seins" (Derais 135).

48. "[V]ous m'avez trouvé en train de lire, allongé sur le divan du living-room, vêtu seulement d'une chemisette et d'un short très court. . . . Sous le prétexte bien faux de vous intéresser à ma lecture, vous rappelez-vous ce que vous avez fait? Nous étions presque seuls, alors dans la grande maison, et il ne s'agissait plus seulement d'épaule" (Derais 137).

49. Though he rejected Gide's advances, Reymond does envisage the possibility that he might have been persuaded to accept: on the two occasions when Gide approached him, he tells the author, "you said absolutely nothing, which is very regrettable. Maybe, who knows, I might have let myself get carried away by your eloquence . . ." [vous ne disiez absolument rien, ce qui est bien regrettable. Peut-être, qui sait, me serais-je laissé emporter par votre éloquence . . .] (Derais 141). In many respects, Reymond is extremely honest about his adolescent interactions with other men: he tells of his sexual experimentation with a male classmate (Derais 238-239), and acknowledges feeling "a certain pleasure . . . , oh! completely momentary, in being courted" by an Arab doctor [un certain plaisir . . . , oh! tout momentané, à être cour-

tisé] (Derais 133). Nevertheless, Reymond takes pains to surround these admissions with extensive anecdotes about his adolescent crushes on young girls, and states emphatically that he did not become a homosexual (Derais 247).

50. "[J]e vous fuyais très soigneusement . . ." (Derais 141); "je craignais fort de vous voir renouveler vos essais" (Derais 177).

51. "Peu à peu, je crois, vous avez compris qu'il ne fallait rien espérer de moi pour vos caprices amoureux. Une méchanceté perfide fit alors place aux avances; j'y répondis sur le même ton, et ce fut un curieux dialogue" (Derais 204).

After reading Reymond's manuscript, Gide wrote a letter addressed to Jean Amrouche but apparently intended for François Reymond's eyes. Though this letter has not been published, Reymond's reply allows us to reconstruct part of its contents. In a letter to Gide dated November 17, 1950 (published as an appendix in *L'Envers du Journal*), Reymond quotes from the author's letter to Amrouche: "'I cannot remember ever having "panted" after anyone'" [« Je n'ai pas souvenir d'avoir jamais « brâmé » après quelqu'un »]—to which Reymond replies: "That's news to me" [Voilà ce que j'ignorais] (Derais 259). Gide apparently incorporated portions of his letter to Amrouche into *Ainsi soit-il*, in which he asserts: "I have never (so far as I can remember) *panted* after anyone" [je n'ai jamais (pour autant qu'il m'en souvienne) *bramé* pour personne] (*So Be It* 162; *Journal 1939–1949* 1241). Gide goes on to state that throughout his life, he immediately ceased his attentions when he realized that his feelings were not reciprocated. Reymond concedes that, if this is the case, "our whole quarrel was based on a misunderstanding" [toute notre querelle se fonda sur un faux-sens] (Derais 259). Nevertheless, he makes it clear that "it was not only the incident of the unsuccessful fondling that made me wish to keep you at a distance" [[c]e n'était pas seulement l'histoire du pelotage raté qui me faisait désirer de vous tenir à l'écart] (Derais 201). "Deep down, I was afraid of you," Reymond explains: "afraid, at first, of your amorous enterprises; then, when I saw that you had more or less given up on them, of your active and continuous hostility . . ." [Au fond, je vous craignais : crainte, d'abord, de vos entreprises amoureuses; puis, quand je vis que vous y aviez à peu près renoncé, crainte de votre inimité active et agissante . . .] (Derais 189).

52. Adopting Reymond's military lexicon, Naomi Segal observes that "[w]arfare was an easier (as well as a more amusing) substitute for a negotiated settlement because neither was able to say a word about what had happened between their bodies" (Segal 340).

53. "[V]os amis . . . nous avaient envahi" (Derais 170–171).

54. "[T]out au long de votre séjour avenue Roustan, je n'ai cessé un instant de vous considérer comme un intrus et un parasite" (Derais 175).

55. In his *Journal*, Gide leads readers to believe that he made a substantial contribution to household expenses: "[Victor] was very much amazed to learn that I share with [Chacha] the daily expenses of the house" [il s'est montré fort étonné en apprenant que je faisais avec elle, pour les frais quotidiens de la maison, bourse commune] (*Journals* 4: 194; *Journal II* 930). This claim does not appear in the *Journal* manuscript (*Journal* ms. gamma 1642, opposite page 28).

56. "[E]ntièrement à la charge de mes parents, et vous avec!" (Derais 174).

57. "[T]out en n'ignorant pas que Chacha n'avait aucune qualité pour disposer de l'appartement" (Derais 166).

58. "[J]e pardonnais mal à ma grand'mère de trahir un peu la famille" (Derais 208).

59. "[Chacha est] épouvantée à l'idée de devoir demeurer seule avec son terrible petit-fils" (*Journal II* 908).

60. Reymond adds that Gide came back to the avenue Roustan apartment "the very day of the liberation" [le jour même de la libération] (Derais 172).

61. "En l'absence de ses parents, Victor se sait maître de la place. Cherche-t-il à me le faire sentir? Il y parvient à force de mauvaise grâce. Je deviens l'intrus, et les prévenances constantes de Chacha ne servent qu'à l'indisposer davantage. Je doute si je pourrai supporter longtemps encore ses bougonneries. Mais où aller?" (*Journal II* 887).

62. Reymond argues, moreover, that he attacked Gide only in self-defense: "I rarely took the first step on the path of new hostilities, but satisfied myself with fiercely counterattacking on the battlefields where you pursued me" [je faisais rarement le premier pas dans la voie d'hostilités nouvelles, me contentant de contre-attaquer férocement sur les terrains où vous me poursuiviez] (Derais 185).

63. "J'appartenais au mouvement de jeunesse vichyste des « Compagnons de France », mais j'étais porté à abandonner ces idées et à me joindre à l'opposition au régime alors régnant; le goût du risque, l'attrait de l'inconnu, et aussi, quoi que vous puissiez en penser, les idées généreuses de justice sociale que l'on me présentait, me décidèrent à cette totale volte-face" (Derais 216).

64. "[Des] mots d'ordre incisifs sur les occupants et leurs valets" (Derais 218).

65. When his offer to procure Gide's own identity papers was rejected as impractical because of the writer's fame and advanced age, François stole the card belonging to Jean Amrouche's wife Suzanne. When he later admitted the theft, Jean and Suzanne replied: "'Why didn't you ask us for it? We would have been glad to give it to you'" [« Pourquoi ne nous l'as-tu pas demandée? Nous te l'aurions volontiers donnée »] (Derais 220–221).

66. "[P]our lire votre *Journal* en cachette et avoir ainsi, sur le moral de l'ennemi, quelques renseignements" (Derais 180).

67. "La seule chose qui m'intéressait était votre *Journal,* et vous le laissiez bien en évidence sur votre bureau" (Derais 186).

68. "[V]ous modifiez un peu votre *Journal* après coup, ainsi que j'ai pu m'en rendre compte par comparaison avec le souvenir de ce que j'en lus furtivement à l'époque" (Derais 124).

69. On March 8, 1943, Gide accused François of locking the six-volume Larousse dictionary in his room (*Journal II* 919; O'Brien's translation omits this anecdote, which was first published in the 1997 Pléiade edition of Gide's *Journal*). Reymond claims that Gide later retracted his accusation, but omitted the retraction from the published version of his *Journal* (Derais 184–185). The March 9 entry—in which Gide admits he had falsely accused the boy—was indeed absent from published versions of the *Journal* until 1997 (*Journal II* 920).

70. "Je ne doute pas que votre renom et votre grand âge ne vous aient habitué à plus de docilité chez les jeunes sujets que le hasard met sous votre main" (Derais 141).

71. "[Que] vous ayez trompé indignement mes parents, abusé de ma confiance en votre prestige de vieillard « auréolé de gloire », y avez-vous seulement pensé . . . ?" (Derais 137)

     Gide's friend Roger Martin du Gard echoes Reymond's charges in his diary entry for November 9, 1940. Recording Gide's indignant reaction—"'*This is odious!*'" ["*C'est odieux!*"]—when a teacher sexually harassed his seventeen-year-old daughter Catherine (Martin du Gard 361), Martin du Gard deems the teacher's behavior less reprehensible than Gide's own:

     > Now, dear old Gide has spent his life committing far more serious breaches of trust! How many times has he introduced himself to a friend's family, increasing his kindness to the parents with the sole intent of approaching the young son of the household, sometimes a schoolboy only thirteen years old, joining him in his bedroom, awakening his sexual curiosity, and teaching him lust! More

clever than Catherine's teacher, more diabolical in his temptations, more daring, too; how many times has he been able to fool the parents, assure himself of a child's complicity, and engage him in tender and perverse games? Then he did not find anything "odious" about the premeditated and elaborate corruption of a young boy whose parents had naively entrusted him to their friend Gide!

[Or, ce bon Gide a passé sa vie à commettre de bien plus graves abus de confiance! Combien de fois s'est-il introduit dans une famille amie, multipliant les amabilités avec les parents, dans le seul but d'approcher le jeune fils de la maison, parfois un écolier de treize ans, de le rejoindre dans sa chambre, d'éveiller ses curiosités sexuelles, de lui apprendre le plaisir! Plus malin que le professeur de Catherine, plus diabolique dans ses tentations, plus hardi aussi, combien de fois a-t-il su embobiner les parents, s'assurer la complicité d'un enfant, et se livrer avec lui à des jeux tendres et pervers? Il ne trouvait alors rien d'« odieux » dans le détournement prémédité et poussé aussi loin que possible du jeune garçon, que ses parents confiaient ingénument à l'ami Gide!] (Martin du Gard 362)

72. "[L]e choix . . . de ses petits complices (enfants du peuple, ne parlant pas sa langue, nègres) avec lesquels aucun échange n'est possible que physique, rétrécit le champ de l'éventuelle déception" (Herbart 23).

73. "[A]u long de ce travail, j'ai senti à chaque instant tout ce que mes pensées, mes réactions, vous devaient, tant à vous-même qu'à votre œuvre. Pourquoi le nier? Ceux que ma jeunesse a respectés, ceux auxquels je dois quelque part de ma formation présente, étaient vos disciples" (Derais 255).

In the early years of the war, Gide was accused of corrupting the youth of France through his literary influence, his Communist sympathies, and his open homosexuality. Though the 1951 *L'Envers du Journal* is not a response to accusations leveled at Gide during *"la querelle des mauvais maîtres,"* François Reymond does demonstrate that, in his individual case, Gide's influence was not negative. As a teenager, Reymond was a great reader, and as an adult he acknowledged Gide as a positive influence on his thinking (Derais 255). Young François did not come to Communism through the writer's influence, but like Gide he was attracted by Communism's "noble ideas about social justice" [idées généreuses de justice sociale] (Derais 216). Like Gide, he later abandoned Communism, declaring in 1951: "I am no longer a Communist, nor even anything at all" [Je ne suis plus communiste, ni même rien du tout] (Derais 248). Finally, though Reymond vehemently protests Gide's sexual abuse, he states that the writer's advances did not influence his sexual orientation: "I did not become a homosexual, far from it; and yet everything predisposed me to become one: an adolescence surrounded by numerous examples, some of them illustrious, plus a few personal experiences" [Je ne suis pas devenu homosexuel, tant s'en faut; j'avais pourtant tout pour cela : une adolescence entourée d'exemples nombreux dont certains illustres, quelques expériences personnelles] (Derais 247). To a certain extent, each of the major areas in which Gide was supposed to have exerted a baneful influence on French youth was played out in the writer's relationship with young François Reymond, and Reymond's memoirs exonerate Gide on all counts.

74. "Ma première démarche fut de porter dans ma chambre deux ou trois de vos livres . . . que je me mis à lire ou à relire, voulant d'abord ainsi profiter de votre présence" (Derais 127).

75. "Eugène K. . . . m'avait demandé avec une curieuse insistance de la voix et des yeux si j'avais lu ses livres [ceux de Gide], ce que j'en pensais, etc." (Derais 131).

76. François "[é]tait resté seul à veiller, certain soir, attendant manifestement mon retour, après avoir lu *Si le grain ne meurt,* mais tout désir de le peloter a vite cédé au désir de

le calotter en entendant ses insolences" (Gide and Martin du Gard 270). Notice how Gide first acknowledges and then swiftly dismisses his desire to fondle the boy.

77. "Ah, vous n'avez jamais su comment je me suis précipité dans la salle de bains, savonné, frotté avec une brosse à laver à m'en faire saigner, de quelle manière, tant j'étais fébrile, je me heurtais aux robinets et aux parois de la baignoire!" (Derais 137).

78. Gide, *Strait* 19-20.

79. "'[E]lle attire contre le sien mon visage, passe autour de mon cou son bras nu, descend sa main dans ma chemise entr'ouverte, demande en riant si je suis chatouilleux, pousse plus avant . . . je m'enfuis; je courus jusqu'au fond du jardin; là, dans un petit citerne [the precise quote is "citerneau" (Gide, *Romans* 500)] du potager, je trempai mon mouchoir, l'appliquai sur mon front, lavai, frottai mes joues, mon cou, tout ce que cette femme avait touché!'

    "On ne saurait mieux dire, Jérôme . . . sauf que vous n'étiez pas une jeune et jolie tante . . ." (Derais 138-139).

80. "[Chacha] parle de « son petit cagibi » où elle s'enferme, comme faisait la Séquestrée de Poitiers de son « cher grand-fond Malampia »" (*Journal II* 881). Bastian referred to her quarters as "my dear little grotto" [ma chère petite grotte] and "my dear big black Malampia" [mon cher grand fond Malampia] (Gide, *Ne jugez pas* 215, 227).

81. "[R]ien n'est plus banal et plus facile à inventer que les traits de cynisme égoïste" (Gide and Martin du Gard 274).

82. "L'eussé-je connu plus tôt, j'aurais enrichi de ses traits le Strouvilhou de mes *Faux-Monnayeurs*" (*Journal II* 878).

83. "Pour la première fois peut-être, un de vos personnages, en partie réel et en partie composé, a pris la parole pour vous répondre, et raconter lui-même son histoire" (Derais 257).

84. "J'ai connu à Tunis, en juin dernier, deux nuits de plaisir comme je ne pensais plus en pouvoir connaître de telles à mon âge" (*Journal II* 826).

85. "Tout son être chantait merci" (*Journal II* 827).

86. "Il semblait si peu se soucier de mon âge que j'en venais à l'oublier moi-même" (*Journal II* 826).

87. "Ah, j'en connais un autre qui s'en est soucié" (Derais 134).

88. While Reymond's co-author Henri Rambaud claims to have confirmation of the brief affair, he points out that the passage was written after the fact (Derais 262), and calls the reader's attention to the date of the *Journal* entry in question: "August 3, 1942, only nine days after his failure with François!" [3 août 1942, juste neuf jours après l'échec avec François!] (Derais 92).

89. "Fâcheuse coïncidence, l'initiale de son prénom est aussi celle du mien; et même est-ce seulement une coïncidence?" (Derais 134).

90. Protesting Gide's efforts to dominate him, Reymond objects to his renaming in the *Journal:* "Why . . . call me Victor when ordinary mortals are referred to by their names or by X.? I don't mind X., but I abhor Victor. In this respect I must recognize that I was indeed 'possessed'" [Pourquoi . . . m'avoir appelé Victor, alors que le commun des mortels est désigné par son nom ou par X.? X. m'est indifférent, mais j'ai Victor en horreur. Là, je dois reconnaître que j'ai été bien « possédé »] (Derais 128-129).

91. "[D]evinant à demi les raisons de mon attitude, vous les avez repoussées en tâchant de vous tromper vous-même" (Derais 248). "Several times I had the feeling that you were about to understand, to discover the exact reasons for our quarrel," Reymond adds [A plusieurs reprises, j'ai eu le sentiment que vous étiez sur le point de comprendre, de mettre à jour les motifs exactes de notre querelle] (Derais 248). He then quotes the *Journal* entry for January 23, 1943: "I should like to know whether he would act in this uncivil way and show the same disregard for anyone whatsoever, or

whether, as I fear, this reveals a particular hostility toward me" [je voudrais savoir s'il se comporterait de cette incivile manière et marquerait le même sans-gêne indifféremment avec n'importe qui, ou si, comme je le crains, ceci témoigne d'une particulière hostilité à mon égard] (*Journals* 4: 160; *Journal II* 887).

92. "De mon attitude odieuse, de ce que j'ai été avec vous insolent, égoïste, menteur, vous donnez diverses explications bien fantaisistes" (Derais 202).

93. "[J]e me persuade qu'il ne faut voir là qu'un effet de sa goujaterie naturelle" (*Journal II* 896).

94. "Comment Victor, qui ressemble tant à son père, supporte-t-il d'être à ce point captif de son hérédité? Il y a peut-être, dans son mutisme envers moi, moins de résolution que de laisser-aller à sa pente" (*Journal II* 937). The manuscript has "hostile resolve" [résolution hostile] (*Journal,* ms. gamma 1642, opposite p. 7).

95. "He does not yet seem very developed from a sexual point of view," Gide wrote on March 27, 1943 [Il ne semble pas encore très développé, sexuellement parlant] (*Journals* 4: 194; *Journal II* 930). "Curious to know whether puberty, which is slow in coming to him, will awaken any feelings of emotion," he wondered on January 8 [Curieux de savoir si la puberté, qui chez lui se fait attendre, éveillera quelques sentiments affectifs] (*Journals* 4: 151; *Journal II* 876). Gide also mentioned François's sexual development in a September 1942 letter to Roger Martin du Gard, calling the boy "[d]elayed in physiological development" [[r]etardataire pour le développement physiologique] (Gide and Martin du Gard 270).

96. "Si je ne veux pas coucher avec vous, ce n'est pas, bien sûr, parce que cela ne me dit rien du tout, mais parce que je suis impubère!" (Derais 250).

97. The confiscated notebook contained Gide's journal entries for January through April 1942. Hope Boutelleau managed to conceal from the Italian police a second notebook, containing the still untranscribed diary for May to December 1942 (*Journals* 4: 184; *Journal II* 916).

98. Gérard Boutelleau was the son of Jacques Chardonne, the writer whose pro-German *Chronique privée de l'an 1940* had jarred Gide out of his *attentiste* [wait and see] position. Chardonne's connections with German authorities in Paris facilitated Gérard Boutelleau's release from the prison camp (Heller and Grand 87).

99. Gide learned that the German authorities were particularly unhappy with the entry for February 7, 1942: "I hold the collaboration Germany is offering us as a piece of trickery wholly to her advantage" [[je] tiens la collaboration que l'Allemagne nous propose pour une duperie tout à son avantage] (*Journals* 4: 101; *Journal II* 802); "it is futile to claim that had we not declared war, Germany would have respected France, which it knew to be . . . weakened, incapable of resisting for long" [il est vain de prétendre que, n'eussions-nous pas, nous, déclaré la guerre, l'Allemagne eût respecté la France qu'elle savait . . . affaiblie, incapable de résister longtemps] (*Journal II* 803 [my translation]).

100. "Que ma propre personne soit recherchée par les autorités allemandes, il n'est pas bien prouvé. Arrêté comme suspect? de quoi? Non, mais, peut-être, de bonne prise, comme témoin susceptible de parler et que l'on préfère ne pas céder aux Anglais. . . . Encore que j'aie du mal à me convaincre que . . . ma personne ou ma voix puisse être de quelque importance, mieux valait ne pas courir la chance d'un voyage et séjour contraints en Allemagne ou en Italie" (*Journal II* 943).

101. "Je laisse pousser ma barbe blanche; j'attends, pour me raser à neuf, la délivrance" (*Journal II* 946).

102. "Nous vivons, ici, sans électricité et, partant, sans nouvelles de la radio; souvent sans eau, sans presque plus d'alcool, ni de gaz, ni d'huile, sur un reste de provisions presque épuisé, mal soutenus par des repas chaque jour plus insuffisants" (*Journal II* 945).

103. "Aucun plaisir; content de rentrer dans ma grotte" (*Journal II* 949).

104. When she was discovered after twenty-five years of confinement, Mélanie Bastian was emaciated and had extremely long hair, and she begged not to be taken away from her "dear little grotto" [chère petite grotte] (Gide, *Ne jugez pas* 223–224, 215). Gide seems to be implicitly comparing his month-long ordeal to Bastian's quarter century of confinement.

105. Gide's private "théâtre fermé . . . débouche sur la délivrance, lorsque l'intime et le public fêtent la même libération" (Sagaert, "Introduction" xxv).

106. According to Éric Marty, "The battle of Tunis, which history books present in its full reality, acquires meaning only retrospectively [in Gide's *Journals*]; yet while it was *taking place,* it was simultaneously almost empty of meaning, ambiguous, without reality, and, as always, mingled with the most profound Gidean intimacy . . ." [La bataille de Tunis, qui a sa réalité dans tous les livres d'histoire, ne prendra de sens [dans le *Journal* de Gide] que rétrospectivement, alors que, tant qu'elle *avait lieu,* elle était tout à la fois pauvre de sens, ambiguë, sans réalité, et mêlée comme toujours à la plus profonde intimité gidienne . . .] (31).

107. "[T]ous les peuples conquis et sous le joug allemand, vont puiser dans cet immense revers de l'oppresseur, un extraordinaire encouragement à la résistance. On peut y entendre l'annonce d'un effondrement général" (*Journal II* 955).

108. All told, Gide's *Journal* entries on the liberation of Tunis appeared seven times between August 1943 and November 1944:

> "La délivrance de Tunis," *La Syrie et l'Orient* [August 1943]
> "La délivrance de Tunis," *Interviews imaginaires, la délivrance de Tunis, pages de Journal* (New York: Jacques Schiffrin and Co., 1943)
> "The deliverance of Tunis," *Imaginary Interviews,* trans. Malcolm Cowley (New York: Alfred A. Knopf, 1944)
> "La libération de Tunis," *La France nouvelle* (October 15, 1943: 7)
> "La libération de Tunis," *Combat* (January 9, 1944: 8)
> "Fragments d'un Journal," *Chroniques interdites II* (Paris: Éditions de Minuit, 1944)
> "La délivrance de Tunis," *Les Lettres françaises* (November 18, 1944: 1)

109. "Je n'ai rien écrit de plus plat; et jamais aucun texte de moi ne rencontra pareil accueil; il ne reste plus qu'à le servir dans les « Morceaux Choisis » pour lycées!" (Gide and Bussy 603).

110. Gide's *Journal* entry reads: "[I] go down with my companions in captivity into the street, where *they* have not dared appear for exactly six months" [[je] descends avec mes compagnons de captivité dans la rue, où *eux* n'avaient pas reparu depuis exactement six mois] (*Journals* 4: 210; *Journal II* 951, emphasis added). The twice-translated article reads: "with my companions in captivity I go down into the street, where *we* have not ventured for exactly six months" [avec mes compagnons de captivité, je descends dans la rue où *nous* ne nous sommes pas aventurés pendant exactement six mois] (Gide, "La libération" 8, emphasis added).

111. The editor of *Combat* acknowledged that the paper was reprinting "La libération de Tunis" without Gide's authorization (Gide, "La libération" 8). Alfred Fabre-Luce made a similar admission in his 1942 *Anthologie de la nouvelle Europe* (267).

112. "Aujourd'hui, la littérature est une arme de guerre. C'est pourquoi je réclame la prison pour André Gide et des poursuites contre le gérant de *L'Arche*" (*Journal II* 1105).

113. "[U]ne pièce majeure dans la main de la propagande ennemie" (Aragon 1).

114. "[Q]u'alliez-vous faire dans cette galère ennemie?" (Gide and Martin du Gard 289).

Friends were dissatisfied not only with the choice of *Les Lettres françaises* but also with the content of "La délivrance de Tunis": in a letter to Maria Van Rysselberghe, Roger Martin du Gard wished that Gide had chosen an irreproachable piece, and one of higher quality, for his literary "rentrée" (Martin du Gard 725).

115. In fact, Gide had authorized *Les Lettres françaises* to publish *Journal* excerpts to be chosen by François Mauriac, Jean Schlumberger, or Jean Paulhan (Gide and Schlumberger 964), but did not specifically give permission to publish "La délivrance."

116. "Toute liberté d'opinion est compromise pour longtemps et c'est en devenant « totalitaires » à notre tour et à notre façon, qu'on lutte et proteste contre le totalitarisme nazi. Qui n'est pas conforme est suspect" (Gide and Martin du Gard 288).

117. "Mes *Pages de Journal* ont paru hier à Alger; petit volume tout mince et réduit, car de violentes attaques communistes m'ont incité à en faire tomber toutes les pages qui pouvaient alimenter leurs accusations" (Gide and Martin du Gard 282). An essentially unexpurgated version was published simultaneously in the United States (*Pages de Journal, 1939–1942,* New York: Pantheon, 1944).

118. "[M]algrè le violent désir que j'ai de vous retrouver, je ne vous conseillerai pas de rentrer tout de suite : les passions sont à leur comble . . ." (Mauriac, *Conversations avec André Gide* 263).

119. Between April 17 and December 17, 1945, Gide neglected his journal (*Journals* 4: 255; *Journal II* 1015).

120. The telegraphic entry on June 6, 1944—"ALLIED LANDING IN NORMANDY" [DÉBARQUEMENT DES ALLIÉS EN NORMANDIE] (*Journals* 4: 242; *Journal II* 991)—is one of Gide's few references to the war after May 1943.

121. To be sure, Gide wrote of other sexual experiences with young boys in his *Journal* and autobiographical works. The case of François Reymond was particularly threatening, though, because Reymond made it clear—first through his actions, and later in his memoirs—that Gide's act was a violation.

122. "[E]n ces temps encore tout déchirés de misères et de catastrophes, ce journal intime risque d'impatienter le lecteur" (Van Rysselberghe 3: 329).

123. "C'est si maladroit, en ce moment où tous les « héros » racontent leur odyssée, et où tant de gens, confrères et lecteurs, ont des souvenirs « héroïques », de publier ce texte d'actualité, ce « journal de guerre » qui ne peut servir qu'à mettre en évidence la différence qu'il y a entre la façon dont Gide a souffert de la guerre, et celle de la majorité des Français!" (Martin du Gard 725).

124. "Il se soumit à la dure discipline que connaissent tous ceux qui, en Europe occupée, vivent en marge des lois allemandes" (Amrouche, [n. pag.]).

125. "[F]aute de mieux et incapable d'écrire quoi que ce soit de neuf « ad hoc » . . . fort déprimé par un mois de claustration avec nourriture tout juste suffisante . . . et défense non seulement de sortir, mais même de mettre le nez à la fenêtre à cause des gens de la maison d'en face" (Gide and Bussy 602-603).

126. "[L]'extrême dévouement des amis communistes qui m'hébergeaient et m'apportaient pitance" (Gide and Bussy 602-603).

127. As late as 1947, Gide's supporter Jacques Galland felt the need to reiterate this point: "[Gide] was taken to safety, to a place where several political notables of the Regency, whose notoriety had made their disappearance desirable, had already found refuge. This is where he spent the last days of the Occupation, cloistered in the company of socialists, Communists, and trade unionists" [[Gide] fut mis en sécurité dans un lieu où plusieurs personnalités politiques de la Régence, dont la notoriété avait rendu l'éclipse désirable, avaient déjà trouvé refuge. C'est là qu'il passa les derniers temps de l'occupation, cloîtré en compagnie de socialistes, de communistes et de syndicalistes] (8).

Works Cited

Amrouche, Jean. "André Gide à Tunis." *Vaincre,* June 18, 1943: n. pag.

Aragon, Louis. "Retour d'André Gide." *Les Lettres françaises,* November 25, 1944: 1+.

Boretz, Eugène. *Tunis sous la croix gammée.* N.p.: Office français d'édition, 1944.

Chauvet, Louis, ed. "Que sera demain la littérature? Réponses de MM. André Gide, Jean Schlumberger, Émile Henriot, Stève Passeur, Blaise Cendrars." *Le Figaro,* October 12, 1940: 3.

Derais, François [François Reymond] and Henri Rambaud. *L'Envers du Journal de Gide: Tunis 1942–43.* 2nd ed. Paris: Le nouveau Portique, 1952.

Fabre-Luce, Alfred, ed. *Anthologie de la nouvelle Europe.* Paris: Librairie Plon, 1942.

Galland, Jacques. "André Gide en Afrique du Nord." *Paru* 27 (February 1947): 5–9.

Gide, André. *Attendu que . . .* Algiers: Charlot, 1943.

———. *Corydon.* Paris: Gallimard, 1924.

———. "Feuillets." *La Nouvelle Revue Française* 322 (December 1940): 76–86.

———. *Journal.* Ms. gamma 1642, Bibliothèque Littéraire Jacques Doucet, Paris.

———. *Journal I, 1887–1925.* Ed. Éric Marty. Paris: Gallimard, Bibliothèque de la Pléiade, 1996.

———. *Journal II, 1926–1950.* Ed. Martine Sagaert. Paris: Gallimard, Bibliothèque de la Pléiade, 1997.

———. *Journal 1939–1949; Souvenirs.* Paris: Gallimard, Bibliothèque de la Pléiade, 1954.

———. *The Journals of André Gide.* Ed. and trans. Justin O'Brien. 4 vols. New York: Alfred A. Knopf, 1947–1951.

———. "Les Juifs, Céline et Maritain." *La Nouvelle Revue Française* 295 (April 1938): 630–636.

———. "La libération de Tunis." *Combat,* January 9, 1944: 8.

———. *Ne jugez pas.* Paris: Gallimard, 1930.

———. *So Be It, or The Chips Are Down.* Trans. Justin O'Brien. London: Chatto & Windus, 1960.

———. *Strait is the Gate.* Trans. Dorothy Bussy. New York: Alfred A. Knopf, 1959.

Gide, André, and Dorothy Bussy. *Correspondance André Gide—Dorothy Bussy III: Janvier 1937–Janvier 1951.* Ed. Jean Lambert and Richard Tedeschi. *Cahiers André Gide* 11. Paris: Gallimard, 1982.

Gide, André, and Roger Martin du Gard. *Correspondance 1935–1951.* Paris: Gallimard, 1968.

Gide, André, and Jean Schlumberger. *Correspondance 1901–1950.* Ed. Pascal Mercier and Peter Fawcett. Paris: Gallimard, 1993.

Gillouin, René. "Responsabilité des écrivains et des artistes." *Journal de Genève,* No. 33, February 7 and 8, 1942: 3.

Heller, Gerhard, and Jean Grand. *Un Allemand à Paris, 1940–1944.* Paris: Éditions du Seuil, 1981.

Herbart, Pierre. *A la recherche d'André Gide.* Paris: Gallimard, 1952.

"La Jeunesse de France." *Le Temps,* July 9, 1940: 1.

Martin du Gard, Roger. *Journal III, 1937–1949. Textes autobiographiques 1950–1958.* Ed. Claude Sicard. Paris: Gallimard, 1993.

Marty, Éric. *L'Écriture du jour : Le Journal d'André Gide.* Paris: Éditions du Seuil, 1985.

Mauclair, Camille. "Pour un assainissement littéraire." *La Gerbe,* January 2, 1941: 7.

Mauriac, Claude. *Conversations avec André Gide.* Paris: Éditions Albin Michel, 1951.

———. *Conversations with André Gide.* Trans. Michel Lebeck. New York: George Braziller, 1965.

Mehlman, Jeffrey. *Legacies of Anti-Semitism in France.* Minneapolis: University of Minnesota Press, 1983.

O'Brien, Justin. "Introduction." *The Journals of André Gide.* By André Gide. Ed. and trans. Justin O'Brien. Vol. 4. New York: Alfred A. Knopf, 1951. v–x.

Paxton, Robert O. *Vichy France: Old Guard and New Order, 1940–1944*. New York: Columbia University Press, 1972.

Pétain, Philippe. *Actes et Écrits*. Ed. Jacques Isorni. Paris: Flammarion, 1974.

Sagaert, Martine. "Introduction." *Journal II, 1926–1950*. By André Gide. Paris: Gallimard, Bibliothèque de la Pléiade, 1997. ix–xxxiii.

———. "Notes et variantes." *Journal II, 1926–1950*. By André Gide. Paris: Gallimard, Bibliothèque de la Pléiade, 1997. 1142–1515.

Segal, Naomi. *André Gide: Pederasty and Pedagogy*. Oxford: Oxford University Press, 1998.

Tournier, Paul, and Robert Tournier. "André Gide en Tunisie." *Bulletin des Amis d'André Gide* 20.96 (October 1992): 453–468.

Van Rysselberghe, Maria. *Les Cahiers de la Petite Dame : Notes pour l'histoire authentique d'André Gide*. 4 vols. *Cahiers André Gide* 4-7. Paris: Gallimard, 1973–1977.

CHAPTER 13

Theseus Revisited: Commitment through Myth[1]

Pamela A. Genova

Gide's relationship to the extraordinarily rich world of Greek mythology is a complex and ambivalent subject, and many modern critical studies have explored various aspects of this relationship, from its presence as a constant aesthetic referent to its potential as a unique discursive framework.[2] Indeed, Gide's interest in myth, as with his attraction to Christian motifs, represents a consistent force throughout his life and a fundamental referential thread throughout his textual corpus, from the 1891 *Traité du Narcisse* through the 1946 *Thésée*. Gide employed a mythic backdrop to explore a variety of generic forms, composing mythologically based texts within such forms as the *récit,* the dramatic text, the *sotie,* the treatise, the essay, and the Socratic dialogue. References to Greco-Roman myth abound as well in his correspondence and his personal papers, in his conversations and his lectures. Clearly Gide felt a deep attachment to the dynamic system of the ancient modes of thought and art; he obviously discovered in the myths of antiquity something more powerful than merely an evocative historical framework or a provocative narrative structure.

In one sense, one can argue that Gide's primary interest in myth is of a personal nature, for it is evident that in many ways, Gide retells the stories of the heroes of myth in order to recount his own adventure, to communicate a personal narrative within a mythic framework. This act of self-expression exists for Gide as a gesture of exploration and inquiry, as a significant move in the enterprise to work towards a more authentic understanding of himself. In the mirror of ancient myth, Gide recognizes a shadowy figure, a double of himself both desired and feared, not unlike the painfully beautiful and inaccessible image that flashes up to Narcissus seated at the water's edge.[3] Thus, myth for Gide fulfills the fundamental purpose of serving as a vehicle for the expression of subjectivity, as a structure within which the author can dramatize conflicts drawn from his own internal stage.

Moreover, Gide's understanding of myth is clearly modern, in the sense that what interests and attracts him in the tales of antiquity is not so much an eternal,

unchanging truth that would convey to the moderns, as we often assume was
the case for the ancients, an immutable fragment of divine wisdom or a cleverly
worded solution to a basic human dilemma. Rather, Gide's interest in myth is
as a partner, indeed as a double to complement himself, and for him the story
of a myth becomes truly powerful and significant only when it joins together
with a unique creative mind, as it takes on new meaning and potential through
an individual reading of its most basic elements. Thus Gide enters the aesthetic
tradition of the *mythe littéraire,* an artistic form embodying the response of a single writer to the encounter of an ancient narrative. Literary myth implies evolution, subversion, and surprise, as an author approaches the antique myth from
a unique, reinvigorated standpoint, manipulating the referent to reveal its hidden, neglected, or censored implications.[4] As the progeny of the union of an
author and a legendary narrative of a prior age, literary myth ensures the continuation of the mythic in the modern world. For without literature, myth
would be lost to human sensibility; without the conscious act of a writer to reac-
tivate the material of ancient myths, the anonymous oral message, structure, and
contexts of the powerful stories of antiquity would no longer hold meaning
today. In the words of Albert Camus, "Myths . . . await our incarnation. If even
one man responds to their call, they offer up their strength intact."[5] Gide himself is not unaware of the active, polyvalent nature of ancient myth; he argues:
"The Greek fable, after Troy, loses its symbolic meaning but takes on a psychological and poetic value, to the great advantage of dramatists. There is no longer
any reason to seek the hidden meaning of those stories; they have ceased to have
anything mythical about them; their admirable pathos must suffice for the ingen-
ious poet" (*Journals* 4: 253).[6]

Interestingly, Gide does not consider the construction of his own *mythe littéraire* as a gesture of rebellion or competition when confronted with a previous
author perceived as an aesthetic rival or a traditional model to be overturned.
Rather, for Gide, his own response to a mythic tale, or to any specific later textual version of that tale, is always already unique, necessarily unlike that which
came before. Regarding the myth of Oedipus, for example, Gide underscores
the fact that he is in no way interested in an attempt to outdo other authors, or
to redo what they have accomplished, but to construct a new and unsuspected
perspective, to uncover an element inherent in the narrative until then unde-
tected. He writes: "You have Sophocles' play and I am not posing as a rival; I
am leaving him the pathos; but here is what Sophocles could not have seen and
understood, though it lay in his subject, and what I understand—not because I
am more intelligent but because I belong to another epoch. . . . I intend not to
make you shudder and weep, but to make you reflect" (*Journals* 3: 254).[7] As is
clear in this passage, Gide does not perceive the individual subject in an isolated,
solitary state, but rather, he contextualizes the standpoint from which the modern author contemplates the mythic referent. In Gide's view, the reason for the
unique nature of his own interpretation of the myth appears grounded primarily in the era to which the writer belongs. The challenge in the enterprise to
construct a truly powerful contemporary literary myth focuses then on the
problem of unifying the ancient figures with the modern atmosphere, and the

individual mind with the collective spirit. Within this framework, elements of individual personality and artistic style combine with factors of social, political, and cultural significance to produce finally a multidimensional text in which the writer paints a portrait of his time, as a spokesman of the culture that he represents. Thus Gidean literary myths embody simultaneously the presentation of a subjective perspective, while these texts also communicate a reflection of the more global questions of the age, and act as a vehicle for a discursive element originating within a given community.

One of the most basic and most ambivalent of such social concerns that characterize the era of Gide's life and that animate the writing of the period is the notion of commitment, of the problematic of individual action during a time grounded in upheaval and change. Throughout his long life, Gide was witness, of course, to two world wars, as well as to numerous forms of conflict and transition at many levels of the human experience. From religious conversions to governmental crises to aesthetic revolutions, Gide found himself surrounded by the dynamics of change and uncertainty, as horizons on all sides promised new unknowns. The unpredictability of the French experience in the first half of the twentieth century is in fact reflected quite closely in Gide's own personal experience, in his infamous moments of hesitation, doubt, contradiction, and reversal. As an artist, for example, he began his literary career within the limited circle of *fin-de-siècle* Symbolism, an aesthetic attitude that he embraced quite fondly early on.[8] Through such texts as *Le Traité du Narcisse* and *Le Voyage d'Urien* (1892), Gide appears to have taken quite seriously the artistic potential of the Symbolist school, as he experimented with both fictional narrative and theoretical discursive writings based on the Symbolist creed. Yet Gide soon tired of the closed atmosphere of the Symbolist *cénacle,* disappointed by what he considered as the refusal on the part of the poets to take part in the world around them, to plunge into the adventure of modernity.[9] Thus he composed his 1895 *Paludes,* for example, which presents the Symbolist poets in a satirical mode, through a critique of the monotony, stagnation, and entropy that Gide considered to be the most dangerous weaknesses of the movement. In the 1897 *Nourritures terrestres,* Gide expands these reflections as he turns to the exterior, singing the praises of a life of passion, adventure, and action as a means to overcome the stiflingly contemplative existence he saw embodied in the Symbolist stance. *L'Immoraliste,* from 1902, continues this inquiry into the power of action and its potentially destructive implications. Indeed, the problem of social and cultural commitment can be traced to his earliest works, and though Gide seems to have come more into his own as the century progressed, as he aimed to present a more unified self-image as a writer, a literary critic, a Nobel Prize laureate, or a husband and father, in truth, his concerns about his sexuality, his religion, and his rightful place in an increasingly more active and complex society continue to plague him until his death.

The question of Gide's attitudes towards political questions and his view of the importance of social concerns to the individual has been hotly debated, due in large part to the author's profound ambivalence in this realm. In certain writings, Gide appears to limit the ultimate value of man's social engagement, arguing for the precedence of ethical problems over political concerns: "political questions interest me less, and I believe them less important, than social questions; and social questions less important than moral questions" (*Journals* 2: 244).[10] Despite the clarity of this particular remark, Gide is rarely consistent on the topic of *engagement,* and from among the many contradictory opinions he expresses, this passage from 1935 illustrates the hesitation and change inherent in his views:

> I had thought, until quite recently, that it was most important first to change man, men, each man; and that this was where one had to begin. This is why I used to write that the ethical question was more important than the social question. Today I let myself be convinced that man himself cannot change unless social conditions first urge him and help him to do so—attention must first be paid to them. But attention must be paid to both. (*Journals* 3: 334)[11]

Some critics argue, in fact, that Gide was an exemplary model of political and social engagement, through his involvement from 1914 to 1916 in the Foyer franco-belge, his interest in the Action française, his eventual denunciation of the cruelties of colonialism in Africa, his exploration of the French judicial system, and his active interest in Communism, culminating in the 1936 journey to Russia that left him wholly disillusioned with what he perceived as the false hopes of Stalin's ideology. In his 1991 study *André Gide : L'Engagement (1926–1939),* for example, Daniel Moutote describes the positive force of Gide's efforts in these terms:

> Gidean commitment carries with it a lesson of courage and solidarity in accord with contemporary moral and political views: courage to reform a religion which had generally become, over time, abstract dogma and rites; courage to pull the population of French Equatorial Africa out of slavery and give it back its humanity when it was being crushed by a colonizing civilization that had in practice adopted colonialism, and courage to speak on behalf of the criminals, the mentally ill, the miserable, and all those abandoned by our society; courage to join the ranks of the people and of the egalitarian regime of the U.S.S.R., and an even more impressive courage to disengage himself from those ranks, once he recognized the undermining of the spirit of the October Revolution by the Stalinist state.[12]

Although Gide never becomes an official member of the Communist Party, he does seem to find early on in the Russia of the 1930s some glimmer of realization of the theories he himself elaborated in his texts, such as the motifs of *bâtardise* [illegitimacy] and *déracinement* [uprootedness]. In 1931, he writes of the U.S.S.R.: "I should like to live long enough to see the success of that tremendous effort; its realization, which I wish with all my soul and for which I should like to work. To see what can be produced by a state without religion, a society without the family" (*Journals* 3: 180).[13] Doubtless, for many of his contemporaries, Gide became a progressively more visible and effective spokesman on issues of human rights and the problem of individual liberty, as he explored the subtleties of the most popular and powerful ideologies of his time, uncovering the potentially dangerous implications of any given political or social system.

However, despite Gide's travels, his work with humanitarian groups, and the publication of works that aimed for a higher social consciousness, such as *Les Nouvelles Nourritures, Geneviève, Retour de l'U.R.S.S., Souvenirs de la cour d'assises, Voyage au Congo,* and the texts written from 1929 to 1935 and collected under the title *Littérature engagée,* Gide did not escape criticism as the incarnation of an aristocratically minded bourgeois, sickened perhaps by the hypocrisy, cruelty, and apathy of his contemporaries, but much too comfortable in the security of his economic and social situation to truly act and to sacrifice his comfort for the oppressed.[14] Germaine Brée has noted what she considers Gide's desire to engage himself in social issues, but concludes that "his voice is without impact and his interventions are those of an amateur. Nothing really profound in Gide seems to be touched when faced with these questions that remain outside of his preoccupations as a writer. . . . Despite his good faith, there is a deep social irresponsibility in Gide."[15] And as Gide himself writes in 1933: "I have already said so: I know nothing about politics. If they interest me, they do so as a Balzac novel does, with their passions, their pettinesses, their lies, their compromises" (*Journals* 3: 275).[16]

As with many other issues, on the question of commitment, Gide appears to be of two minds, and in fact, this impression of duality, of a profound anxiety produced by fundamental contradiction, has come to be known as a characteristically Gidean trait. Much has been written on Gide's innate duality, on the series of paradoxes he embraced, the oppositions that make it so difficult to pin him down to any consistent system of belief or principle. Torn between a plethora of fundamental contradictions, between sensuality and morality, pleasure and asceticism, paganism and Christianity, it is hardly surprising that Gide's world view is characterized by an incessant tension of opposition and conflict. As Jean-Paul Sartre has written in a celebrated passage:

> Courage and prudence: this carefully measured mixture explains the inner tension of his work. Gide's art aims to establish a compromise between risk and regulation. Within it are balanced Protestant law and homosexual nonconformity, the proud individualism of the bourgeois and the Puritan inclination towards social constraints; a certain harshness, a difficulty with communication, and a humanism of Christian origin, an active sensuality that presents itself as innocent. The compliance with rules unites in Gide's work with the quest for spontaneity.[17]

If it can be argued that Gide failed in his attempt to involve himself fully in human political affairs, incapable of genuine social commitment as he conceived of the notion on a theoretical level, might there not be another kind of experience, as valuable and complex as that of concrete adventure in the world of

politics, available to the writer who rejects a more traditional understanding of
commitment as a public declaration to save the world? Maurice Blanchot, in his
essay "Gide et la littérature d'expérience," describes "the power to test oneself,
. . . to pursue an experience through which, in relation both to oneself and to
one's world, the overwhelming sense of the human condition will be
revealed."[18] For Gide, this experience of the totality of human existence may
not come directly from human history, or from social action in the streets, or
from unwavering religious conviction, but from art itself, from the creation of a
subtle and unexpected discourse in his writing that transmits an effective and
subversive power. One way to uncover this oblique discourse, to unveil it by
removing its often cryptic camouflage, is to plunge directly into the Gidean
labyrinth, following Ariadne's thread quite simply back into the realm of myth.
For myth is the original place of paradox, of contradiction and conflict, where
the attraction of opposites can produce a rich, synthetic harmony, a unity born
from difference; in the words of Gilbert Durand, "Myth is the ultimate discourse
in which antagonistic tension, fundamental to all discourse, that is, to all 'development' of meaning, is constituted. The myth that makes up Greek thought is
the story of the antagonism between Apollonian and Dionysian forces."[19]
Indeed, the complexities of myth mirror the elusiveness of Gide's belief system
and the intricacies of his writing style; the power of myth to engage both sides
of a seeming contradiction could hardly fail to attract the attention of a writer
who proclaims: "we must protect in us all the natural antinomies and realize that
it is only thanks to their irreducible opposition that we are alive" (*Journals* 2:
367).[20] The question now to be considered concerns the specific nature of that
subversive message, the aim and direction of the provocative design hidden
within the Gidean mythic text.

In her essay "Homotextual Counter-Codes: André Gide and the Poetics of
Engagement," Emily Apter examines the problem of Gide's relationship to the
issue of social commitment, and suggests that although we can discover traces of
actively political commitment in his life, it is more valuable perhaps to see Gide
as a liberator of a different kind, working toward a different freedom, that of sexuality. Apter suggests further that in such texts as *Les Nourritures terrestres, Les
Nouvelles Nourritures,* and *Si le grain ne meurt,* "the subversiveness of form matches
the subversiveness of content, generating what might be characterized as a
counter-code, in turn comprised of homosexual signs" (77).[21] It is quite true
that in the texts Apter analyses, as well as in others with a more direct homoerotic motif, such as *Corydon* and *Les Faux-Monnayeurs,* Gide speaks out for a
freedom quite obviously underrepresented in his time. It could be argued, of
course, that Gide's sense of commitment in the realm of sexual politics is hardly
momentous in changing laws or guaranteeing freedoms, and predictably, in his
literary statements on homosexuality, he does not succeed at escaping the anxiety and doubt that haunted him continually; one needs only to think of his hesitation to publish his most directly homosexual work, *Corydon,* to find an
illustration of his deep ambivalence.[22] Yet, as Apter argues, his message does not
go unheard; his creative work can be seen as emerging finally as socially significant and ideologically rebellious, most effectively, in fact, in his *mythe littéraire:*

"Both Greek myth and Biblical parable are transformed and instrumentalized as effective didactic vehicles for purveying ideological norms, specifically the primacy of sexual liberty and license" ("Homotextual Counter-Codes" 81). Gide himself is aware of the potentially revolutionary nature of myth, and he directly accents the connection among the discrete elements of homoerotic sexuality, politics, Greek culture, and an authentic sense of individual harmony:

> No people had greater sense and understanding of harmony than the Greeks. Harmony of the individual, and of manners, and of the city. And it is from a need for harmony (intelligence as much as instinct) that they admitted uranism. This is what I tried to bring out in *Corydon*. This book will be understood later on, when it is first understood that a large share of the upset of our society and our dissolute morals come from this: that we try to banish uranism, which is indispensable to the constitution of a well-regulated society. (*Journals* 3: 117)[23]

Obviously Gide was no stranger to homosexuality, yet perhaps his outlook could be considered as strange indeed. While he authored such texts as *Corydon, L'Immoraliste,* and *Les Faux-Monnayeurs,* in which the motif of homosexuality is undeniably manifest, it must also be admitted that he extended much energy and penned many lines in the endeavor to cover his tracks, to deliberately weave a veil of mystery and create a code of silence to cloak his own persona. Much recent Gide criticism has focused on the problematic nature of sexual identity in Gide's life and work, as in such studies as Apter's 1987 *André Gide and the Codes of Homotextuality,* Patrick Pollard's 1991 *André Gide: Homosexual Moralist,* and Michael Lucey's 1995 *Gide's Bent.* These critics identify the dynamics of a homosexual discourse in Gide's corpus as a creative leitmotif often so subtle as to escape notice. This subversive voice returns throughout Gide's writing, from *Le Traité du Narcisse* to *Le Prométhée mal enchaîné,* from *Les Nourritures terrestres* to *Oscar Wilde.* Yet there remains one text with a homosexual paradigm that has occasioned little discussion, one book that nevertheless integrates on a fundamental level the problematics of gender identity and sexual preference: *Thésée.* In many ways considered one of the most political of Gide's fictional writings, through its reflections on humanism, on the founding of the state and the formation of a statesman, and on the contract established between an individual and the government of his society, *Thésée* can also be considered a powerful statement on sexual liberty, uniting the elements of will, power, identity, and desire into a productive and subversive homoerotic framework.

The literary myth of Theseus is one of the richest and most diverse of those handed down from antiquity, a legend whose principal elements came together over a long period of gestation, and from a variety of sources. Unlike the hero tales of Prometheus and Narcissus, for the Theseus myth there is no specific original text that can be identified as its sole progenitor, and by the very indeterminacy of its origin, the myth adopts a more deeply universal and archetypal aura, as a cultural voice belonging to many periods and many peoples. As Marguerite Yourcenar has written: "The Greco-Cretan adventures of Theseus, his struggle with the Minotaur, his love affair with the two sisters of the monster . . . , rank among the ancient legends that contain the greatest number of obvious parallels with the fables and folk tales of every country and every age."[24] Over the centuries, many authors have composed their own versions of the literary myth of Theseus, such as Plutarch, Euripides, Sophocles, Ovid, Callimachus, Seneca, Chaucer, Boccaccio, Shakespeare, Racine, Ruskin, and Butor, all of whom highlight different aspects of the narrative, each author bringing to the myth new cultural and aesthetic variables. Thus, throughout literary history Theseus has become a protean figure, an ambivalent hero who incorporates many fragmented antithetical characteristics, depicting in various texts the champion over monsters, judge of criminals, faithful friend, unfaithful lover, tragic hero, or triumphant statesman. He seems indeed a man for all seasons, a chameleon of mythic lore.

In 1946, Gide publishes his *Thésée,* the text that would be his last, and as he would have it, his *testament.*[25] However, as early as 1911, Gide notes in his *Journal* the power of attraction he recognizes in the Theseus myth, specifically in relation to the themes of personal freedom and self-identity when confronted by the moral constraints imposed by others: "In the *Thésée* this must be brought out—the apron-string, to express it vulgarly. After having conquered the Minotaur, he would like to go on. — He is held—obliged to return" (*Journals* 1: 302).[26] The Theseus Gide ultimately creates stands as a complex cultural figure who harks back to his own aesthetic namesakes, notably those of Plutarch, Sophocles, and Racine, and embodies a multidimensional textual consciousness constructed upon linguistic and discursive forms of play, especially the rhetorical figures of condensation, litotes, and amplification.[27] In this way, Gide allows his readers to perceive the echoes of the legend's past, while he formulates his own modern voice through the self-affirmation of his hero, through his constant desire for freedom and authenticity, with the aim always to *passer outre* [go beyond].

From this perspective, Gide's Theseus text may appear at first glance to rely heavily on its sources; following the basic lines of the myth, the Gidean Theseus undergoes many of the same adventures as his forerunners: he clears the countryside of thieves, murderers, and monsters; he travels to Crete, enters the labyrinth, and triumphs over the Minotaur; he encourages rumors that the god Poseidon is his real father; he kidnaps Phaedra and toys with Ariadne, whom he abandons on the island of Naxos; and he is responsible for the suicide of his father, Aegeus, who leaps to his death when he sees that the flags on Theseus's ship are black, the signal established between father and son to indicate Theseus's own death—the young hero admits he apparently "forgot" to change the flags, and is rewarded for his forgetfulness with the kingdom of Athens upon his return. Thus far, Gide's hero follows closely in the footsteps of his past namesakes, and the reader may expect him to remain as solidly conventional, as clearly established in the straight and narrow path as his predecessors.[28] Yet in Gide's text, such seeming conventionality soon becomes suspect, and in fact the author subverts the traditional literary myth of Theseus in many ways, primarily through language, also through irony, reversals, parody, pastiche, and other comic devices, as the hero recounts his exploits. Gide also transforms the structural framework of the narrative, adding two episodes never before directly included in the Theseus legend, the first a long *mise en abyme* focusing on Daedalus, the inventor of the labyrinth, and on his son, Icarus, who "flew too close to the sun" and has fallen deep into madness. The second episode involves the meeting of Theseus and Oedipus, the two heroes representing a series of oppositions regarding self, family, and city, two antithetical positions from *le bâtard* and *le père de famille* on such notions as happiness, responsibility, plenitude, and parricide.[29] These many elements are provocative and significant, worthy of debate and analysis, but perhaps to uncover the most potentially powerful manner in which Gide makes Theseus a figure of social and sexual liberty, it may prove most useful to focus first on the ambiguities of Theseus's own personality, on the dualities and mirror images of his individual character, manipulated by Gide both to renew the ancient mythic material and to construct a hero of his own time.

Throughout his mythic and literary career, Theseus had been consistently portrayed as the epitome of manliness, of a virility, strength, and heterosexuality seemingly far beyond suspicion. Among Gidean heroes, Theseus may stand apart most distinctly through his loud proclamation of his unwavering heterosexuality. When he and his friend Pirithoüs are planning the kidnapping of Phaedra, he enthusiastically asserts his unswaying preference for the female sex: "But though I am a Greek, I do not feel myself drawn in any way toward people of my own sex, however young and attractive *[jeunes et charmants]* they may be . . ." (*Two Legends* 90).[30] Although these words are undeniably printed on the page, and although some critics have seen no reason not to accept them at face value, as in Pollard's assertion that Theseus "is egotistically heterosexual, and there is no hint that he has other inclinations" (*André Gide: Homosexual Moralist* 396), perhaps there is more to this statement than appears obvious, something in it that can be seen as a challenge to the reader to unearth a more elusive level of meaning.[31]

Indeed, the motif of homosexuality represents a vital element in the overall aura of the Theseus text, permeating the entire narrative, surrounding the mythic core much like the sweet smoke that envelopes and enchants those who wander into the Gidean maze. The multiform nature of human sexuality is reflected throughout the text, as Gide manipulates the clichés that cloak the myth to uncover the complex ambiguity of the subject hidden within. Gide first targets the seemingly opaque, polished surface of sexual identity traditionally associated with Theseus, revealing his disguise as fragmented and transparent, a cracked mask to be deconstructed. Theseus is sent to Crete as a member of a group of sacrificial victims, seven young men and seven young women, who represent the obligatory token offering of Athens to Crete. Within this group is Pirithoüs, Theseus's closest friend, with whom it is hardly impossible to imagine that he carries on an *amitié particulière,* in the time-honored tradition of Greek culture, illustrated by such heroic couples as Achilles and Patroclus, or Orestes and Pylades.[32]

Moreover, Gide makes a point in this text to highlight the ubiquitous presence of homosexuality on the island of Crete, as he situates the action of his narrative in a land of sexual indeterminacy. At one point, Pirithoüs tries to explain to Theseus that he could take Glaucus as a lover, both to flatter the young man's father, King Minos, and to spare Glaucus the humiliation of being neglected by the more mature men of Crete:

> You know that Minos and Rhadamanthus, those two model legislators, have drawn up a code of morals for the island, paying particular attention to pederasty. As you know, too, the Cretans are especially prone to this, as is evident from their culture. So much so, in fact, that every adolescent who reaches manhood without having been chosen by some older admirer becomes ashamed and regards his neglect as dishonorable; for if he is good-looking, people generally conclude that some vice of heart or mind must be the cause. (*Two Legends* 90)[33]

From the very setting Gide chooses for his text, the theme of homoeroticism bathes the action in overtones of alternative sexual practices, as his hero debarks onto an island of openly acceptable homosexual desire and practice.

The figure of Gide's Minotaur, along with the labyrinth that enslaves him, has produced much speculation in critical circles, and the maze has come to symbolize a variety of elements, from a concrete representation of the unknown, to an icon for the complexities of identity, to the symbol of all doctrines that limit individual freedom. In Gide's version, legend has it that the young Athenian victims must be sent "to satisfy, it was said, the appetites of the Minotaur" (*Two Legends* 55),[34] and yet, as Gide's Daedalus later remarks of the monster: "They used to say that he lived on carrion; but since when has a bull eaten anything but grass?" (*Two Legends* 83).[35] The text leaves open the fate of the would-be victims, and posits the strong suggestion that the Minotaur's appetite may well be of a nature more sexual than nutritional. In fact, in his essay "Considérations sur la mythologie grecque," Gide directly addresses this significant ambiguity of the legend, and writes: "[Theseus] embarks . . . with the band of twenty youths and twenty maidens which Greece paid in annual tribute to Crete to be devoured by the Minotaur, so says the old wives' tale; personally, I think that the monster in the depths of the labyrinth counted on them for his seraglio. Why so? Simply because I do not see such carnivorous tastes as inherited from Pasiphaë or the bull progenitor—I see it as lust" ("Thoughts on Greek Mythology" 231).[36] When Theseus enters the labyrinth and discovers the Minotaur reclining provocatively on a bed of flowers, he hesitates, disarmed by the beauty of the beast:

> Facing me . . . lay the Minotaur. As luck would have it, he was asleep. I ought to have hurried forward and taken advantage of this, but something held me back, arrested my arm: the monster was beautiful. As happens with centaurs also, there was in his person a harmonious blending of man and beast. On top of this, he was young, and his youthfulness gave an indefinable bloom to his good looks; and I am more vulnerable to such things than to any show of strength. When faced with them, I needed to call

upon all my reserves of energy. . . . I even stood still for some time and just looked at him. (*Two Legends* 86–87)[37]

The indeterminate nature of the Gidean Minotaur, a creature as gracefully double as a hermaphrodite à la Lautréamont, captivates Theseus who, once the monster awakens, "triumphs" over him. Further, the erotic implications of this act of power are in no way refuted by Theseus's own ambivalent description of what exactly took place between them: "What I did next, what happened, I cannot exactly recall. . . . [A]nd if in spite of this I vanquished the Minotaur, my recollection of the victory is confused, though on the whole somewhat voluptuous" (*Two Legends* 87).[38] In an overwhelming sense, this episode represents a metaphysical and sexual rite of passage through which Theseus must venture, the labyrinth an image of the complications of his own desire, the force symbolized in the monster. Ben Stoltzfus writes of this *épreuve* [test] as a "lustful encounter with so handsome a beast," and sees in their coupling a characteristically Gidean act: "this symbolic labyrinth of man's in which Theseus gladly makes love to the monster who now has him in its thrall is a dilemma of many Gidean characters" (152). The struggle with the beast thus incorporates elements not only of mind and soul, but also of body, as the Gidean process of initiation and becoming involves the indispensable aspect of sexual maturity as well as emotional and intellectual development.[39] Moreover, in Theseus's appreciation of the physical beauty of the Minotaur, of the beast's innate corporeal sense of antique harmony, we can uncover a parallel to his awareness of the attractiveness of the *jeunes* and *charmants* boys of Greece. Through his hero's sensitivity to the physical grace of young men, Gide has couched a central theme of Greek homosexuality, based specifically on the comely nature of young, inexperienced boys. As Apter points out, the connection between Gide's conception of male beauty and the classical origins of the aesthetic nude is key in the homoerotic resonance of the writing: "Gide's poetics of nudity was based on classical standards of beauty, in particular the hellenistic beauty of the male nude as canonized by Renaissance sculpture and the aesthetics of Winckelmann, a tradition that joins the idealization of the young male form to its eroticized homosexual implications" (*André Gide* 95).[40]

Apart from Theseus's dealings with men, and with creatures who are half-men, his relationship to women is no less revealing in the establishment of his complex, ambivalent sexual persona. In spite of his many female conquests, or perhaps indeed because of his prowess with women, Theseus manifests an incontestable disdain for the female sex, and much of his attitude can best be described as purely misogynist; as Watson-Williams has noted: "For Theseus, the legendary philanderer, the casual affairs and the sexual relationships formed in Crete with Ariadne and Phaedra are simply means to an end" (133).[41] Ariadne, of course, receives his most malicious scorn, and after a night spent in her bed, he concludes with distaste: "The hours passed slowly for me, I must admit" (*Two Legends* 70).[42] As she falls in love with him, he scoffs at her attention, and when she declares that she can no longer do without him, he sarcastically remarks: "This made me think all the time of how to get rid of her" (*Two Legends* 71).[43]

Other female figures are dismissed, debased, or simply absent from the text. The-seus's mother, Aethra, conventionally a key figure in the myth, is practically erased from the narrative, and Pasiphaë, the mother of Ariadne and Phaedra, is portrayed in a manner that can only be described as grotesque. Notice the sub-tle use of one particular adjective to recall Pasiphaë's celebrated sexual adven-ture with the bull: "She had the lips of a glutton, an upturned nose, and huge empty eyes, whose expression one might have called *bovine*" (*Two Legends* 59, my emphasis).[44] It is worthy of note that the two women for whom Theseus does seem to feel genuine affection are described through strikingly masculine images. The first, the one-breasted Amazon warrior Antiope, overpowers him in her embrace and matches him blow for blow in battle. The other, Phaedra, may well interest Theseus in part because of her striking likeness to her younger brother, Glaucus, whom she resembles as an "absolute double" (*Two Legends* 90).[45] Gide's hero shows no sign of reluctance or concern for his reputation as a ladies' man when, in order to kidnap Phaedra from Crete, she must be dis-guised as a man, to respect the homosexual mores of the island.[46]

The code of multiple sexuality is not limited in the text to Theseus alone, and to further highlight the ambivalence in his narrative, Gide accents the ambiguously sexual past of several other characters, especially among Minos's relatives.[47] Pollard notes the anomalies of sex in this curious family: "In Gide's book several members of Minos' family have experience of sexual irregularities: Minos' mother, Europa, was carried off by a bull, and Pasiphaë, his wife, made love to another one. Léda, whom Pasiphaë calls her 'cousin' . . . , had inter-course with a swan" *(André Gide: Homosexual Moralist* 397). In an imaginative intertextual move, the intricate workings of sexual attraction in Minos' family recall the epilogue from Gide's own 1899 text, *Le Prométhée mal enchaîné,* in which Pasiphaë comments on her own unconventional sexual history, through a remark charged with ambivalence: "What can I say? I don't like men."[48] Gide thus calls to the mind of the reader this unusual variety of sexual practices with the aim of problematizing the conventionally clean, even gratuitous seamlessness of the myth. In this vein, another unique adaptation of the ambivalence of sex-ual identity and the dynamic nature of gender in *Thésée* revolves around the character of Icarus. As a legendary figure of transcendence, the young mind who reaches too high returns from his adventure in the realm of the azure marked by madness, by a mysticism so extreme as to constitute lunacy. Yet what he has seen, far above the limits of the average human consciousness, directly addresses the question of sexual identity. He brings back from the beyond the image of a pri-mordial unified sexuality, undivided, all-encompassing, whole: "Who came first: man or woman? Can the Eternal One be female? From the womb of what great Mother have you come, all you myriad species? And by what engendering cause can that womb have been made great? Duality is inadmissible" (*Two Legends* 79).[49] The contingent multiple forms of an archetypal Platonic pansexuality are all reflected in any earthly body and intangible soul. Simplistic dualities are revealed to be unacceptable, while authentic human eroticism reveals itself to be many-sided, complex, elegantly unpredictable.[50]

In the end, Gide does not simply transform the traditional, conformist Theseus into a purely homosexual character, nor does he leave him marked with an oblique, ambiguous bisexuality, as one might argue of his Prometheus. The truly interesting work of the author is the construction of a figure who has always actively been double, translating the multiplicities of the myth itself into the personality and sexual identity of the hero. In perhaps his most original move, Gide allows his own sexually ambivalent Theseus to continue to fulfill his traditional social, political, and cultural roles, as he successfully carries out his rites of initiation, travels the world, becomes a brilliant statesman, and fathers a son. It is thus within the framework of this hero's conventional portrayal that Gide's Theseus takes on the ultimate incarnation of the double, in a harmonious incorporation of divergent facets of a subject both manly and effeminate, trustworthy and suspect, true and false, gay and straight. In his quest for authenticity, Gide's final hero leaves behind the simplistic psychic cohesiveness that characterizes his forebears; indeed, *il passe outre* [he goes beyond], as he comes to embrace both sides of his genuinely ambivalent nature, to welcome both faces of his identity, standing as an icon of the complex, enigmatic, and ambiguous totality of the modern subject. As Albérès has suggested, "As a free and adventurous hero, Theseus sums up for Gide all human adventure."[51] Indeed, Theseus embodies for Gide the author's final answer, the ultimate incarnation of human potential, intellectually, spiritually, and sexually.[52] When, at the end of the text, Theseus remarks, "[W]hat else is there to think about, except mankind?" (*Two Legends* 101),[53] he offers Gide's own response to the culture that besieges him, to the demands of an ungrounded society, of opposing ideologies, political pressures, and the moral dilemmas of his time. In 1911, Gide writes of one of his most controversial texts, *Corydon:* "I do not want to move to pity with this book; I want to embarrass" (*Journals* 1: 296).[54] Thus, Theseus incarnates finally Gide's elusive sense of *engagement,* the spirit of forthright involvement, authenticity, and individual liberty, a hero of ambiguity who awakens the reader to a new conception of action and commitment.

Notes

1. Portions of this essay have appeared in my article "André Gide: Myth as Individual History," *Dalhousie French Studies* 33 (1995): 55–70.
2. For a variety of perspectives on the relationship between Gide and Greek mythology, see Albouy, Genova, Germain, and Watson-Williams.
3. On the connections among the elements of myth, self-identity, and the power of writing, see Yves Bonnefoy: "Isn't writing always mythology, the division of the mythic self brought to life through writing and the subject questing . . . after its own self?" [L'écriture n'est-elle pas toujours mythologie, clivage du moi mythique qu'elle fait vivre et du sujet qui tâtonne . . . à la recherche de soi?] (142).
4. For an overview of the *mythe littéraire,* particularly in relation to the history of French letters, see Albouy, Brunel, Eigeldinger, and Sellier. For a basic definition, Albouy offers this succinct description: "the elaboration of a traditional or archetypal given, through a style characteristic of the author and the work, which releases multiple meanings likely to bring about a collective action of exaltation and defense, or to express a particularly complex state of mind or soul" [l'élaboration d'une donnée traditionnelle ou archétypique, par un style propre à l'écrivain et à l'œuvre, dégageant

des significations multiples, aptes à exercer une action collective d'exaltation et de défense, ou à exprimer un état d'esprit ou d'âme spécialement complexe] (301).

5. "Les mythes . . . attendent que nous les incarnions. Qu'un seul homme au monde réponde à leur appel, et ils nous offrent leur sève intacte" (123). See also Michel Tournier, who suggests: "The function of literary or artistic creation is all the more important given that myths . . . need to be nourished and renewed, or they will die. And a dead myth is called an allegory. The function of the writer is to prevent myths from becoming allegories" [Cette fonction de la création littéraire et artistique est d'autant plus importante que les mythes . . . ont besoin d'être irrigués et renouvelés sous peine de mort. Un mythe mort, cela s'appelle une allégorie. La fonction de l'écrivain est d'empêcher les mythes de devenir des allégories] (193).

6. "La fable grecque, à partir de Troie, perd sa signification symbolique, mais se charge de valeur psychologique et poétique, pour le profit des dramaturges. Il n'y a plus lieu de chercher le sens secret de ces histoires; elles n'ont plus rien de mythique; leur pathos admirable doit suffire au poète ingénieux" (*Journal* 2: 283–284). In a 1949 interview, Gide adds: "all Greek myths almost lose their interest if we conceive of them as accidental and involuntary things, while they suddenly take on an extraordinary meaning when we understand them as conscious and deliberate acts" [tous les mythes grecs perdent presque leur intérêt si on en fait des choses accidentelles ou involontaires, et prennent brusquement une signification extraordinaire lorsqu'on en fait des actes conscients et délibérés] (Marty 311).

7. "[V]ous avez la pièce de Sophocle et je ne me pose pas en rival; je lui laisse le pathétique; mais voici [dans ma pièce] ce que lui, Sophocle, n'a pas su voir et comprendre et qu'offrait pourtant son sujet; et que je comprends, non parce que je suis plus intelligent, mais parce que je suis d'une autre époque. . . . Je me propose, non de vous faire frémir ou pleurer, mais de vous faire réfléchir" (*Journal* 1: 1151). See Gide's remarks in "Considérations sur la mythologie grecque," where he extends the multiplicity and polyvalence of myth to all forms of art: "The complete work of art has the miraculous quality of offering to us always more than was imagined by the author; it permits us continually a richer interpretation" [L'œuvre d'art accomplie a ceci de miraculeux qu'elle nous présente toujours plus de signifiance que n'en imaginait l'auteur; elle permet sans cesse une interprétation plus nourrie] ("Thoughts on Greek Mythology" 230; "Considérations sur la mythologie grecque" 150).

8. See his 1891 letter to Paul Valéry: "I am a Symbolist, and I want you to know it. . . . Mallarmé for poetry, Maeterlinck for drama—and although next to those two I feel a little puny, I add Me for the novel" [je suis Symboliste et sachez-le. . . . Mallarmé pour la poésie, Maeterlinck pour le drame — et quoique auprès d'eux deux, je me sente un peu gringalet, j'ajoute Moi pour le roman] (46).

9. Gide's criticism of Symbolism, and of his own young naiveté, is reflected in many texts, as in this passage from *Si le grain ne meurt*: "The movement was organized as a reaction against realism, with a backlash against Parnasse, as well. Sustained by Schopenhauer, . . . I held as 'contingency' . . . everything that was not 'absolute,' all the prismatic diversity of life. . . . The error was not in seeking to unveil some general truth or beauty from the inextricable mess presented at that time by 'realism,' but rather, to deliberately turn our backs on reality. I was saved by gluttony . . ." [Le mouvement se dessinait en réaction contre le réalisme, avec un remous contre le Parnasse également. Soutenu par Schopenhauer, . . . je tenais pour « contingence » . . . tout ce qui n'était pas « absolu », toute la prismatique diversité de la vie. . . . [L]'erreur n'était pas de chercher à dégager quelque beauté et quelque vérité d'ordre général de l'inextricable fouillis que présentait alors le « réalisme »; mais bien, par parti pris, de tourner le dos à la réalité. Je fus sauvé par gourmandise . . .] (535; last ellipsis Gide's). On the complex relationship of Gide to Symbolism, see Brosman and Brontë.

10. "[L]es questions politiques m'intéressent moins, et je les crois moins importantes que les questions sociales; les questions sociales moins importantes que les questions morales" (*Journal* 1: 668). See Gide's related comment: "Social question? Yes indeed. But the ethical question is antecedent. Man is more interesting than men. God made *him* and not them in his image. Each one is more precious than all" [Question sociale? — Certes. Mais la question morale est antécédente. L'homme est plus intéressant que les hommes; c'est lui et non pas eux que Dieu a fait à son image. Chacun est plus précieux que tous] (*Journals* 1: 76; *Journal* 1: 93).

11. "[J]'avais cru, jusqu'à ces derniers temps, qu'il importait d'abord de changer l'homme, les hommes, chaque homme; et que c'était par là qu'il fallait commencer. C'est pourquoi j'écrivais que la question morale m'importait plus que la question sociale. Je me laisse persuader aujourd'hui que l'homme même ne peut changer que d'abord les conditions sociales ne l'y invitent et ne l'y aident — de sorte que ce soit d'elles qu'il faille d'abord s'occuper. Mais il faut s'occuper des deux" (*Journal* 1: 1241).

12. "L'engagement gidien porte une leçon de courage et de solidarité en accord avec les vues morales et politiques actuelles. Courage de réformer une religion devenue avec le temps généralement rites et dogmes abstraits. Courage de tirer d'esclavage et de rendre à son humanité cette population d'Afrique Équatoriale Française qu'écrasait une civilisation colonisatrice devenue à l'usage colonialiste, et courage de parler pour les criminels, les fous, les malheureux et tous les laissés pour compte de notre société. Courage de se ranger auprès du peuple et du régime égalitaire de l'URSS et courage plus grand encore de se dégager une fois reconnue la trahison de l'esprit de la Révolution d'Octobre par l'État stalinien" (271). For a discussion of Gide as an engaged writer, see also Deschodt, who traces Gide's evolution as a social figure through such endeavors as the founding of the *Nouvelle Revue Française,* his journeys through the Congo, and his work within the judicial system of his time. For his part, Fernandez examines Gide's interpretation as a literary critic of the impact of moral and social issues on the individual.

13. "Je voudrais vivre assez pour voir la réussite de cet énorme effort; son succès que je souhaite de toute mon âme, auquel je voudrais travailler. Voir ce que peut donner un État sans religion, une société sans famille" (*Journal* 1: 1066). See also these remarks, from among numerous others, made in 1932: "I read with the greatest interest Stalin's new speech, which exactly answers my objections and fears . . . ; consequently I rally to it with all my heart" [Je lis avec le plus vif intérêt le nouveau discours de Staline, qui précisément répond à mes objections, à mes craintes . . . ; je m'y rallie donc de tout cœur] (*Journals* 3: 224; *Journal* 1: 1117).

14. Gide expresses an almost amusing ambivalence about his privileged economic status through such comments as this one from 1935: "I feel today, seriously, painfully, that *inferiority*—of never having had to earn my bread, of never having had to work to keep body and soul together" [Je sens aujourd'hui, gravement, péniblement, cette *infériorité,* — de n'avoir jamais eu à gagner mon pain, de n'avoir jamais travaillé dans la gêne] (*Journals* 3: 316; *Journal* 1: 1221).

15. "[S]a voix reste sans résonance et ses interventions sont des interventions d'amateur. Rien de réellement profond en Gide ne semble s'émouvoir devant ces questions qui restent extérieures à ses préoccupations d'écrivain. . . . [M]algré sa bonne volonté, il y a chez Gide une irresponsabilité sociale profonde" (17). Brée continues: "Because he never had to share directly in the misery of a group of men, Gide also lost out on the experience of compassion, originating in solidarity, and which is at the root of the feeling of fraternity. Gide's work, then, has social content only indirectly and by default" [Gide, n'ayant jamais partagé directement la misère d'un groupe d'hommes, n'a pas éprouvé non plus cette compassion, née dans la solidarité, qui est à la base du

sentiment de la fraternité. L'œuvre de Gide n'a donc qu'indirectement et par défaut un contenu social] (19).

16. "Je l'ai déjà dit : je n'entends rien à la politique. Si elle m'intéresse, c'est à la manière d'un roman de Balzac, avec ses passions, ses petitesses, ses mensonges, ses compromissions" (*Journal* 1: 1175).

17. "Courage et prudence : ce mélange bien dosé explique la tension intérieure de son œuvre. L'art de Gide veut établir un compromis entre le risque et la règle; en lui s'équilibrent la loi protestante et le non-conformisme de l'homosexuel, l'individualisme orgueilleux du grand bourgeois et le goût puritain de la contrainte sociale; une certaine sécheresse, une difficulté à communiquer et un humanisme d'origine chrétienne, une sensualité vive et qui se voudrait innocente; l'observance de la règle s'y unit à la quête de la spontanéité" (1539). Note the echoes of Sartre's remark in this comment by Roland Barthes: "Certain people choose one path and stick to it; others change paths, each time with equal conviction. As for Gide, he remained at a crossroads, constantly, faithfully, at the most important, most well-worn crossroads ever, through which pass the two greatest roads of the West, the Greek and the Christian; he preferred this *total* situation, where he could take in both lights, both inspirations" [Certains choisissent une voie et la gardent, d'autres en changent, chaque fois avec autant de conviction. Gide, lui, s'est tenu à un carrefour, constamment, fidèlement, au carrefour le plus important, le plus battu, le plus croisé que soit, par où passent les deux grandes routes d'Occident, la grecque et la chrétienne; il a préféré cette situation *totale*, où il pouvait recevoir les deux lumières et les deux souffles] (94).

18. "[L]e pouvoir de s'essayer soi-même, . . . poursuivre une expérience où sera mis à découvert, par rapport à lui et au monde qui est le sien, le sens de la condition humaine dans son entier" (211).

19. "Le mythe est le discours ultime où se constitue la tension antagoniste, fondamentale à tout discours, c'est-à-dire, à tout « développement » de sens. . . . Le mythe qui constitue la pensée grecque est le récit de l'antagonisme entre les forces apolliniennes et les forces dionysiaques" (28).

20. "[N]ous devons protéger en nous toutes les antinomies naturelles et comprendre que c'est grâce à leur irréductible opposition que nous vivons" (*Journal* 1: 802).

21. Apter also argues that "Gide's trip to the U.S.S.R. in 1936 marked a radical departure from his former posture as a consummately literary and fundamentally disengaged writer. However, it appears to be less of a departure when one considers his early and courageous effort to champion homosexual rights. . . . One might try then to situate the question of Gide's 'engagement' and in particular his 'conversion' to Communism in the thirties, in relation to his long-term commitment to sexual liberation and its formal, or rather textual, representation in his prose fiction" ("Homotextual Counter-Codes" 75).

22. As Gide writes in 1922: "I wanted to be sure that what I put forth in *Corydon,* which perhaps seemed to me venturesome, I was not soon to deny. But in this case my thought has only grown more vigorous, and what I now reproach my book with is its prudence and timidity" [Je voulais être sûr que ce que j'avançais dans *Corydon,* qui me semblait aventuré peut-être, je n'allais pas devoir le renier bientôt. Mais ma pensée n'a fait ici que s'affermir, et ce que je reproche à présent à mon livre, c'est sa prudence et sa timidité] (*Journals* 2: 246; *Journal* 1: 740).

23. "Nul peuple n'eut plus le sens et l'intelligence de l'harmonie que le peuple grec. Harmonie de l'individu, et des mœurs, et de la cité. Et c'est par besoin d'harmonie (intelligence autant qu'instinct) qu'ils donnèrent droit de cité à l'uranisme. C'est ce que j'ai tâché de faire voir dans *Corydon*. On comprendra ce livre plus tard, lorsqu'on aura compris, d'abord, qu'une grande part du malaise de notre société et du dérèglement de nos mœurs vient de ceci : qu'on en prétend bannir l'uranisme, indispensa-

ble au tempérament d'une société bien réglée" (*Journal* 1: 996). See also Gide's enthusiastic remark on the implications of Greek homoerotic culture for all later human civilization: "Had Socrates and Plato not loved young men, what a pity for Greece, what a pity for the whole world!" [Socrate et Platon n'eussent pas aimé les jeunes gens, quel dommage pour la Grèce, quel dommage pour le monde entier!] (*Journals* 2: 308; *Journal* 1: 671).

24. "Les aventures gréco-crétoises de Thésée, ses amours avec les deux sœurs du monstre . . . , comptent parmi les légendes antiques qui comportent le plus d'éléments immédiatement comparables à ceux du conte populaire par tous pays et dans tous les temps" (165).

25. It was with great joy and relief that Gide finished a draft of his text in 1944: "Today, 21 May, I finished *Thésée*. There still remain large parts to rewrite, and particularly the beginning, for which I had not yet managed to find the proper tone. But now the entire canvas is covered. For the past month I have daily and almost constantly worked on it, in a state of joyful ardor that I had not known for a long time and thought I should never know again. It seemed to me that I had returned to the time of *Les Caves* or of my *Prométhée*" [Aujourd'hui, 21 mai, j'ai achevé *Thésée*. Il me reste de grands morceaux à récrire; et, en particulier, le début, pour lequel je n'avais pas pu d'abord trouver le ton. Mais, à présent, toute la toile est couverte. Depuis un mois, j'y ai quotidiennement, et presque constamment, travaillé, dans un état de ferveur joyeuse que je ne connaissais plus depuis longtemps et pensais ne plus jamais connaître. Il me semblait être revenu au temps des *Caves,* ou de mon *Prométhée*] (*Journals* 4: 240; *Journal* 2: 269–270).

26. "Dans le *Thésée,* il faudra marquer cela — le fil à la patte, soit dit vulgairement. Il voudrait, après avoir dompté le Minotaure, continuer. — Il est tenu — contraint de revenir" (*Journal* 1: 347).

27. On Gide's utilization of antecedent texts, see Pollard's 1970 study, "The Sources of André Gide's *Thésée.*"

28. Some critics argue, in fact, that Gide's *Thésée* shows very little originality. See Magny: "*Thésée,* which aims to make a significant contribution to versions of the myth, is in no way an absolute innovation: neither in respect to its subject (the Gidean interpretation of the myth remaining generally faithful to the tradition, albeit not without some coquetry), nor in relation to Gide's own earlier work" [L'intervention du *Thésée* n'est d'ailleurs en aucune façon une innovation absolue : ni par rapport au sujet (l'interprétation gidienne du mythe restant en gros, non sans quelque coquetterie, fidèle à la tradition), ni par rapport à l'œuvre antérieure de Gide lui-même] (83).

29. On the meeting of Theseus and Oedipus in Gide's text, see Ireland, Lévy, and Watson-Williams. Gide himself declares in an interview: "It is clear that Theseus was more or less my spokesman, while I imparted to Oedipus opinions that I find admirable, and for which I had a great deal of respect, but which were not my own opinions, mystical opinions" [Il est évident que Thésée a été plus ou moins mon porte-parole tandis que pour Œdipe, je lui prêtais des pensées que je trouve admirables, pour lesquelles j'étais plein de respect, mais qui n'étaient pas les miennes, des pensées mystiques] (Marty 310).

30. "[B]ien que Grec, je ne me sens aucunement porté vers ceux de mon sexe, si jeunes et charmants qu'ils puissent être . . ." (*Thésée* 1441).

31. Pollard adds: "If specifically homosexual, these desires must be the author's own, for if they mean anything in Thésée's case they can only be more general, standing for curiosity and appetites which lead him away from his central heroic purpose" (*André Gide: Homosexual Moralist* 398). Could it not be argued, in fact, that this curiosity represents a key element in Theseus's very heroism?

32. On the relationship between Theseus and Pirithoüs, Pollard comments that "there is nothing overtly homosexual between them" (*André Gide: Homosexual Moralist* 398). Perhaps not; yet perhaps, too, the key word in this remark is "overtly." Gide himself certainly appears to have left the question open.

33. "Sache que Minos et Rhadamante, ces deux très sages législateurs, ont réglementé les mœurs de l'île, et particulièrement la pédérastie, à laquelle tu n'ignores pas que les Crétois sont fort enclins, comme il appert de leur culture. C'est au point que tout adolescent qui atteint la virilité avant d'avoir été choisi par un aîné prend honte et tient à déshonneur ce mépris; car l'on pense communément, s'il est beau, qu'alors quelque vice d'esprit ou de cœur en est cause" (*Thésée* 1441).

34. "[P]our satisfaire, disait-on, aux appétits du Minotaure" (*Thésée* 1419–1420).

35. "On a dit qu'il se nourrissait de carnage; mais depuis quand les taureaux n'ont-ils dévoré que des prés?" (*Thésée* 1437).

36. "[Thésée] s'embarque . . . avec ce troupeau de vingt jeunes garçons et de vingt jeunes filles, que la Grèce payait à la Crète en tribut annuel pour être dévorés par le Minotaure . . . ; pour moi je pense que le monstre au fond du labyrinthe s'en devait former un sérail. Pourquoi? Oh! simplement parce que cette carnivoracité je ne la vois héritée ni de Pasiphaë, ni du taureau progéniteur, mais bien un appétit de luxure" ("Considérations sur la mythologie grecque" 151–152).

37. "[J]e vis le Minotaure couché. Par chance, il dormait. J'aurais dû me hâter et profiter de son sommeil, mais ceci m'arrêtait et retenait mon bras : le monstre était beau. Comme il advient pour les centaures, une harmonie certaine conjuguait en lui l'homme et la bête. De plus, il était jeune, et sa jeunesse ajoutait je ne sais quelle charmante grâce à sa beauté; armes, contre moi, plus fortes que la force et devant lesquelles je devais faire appel à tout ce dont je pouvais disposer d'énergie. . . . Je restai même à le contempler quelque temps" (*Thésée* 1439).

38. "Ce que je fis alors, ce qui se passa, je ne puis le rappeler exactement. . . . [E]t, si pourtant je triomphai du Minotaure, je ne gardai de ma victoire sur lui qu'un souvenir confus mais, somme toute, plutôt voluptueux" (*Thésée* 1439).

39. One is reminded here of Michel, the protagonist of *L'Immoraliste,* whose program to reconstitute his deepest psyche is clearly grounded in the realm of the physical, as he trains his body to respond to the demands of nature at its harshest.

40. As Michel Foucault has argued, the exaltation of the beauty of young boys is a common motif in the oldest traditions of the homosexual code: "The adolescent physique became the object of a sort of extremely insistent cultural valorization. The fact that the male body could be beautiful, far beyond its first charms, was hardly unknown to or forgotten by the Greeks. . . . But in sexual morality, it is the juvenile body, with its own charms, that is regularly proposed as the 'good object' for pleasure" [Le physique adolescent est devenu l'objet d'une sorte de valorisation culturelle très insistante. Que le corps masculin puisse être beau, bien au-delà de son premier charme, les Grecs ne l'ignoraient ni ne l'oubliaient. . . . Mais dans la morale sexuelle, c'est le corps juvénile avec son charme propre qui est régulièrement proposé comme le « bon objet » de plaisir] (220–221).

41. On the restrictive role of women, see Gide's related 1927 remark: "Whoever starts out towards the unknown must consent to venture alone. Creusa, Eurydice, Ariadne, always a woman tarries, worries, fears to let go and to see the thread break that ties her to her past. She pulls Theseus back and makes Orpheus look back. She is afraid" [Qui se dirige vers l'inconnu, doit consentir à s'aventurer seul. Créüse, Eurydice, Ariane, toujours une femme s'attarde, s'inquiète, craint de lâcher prise et de voir se rompre le fil qui la rattache à son passé. Elle tire en arrière Thésée, et fait se retourner Orphée. Elle a peur] (*Journals* 2: 403; *Journal* 1: 840). See also *Journal* 1: 1091 and 1094, in the original, and *Journals* 3: 202 and 205, for the English translation.

42. "Le temps, il me faut l'avouer, me parut long" (*Thésée* 1429).

43. "Ce qui fit que je ne songeais plus qu'à me passer d'elle" (*Thésée* 1429).

44. "Elle avait les lèvres gourmandes, le nez retroussé, de grands yeux vides, au regard, eût-on dit, *bovin*" (*Thésée* 1422).

45. "[C]omme un double" (*Thésée* 1441). He adds that "the two were of exactly the same build . . ." [Tous deux étaient exactement de même taille . . .] (*Two Legends* 92; *Thésée* 1443).

46. As Pirithoüs explains to Theseus, "one of the customs of the island, and one that Minos himself instituted, is that the lover assumes complete charge of the child whom he covets, and takes him to live with him, under his roof, for two months; after which period the child must announce publicly whether or not his lover has given him satisfaction and treated him properly" [une des coutumes de l'île, instituée par Minos lui-même, veut que l'amant s'empare de l'enfant qu'il convoite, qu'il l'emmène vivre avec lui, chez lui, durant deux mois; à la suite desquels l'enfant déclare publiquement si son amant lui plaît et se comporte avec lui décemment] (*Two Legends* 91; *Thésée* 1442).

47. As regards the familial relations of this royal clan, Apter emphasizes the cultural significance of Gide's nonconformist reading of ancient systems of hierarchy and power: "Gide's subversive transformation of Greek myths and biblical parables, particularly those that underscore the violation of taboos or the testing of blood ties, implies a radically new society grounded on open sexuality, a kind of homosexual utopia, ideologically compatible with Marxist ideals of individual self-realization" (*André Gide* 102).

48. "Que veux-tu? Moi, je n'aime pas les hommes" (341). On a humorous note, in *Le Prométhée mal enchaîné,* Gide underscores the pragmatic side of Pasiphaë's act of bestiality, and has her complain: "It's pretty irritating (and it wasn't easy!); I was hoping that a God was hidden in the bull. — If Zeus had been involved, I would have given birth to one of the Dioscuri; thanks to that animal, I only brought forth a calf" [C'est assez vexant (et ça n'a pas été facile!) j'espérais qu'un Dieu s'y cachait. — Si Zeus s'en fût mêlé, j'eusse accouché d'un Dioscure; grâce à cet animal je n'ai mis au monde qu'un veau] (341).

49. "Qui donc a commencé : l'homme ou la femme? L'Éternel est-il féminin? Du ventre de quelle grande Mère êtes-vous sorties, formes multiples? Et ventre fécondé par quel engendreur? Dualité inadmissible" (*Thésée* 1434).

50. Icarus also plays a useful role in the establishment of the homosexual code, for Theseus is not unmoved by his beauty; his description of Icarus's charms is echoed in his memories of his own comely but ill-fated son, Hippolytus.

51. "Héros désinvolte et aventureux, Thésée résume pour Gide toute aventure humaine" (269).

52. In an interview, Jean Amrouche remarks to Gide: "But the supreme value of Theseus lies in the fact that it appears he alone was able to succeed in establishing a balance among the diverse faculties of man, and that these diverse faculties must lead to action, and to the work of art." Gide's response, "Exactly," needs no commentary. [Mais la suprême valeur de Thésée réside en ceci que lui seul, semble-t-il, ait réussi à établir l'équilibre entre les diverses facultés de l'homme et que ces diverses facultés doivent aboutir à l'action, à l'œuvre. / Parfaitement] (Marty 312).

53. "[D]e quoi s'occuper, que de l'homme?" (*Thésée* 1448).

54. "Je ne veux pas apitoyer, avec ce livre; je veux GÊNER" (*Journal* 1: 340); similarly, in 1949, he declares his role as that of an *inquiéteur:* "But I've said it over and over throughout all my work, that I believe that there are truths which are subjective, and I believe that diversity is a truly human thing. My role is that of a provocateur. I want to trouble my readers and make them think by themselves" [Mais je l'ai dit et répété

à travers toute mon œuvre, je crois qu'il y a des vérités subjectives et je crois que la diversité est une chose profondément humaine. Mon rôle est celui d'un inquiéteur. Je veux inquiéter mes lecteurs et les faire penser par eux-mêmes] (Marty 315).

Works Cited

Albérès, R.-M. *L'Odyssée d'André Gide*. Paris: Albin Michel, 1951.

Albouy, Pierre. *Mythes et mythologies de la littérature française*. Paris: Colin, 1969.

Apter, Emily. *André Gide and the Codes of Homotextuality*. Saratoga, CA: Anma Libri, 1987.

———. "Homotextual Counter-Codes: André Gide and the Poetics of Engagement." *Michigan Romance Studies* 6 (1986): 75–87.

Barthes, Roland. "Notes sur André Gide et son journal." *Bulletin des Amis d'André Gide* 13.67 (July 1985): 85–105.

Blanchot, Maurice. "Gide et la littérature d'expérience." *La Part du feu*. Paris: Gallimard, 1949. 208–220.

Bonnefoy, Yves. *Entretiens sur la poésie*. Neuchâtel: La Baconnière, 1981.

Brée, Germaine. *L'Insaisissable Protée*. Paris: Les Belles Lettres, 1970.

Brontë, Diana. "Le Symbolisme dans l'œuvre d'André Gide jusqu'à *L'Immoraliste*." *Cahiers André Gide* 1. Paris: Gallimard, 1969. 225–240.

Brosman, Catharine Savage. "Gide's Criticism of Symbolism." *Modern Language Review* 61.4 (October 1966): 601–609.

Brunel, Pierre, ed. *Dictionnaire des mythes littéraires*. Paris: Éditions du Rocher, 1989.

Camus, Albert. *L'Été*. Paris: Gallimard, 1959.

Deschodt, Éric. *Gide, « le contemporain capital »*. Paris: Perrin, 1991.

Durand, Gilbert. *Figures mythiques et visages de l'œuvre*. Paris: Berg, 1979.

Eigeldinger, Marc. *Mythologie et intertextualité*. Geneva: Slatkine, 1987.

Fernandez, Ramon. *Gide ou le courage de s'engager*. Paris: Klincksieck, 1985.

Foucault, Michel. *L'Usage des plaisirs*. Vol. 2 of *L'Histoire de la sexualité*. Paris: Gallimard, 1984.

Genova, Pamela A. *André Gide dans le labyrinthe de la mythotextualité*. West Lafayette, IN: Purdue University Press, 1995.

Germain, Gabriel. "André Gide et les mythes grecs." *Entretiens sur André Gide*. Ed. Marcel Arland and Jean Mouton. Paris: Mouton, 1967. 41–67.

Gide, André. "Considérations sur la mythologie grecque." *Œuvres complètes*. Vol. 9. Ed. Louis Martin-Chauffier. Paris: Gallimard, 1935. 147–154.

———. *Journal*. 2 vols. Paris: Gallimard, Bibliothèque de la Pléiade, 1951, 1954.

———. *The Journals of André Gide*. Ed. and trans. Justin O'Brien. 4 vols. New York: Alfred A. Knopf, 1947–1951.

———. *Le Prométhée mal enchaîné*. *Romans, récits et soties, œuvres lyriques*. Ed. Yvonne Davet and Jean-Jacques Thierry. Paris: Gallimard, Bibliothèque de la Pléiade, 1958. 301–341.

———. *Si le grain ne meurt*. *Romans, récits et soties, œuvres lyriques*. Vol. 2. Paris: Gallimard, Bibliothèque de la Pléiade, 1954. 349–616.

———. *Thésée*. *Romans, récits et soties, œuvres lyriques*. Ed. Yvonne Davet and Jean-Jacques Thierry. Paris: Gallimard, Bibliothèque de la Pléiade, 1958. 1413–1453.

———. "Thoughts on Greek Mythology." *Pretexts*. Trans. Jeffrey J. Carre. New York: Delta, 1959. 227–233.

———. *Two Legends: "Oedipus" and "Theseus."* Trans. John Russell. New York: Vintage, 1958.

Gide, André, and Paul Valéry. *Correspondance André Gide—Paul Valéry*. Ed. Robert Mallet. Paris: Gallimard, 1955.

Ireland, G. W. *André Gide: A Study of His Creative Writings*. Oxford: Clarendon, 1970.

Lévy, Zvi H. "André Gide entre Œdipe et Thésée." *French Studies* 44.1 (January 1990): 34–46.

Lucey, Michael. *Gide's Bent: Sexuality, Politics, Writing.* New York: Oxford University Press, 1995.

Magny, Claude-Edmonde. "A propos du *Thésée* : l'éthique secrète d'André Gide." *Poésie* 36 (December 1946): 82–94.

Marty, Éric. *André Gide : Qui êtes-vous? avec les entretiens Jean Amrouche et André Gide.* Lyon: La Manufacture, 1987.

Moutote, Daniel. *André Gide : L'Engagement (1926–1939).* Paris: SEDES, 1991.

Pollard, Patrick. *André Gide: Homosexual Moralist.* New Haven: Yale University Press, 1991.

———. "The Sources of André Gide's *Thésée.*" *Modern Language Review* 65.2 (April 1970): 290–297.

Sartre, Jean-Paul. "Gide vivant." *Les Temps Modernes* 65 (1951): 1537–1541.

Sellier, Philippe. "Qu'est-ce qu'un mythe littéraire?" *Littérature* 55 (October 1984): 112–126.

Stoltzfus, Ben. *Gide's Eagles.* Carbondale, IL: Southern Illinois University Press, 1969.

Tournier, Michel. "La dimension mythologique." *Le Vent Paraclet.* Paris: Gallimard, 1977. 151–210.

Watson-Williams, Helen. *André Gide and the Greek Myth.* Oxford: Clarendon Press, 1967.

Yourcenar, Marguerite. "Aspects d'une légende et histoire d'une pièce." *Théâtre II.* Paris: Gallimard, 1971. 165–179.

NOTES ON THE
CONTRIBUTORS

Tom Conner earned his Ph.D. from Yale University and is Associate Professor of French at St. Norbert College. He has previously published *Chateaubriand's "Mémoires d'outre-tombe": A Portrait of the Artist as Exile* and edited a book of essays entitled *Dreams in French Literature*. His current research focuses on French and German left-wing intellectuals in the 1930s.

Peter F. DeDomenico received his Ph.D. in French at the University of California, Berkeley. His dissertation, which dealt with literary and political debates in France between the Wars, was entitled "Militant Aesthetics: Polemics and the French Novel of the 1930s."

Jeffrey Geiger earned his Ph.D. from the University of California, Los Angeles, and now teaches film studies at the University of Essex, UK. His recent work has focused on the connections between documentary film and colonial politics, the influence of ethnographic writing and film on Hollywood, and masculinity in African-American literature. He is currently working on a book dealing with U.S. representations of the South Pacific during the modernist period.

Pamela A. Genova received her B.A. (1983) from the University of Kansas, and her M.A. (1986) and Ph.D. (1991) from the University of Illinois. She is currently Associate Professor of French in the Department of Modern Languages and Associate Dean of the College of Arts and Sciences at the University of Oklahoma.

M. Martin Guiney received his Ph.D. in Comparative Literature from Yale University and is currently Associate Professor of French at Kenyon College. He has published articles on Gide, Rilke, Madame de Staël, and French national education policies in the nineteenth century. He is currently writing a book on the teaching of literature and the cult of the nation in the French Third Republic.

Paul Hollander teaches sociology (including the sociology of literature and political sociology) at the University of Massachusetts, Amherst. He is the author of *Soviet and American Society: A Comparison; Political Pilgrims: Travels of Western Intellectuals to the Soviet Union, China, and Cuba, 1928–1978;* and *Anti-Americanism: Critiques at Home and Abroad, 1965–1990,* in addition to three volumes of collected essays. His interpretation of the collapse of Soviet Communism, *Political Will and Personal Belief,* was published by Yale University Press in 1999.

John Lambeth is Associate Professor of French and Director of the Honors Program at Washington and Lee University, where he teaches courses on the nineteenth- and twentieth-century French novel, African Francophone literature, and the history of French cinema. He has published articles on Zola, Gide, and Camus and is currently working on a book about Zola and amateur photography in France in the 1890s.

Michael Lucey is the author of *Gide's Bent: Sexuality, Politics, Writing* and is currently completing a book on Honoré de Balzac, entitled *The Misfit of the Family: Balzac and the Social Ground of Sexuality.* He teaches French, Comparative Literature, and Queer Studies at the University of California, Berkeley.

Daniel Moutote was Professor Emeritus at the Université Paul Valéry in Montpellier and an authority on Gide. His many books on Gide include the much acclaimed *Le Journal de Gide et les problèmes du moi (1889–1925)* and *André Gide : L'Engagement (1926–1939).*

Walter Putnam is Professor of French and Chair of the Department of Foreign Languages and Literatures at the University of New Mexico. He completed his doctoral work in Comparative Literature at the Université de Paris III (Sorbonne Nouvelle). His publications include two books (*L'Aventure littéraire de Joseph Conrad et d'André Gide* and *Paul Valéry Revisited*) and numerous articles on French literature from Baudelaire to Le Clézio. His current work on French literary colonialism focuses on the written representations of the colonial project among established French writers of the nineteenth and twentieth centuries.

Naomi Segal is Professor of French Studies at the University of Reading, UK, and is the author of numerous articles and eight books, most importantly *Narcissus and Echo: Women and Men in the French Récit; The Adulteress's Child: Authorship and Desire in the Nineteenth-Century Novel;* and *André Gide: Pederasty and Pedagogy.* She has also co-edited *Scarlet Letters* and *Coming Out of Feminism?* In addition, she has published articles on *style indirect libre* and stream of consciousness, *Fatal Attraction* and *The Piano,* and Princess Diana. Her current research projects include an edition in French of a collection of papers by Gide and a co-edited book of essays on the indeterminate body.

Roger Shattuck is University Professor Emeritus at Boston University. He has also served as President of the Association of Literary Scholars and Critics. He is the author of *The Banquet Years: The Origins of the Avant-Garde in France, 1885 to World War I,* as well as many other books, including *Forbidden Knowledge: From Prometheus to Pornography; Candor and Perversion: Literature, Education, and the Arts;* and *Marcel Proust.*

Jean-François Sirinelli is Professor of Contemporary History at the Université Charles de Gaulle-Lille III and an authority on the history of French intellectuals. He is co-author of *Les Intellectuels en France, de l'Affaire Dreyfus à nos jours* and author, most recently, of *Sartre et Aron.*

Jocelyn Van Tuyl received her Ph.D. from Yale University, where her research on Gide focused on the poetics of the literary voyage. She is currently completing a book on Gide and World War II, thanks to a fellowship from the National Endowment for the Humanities. She teaches at New College of the University of South Florida, the honors college of the state university system of Florida.

INDEX

Note: To save space, consecutive pages on which a particular item appears are grouped together, rather than listed separately; for instance, Auguste Anglès is briefly mentioned on pages 54, 55, and 56, which the index represents as 54-56.

All works by Gide are listed under "Gide, André." The pages specified there may not mention a particular work by name but may, instead, include a quotation from it or refer to a character. The only characters listed elsewhere in the index are those appearing in classical mythology. *Voyage au Congo* and *Le Retour du Tchad* are listed separately, even though many references in the essays are to pages in a combined edition. In Walter Putnam's essay, all page references up through 255 are to *Voyage*; references thereafter are to *Retour*. In Jeffrey Geiger's essay, all page references to the English translation *Travels in the Congo* up through 199 are to *Voyage*, as are all references in the French edition up through 285; references thereafter are to *Retour*.